PERSPECTIVES ON SOUTHERN AFRICA

1. THE AUTOBIOGRAPHY OF AN UNKNOWN SOUTH AFRICAN, by Naboth Mokgatle (1971)
2. MODERNIZING RACIAL DOMINATION: *South Africa's Political Dynamics,* by Heribert Adam (1971)
3. THE RISE OF AFRICAN NATIONALISM IN SOUTH AFRICA: *The African National Congress, 1912–1952,* by Peter Walshe (1971)
4. TALES FROM SOUTHERN AFRICA, by A. C. Jordan (1973)
5. LESOTHO 1970: *An African Coup Under the Microscope,* by B. M. Khaketla (1972)
6. TOWARDS AN AFRICAN LITERATURE: *The Emergence of Literary Form in Xhosa,* by A. C. Jordan (1972)
7. LAW, ORDER, AND LIBERTY IN SOUTH AFRICA, by A. S. Mathews (1972)
8. SWAZILAND: *The Dynamics of Political Modernization,* by Christian P. Potholm (1972)
9. THE SOUTH WEST AFRICA/NAMIBIA DISPUTE: *Documents and Scholarly Writings on the Controversy Between South Africa and the United Nations,* by John Dugard (1973)
10. CONFRONTATION AND ACCOMMODATION IN SOUTHERN AFRICA: *The Limits of Independence,* by Kenneth W. Grundy (1973)
11. POWER, APARTHEID, AND THE AFRIKANER CIVIL RELIGION, by Thomas D. Moodie (1973)

Confrontation and Accommodation in Southern Africa

PUBLISHED FOR THE CENTER ON
INTERNATIONAL RACE RELATIONS,
UNIVERSITY OF DENVER

Confrontation and Accommodation in Southern Africa

The Limits of Independence

Kenneth W. Grundy

UNIVERSITY OF CALIFORNIA PRESS
BERKELEY · LOS ANGELES · LONDON

UNIVERSITY OF CALIFORNIA PRESS
BERKELEY AND LOS ANGELES, CALIFORNIA
UNIVERSITY OF CALIFORNIA PRESS, LTD.
LONDON, ENGLAND

ISBN: 0-520-02271-8
LIBRARY OF CONGRESS CATALOG CARD NUMBER: 72-78950
PRINTED IN THE UNITED STATES OF AMERICA

To Marty,
She knows why

Contents

	List of Illustrations	viii
	List of Tables	ix
	Preface	xi
1.	Ideological Positions and the Racial Motif	1
2.	Economic and Transport Relationships	28
3.	The Political and Diplomatic Networks	83
4.	The "Bridge Builders"	118
5.	Revolutionary Thought and Revolutionary Practice	152
6.	Lifelines and Tensions: The International Relations of Guerrilla Warfare	191
7.	South Africa's "Outward-Looking Policy" in Africa	228
8.	Conclusions: Hardened Positions and Pragmatic Responses	276
	Appendix 1. Some Notes on the Analysis of Regional Sub-Systems	303
	Appendix 2. Manifesto on Southern Africa Adopted by the Fifth Summit Conference of East and Central African States Held in Lusaka, Zambia—April 14–16, 1969	315
	Bibliography	325
	Index	345

Illustrations

FIGURES

1. Formal Diplomatic Representation, 1969–71 85
2. Intra-Regional Diplomatic Visits, 1966–71 91
3. The Dialogue Question 144
4. Some Types of Intermediary Relationships 150
5. African National Congress View of Vorster's African Policy 250
6. The Nationalist Party Split between *Verligte* and *Verkrampte*. 254
7. "They've Come to Install the New Hot Line!" 268

MAPS

1. Principal Railway Routes, Southern Africa 52
2. Migration of Foreign Africans 61
3. Principal Areas of Guerrilla Presence, Routes of Infiltration, and External Training and Transit Bases 172

Tables

1. Gross Domestic Products: Southern Africa 30
2. Intra-Regional Trade Directions, 1964 33
3. Trade with South Africa and White Southern Africa by Regional States, 1964 and 1968 35
4. Representative Proportions of Ordinary Government Revenues from Customs and Excise: Botswana, Lesotho, and Swaziland 37
5. Zambia's External Transport Patterns, 1967 51
6. Total Foreign-Born African Residents 60
7. Botswana Labor Force, 1950–65 63
8. Summit Conferences of Heads of State and Government of East and Central African States 114

9*A*. Political and Military Wings of the Principal Southern African Revolutionary Movements 155

9*B*. Basic Data 156

10. International Associations of Revolutionary Nationalist Movements, Southern Africa 193
11. Refugees from Southern Africa: Major Host Countries and Sources 201
12. Approximate Military Force Levels, 1970–71 216
13. South African Exports to Africa 252
14. Southern Africa, Various Groupings 311
15. A Two-Dimensional Matrix for the Study of International Politics 314

Preface

> If you tell people to live together, you tell them to quarrel. —*Congo*

In an era marked by war in Southeast Asia, the rise of the Chinese People's Republic, the conflagration in Northern Ireland, the constant crisis in the Middle East, and the war between India and Pakistan it is small wonder that southern Africa does not command the attention it deserves outside the region. It takes no prescience to maintain that such a status for southern African issues is merely a temporary condition hidden by the relatively superficial calm that glosses over profound social divisions. There have, of course, been smouldering guerrilla wars and civil unrest in southern Africa for more than a decade, but the extent of the coverage in non-African news media has been marginal. This is not to say that it is desirable to be in the headlines or that southern Africa will necessarily explode within the next few years. For years journalists, statesmen, and scholars have foreseen a violent future in the region, especially for the Republic of South Africa. But Armageddon has not arrived. Nevertheless, it is this inherent potential for violence, on a domestic as well as an international scale, that lends greater urgency to our efforts to understand regional affairs there. There is a marked tendency for fundamentally opposed contestants for power to seek to improve their political and strategic positions by, depending on internal and external distributions of power, either internationalizing or localizing the contest. The weaker side, in particular, tends to search about for support, and this in turn may lead to expanding the impact of the competition and perhaps to affecting its intensity, duration, and violence. Conversely, external forces may seek to exploit the unrest in particular areas or states. As a result, any potential or real unrest in southern Africa may be expected to involve other than regional participants, just as present political, military, diplomatic, and economic maneuverings go beyond the geographic confines of southern Africa to enmesh dozens of intrusive and invited states.

Southern Africa is important for another reason. Its distinctive racial characteristics provide us, in some ways, with a caricature of the racial situation over the world. This is particularly the case when we note the overlay of racial and economic variables. In that the United States, especially, is confronted by racial problems that we have been unable or unwilling to deal with equitably, the southern African experience provides us with comparative cases for consideration. Even though the southern African racial situation is manifestly distinct from the American, its political and ideological ramifications cannot be discounted. The racial component in international affairs as distinct from domestic affairs, particularly on a regional level, deserves more study than it has heretofore received.

There are, moreover, a number of vexing moral and philosophical issues, related to cultural and racial interaction, intervention, and penetration, and to super- and subordination, violence, and the basis of governmental legitimacy that are posed by various southern African conditions and practices. Foreign policy is in many ways an effort by a government to adapt to or alter its external environment in order to improve domestic circumstances. Hence, these knotty issues, if they are faced by policy makers, affect and are affected by the values of the policy maker, and the practical limitations of policy, in turn necessitate adjustments in the perceived values of officials.

We can see, in this study of regional international relations, how the racist states of southern Africa—Portugal, Rhodesia, and South Africa—contend with their immediate, often expressly antagonistic environment. By making certain domestic adjustments, by involving themselves with regional neighbors, by attempting to cultivate more powerful friends elsewhere, by seeking to penetrate and isolate their more hostile neighbors, and by trying to stir divisive debate within the larger continent, they hope to prevent the creation of a unified, global community dedicated to the revision of societal norms in their countries. In this way they pursue their desire to preserve and strengthen the status quo in a world that rejects the very foundations on which that status quo is founded. Conversely, some regional actors, both states and groups within states, have sought to resist this pattern of interaction. They endeavor to support policy linkages of the sort that tend to undermine a system of relationships dominated by white-governed states, and to sever relationships that would define their foreign and domestic policy alternatives narrowly. Such linkages are woven throughout the pattern of interactions that are described in this study. In one perspective they might be regarded as a set of tentacles that enable the white-dominated states to control the entire region. In another, they are defended as the very lifelines of the region, giving it structure, holding it together, and assuring its continuation and growth. In still another, they are seen as disruptive of regional cohesion and cooperation. In any case, this is the very essence of the regional sub-system providing us with a variety of data on patterned interactions.

Perhaps a word about the phrase *regional sub-system* may be in order. One can conceive of the total, world picture of international relations as a complex and complete system, much like a gigantic electrical circuit, although not nearly so predictable. An action at one point in that circuit sets off a reaction elsewhere in the system, and so forth. Certain actions and reactions occur regularly. In the context of international relations this might be, for example, the transfer of goods from one territory to another. So frequently do they occur that special machinery is created to deal with them. They may become routinized. In this regard we may speak of patterned interactions or patterns of interaction. Frequently, when we survey the total picture of international relations, it becomes evident that some actors deal with others more regularly and more intensely. These patterns of interaction can, when sufficient comparable data are available, be tabulated and plotted. They are often obvious, without the need for statistical verification. We may have, in that case, a recognizable sub-system of the global system. Frequently such patterned relationships are identified with a specific geographic region, hence we can speak of a regional subsystem. This is not to say that a regional sub-system is isolated from actors outside the sub-system. Certainly this is not so with regard to southern Africa. Rather it means that the preponderant pattern of relationships is regionally defined. Southern Africa may well be such a regional sub-system. This study endeavors to explore that proposition, to define more precisely the nature of regional interactions, and to describe them more fully. Professional social scientists more familiar with the nomenclature of systems analysis are referred to Appendix 1 for further discussion of this approach in the context of southern African affairs.

Since we are concerned with a regional sub-system, it becomes necessary to delimit the boundaries of our subject matter. This task will occupy an important portion of the concluding chapter. Meanwhile, for purposes of data collection and organization, we shall first arbitrarily define and delineate our region in broad geographical terms. Southern Africa, for our purposes, will include all territories south of the Zambezi River and its tributaries, plus those black-governed states that share boundaries with white-governed territories. Southern Africa thereby is comprised of some thirteen territories (regarding South West Africa or Namibia as separate from the Republic of South Africa) ranging southward from the Congo-Tanzania belt across the continent. (The fact is, however, that Namibia has no identifiable international behavior distinct from that of South Africa, unless we consider the activities of liberation movements, states sympathetic to them, and international organizations.) Thus we have included the following states and territories: Angola, Botswana, Lesotho, Madagascar, Malawi, Mozambique, Rhodesia (Zimbabwe), Swaziland, South Africa, South West Africa (Namibia), Tanzania, Zaïre—usually referred to as the Congo

[Kinshasa] in this study, and Zambia. The island of Madagascar is included although for years its policies were oriented toward France and Europe and away from its geographical neighbors. Madagascar is beginning to play an increasingly crucial part in African and southern African affairs, and hence some facets of its foreign policy deserve discussion.

Thus southern Africa presents a relatively compact geographic region which, under detailed study, may provide us with greater insight into larger questions regarding regional subsystems and their relationships with the global international system or segments thereof. This is why a country-by-country coverage has been rejected and a regional perspective assumed. This study seeks, therefore, to focus on the interplay of numerous variables, especially the economic, political, diplomatic, racial, geographic, and military. Regional relationships in this regard are multidimensional. There exists, side by side, but not in isolation, a tremendous variety of regional "sub-systems" within the same geographic region. In Appendix 1 there is a discussion of criteria for defining relationships. Depending on which set of relationships is studied, the component parts will differ. It can be shown, relatively easily, that a southern African regional sub-system based on diplomatic-organizational criteria differs markedly from regional relationships based upon economic criteria. Likewise, if we were to concentrate on, let us say, sociocultural criteria, it would matter greatly whether we chose to emphasize inter-state relations or relationships among actors that do not encompass an entire state. For example, though there are practically no official governmental relationships between Rhodesia and Zambia, there are still vital and intense relationships between their various sub-state groupings and sociocultural communities.

A further problem relates to the choice of focus for the study. We have decided to concentrate on the region and to use, as our central unit of analysis, the state and territory. However, it may occasionally be necessary to focus on the wider world, or, to move in the opposite direction, on affairs within the state, on groups of actors below the state level, and even on individual personalities. Thus we face difficulties with regard to which unit and level of analysis is best suited to shed light on our subject. General advice offered by students of the level-of-analysis problem is to avoid shifting from one level to another. To some extent, this is unavoidable, but provided the scholar is aware of his drifting focus, he can at least minimize a tendency to translate properties or relations from one level of analysis to another. Throughout the body of this study we are constantly faced with the complexity of these issues and the necessity to move, from time to time, from one level of analysis to another, from one unit of analysis to another, and from one substantive dimension to another. Although the exploratory nature of this exercise is no excuse for the shifts, we can only hope to be on guard against the pitfalls inherent in the multidimensionality of the subject matter.

For one searching through mountains of reports and collected data and seeking to discern patterns from which generalizations can be abstracted, frustration comes easily when constant and abrupt change prevails. The task of finding order and pattern in international events is difficult enough. But to compound that task by the repeated injection of new actors, forces, and conditions seems capricious to the uninitiated and wicked to the suspicious. Over-time data is an important comparative analytical ingredient. But the constitutional and structural alterations stemming from the demise of colonial rule has made this sort of comparison difficult. The dissolution of the Federation of Rhodesia and Nyasaland in 1963 and the successive negotiated and declared independence of its component parts in 1964 and 1965 is one such example. The same situation exists with regard to the transformation of the British High Commission Territories. At least, radical governmental changes in these entities have not added to our confusion, although constitutional gymnastics in Lesotho in 1970 may yet impede over-time comparison. Nevertheless, it is clear that in many of the newly independent states of black Africa and in the racist regimes in southern Africa there is an absence of long-standing and widely (i.e., cross-culturally) agreed-upon patterns of political interaction that could be translated into stability and governmental security. Politics in many of these states is still a fundamental struggle over the ground rules by which to structure sociopolitical order and to direct change. Irregular domestic change is bound to have its counterpart in foreign policy. Thus the sets of relationships we shall describe are fluid, embryonic, and incomplete, and the profile of regional relations that emerges is amorphous and analytically elusive. If there is an element of continuity and regional cohesion it is as much the result of a low level of power within the sub-system and on its surrounding periphery as of well understood and popularly accepted patterns of interaction. In a relative sense, the southern African regional sub-system operates in a vacuum. It may not be as isolated as the Americas in the nineteenth century, but southern Africa is removed from direct great power confrontation to an unusual degree in the second half of the twentieth. Certainly this is the case if we were to compare southern Africa with Southeast Asia, Central Europe, the Middle East, and the Indian subcontinent.

The primary focus of this study is upon the intra-regional patterns of international relations. Insofar as these patterns are dependent upon the intrusive behavior of extra-regional actors we shall explore external factors. Certainly, the ultimate desire would be to relate the regional sub-system to the international system as a whole. But this is another project in itself, and one which, regardless of its importance, will not occupy center stage in this book. Our perspective is fairly parochial, at least in a geographic sense.

In Chapter 1, we shall explore some of the more intangible yet profound issues of regional international relations. What role does race play in international behavior? What are the ideological postures of the participants? How deep are the commitments so derived? What is the place of violence in regional affairs and in the perspectives of the respective actors? Chapter 2 concentrates on economic and transport relationships that exist or are in the process of being developed. Here we discuss the overwhelming regional economic strength of South Africa, regional trade patterns, functional economic cooperation, private business relationships, transport routes, the effects of labor supply and migration, economic aid, and finally the meaning of economic influence in international affairs.

Chapter 3 describes the political and diplomatic network that has emerged regionally. Have patterns been given organizational expression? Do extra-regional international organizations affect the region? What forms of diplomatic exchange occur outside the formalized representational channels? What sort of behavior characterizes those states that seek to transcend intraregional division? Chapter 4 is devoted to the important place of the "bridge builders," those states who see their foreign policy role as encouraging interaction and dialogue between the white and black states of Africa. The subjects of guerrilla warfare and politico-military confrontation are treated in Chapters 5 and 6. Theories of guerrilla warfare and patterns of fighting and organization are discussed. But a primary concern throughout is the international ramifications of guerrilla struggle, for those who support guerrilla movements and the guerrillas themselves, and for the white states and their external allies. Given South Africa's keystone position in the region, the concluding chapter is a case study of the republic's "outward policy," its roots, first efforts, the potential for "outwardness," the domestic political considerations, and its future.

To some extent the coverage in this volume is uneven. For example, considerable space is devoted to describing the diplomatic patterns that have evolved, but relatively little effort is made to detail the succession of resolutions passed by the United Nations General Assembly and Security Council. In most instances the reason for this unevenness is easily explained. I have attempted to give more elaborate coverage to those facets of international relations in the region about which little of a descriptive or analytical nature has been published. Where omissions seem glaring—that is, where important subjects seem to have been glossed over, descriptively at least—it is because there exists a relatively large body of literature about them and I would prefer to place them in their analytical contexts rather than repeat or abstract the work of others. In these cases, efforts have been made to cite the significant materials to which the reader may turn, though it is hoped that sufficient background information has been included to maintain continuity.

A book passes through many stages in its transformation from an idea to a finished product. En route the author becomes so deeply in debt, intellectually speaking, that it would be impossible to repay everyone responsible for some form of assistance and encouragement. Nevertheless, it is with a great deal of joy that I extend warm thanks to some of those whose help was indispensable. The persons and organizations whose names appear below bear no responsibility for errors of fact or judgment that may appear in this study.

While teaching at Makerere University College of the University of East Africa in 1967–68 I was invited to read a paper on "The 'Southern Border' of Africa" at an international conference on "African Boundary Problems," held in Uppsala, Sweden. The Rockefeller Foundation, together with the Department of Political Science and Public Administration of Makerere and its chairman, Professor Ali A. Mazrui, made available travel funds that took me to Dar es Salaam and to Zambia to gather data for that paper. But it was the conference's sponsoring organization, the Scandinavian Institute of African Studies, and its director, Professor Carl Göstra Widstrand, who planted the seed for a study of this question. Several of the participants at that conference also encouraged me to pursue the study and suggested ways that it might be expanded and improved.

In 1969 I returned to Africa, this time to southern Africa, thanks to a generous grant from the Center on International Race Relations of the University of Denver. Professor George W. Shepherd, Jr., its director, provided the impetus to continue my work, as he did the following summer, by supporting my research and writing. I am honored that this study can be brought out under their auspices. Dr. Denis Worrall, then of the University of South Africa and now of the University of the Witwatersrand, helped immeasurably during my stay in South Africa, by securing interviews and by arranging meetings with numerous political, governmental, journalistic, and academic figures.

Again in 1970 I got an opportunity to pull my thoughts together by presenting a paper at a colloquium on "International Law and Development in Southern Africa" at the African Studies Center of the University of California, Los Angeles. I should like to thank Dr. Henry J. Richardson III, and Professor Richard Sklar for making my presence at the colloquium possible, and Professor Michael Lofchie for commenting on my paper. I am grateful to the other participants whose papers had been circulated for the other sessions, and to those who participated in the discussion after my presentation.

Later in 1970 Professor Shepherd once again kindly invited me to present some of my work, essentially the second section of Chapter 1, to an international conference on "The Role of Public Policies in the Elimination of Racial Discrimination," sponsored by the Center on International Race Relations, the United Nations Institute for Training and Research, and the Aspen Institute for Humanistic Studies. Intensive discussions with several of the participants helped immensely in sharpening my ideas.

Many others have read all or parts of my manuscript, commented upon it, supplied me with materials, data, and ideas, or discussed southern African regional affairs with me at length. I would like to thank particularly Douglas Anglin, Ian Baldwin, Jr., Larry W. Bowman, Leon Gordenker, Kevin Maguire, John Marcum, James Mittelman, and I. William Zartman for their timely help. Dozens of others in the United States and abroad deserve my gratitude. I regret that I cannot thank them all individually here.

Mrs. Anne Miller shepherded this manuscript through several drafts. Her diverse secretarial skills have been a continuous source of help.

In addition, I wish to acknowledge with thanks the following organizations for permission to use maps, data, and cartoons that appear in this book: the Africa Institute of South Africa, Pretoria; *Africa Quarterly*, New Delhi; *The Argus*, Cape Town; Econburo (Pty.) Ltd., Pretoria; *Sechaba*, London, the official organ of the African National Congress, South Africa; *The Star*, Johannesburg; and the *Sunday Times*, Johannesburg. I should also like to thank the Peter Pauper Press for permission to use the proverbs heading each chapter. They appear in *African Proverbs* (1962), compiled by Charlotte and Wolf Leslau. I thank Grossman Publishers for permission to use materials that appear in slightly different form in my *Guerrilla Struggle in Africa*, copyright 1971 by the World Law Fund.

My wife, to whom this book is dedicated, has been through the manuscript probably as many times as I have. That is indeed uncalled-for devotion. More, her unfailing extra-editorial sacrifices and considerations have provided me with the loving atmosphere that made my work a pleasure and her contribution indispensable.

I

Ideological Positions and the Racial Motif

> A white dog does not bite another white dog. —*Kenya*

The first order of business, before we can plunge into a detailed description and analysis of patterned relationships among the states and territories in southern Africa, is to examine the underlying attitudes and ideological commitments currently accepted by political elites in the region. To be sure, it is unwise to concentrate solely on elite attitudes, especially when dealing with the themes of racial prejudice and violence. This is particularly so when treating the nature and prospects of domestic political violence and guerrilla warfare. Without truly popular support, the effectiveness of such movements suffers. Nevertheless, our primary interest is in the field of international, and particularly inter-state relations, and consequently, the views and ideological orientations of relevant elites merit weighted examination. Moreover, it is not easy, given the intellectual atmosphere in much of the region, to research popular attitudes on such questions, particularly among the African populations. Those studies that exist are, with some important exceptions, outdated or poorly constructed. The thesis to be developed in this chapter is not necessarily new or unusual. It would appear, viewing the developments of the past two decades, that we are witnessing a steady polarization and hardening of attitudes and attending ideological doctrines, and that this polarization seems to be dividing along racial lines and leading to an increasing fatalism and in numerous cases commitment to the efficacy of violence to fulfill political aspirations or to maintain privilege. If there is any pervasive theme in the southern African subsystem, it is the intransmutability of race as a primary determining factor in intra-state and inter-state political relations. Political power is widely conceived of in racial terms, and, although there are exceptions to this theme, they are most often confined to the realm of the inconsequential, the unattainable, the unintended, the academic, or the embattled. Throughout the region advocates of a truly nonracial society find themselves on the defensive—in Rhodesia, in South Africa, in the Portuguese territories notwithstanding official Portuguese doctrine, and even on occasion in black African-governed states.

Institutionalized Racism and Uncompromisable Anti-Racism

Racism is one major element responsible for tension and conflict (as well as cooperation among core states and among some peripheral actors) in international politics in southern Africa. Racism in this context means the attribution of either normative qualities of superiority or inferiority, or immutable behavioral (as distinct from physical) differences, or both, to a "statistical aggregate of persons who share a composite of genetically transmissible physical traits."[1] Racism is usually associated with political power and logically includes the pursuit of policies based on these putative characteristics. Although it would be difficult to sustain an argument that even physically demonstrable attributes, as fuzzy as they may become, are necessarily helpful in the analysis of sociocultural and political affairs, the fact remains that peoples and governments do behave as though such characteristics were important and analytically

1. Rose, *They and We*, p. 8.

Note: For abbreviations used in footnotes see the list at the beginning of the Bibliography.

precise. Thus the social scientist interested in human behavior must become conversant with racial modes of cognition. In contemporary South Africa racism in the context of racial superiority and inferiority is not officially in vogue, although the white population may not behave accordingly. Rather, racial domination has assumed a more marketable and insidious image, one that stresses the differences between races and hence maintains that social peace can be achieved only by separating racial groups. Nevertheless, the underlying behavior patterns are racist in that they perpetuate advantage and disadvantage stemming from supposed racial distinctions.[2]

The most obvious social fact in the region is that racial patterns have evolved and become hardened. Such patterns easily find projection in the foreign policies of the actors. So ingrained are racial distinctions in the thought of white southern Africans that the all-too-vague distinctions of race have, nonetheless, become legitimized as the basis for social organization. Thus, an ideology of exclusion based on perceived racial differences has become pervasive and firmly implanted in sociopolitical custom and law.[3] Despite its attendant analytical problems, race is reified, and racism is raised to the guiding principle of sociopolitical organization. Illustrative of this all-consuming preoccupation with race are the words of former Prime Minister J. G. Strijdom. "Our task in South Africa," he said, "is to maintain the identity of the white man; in that task we will die fighting." The "identity of the white man" is one thing. Dr. Verwoerd and others have not been reluctant even to use the phrase "the supremacy of the white man" with approval.[4] A pale though no less committed reflection of this image is supplied by Rhodesian Prime Minister Ian Smith, who maintains:

2. Adam, *Modernizing Racial Domination.*

3. The definitive and still valuable study is: MacCrone, *Race Attitudes in South Africa*; see also Brett, *African Attitudes*; and the forthcoming study of elite attitudes directed by Professor H. W. van der Merwe of the Abe Bailey Institute for Inter-Racial Studies at the University of Cape Town.

4. Strijdom quoted in Vatcher, *White Laager*, p. 149. Verwoerd in RSA, House of Assembly, *Debates (Hansard)*, January 25, 1966, cols. 46–47. Hereinafter cited as RSA, Assembly, *Hansard*.

"If we ever have an African majority in this country we have failed in our policy, because our policy is one of trying to make a place for the white man."[5] The superiority of that place may not be stated, but it is clearly intimated. To the outside world, white South African nationalists argue: "We claim the right of survival, not, as is so often charged, as a master race, but as a distinctive race."[6]

To these ends the massive apartheid structure is constructed, modified, and defended. And this ideology has a ready corollary in a distinctive outlook on foreign affairs. Dr. Piet J. Meyer, an influential Nationalist Party member and head of the South African Broadcasting Corporation and of the Broederbond (the secret leadership society within the Afrikaner community), has put it this way: "South Africa will make a decisive contribution to the consolidation of the entire West as a White world united in its struggle against the forces of the Yellow and Black races." He added that once America overcame its "transitional sickness" regarding its professed commitment to racial equality and integration and assumed "leadership of the whole White world," the West would be "very favorably placed to win the racial struggle on a global scale."[7] This orientation took practical form in South Africa's response to Rhodesia's "unilateral declaration of independence," or UDI. In the view of Dr. Verwoerd, South Africans could not ignore the threatened position of a white Rhodesia. In a clear-cut slur at Great Britain, he put it this way: "We have blood relations over the border. However others may feel or act towards their kith and kin, when their international interests are at stake, South Africans on the whole cannot coldshoulder theirs."[8]

With this mentality prevalent, it followed that racism would become institutionalized in the white South. It is no less understandable that race consciousness, once raised to this level by the minority population, envelops also the majority popula-

5. As quoted in Hall, *The High Price*, p. 56.
6. As quoted in Vatcher, *White Laager*, p. 149. For a more complete explication of the roots of apartheid philosophy see Rhoodie and Venter, *Apartheid.*
7. As quoted in *Africa Digest*, XII (1965), 131.
8. RSA, Assembly, *Hansard*, January 25, 1966, col. 49.

tion, a population that somehow must adjust to and survive in a racialistically attentive society.[9] Characteristic of this counter-response to institutionalized white racism is the ideology of the Pan-Africanist Congress of South Africa, which maintains that there is no basis for cooperation between black and white, and therefore that racial conflict—not class conflict—and racial exclusiveness within the liberation movement are the only viable strategies to gain majority rule in South Africa.[10]

Despite the comprehensible tendency for institutionalized racism to spawn a counterracism, African leaders throughout black southern Africa have displayed an amazing restraint in rejecting racism and its by-products. It is not that they are unaware of the political ramifications from and the possibility of, indeed even likelihood of, some form of racial war. Rather, their goal is for popular indigenous governments to emerge in the region. Thus, a far more internationally acceptable rallying cry is majority rule. Black racism might not only alienate potential support from the West and Russia, but could well debase whatever support might be forthcoming from liberal elements within the white populations in the region. Moreover, the present balance of military force in the region is heavily weighted in favor of the white South. Thus it would be wise to avoid a racial war at this time. In addition to the many practical reasons why black Africa's leaders seek at present to shun such a frontal encounter, there is every reason to believe that they find such a posture morally repugnant and out of character. Not only is racial conflict unwise in the eyes of black African leaders, but it is contrary to all they believe to be right. Men such as Kenneth Kaunda and Julius Nyerere have spent much of their adult lives attempting to demonstrate the unity of the human race, not its diversity. There is little evidence to contradict the reality of their commitment to nonracialism and humanism,[11] notwithstanding their evident dedication to policies which they

9. For a thought-provoking treatment of these issues see Halpern, *Applying a New Theory*.
10. See particularly Kuper, *An African Bourgeoisie*, esp. pp. 364–87.
11. For example, Kaunda, *A Humanist in Africa*, esp. pp. 61–80, and Nyerere, *Freedom and Socialism*, esp. pp. 132–33.

feel will lead to the liberation and self-rule of all Africans in the white-ruled countries of southern Africa. Thus one of the key passages in the Lusaka Manifesto of April 1969, reads:

> Our stand toward Southern Africa thus involves a rejection of racialism, not a reversal of the existing racial domination. We believe that all people who have made their homes in the countries of Southern Africa are Africans regardless of colour of their skins; and we would oppose a racialist majority government which adopted a philosophy of deliberate and permanent discrimination between its citizens on grounds of racial origin.[12]

This position was endorsed in September of that year at Addis Ababa by the Organization of African Unity's Heads of State and Government. Not only are responsible heads of state and government openly opposed to the entrenchment of racialism in Africa, but many of the liberation movements, those with far more to gain by appealing to emotional racism, publicly adopt a tolerant attitude—tolerance toward all men, but not tolerance of racist doctrines and policies. The Zimbabwe African National Union (ZANU), for example, issued a warning that those "who would seek refuge in militant racism ('we must have our country from the white men') must be exposed with courage for the opportunists they are, because of such stuff are born the wealthy black bwanas of the era of post independence."[13] A peculiar twist to the acceptance of white settlers in southern Africa is offered by President Banda of Malawi. He argues that whites in southern Africa have as much a right to reside in Africa as do the Arabs of northern Africa. On occasion he seems to indicate that Arabs do not belong in Africa, and has even implied, though rarely, that white settlers should not reside there. Of Arabs and whites he has said: "They are all settlers, they are both imperialists, they are both colonialists, they are both foreigners."[14] Nevertheless, the thrust

12. The "Manifesto on Southern Africa" is reprinted in full in Appendix 2.
13. *Zimbabwe News*, Lusaka, IV, 2, December 31, 1969.
14. Banda, *Opening of Lilongwe Convention, September 16, 1968*, pp. 36–37. For a more detailed discussion of this point see the following section of this chapter.

of his repeated messages is clear—white southern Africa is a fact of life, and a cooperative modus vivendi must be established. Unfortunately, race is a ubiquitous issue. One might argue that there is a sort of Gresham's law of racialism. When one side insists on imposing a racist cast to all political problems, the other side, in self-defense, seems to feel the need to respond in kind. Despite a commitment to nonracialism, there is no question that black Africa's leaders are acutely sensitive to racial issues. Though they would prefer not to be faced constantly with political questions that are posed in racial terms, they cannot avoid such considerations. And their responses, on occasion, assume the coloration of racist responses, though their preferences are clearly against such a posture. But responsive, defensive decisions ought not to be regarded as racist in this context. For the primary distinction is that white governmental leaders in southern Africa aspire to create and defend racially based polities, with privilege retained in minority hands, while black Africans reject such an outcome in principle as well as in fact.

Dedication to the ideals of nonracialism puts black African governments in direct opposition to the policies of racial separation and racial super- and subordination, as legitimized in white southern Africa. In this fundamental conflict the political battle lines are drawn, the issues and positions hardened, and compromise increasingly becomes a fleeting and idle fancy. Indicative of the widening gap between the governments in the region have been the United Nations activities and resolutions (particularly those prompted by black African initiatives) relating to human rights in South Africa and Rhodesia, to the status of Namibia (South West Africa) and Rhodesia, and to colonialism in Portuguese Africa.

Early in its history, the UN was asked to consider discriminatory racial policies in the Union of South Africa. At first, in 1946, it was the issue of discriminatory legislation aimed at South Africans of Indian origin. That same year, South Africa had requested the General Assembly to permit its incorporation of South West Africa, which it had held since 1919 under a Class C mandate from the League of Nations. The General

Assembly not only refused, but recommended that the territory be placed under an international trusteeship of the UN.[15] Later UN resolutions (since 1952) were aimed directly at the policies of apartheid. Commissions and committees were established regularly to study and report on the issue to the General Assembly and the Security Council. South Africa has refused to recognize these bodies, claiming that they are contrary to Article 2(7) of the UN Charter, which precludes intervention by the UN in the internal affairs of member states. In the face of continual frustration, General Assembly resolutions became increasingly severe as Arab-Asian and then African states exerted voting strength. Later the Security Council added to the pressure on South Africa.

A similar progression of actions and resolutions followed regarding Rhodesia (since 1962) and the Portuguese colonies (since 1969), those applying to Rhodesia being by far the more stringent and demanding. Sanctions have been "recommended" and some have been made "mandatory" on sales of weapons to white governments in Africa, and member states have been requested to break off diplomatic and trade relations with South Africa and Rhodesia and to close ports and airports to their vessels and planes. But although the rhetoric of frustration paid dividends in the coin of international resolution and ridicule, that coin was not easily convertible in the exchanges of power and development.

General efforts to isolate white South Africa from continental and international scientific, sports, cultural, and functional bodies have been successful. On the legal front, the International Court of Justice (ICJ) has been requested several times to consider the status of South West Africa. First in a 1950 advisory opinion, then in 1962 and again in 1966, the ICJ failed to clarify the legal questions and contributed to the political confusion.[16] The independent black African states began to

15. *International Status of South West Africa, Advisory Opinion, I.C.J. Reports 1950*, p. 128.
16. *South West Africa Cases, Preliminary Objections, Judgment, I. C. J. Reports 1962*, and *South West Africa Cases, Second Phase, Judgment, I. C. J. Reports 1966.*

despair of a peaceful conclusion to their demands. They moved progressively closer to the position of the liberation groups that long had been convinced of the inefficacy of nonviolent responses to the white South. In their minds, the conflict was a noncompromisable one. Most of them have attempted, since their entry into the international community, to isolate, embarrass, weaken, and otherwise bring international legal and political pressure and sanction upon the white South. But though they have been successful in gaining widespread support in the form of votes for resolutions and public criticisms of racism, and in the 1971 advisory opinion of the ICJ, the results have not been rewarding in terms of compromise or cooperation from or replacement of the target governments. On the contrary, although the white-governed states have been relatively silent about the pressure, they have repeatedly refused to comply with the resolutions and findings; indeed, they have reacted by redoubling their policies of racial separation domestically and their military posture internally and externally. Dedicated racists in these societies have used external pressures to isolate moderates and governmental opponents.[17] In the short run at least, direct and potential as well as actual violent confrontation has been counterproductive, isolating and silencing sympathetic whites, and further weakening internal black support for reform or revolution. Simply put, white minorities can adapt to and raise their level of tolerance for value deprivation. To a degree, then, if the conditions are right, external pressure and opprobrium can strengthen the parties in power. Actually, this is only partly accurate, for what has probably happened is that the white governments merely responded by accelerating the process that all along seemed to be unidirectional and nonreversible. Thus, there was little that the committed opponent of racism could do in this situation. Silence would represent self-emasculation. Organized opposition would merely contribute to the already deteriorating process. In the end, I suspect,

17. See Mudge, "Domestic Policies and UN Activities," *International Organization*, XXI (1967), 55–78, and Galtung, "On the Effects of International Economic Sanctions," *World Politics*, XIX (1967), 378–416.

independent black African statesmen did what they could at the international organizational level to speak out against an intolerable situation.

The intensity and extent of their emotional rejection of the reality of colonial and white minority rule is undeniable. If their public statements have been intemperate and their actions irresolute it can be understood more easily if one could survey the history of measured appeal and repeated rebuff and frustration.[18] Bearing this in mind, it is all the more commendable that black African diplomats have displayed a sense of responsibility—an awareness of political realities—in their UN maneuverings. They have sought not merely to force the passage of resolution after resolution, but have accepted, indeed even sought out, modifications in draft resolutions so that they might achieve as nearly unanimous acceptance as possible, especially the support of the United States and the United Kingdom, even at the risk of weakening their ultimate desires.[19] There is little point in detailing the progression of resolution and reaction. The drifting apart of black and white Africa is a matter of record. UN and Organization of African Unity (OAU) resolutions are merely a testimony to a polarization that is, in ideological and political terms, *almost* complete.

There are, however, a few black statesmen in independent black Africa who, though they claim to be opposed to apartheid and racism in principle, feel that the only effective way to deal with the white South is to open and expand contacts, and to encourage greater exchange. Thus, they argue, to bring down apartheid and minority governments it is first necessary to expose the white Southern officials to black states that are friendly, orderly, and tolerant to a white presence on the continent and thereby demonstrate the folly and futility of racism. It is to the views of these statesmen, the self-professed "bridge builders," that we now turn. If it appears that they are accorded an un-

18. See, for example, Pratt, "African Reactions to the Rhodesian Crisis," *International Journal,* XXI (1966), 186–98.
19. Hovet, "African Politics in the United Nations," in Spiro, ed., *Africa,* 146–49. See also Cefkin, "The Rhodesian Question at the United Nations," *International Organization,* XXII (1968), 649–69.

deservedly lengthy coverage, it is because they are unusual in their policies and because, to a great extent they are in power in pivotal states that do represent both a chink in the united black front and a potential wedge aimed at the heart of the racist South. What is more, such a discussion affords us an opportunity to examine some of the knotty questions regarding the importance of race in international relations. Our concentration at this point is not with the substance of relations between the bridge builders and the white South. Rather we shall concentrate on the matter of perspectives on and philosophies of race relations which shape and rationalize dealing openly with white minority governments. Substantive contacts will be treated in further detail in Chapters 3 and 4.

The Rationalization of International Tokenism

Most Americans are familiar with that strategy of race relations known as tokenism. It is a strategy that few would openly admit to, but one which has been implicitly accepted by elements of the black middle class, by many professedly liberal whites, by most moderate conservatives, and even by some reluctant but resigned segregationists.

Yet tokenism is at once an implicit strategy of those who seek change and those who resist change. The very word smacks of derision and contempt. Tokenism is a compromise approach to change (or to the defense of the status quo). And compromise on moral issues prompts disdain from purists of all degrees. Yet the American political style has always placed a premium on compromise and problem solving. To be radical, even on moral issues, has in the past served to isolate most noncompromisers in America. Americans have been a people of proximate solutions to profound problems.

Despite its importance in American racial thought and practice, tokenism as a philosophy and strategy of race relations has never been fully articulated. Without a clear, comprehensive statement of tokenism it becomes necessary to reconstruct such a statement, at least insofar as it applies to racial relations in the United States.

What then is tokenism and what is the strategic essence of it? It is necessary to discuss tokenism from two perspectives—that of those who desire change and that of those who are committed to resisting change. The tokenist who seeks change reasons that the symbolic act of forcing minimal change on what had heretofore been a monolithic, unapproachable community, in any way, no matter how small, represents a political victory of far greater significance than its absolute magnitude might suggest. After all, you have to begin somewhere. Once the rationale of convinced segregationists or purists who gained encouragement and support from the philosophy of "never" had been punctured, it was felt that the entire system of segregation would crumble and the barriers would fall with far less proportionate effort. Moreover, if the very "best" test cases were advanced first, the act of token integration would enable the black integrators to "prove" that they were worthy of admission, that they were "respectable," or "human," or "American," and thus deserving of open and fair treatment. This act then would lead to a changed attitude on the part of the dominant community, thereby facilitating further, more complete and more rapid integration in the future. From this perspective, token change is a first step.

From the perspective of the conservator who seeks to defend the existing system of racial super- and subordination, it could be argued that token change is better than radical change. To be sure, this is a counsel of last resort, one of resignation that some sort of change is inevitable or else collapse may ensue. So he rationalizes that this ploy will not fundamentally alter the environment, only a facet of it, and that within marginally tolerable limits. Better this than rebellion, he would conclude. If he is able to swallow the embarrassment of symbolic change, he may be able to assure minimum physical restructuralization of the system. For him, token change is a final, not a first step.

There is a stunning identity between the premises of both positions. Both are fundamentally conservative positions. Both see the necessity for conserving the cultural dominance of what might be called white middle-class values. The segregationist recognizes that it is a white man's world and openly seeks to prevent black entry into it. Failing that, he permits limited entry, according to the terms he sets and through a gateway he polices. But the token integrationist encourages the black to enter a system that still remains the same white man's world. By gaining admission, blacks will thus be "raised up" to white standards. That whites might gain from a shared acculturation process is rarely admitted, by either side. The black who enters is still faced with his traditional problem, that of being black in white America. Likewise, both viewpoints are founded on a naïve optimism. They are unwilling to face the prospect of conflict. Even though the threat of violence underlies all such political situations, the tokenist counsels symbolic change because he rejects the possible need for violent or potentially violent confrontation.

Tokenism also has its advocates as an approach to problems of *international* race relations. Representative of this mentality is the professed rationale of the self-styled bridge builders of black Southern Africa—those statesmen of Malawi, Madagascar, Lesotho, and Swaziland who feel that the Republic of South Africa's "outward policy" ought to be encouraged and that efforts should be made by black Africa to establish diplomatic, economic, and cultural relations with white governments.[20] This, rather than force, they argue, will really bring about the dissolution of apartheid and its derivatives in white Southern Africa. Obviously, this approach is not shared by the majority of African statesmen.

Let us take, for example, the position the president of Malawi, Dr. H. Kamuzu Banda, the most vocal proponent of the bridge-building philosophy. Basic premises of his thinking are the views that Europeans in southern Africa have a right to be in Africa, that their existence there must be recognized as legitimate, and that their governments must be dealt with openly and cordially. "To me," he has stated, "if the whites in South Africa, Rhodesia, Mozambique, Angola and South West Africa

20. In Chapter 3 a distinction is drawn between "bridge building" and the less pretentious and demanding policy of establishing expanded relations with white southern Africa. It is the latter, despite what its proponents call it, that is treated here.

have no right to be there because they come from Holland, Germany, France, Britain and other European countries, so too, have the Arabs no right to be in the Sudan. . . . Therefore, there is no differen[ce] whatsoever between the whites in South Africa, whites in Rhodesia, whites in Angola, whites in Mozambique and the Arabs in North Africa."[21] He rejects the views of those who say that black Africans must have nothing to do with white southern Africa. "To me," he continues, "Mozambique, Rhodesia, South Africa are facts of geography and history which we cannot wish out of existence or boycott or isolate out of existence."[22] To ignore or challenge them, the argument runs, would be to contribute to conditions which lead to heightened tensions. Racial animosity grows out of misunderstanding and fear. Only by direct contact can these fears be allayed.[23] Whites must be assured that their future in Africa is secure, and they must be given the opportunity to see how the black states in Africa have managed racial affairs in their own territories.[24] When foreign policy activism in black Africa began to be expressed in hostility toward the white South and open assistance to its coercive enemies, the white South responded not only with threats and acts of retaliation but with hints of contemplated preemptive strikes.[25] The potential for the continuous injection of violent behavior at the inter-state level in southern

21. Banda, *Opening of the Lilongwe Convention, September 16, 1968*, p. 36. See also Houphouet Boigny's similar views as quoted in *The Star*, Johannesburg, May 8, 1971, p. 7. All citations from *The Star* are from the weekly air edition unless otherwise noted.
22. Malawi, *Debates*, Parliament *(Hansard)*, 6th sess., 4th meeting, 1st day, July 29, 1969 (unrevised edition), p. 390.
23. Ibid., 3d day, July 31, 1969 (unrevised edition), pp. 424–25; *Malawi News*, Blantyre, July 8, p. 1.
24. For similar views see the remarks of the prime minister of Ghana, Kofi Busia, in *West Africa*, no. 2737, November 15, 1969, p. 1386; also *ARB*, VI, 1671C, March 15, 1970.
25. For example, Dr. P. van der Merwe, chairman of the Nationalist Party's Foreign Affairs Committee, has publicly stated that in the future South Africa might have to cross borders "to destroy her enemies." He specifically mentioned Zambia and Tanzania and cited the Israeli example approvingly. *The Star*, March 21, 1970, p. 9. See also pp. 168–69 and 207–10, below.

Africa is staggering. The prospects for minimizing its ultimate employment are meager. That it will be employed intensively is less likely, but extensive, sporadic, low-level use of violence will continue to be super-imposed on regional international relations.

President Banda contends that not only is his conciliatory policy a sensible one for Malawi, but that it is also one that will, in the long run, yield changes in the white societies. He would, no doubt, concur in the view of President Tsiranana of Madagascar:

> I condemn racism, perhaps more than do those people who make such a lot of noise about it. But we know very well that we cannot fight these three countries [Rhodesia, Mozambique, and South Africa] with arms. So, rather than excite them, which could harm our African brothers, I prefer to use a revolutionary but specific method which will make headway.[26]

At a state banquet honoring Tsiranana, Banda echoed those views:

> The White people of South Africa and Rhodesia are afraid of Africans. We will not cure them of apartheid by boycotting them or denouncing them at a distance. We have to let them come here and mix with us and let them see how it is to live under Black government. This is an honest, sincere, religious belief about apartheid. We African leaders will help Africans in South Africa much better if we let Whites come in and see how Black, Brown, and White people live together.[27]

In an ensuing communiqué the two emphasized that only through example, persuasion, and "liberalism" could the struggle against racism be effectively pursued.

Thus, such officials seek to encourage the "outward policy" of South Africa and even to deal, where necessary, with Rhodesia. Their position is predicated on the conviction that "South Africa has no imperial or colonial ambitions in Africa" and therefore they are not alarmed by growing South African mili-

26. *ARB*, VI, 1374A, May 15, 1969.
27. Ibid.

tary power or involvement in Rhodesia, Portuguese Africa, and nearby black states.[28]

What sort of political order would President Banda like to see established in white southern Africa? He is not necessarily in favor of white rule in South Africa. Rather he claims to prefer "rule for all the people; a rule that is neither white nor black, but for all the people. But I do not say that white people have no business ruling here; that is the point. . . . We want to establish here a government of partnership between races."[29] But, in fact, little partnership exists in white-ruled states. According to Banda, changes must be brought about, but gradually, taking care not to set off the racial conflict so close beneath the surface.

The essence of Banda's token or gradualist approach is embodied in his advice to black Rhodesian politicians.[30] He opposes the appeal to guerrilla warfare. He feels that even in contemporary Rhodesia, Africans can reach their political goals by working within the constitution. Using his own experience in negotiating with the British as a model, he urges Rhodesian blacks not to boycott Rhodesian elections and politics, but to get involved, contest electoral seats that are allocated them, make their peace with the chiefs, and organize themselves, especially in the villages. To this end he has cooperated with the official African opposition in Rhodesia, the National People's Union, invited their officers to various meetings and congresses in Malawi, and used his country's diplomatic offices to gain entry to black Africa for their officials and parliamentarians. By working within the system, "step by step and step by step, they will get there where they want to be." Cooperation between races is crucial in Rhodesia. The presence of large numbers of white settlers precludes any sort of all-black government. "The best we can look forward to in Rhodesia is a government for all the people. . . . There are . . . many Europeans who are willing to work with the Africans in Rhode-

28. See, for example, Banda, *Press Conference at Chichiri House, July 8th, 1969*, pp. 9–10.
29. Ibid., pp. 13–14.
30. His viewpoint is detailed in ibid., pp. 21–33.

sia. . . . If you use force . . . then you drive all these Europeans away from their liberal attitude . . . . I want to encourage those whites . . . who are liberal in intention, by treating them like human beings; by not isolating them, by not boycotting them and by not denouncing them." In the life of a nation, he persists, ten years, twenty years, even a hundred years is nothing. As a self-admitted "visionary" he concludes:

> I can visualize a time . . . when the children or grandchildren or great-grandchildren of the present European political leaders in South Africa, Rhodesia, Mozambique and Angola, and the great-grandchildren of the present generation of African leaders in this country, embrace each other as we, the present generation of African leaders and the Arab leaders are doing today.

In the long, long run, racial amity will prevail and integration will be achieved. Thus, in President Banda's own repetitious, ponderous, patronizing, and parental rhetoric, a philosophy of tokenism emerges in a most unusual context—that of a poor African state dealing with adamant racist minority governments. So convincing is Banda to some white South Africans that he has been denounced as too revolutionary. In South Africa, at least one Herstigte Nasionale Party candidate in the 1970 election campaign accused Banda of trying, under the guise of being an ally, to destroy apartheid by sending black diplomats to the country.[31] He was convinced that Banda's sympathies lay with the black Africans who opposed South Africa. Unfortunately for Banda, his integrity and ultimate purposes are also questioned by his black colleagues to the north.[32] There is some truth, nevertheless, to his often repeated claim that other black African leaders agree with him although they would not, at this stage, admit it publicly.

It should not be inferred from the preceding discussion that the principal reason for Malawi's willingness to deal with white southern Africa is to attempt to alter racial patterns to the south.

31. *The Star*, April 4, 1970, p. 2, and August 7, 1971; also *NYT*, November 16, 1969, p. 12.
32. Representative samples of anti-Banda invective can be found in *ARB*, IV, 859A–B, October 15, 1967, and *The Nationalist*, Dar es Salaam, April 16, 1969.

Far from it, that is only an incidental rationale for the policy. The principal reason is probably Banda's belief that by dealing with white southern Africa, Malawi, its citizens, and his government will benefit. Whether this is the case, in the long or short runs, is a question that must be answered separately.

There are important moral and philosophical problems in the application of tokenism to international southern African race relations. First, tokenism represents the counsel of compromise and accommodation. In a real sense all it asks of the dominant group is that it alter its attitudes in the direction of some acceptance of selected elements of the subordinate segment of society. But fundamentally, society is not restructured. Patterns of political dominance remain essentially unchanged. In white southern Africa, white dominance is not changed. Tokenism thus may be regarded as a stabilizing policy, not really revolutionizing a situation where a few people exercise political authority over the many. Tokenism is based on a nonrevolutionary type of optimism. The notion, by men like Banda, is that somehow integration is inevitable—but always it is in the future, always over the horizon. This attitude rejects the reality of a conflict situation and as such is far less realistic than is claimed. That this strategy toward white southern Africa may be a sensible foreign policy for some black states with fewer options is at least possible. That it will change the sociopolitical structures of white southern Africa is a delusion.

The chief problem with tokenism centers on the issues of cultural identity and assimilation. In any sociopolitical system, someone or some group within the system sets the standards for social values, styles, and behavior. In southern Africa, this standard is, at present, a white, European standard set and controlled by the minority yet dominant community. An underlying premise of tokenism is assimilation into the dominant (i.e., white) social framework. Implicit in the pronouncements of Banda, Chief Jonathan, and like-minded leaders is the view that white European standards will continue to be the social standards to which black Africans will and should aspire. The standards are not amalgamated standards drawing broadly from the various components of the population. On the contrary, cultural standards are rarely integrated or applied equitably. The unexpressed end of this philosophy is to achieve a white-like or "honorary white" status, as has been granted to non-white diplomats and to Japanese and, in some individual cases, black businessmen. This might be regarded as an internationalized version of the "passing for white" strategy within South African society, which, though more difficult than once was the case, is still the dream of many Coloured people.[33] In another context, the late Eduardo Mondlane put it bitterly when he wrote: "The most that the *assimilado* system even sets out to do is to create a few 'honourary whites,' and this certainly does not constitute non-racialism."[34]

Although an assimilationist philosophy is theoretically not a racialist philosophy, in practice it often is. Even if the acceptance of a measure of tokenism by the dominant community represents an incremental setback for the philosophy of racial arrogance, it represents, in turn, a vindication of the philosophy of cultural arrogance. In interpersonal relations it makes little difference to the sufferer whether his loss of dignity and self-respect comes from racial or cultural arrogance. The cultural variety could well be more pernicious since it functions under the pretense that it is not discriminatory and arbitrary, and that it is liberal, that is, admitting of some social change. It is a cliché that imitation is the highest form of flattery. But to some degree it also represents a tacit admission of cultural inferiority. The principle of assimilation could admit of some efficacy when applied to a minority group that was divorced from its roots and being assimilated into a dominant majority group. But when a superordinate minority insists that the majority must adopt its culture (as in Portuguese Africa at its theoretical best) and moreover refuses to provide the vast majority with opportunities to adapt, then the integrity of the assimilation effort is doubtful. It simply reflects a recognition by forces of the status quo that it is strategically less disruptive to comply symbolically by admitting a few "Europeanized" blacks into white institutions than

33. Watson, "The Process of Passing for White in South Africa," *Canadian Review of Sociology and Anthropology*, IV (1967), 141–47.
34. Mondlane, *The Struggle for Mozambique*, p. 50.

it would be to resist uncompromisingly by fighting external and internal pressures to the bitter end. Even if assimilated fully into the European culture, these Africans would be little more than refugees from an "inferior" culture. This token approach never really comes to grips with the problem of racial diversity and exploitation in Africa. In the Republic of South Africa even this minimal approach to interracial exchange is ideologically rejected and separateness is raised to the level of the sacred.

It is impossible to abstract racial issues from their economic, demographic, and political contexts. Racial separation, discrimination, and exploitation are matters of power, wealth, and status. Such systems invariably rest on institutionalized structures of super- and subordination. The philosophies of apartheid and separate development tolerate no compromise. Tokenism could never lead to radical change in South Africa because the first token steps would never be permitted. The legal norms of the South African state are even abandoned in dealing with elements of the European population. They reject even the right of token integration. In the United States at least there was a strong historical strain of constitutional interpretation that was to become the law of the land in various fields of interracial contact in the 1940s and 1950s and into the 1960s. In South Africa the sanction of the legal structure precludes tokenism. It is unlikely that policies of cooperation with white southern Africa will really alter conditions for blacks in white-governed territories. Tokenism is a strategy of the minority outside group that wants to be admitted into the system. When a majority group is forced or agrees to accept tokenism, it is allowing the minority to shape the environment to its own interests and advantages. And a culturally dominant group, no matter how small, always has a psychological advantage.

Although tokenism may bring direct benefits to those who deal with white Africa and even to their constituencies (at the expense of their racial brothers within white southern Africa), it cannot work to free their brothers or to reshape the constellation of power and wealth in southern Africa. It may indeed address itself to issues of war and peace, economic development and retardation, in an opportunistic and parochial sense, but it will not alter markedly the racial attitudes and tensions prevailing in the region.

The Role of Violence in Intraregional Affairs

A crude measure of the intensity of the commitment to the alteration of the racial status quo in southern Africa can be distilled from the various pronouncements by southern Africans, black and white, on the place of violence in their sociopolitical models. Historically there has been a steady evolution in the willingness of responsible black African officials to employ violent means in order to deal with white racism. Today the selective utility of violence has come to be widely recognized in Africa. Over the past twenty years or more, black Africa's leaders have abandoned Gandhian thought patterns regarding violence and have increasingly mirrored Fanonesque ones. The general temper of independence and liberation movements and the views of officials and leaders in independent states have become orchestrated. Even when circumstances of particular issues lead such persons to abstain from a violent policy in the specific, a willingness to admit the doctrinal efficacy of violence in the abstract is broadly held.

Throughout the forties and fifties and even into the sixties there seemed to be a widespread dedication to nonviolence. The influence of M. K. Gandhi had been profound throughout black Africa. Nyerere, Kaunda, and various South African and Rhodesian black nationalists were, early on, of this persuasion in their strategies for racial equality.[35]

This overall predisposition was generally reflected in the statements and resolutions deriving from early Pan-African meetings. For example, at the first All-African Peoples' Conference in Accra, Ghana, in 1958, the Algerians sought to persuade the delegates to approve of their use of violence in their

35. For a discussion of a similar orientation of those opposing Portuguese colonialism and their frustrations see Marcum, *Angolan Revolution*, pp. 13–120.

war against France.[36] A large majority of the delegates felt that "violence as a policy could not work," but reasoned that a nationalist movement would not employ violence unless driven to it. Thus they grudgingly resolved to support "all those who resort to peaceful means of non-violence and civil disobedience as well as to all those who are compelled to retaliate against violence to attain national independence and freedom for the people."[37] Nevertheless the conference rejected violence as a considered means of struggle.

Later in 1958 an even more positive stand was assumed by the Pan-African Freedom Movement of East and Central Africa (PAFMECA). In its original constitution, one of the five aims of the organization was "To champion nonviolence in the African nationalist struggles for freedom and prosperity."[38] The nonviolent persuasion continued to prevail at the Accra Conference on Positive Action and Security, in April 1960, largely owing to Kwame Nkrumah's Gandhian penchant and his high status in the early Pan-African movement.

But this perspective was being undermined by changing conditions. Two conferences at Addis Ababa, in 1962 and 1963, marked most clearly the transition in attitudes. The first was a conference at which PAFMECA was expanded to include the southern African liberation movements and a new organization, the Pan-African Freedom Movement of East, Central and Southern Africa (PAFMECSA), was born. The influence of new, more southerly participants and their more militant experiences was apparent. A call to arms by Nelson Mandela of the African National Congress (ANC) of South Africa received approval from the delegates.[39] The only delegate who reportedly

36. Mboya, *Freedom and After*, p. 50. Mboya was chairman of the conference.

37. Legum, *Pan-Africanism*, pp. 229 and 43.

38. See Appendix B of Cox, *Pan-Africanism in Practice*, p. 83.

39. This account of the delegate response is drawn from ibid., pp. 51–58 and 36–38. The Mandela address appears in *PAFMECSA, Addis Ababa Conference, February 2–10, 1962*, pp. 29–35. Peter Molotsi of the Pan-Africanist Congress of South Africa directly attacked the PAFMECA constitutional pledge to "champion non-violence." He regarded it as unrealistic and in conflict with then current thinking of the UN and the All-African Peoples' Congress (p. 40). This clause was

did not seem caught up in the infectious enthusiasm was Kenneth Kaunda, the president of the United National Independence Party of Northern Rhodesia (Zambia).

The second Addis Ababa meeting, in May, 1963, established the Organization of African Unity. Embodied in the first resolutions of the OAU (resolutions 10–15) are provisions for the creation and operation of a committee to coordinate and finance liberation activities among the various nationalist movements. By this time, African Gandhism was "nearly dead."[40]

This shift from African Gandhism was obvious, but not always eagerly approved. Julius Nyerere spoke for many leaders when he said:

> Our preference, and that of every true African patriot, has always been for peaceful methods of struggle. We abhor the sufferings and the terror, and the sheer waste, which is involved in violent upheavals, and believe that peaceful progress is worth some sacrifice in terms of time. But when the door of peaceful progress is slammed shut and bolted, then the struggle must take other forms; we cannot surrender.[41]

Nevertheless, driven to this position, leaders did not hesitate to make the difficult decision. The various resolutions at international conferences are basically a reflection of the views of a number of the more active and vocal leaders. Resolutions on violence increasingly reflected the changing circumstances of the struggle for independence. The growing disillusionment with nonviolent approaches became evident as leaders came to face more intractable white governments in central and southern Africa. President Kaunda seemed to make perhaps the most significant about-face. No stronger proponent of nonviolence had risen to such a high governmental level in Africa.[42] His

---

eliminated from the proposed constitution of the new body, PAFMECSA (pp. 88–89).

40. Mazrui, *Violence and Thought*, p. 36.

41. Nyerere, *Tanzania Policy on Foreign Affairs*, p. 9.

42. Kaunda appears to have been won over to absolute nonviolence in the first instance in the period between the mid-1950s and his restriction in rural Zambia and imprisonment in Salisbury in 1959. See Hall, *The High Price*, pp. 43–51.

conception of "humanism" had been founded on a respect for the dignity and individual worth of every man. By his own interpretation he sought to combine Gandhi's policy of nonviolence with Nkrumah's "positive action."[43] The Rhodesian UDI contributed to Kaunda's transformation. The intransigence of racism, in his view, drove him to it.

Curiously, though African Gandhism might have been dead, at least one militant revolutionary body, the ANC of South Africa, felt the need to reconcile its violent stance with Gandhi's doctrine. After all, Gandhi has played a vital role in the creation of Indian and African political activism in South Africa. In an unsigned article, "From Gandhi to Mandela," in the ANC's official organ a spokesman noted that Gandhi never resolved, "except abstrusely," the problem of disarming the people in the face of an enemy determined to rule by force. On the contrary, the article quoted Gandhi favorably and at length to the effect that:

> Where the choice is set between cowardice and violence I would advise violence. . . . This is because he who runs away commits mental violence; he has not the courage of facing death by killing. I would a thousand times prefer violence than the emasculation of a whole race. I prefer to use arms in defence of honour rather than remain the vile witness of dishonour.[44]

Thus, despite the distortion of the spirit and total thrust of Gandhian teaching, the ANC contends that by taking up arms it is not acting in contradiction of Gandhi.

The ANC and some others see violence as a natural "extension" of the forms of political action attempted in the past. According to one former PAC official:

> Force is an extension of all the possible non-violent avenues that have been tried and have failed; thus, force is a logical sequence in the progression of trying to obtain objectives. Force and nonviolence are interdependent.[45]

43. Kaunda, *Zambia Shall Be Free*, pp. 140, 152, 88–91. See also Kaunda, *A Humanist in Africa*.
44. "From Gandhi to Mandela," *Sechaba*, London, III (May 1969), 10.
45. Morley Nkosi, in Davis and Baker, eds., *Southern Africa in Transition*, p. 280; see also Oliver Tambo (ANC), ibid.

This Clausewitzian doctrine of violence views the independence struggle as a form of escalatory politics by which revolutionary forces employ at each successive stage the political means which they deem adequate to carry the people with them and maintain their revolutionary fervor and base. At each stage, however, they are foiled and therefore the stakes and the level of political conflict are raised. Apparently, when these ideas are applied, there is no qualitative transition from nonviolent to violent means.

Actually, this sort of view is not common among southern African thinkers and leaders. More frequently they tend to be more pragmatic and practical, and to recognize the qualitative distinction between the two varieties of behavior. Nonviolence thereby succeeds or fails depending upon the nature of the opposition and the political environment within which it operates.[46] And that environment has two contexts—internal and international. Nonviolence as a political strategy embodies, at heart, an appeal to moral conscience. If the ruling power has no sensitivity to moral suasion, nonviolence is left without any impact, in a localized sense. But leaders still might fruitfully employ nonviolent techniques if they thought such tactics might attract attention and support externally. To be sure, "no outside person, however sympathetic, can make a people free," to borrow the words of President Nyerere.[47] But the direct support that outsiders could render a liberation movement and the pressure that they might bring to bear on the target government are not inconsiderable. Herein lies the tragedy of the first nonviolent steps toward independence in southern Africa. The essential insensitivity of the outside world has not gone unnoticed by Africa's black leaders. There are built-in rewards for violent behavior. Violence, because it is newsworthy, helps create the conditions in which the world takes notice of the sufferings of those under colonial rule. Experience shows, the late Tom Mboya wrote, that the world only helps African nationalists

46. See, for example, statements by Arthur N. L. Wina and Ndabaningi Sithole, ibid., p. 240.
47. Nyerere, *Tanzania Policy on Foreign Affairs*, p. 10.

when they have become active, and never before.[48] The demonstration effect of violent behavior has many dimensions, not the least of which is the impact it makes on opinion and policy abroad.

There are other reasons for the resort to violent means. Most African leaders would contend that violence is not of their own instigation. Rather, violence is an integral part of the established order in minority-dominated states. Such was the view expressed by ANC leader Nelson Mandela at his 1962 trial in Pretoria. He said then: "They [the white government] set the scene for violence by relying exclusively on violence with which to answer our people and their demands. . . . We have warned repeatedly that the government, by resorting continually to violence, will breed, in this country, counter-violence amongst the people, till ultimately, the dispute between the government and my people will finish up by being settled in violence and by force."[49] Drawing upon the examples of Algeria, Kenya, and Angola, Tom Mboya once framed a rule that "in any colony where there has been considerable white settlement, violence has become inevitable, although it was not the original policy of the nationalist party."[50] White settlers invariably seek to prevent majority rule. In short, violence does not originate with the black Africans. Their violence is frequently a reaction to forceful provocation by the ruling power. On the other hand, this explanation and rationale, though often accurate, ignores much of sociological theory regarding violent behavior. Violence may indeed feed on itself. And repeated acts of forceful repression do invite retaliation and serve as catalysts for counter-violence. But the sort of foreign policy that encourages violence within another state or contemplates the direct utilization of armed forces for policy ends is more often at heart a result of a genuine conflict of interests.

Still the privileged order may, in order to protect its privi-

48. Mboya, *Freedom and After*, pp. 50–52.
49. As quoted in "What Nelson Mandela Said about Dialogue," *Sechaba*, V (July 1971), 6.
50. Mboya, *Freedom and After*, p. 50; see also F. Jariretundu Kozonguizi in Davis and Baker, eds., *Southern Africa in Transition*, p. 80.

leges, engage in preemptive violence, sensing that to hestitate might lead to a disadvantageous redistribution of power. To have a vested interest in the status quo is not always to be committed to the absence of violence. Such a view assumes that the underprivileged instinctively are more violent than the privileged. Yet at the individual level, the protective instinct can lead to violent behavior more readily than the acquisitive one. Group conceptions of protection and conservation are probably not much different. The insecure ruling group is a more dangerous animal than the ambitious poor.[51] Despite the tendency of the established governments to urge nonviolence and order, in practice coercion has been a frequent and ready ally of the insecure status quo.

51. See the excellent discussion of these points in Mazrui, *Towards a Pax Africana*, pp. 144–45.

2

Economic and Transport Relationships

If a little tree grows in the shade of a larger tree, it will die small. —*Senegal*

Political attitudes and doctrinal pronouncements may be important indicators of preference, and to some extent they tell us much about the foreign policies of states, but they are only two among several such indicators of foreign policy behavior. Given the ambiguities of doctrine and ideological preference, such indicators can, at times, be less than helpful in an effort to discern relational patterns. Because doctrine may obfuscate policy, it becomes necessary to look for more direct, comparable, and precise indicators. The next six chapters will attempt to sketch a more concrete picture of international behavior in southern Africa.

Which indicators are the more reliable manifestation of overall patterns is an open question. Simply answered, it depends on which facet of the regional system one wants to understand. It is hoped in this study that by overlaying the several "maps" of the system, the more salient patterns will become more obvious. As a study in political relational patterns, it will concentrate on political factors in a broad sense—those issues of conflict and cooperation by which influence, control, and persuasion are exercised. Unfortunately, it is sometimes necessary to get at these issues indirectly. Economic, diplomatic, and military data are but unrefined indicators of overall regional political relations. Insofar as they can be, they will be treated separately, but it must be borne in mind that the chief concern is to see them as part of a larger, more basic pattern of interaction.

In many respects, postcolonial relations in southern Africa have not developed from scratch. Rather they are conditioned, some would say predetermined, by an already routinized set of patterned economic relationships that must first be considered before radical political transformation could be contemplated. These relationships, shaped originally by and for the convenience and profit of the colonial interests and governments, or by and for the minority settler regimes, work almost entirely to the advantage of present white-governed states in southern Africa. Except for the massive copper resources of Zambia and the Congo, and the ports of Tanzania and the Congo, black southern Africa is, generally speaking, landlocked, without easily exploitable natural resources, undereducated, and undercapitalized. These are the factors that in some instances circumscribe the foreign policy decisional latitude of the economically weaker black states in the region. In this chapter we will examine those economic patterns that emerged from the colonial milieu. These economic realities set the tone for the perception of political alternatives upon which foreign policies are based. In the concluding section of this chapter an effort will be made to speculate on the relationships between economic power and political influence in international affairs.

South African Economic Hegemony

The most imposing structural characteristic of southern African affairs is the virtually unchallenged economic domination of the Republic of South Africa (RSA).[1] This, more than any other single fact, has determined the economic, military, and

1. Early documentation of this view appears in Green and Fair, *Development in Africa* and more recently in Lombard et al., *The Concept of Economic Co-operation in Southern Africa.*

diplomatic networks that are being constructed in the region. This domination, or imbalance, is evident in a comparison of gross domestic product data for the states in the region (table 1).

TABLE 1
GROSS DOMESTIC PRODUCTS, SOUTHERN AFRICA

Country	*Total in millions of US dollars and year*	*Percent of regional total*
South Africa	15,786.4 (1969)	65.5
Congo (Kinshasa)	1,440.8 (1968)	6.0
Zambia	1,369.2 (1968)	5.6
Rhodesia	1,337.0 (1969)	5.5
Mozambique	1,027.6 (1965)	4.3
Angola	834.4 (1965)	3.5
Tanzania	821.6 (1968)	3.4
Madagascar	655.4 (1967)	2.7
Malawi	328.4 (1969)	1.5
South West Africa	299.6 (1966)	1.2
Swaziland	74.8 (1967)	0.3
Lesotho	69.3 (1966)	0.3
Botswana	59.1 (1967)	0.2
Regional total	24,103.6	100.0

SOURCES: Figures from Angola and Mozambique are from J. A. Lombard et al., *The Concept of Economic Co-operation in Southern Africa* (Pretoria: Econburo, Pty., Ltd., 1969), table IV. The South West Africa figure is from Colin Legum and John Drysdale, eds., *Africa Contemporary Record—1969–1970* (Exeter: Africa Research Ltd., 1970), p. B317. All other figures are from United Nations, Statistical Office, Department of Economic and Social Affairs, *Statistical Yearbook, 1970* (New York: United Nations, 1971), table 179.

South Africa accounts for two-thirds of the combined gross domestic production of southern Africa. The white-governed states together account for about 80 percent. Even though the comparability of the data may be subject to some controversy, the crude indicators are incontrovertible. In relative, regional terms South Africa is an economic giant. The economic patterns that emerge cannot help but be asymmetrical. The political ramifications are equally distorted.

Likewise, South Africa is the only industrialized country in the region. The present distribution of gross domestic products in the other states and the distribution of economically active populations indicate economic structures that are limited to the production of crude primary products, often of a single important commodity in each territory. Mining activities predominate in Zambia (40 percent of GDP), South West Africa (47 percent), and the Congo. Agriculture is dominant in Malawi, Mozambique, Angola, Swaziland, and Tanzania. The export of labor ranks foremost in Lesotho and Botswana. Except for Rhodesia, which is establishing more manufacturing and tertiary enterprises as a result of the imposition of sanctions,[2] South Africa stands almost alone regionally in the production of manufactured goods for export and domestic consumption. In the generation of investment capital and the production of technically trained and experienced personnel South Africa is in an advantageous position to make available to other countries in the region two key ingredients in capitalist enterprise. This is not to say that South Africa can do this easily, or without any necessary sacrifice to its own economic activity, but in relative, regional terms, it alone has the capability.

Aware of these economic facts, South African industrialists, and increasingly her governmental officials and citizenry have begun to picture the RSA as a potential industrial and economic heartland of southern Africa. One Nationalist Party politician in an unveiled slap at Great Britain referred to the RSA's becoming the France of Africa. The fact is that South Africa's leaders and people see the economic strength of the country as a tremendous advantage in conducting foreign policy, and they reason that it gives them leverage for a vigorous regional policy. In another regard, *verligtes* (South Africans who prefer a pragmatic approach to foreign affairs and domestic race issues) see a vigorous foreign policy as necessary if continued economic

2. *Economic Survey of Rhodesia, 1969,* pp. 1–11; Barnekov, "Sanctions and the Rhodesian Economy," *Rhodesian Journal of Economics,* III (March 1969), 44–75; McKinnell, "Sanctions and the Rhodesian Economy" *JMAS,* VII (1969), 559–81.

growth is to be assured. Thus economic strength and the "outward policy" go hand-in-glove: one without the other would be less than satisfactory. By reaching out to neighboring black states, particularly in mercantile terms, the present government tends to bring greater unity among the various segments of South Africa's white population. To them it represents a profitable or potentially profitable "liberalization" that necessitates minimal change of the domestic racial apparatus. Even some committed to profound domestic change see the "outward policy" as a harbinger of a relaxation of racial tensions regionally and an abandonment of racial separation internally.

Regional Trade Patterns

The patterns of regional economic dominance by white southern Africa, and particularly by the RSA, are strongly apparent in trade patterns (table 2). Among those black states most obviously in the geographical context of southern Africa it can be seen that their inter-state trade has been negligible, while their trade with white southern Africa has been vital. On the other hand, trade with regional black states constitutes only a small portion of white southern Africa's trade. With the single exception of Rhodesia's exports (a situation corrected after the unilateral declaration of independence, or UDI), in every instance trade with white regional states is far and away more important than trade with regional black states. More up-to-date comparable data would, if they were available, duplicate these patterns.

Unfortunately the policies of the South African government, with regard to country-by-country trade data, does not facilitate analysis or updating. The last year for which the Department of Customs and Excise provided a complete breakdown for African countries was 1962. In 1963 and 1964 the published data by country in Africa were sketchy and incomplete. By 1965 all African trade was lumped together under a single category, "Africa." Data for all other parts of the world are still presented in a country-by-country format. We can assume that the government

TABLE 2
INTRA-REGIONAL TRADE DIRECTIONS, 1964
(In thousands of South African rands)

Country		*Imports*	*Exports*
Angola	BSA	14	932
	WSA	5,069	3,557
	Total	127,278	158,436
Botswana	BSA	108	311
	WSA	8,629	4,727
	Total	9,329	10,173
Lesotho	BSA	—	—
	WSA	15,217	4,943
	Total	16,900	5,200
Malawi	BSA	927	930
	WSA	16,015	5,072
	Total	28,464	24,142
Mozambique	BSA	384	662
	WSA	22,758	12,302
	Total	121,257	82,161
Rhodesia	BSA	14,846	99,991
	WSA	62,872	24,861
	Total	221,390	294,218
South Africa	BSA	40,592	69,046
	WSA	105,829	206,333
	Total	1,665,488	1,138,415
South West Africa	BSA	35	43
	WSA	126,120	75,595
	Total	140,000	146,773
Swaziland	BSA	13	95
	WSA	16,016	9,963
	Total	19,000	22,695
Zambia	BSA	1,321	1,078
	WSA	115,197	31,268
	Total	158,038	349,418

BSA=black-ruled southern Africa. WSA=white-ruled southern Africa. The totals are for trade with all countries, not BSA and WSA only.

SOURCE: Data drawn from Table I of: Eschel Rhoodie, *The Third Africa* (Cape Town: Nasionale Boekhandel, 1968), table 1, p. 287.

intentionally seeks to obfuscate the extent of South African trade with individual African countries.[3] Thus, less pressure can be brought to bear on those countries that do trade with South Africa. Rhodesia, as well, does not publish directions of trade data. Indeed, to disclose information regarding the extent of and techniques for violation of UN sanctions is a felony in Rhodesia. Nevertheless some black countries are themselves publishing data on their trade with South Africa and Rhodesia, and we can to some extent reconstruct a fairly complete though not always uniform or comparable picture of white southern African trade with black neighbors.

Using what 1968 data we can locate, in all cases except the Congo and Angola, we can see that South Africa provides more than 5 percent of the imports of regional states (see table 3). In contrast, though regional trade is important to South Africa, it is not especially vital in the total picture. Rather, the bulk of the RSA's foreign trade is still with Europe and the United States. Its exports to Africa have not exceeded 20 percent of total exports in the past two decades, and if one includes total trade that figure is reduced significantly. But even though the regional figures are not impressive, South Africa's trade with the rest of Africa is important since Africa is the only continent with which the RSA shows a favorable balance of trade. It is this picture that South African government officials and businessmen seek to improve upon, and they are indeed improving it. The economic byproducts of the outward policy spell profits as well as increased contact and, eventually, economic dependence. It would be this economic dependence they seek to parlay into political acceptance and ultimately, through increasingly narrowed alternatives, into foreign policy clientage.

In some respects these patterns of trade and economic contact have been formalized. The Customs Union between Botswana, Lesotho, Swaziland, and South Africa is based upon an agree-

3. RSA, Department of Customs and Excise, *Foreign Trade Statistics,* 1961 and subsequent years. For a brief account of trade between South Africa and some West African countries see John Edlin, "The Revealing Voyage of Nahoon," *The Star,* June 5, 1971, p. 11.

TABLE 3
TRADE WITH SOUTH AFRICA AND WHITE SOUTHERN AFRICA BY REGIONAL STATES, 1964 AND 1968
(In percentage of monetary value)

Country		*1964*		*1968*	
		With RSA	*With WSA*	*With RSA*	*With WSA*
Botswana	Exports	40	47	50[a]	55[a]
	Imports	50	92	65	92[b]
	Total	45	69	58[a]	72[a]
Lesotho	Exports	95	95	95[a]	95[a]
	Imports	90	90	84	84[a]
	Total	91	91	86[a]	86[a]
Swaziland	Exports	36	37	15	16[a]
	Imports	83	84	91	92[a]
	Total	57	58	49	50[a]
Malawi	Exports	6	22	5	10
	Imports	6	46	11	29
	Total	6	35	9	21
Zambia	Exports	8	12	2	2
	Imports	21	60	23	30
	Total	12	27	10	13
Congo	Exports	1	1	3[b]	3[b]
	Imports	3	5	4[b]	6[b]
	Total	2	3	3[b]	5[b]
Mozambique	Exports	11	18	8[c]	14[c]
	Imports	13	17	11[c]	16[c]
	Total	12	17	10[c]	15[c]
Angola	Exports	1	2	2	3
	Imports	2	4	3	4
	Total	1	3	2	4
Rhodesia	Exports	7	8	29[a]	31[a]
	Imports	24	25	54[a]	56[a]
	Total	15	16	42[a]	44[a]

RSA=Republic of South Africa. WSA=White-ruled southern Africa (including RSA). [a]Estimated. [b]1966 figures. [c]1967 figures.

The 1964 data are based upon Eschel Rhoodie, *The Third Africa*, (Cape Town: Nasionale Boekhandel, 1968), table I, p. 287. The 1968 data are calculated from a great variety of sources.

ment entered into by the Union of South Africa and the United Kingdom (on behalf of their High Commission Territories) in 1910. It originally provided that South African currency be legal tender and that all this area be treated as a single entity for purposes of customs regulations and restrictions. The Union of South Africa, in effect, fixed tariffs for the High Commission Territories (HCT's). Then fixed proportions of its gross customs and excise revenue, based upon the volume of its imports and those of the HCT's, and upon the relative sizes of their economies in 1910, were distributed to the latter. In 1965–1966 the percentages were revised to distribute 0.47093 percent to Lesotho, 0.30971 percent to Botswana, and 0.53033 percent to Swaziland.[4] With the steady growth of the South African economy and the relative stagnation of the economies of the other states, the latter have probably received more than they would have had their customs revenues been self-regulated.

On the other hand, the disadvantages of the arrangement have been frustrating and economically debilitating. These HCT's and their successors were made dependents of South Africa for a large part of their governmental revenues (see table 4). Moreover, changes in tariff structure and the introduction of a South African sales tax were authorized by and in the interests of the South African government, and could be harmful to the economies of the former HCT's.

For these reasons, among others, drawn-out negotiations to review and update the customs union led to a new agreement signed in December 1969 and effective on March 1, 1970. It includes a revised, self-adjusting formula for calculating the division of customs, excise, and sales tax revenue whereby economic growth in the individual countries will lead to their receiving a greater proportionate share of the gross revenue. The result in its first year of operation is that total funds distributed were trebled. The agreement also provided for the establishment of a Customs Union Commission for inter-governmental consultation on the imposition and amendment of customs

4. See Robson, "Economic Integration in Southern Africa," *JMAS*, V (1967), 473–80; also Turner, "A Fresh Start for the Southern African Customs Union," *African Affairs*, LXX (1971), 269–76.

TABLE 4
REPRESENTATIVE PROPORTIONS OF ORDINARY GOVERNMENT REVENUES FROM CUSTOMS AND EXCISE: BOTSWANA, LESOTHO, AND SWAZILAND
(In percentage of total)

Country	*1959–60*	*1965–66*	*1968–71*
Botswana	25	21	20 (1968–69)
Lesotho	50	35	43 (1970–71)
Swaziland	11	32	47 (1969–70)

SOURCES: Figures for 1959–60 are from Jack Halpern, *South Africa's Hostages: Basutoland, Bechuanaland and Swaziland* (Baltimore: Penguin Books, 1965), p. 233, and for 1965–66 from Peter Robson, "Economic Integration in Southern Africa," *Journal of Modern African Studies*, V (1967), 470. In the third column, the Botswana 1968–69 figure (provisional) is from Republic of Botswana, Central Statistical Office, Ministry of Development Planning, *Statistical Abstract, 1969* (Gaberone: Government Printer, August 1969), p. 66; the Lesotho 1970–71 and Swaziland 1969–70 figures are from *Annual Economic Review: Botswana, Lesotho, Swaziland* (London: Standard Bank Group, October 1970), pp. 12 and 18, and Colin Legum and John Drysdale, eds., *Africa Contemporary Record, 1969–1970* (Exeter: Africa Research Ltd., 1970), p. B235.

duties, the unilateral imposition of additional duties to protect infant Botswana, Lesotho, and Swaziland industries, and the maintenance or increase of certain external tariffs needed to protect specified industries in those three countries. The commission, however, may only monitor, recommend, and mediate. It has no executive, legislative, or judicial powers. The formal economic terms for the weaker states have been improved but the by-product is a more intimate economic collaboration with South Africa. For this reason *The Star* of Johannesburg was led to comment: "This is the outward policy in action. We all want more of it."[5]

The three countries want to go a step further. They have proposed a new monetary agreement that would transform the relationship between South Africa and the other states in the rand currency area. They want: (1) a direct voice in exchange control and other fiscal policies designed to protect the rand; (2) a

5. December 13, 1969, p. 11. Turner, op. cit., argues that the new agreement is so different from the old one that it is correct to say that the old customs union no longer exists.

share of the interest on securities held in the South African Reserve Bank; and (3) the right to raise capital by the sale of government bonds and treasury bills on the open market. Again, however, the price to be exacted for improved financial arrangements of this sort would be closer association with a state whose domestic system they find repugnant and whose economic power is, to them, overbearing. Failing to achieve these aims they may consider establishing their own reserve and development banks and issuing their own currencies, chiefly to gain independence from monetary policies pursued by South Africa.

Further evidence of expanding regional trading relationships appeared in the Malawi-South Africa trade agreement signed in March 1967. It provides for duty-free import into South Africa of some key Malawian commodities, including essential oils, tobacco, and tea, and for most-favored rates on additional products. Since then, however, Malawi's exports to South Africa have not risen appreciably, though imports from there have risen from 7 percent of Malawi's total in 1966 to 15 percent in 1969.

Some circles in southern Africa would like to intensify these relationships. Sometimes their desires are expressed as the creation of a "co-prosperity sphere." At other times the phrase "common market" is used. Usually the emphasis is placed on expanding bilateral trade and economic relationships with actual and potential African markets.[6] In all cases, however, proponents urge that South Africa be the industrial core and the motivating force behind greater economic cooperation.

The idea for closer regional economic collaboration has been repeated often in South African governing circles. Some, like Prime Minister Verwoerd, have seen cooperation as a potentially effective substitute for diplomatic or political ties. In most cases, Verwoerd specifically deemphasized the political component of such relationships, stating that a multiracial common

6. Financial journals in South Africa regularly devote special supplements to such countries, often with specific sections on how to expand exports. See, for example, the supplements on Malawi in *Financial Mail*, Johannesburg, January 12, 1968; on Angola and Mozambique, ibid., August 15, 1969, and *Standard Bank Review*, no. 618, September 1970; and on Madagascar, ibid., no. 619, October 1970, pp. 13–20.

market in southern Africa ought to mean that none of the members would exercise political control over any of the others.[7] The concept of a regional common market is generally attributed to him. By and large, however, even among those favorable to the concept there is little agreement as to the structural form that arrangements should take. In 1965 the South African minister for planning told an international conference in Johannesburg that intra-regional marketing arrangements would benefit all the people of the participating states. While mentioning favorably the examples of the European Common Market, the European Free Trade Area and the Central American Common Market, he was quick to add that the European Common Market was designed to foster political unity as well as economic integration. This, he insisted, was not the aim of South Africa.[8] Other South African officials have also insisted on the political unimportance of their economic plans.[9] Likewise, most South African economists have opposed a regional customs union, favoring instead greater cooperation by a series of bilateral arrangements specially tailored for each country.[10] Several African heads of state, including Dr. Banda and Chief Jonathan, have also endorsed the idea. Although there is support in important places for broadened schemes of trade in the region, and blue-ribbon study groups continue to explore the possibilities, so far discussion has been more vague than specific, and formal proposals for multilateral trade arrangements have not yet followed discussion. The basic reserve of governmental officials has not deterred some commentators. The *Star* was even willing to suggest that a "co-prosperity sphere" might lead to "closer political and possibly military ties" which would serve to deter those African states that were "casting covetous eyes on South Africa as the richest and most developed part of the conti-

7. An August 1964 statement quoted in Spence, *Republic Under Pressure*, p. 77.
8. As quoted in Rhoodie, *The Third Africa*, pp. 214–15.
9. See Dr. N. Diederich's statement, *South African Financial Gazette*, April 28, 1967. This entire issue is devoted to the subject. See also *The Star*, July 17, 1971, p. 1.
10. Lombard et al., *The Concept of Economic Co-operation*, especially pp. 34–44.

nent."[11] Despite this optimism, it is unlikely that formal commercial arrangements in the southern African cross-racial context would necessarily lead to extensive political cooperation. Nevertheless, the repeated denials of the political implications of increased economic interaction should not be taken at face value. Virtually everyone concerned is silently and on occasion openly reading political leverage into these contacts.

Multilateral regional cooperation has actually lessened since the black states became independent. The only existing regional organization is SARCCUS, the Southern African Regional Committee for the Conservation and Utilization of Soil, established in 1950. It is concerned mainly with forestry, hydrology, land use, and other aspects of natural conservation and animal health and production. But various regional proposals, and expanding bilateral functional cooperative endeavors (especially with Malawi and the Portuguese territories), hint that the trend of South Africa's economic disengagement is being reversed.

Note must also be taken of a parallel process, perhaps not as advanced or as potentially important in the short run regarding regional commercial relationships. Some black states of southern Africa have attempted to open further trade contacts with black states to the north. Zambia, for example, has applied for membership in the East African Economic Community. Negotiations are presently at an advanced stage. Prime Minister Dhlamini of Swaziland has expressed his country's interest in becoming an associate member of that organization. Bilateral trade agreements have been signed between Swaziland and Zambia, Swaziland and Malawi, Malawi and Zambia, and other regional and extra-regional African states. But these have been little more than gestures toward the principles of continental economic cooperation and away from total dependence upon trading partners in the white South.

Functional Cooperation

The same factors and forces that stimulate further moves toward regional commercial integration have prompted increas-

11. As quoted in Spence, *Republic Under Pressure*, p. 77.

ing functional cooperation in economic projects. By and large, arrangements that have proceeded beyond the talk stages have been bilateral and—with one major exception, the Tan-Zam railway—have involved at least one white southern African state, through either the government or a private enterpreneur (or consortium) in that state.

CABORA BASSA

At the present time, four major hydroelectric schemes with international political ramifications are in advanced planning stages, under contract, under construction, or in operation. The most important, in projected size and in the number of states participating in financing and construction and the purchase of the electricity, is the Cabora Bassa project, on the Zambezi River in Mozambique.[12] At a cost of some $385 million (a figure that could easily grow), the project will be the largest dam in Africa and among the largest in the world. Its first stage (the main dam and generating plant) is scheduled for completion in 1975 and the second and third stages in 1977 and 1979. The Portuguese see it as the key to Mozambique's economic development and as tangible evidence of Portugal's intention to remain in Africa. But the deeper regional political implications bear scrutiny.

Companies interested in the project grouped themselves into three consortiums, each of which bid for the contract. Significantly, South African companies featured prominently in all three. In 1969 the contract for construction of the dam was awarded to ZAMCO, the Consórcio Hidroeléctrico do Zambeze, organized by the Anglo-American Corporation of South Africa and including French, German, South African, Portuguese, Italian, and Swedish firms. On the same day agreements were signed with the South African government and ESCOM, the

12. For details and varying perspectives see Abshire, "Minerals, Manufacturing, Power, and Communications," in Abshire and Samuels, eds., *Portuguese Africa*, pp. 311–13; "Building for the Future," Angola-Mozambique supplement, *Financial Mail*, August 15, 1969, pp. 49–53; "High Stakes at Cabora Bassa," *Sechaba*, III (December 1969), 14–18; World Council of Churches, *Cabora Bassa*. The Kunene project is treated in World Council of Churches, *Cunene Dam Scheme*.

Electricity Supply Commission of South Africa, who will be the chief customers for the power to be generated by the first stage. Basically, South Africa does not need this power. It is expected to cost, at first, more than would power from an additional thermal station in the republic. Under pressure from the Department of Foreign Affairs, however, ESCOM agreed to participate.[13] One can conclude that widespread and massive international financial backing also implies support for Portugal in Africa, and for Portugal's intention to develop the Zambezi Valley and to encourage more European immigrants. It is unlikely that Portugal would easily be abandoned by its supporters after the investments were made, or opposed after the promise of return was realized.

Knowing this full well, those opposed to Portuguese colonial rule have vowed to destroy the project:—the Frente Libertação de Moçambique (Liberation Front of Mozambique)—FRELIMO and its allies by the use of force,[14] and statesmen from independent Africa by political and economic pressure. Early persuasion by the government of Sweden forced Swedish participants to withdraw in 1969. Not only has Zambia refused to participate in the project or to purchase its power, but President Kaunda has assumed the lead in trying to prevent the project from being launched. In 1970 he traveled to Europe to urge those governments whose financial and industrial firms were involved to join an international financial boycott of the project. He sought to get the governments not to approve the financial guarantees to their firms or better, to order their corporations to withdraw from the consortiums. Portugal and South Africa countered with diplomatic overtures of their own. Despite a sympathetic hearing at high levels, Germany and France refused Kaunda's request, stating in effect that although they supported the idea of self-determination, they considered the Cabora Bassa project a "peaceful" effort to improve the living standards of all the people in the area, including the Africans. In late

13. *Financial Mail*, August 15, 1969, supplement, p. 49.

14. Mondlane, *The Struggle for Mozambique*, pp. 161–62; *Sechaba*, III (December 1969), 14–18; *The Star*, October 24, 1970, p. 3, and May 22, 1971, p. 1.

1970, however, the Milan-based Societa Anonima Eletrificazione (SAE) apparently withdrew after the Italian government and an international bank refused credit for its participation.[15] In 1971 the West German government informed German banks that it would no longer guarantee supplier credits to German companies taking part in future schemes in southern Africa. This could have the effect of dissuading German industrialists from making large investments in the region. Though the government had decided not to force German participants in Cabora Bassa to withdraw, its future position was clear.[16] Thus Kaunda's appeals and interventions produced a delayed change of policy on the part of the West German and Italian governments.

Despite numerous resolutions passed by the OAU, by the Conferences of the Heads of State and Government of East and Central Africa, and by the occasional conferences of non-aligned states, construction has begun and is progressing according to schedule. Among Mozambique's neighbors, Malawi and Rhodesia enthusiastically approve its construction and completion.[17]

Cabora Bassa presents a good illustration of South African leadership in regional affairs. Dr. H. J. van Eck of the Industrial Development Corporation has been one of the principal proponents of greater regional economic integration. Early on he saw Cabora Bassa as a vehicle for stimulating and accelerating this integrative tendency. He was instrumental in channeling Portuguese thinking about the project along the lines it ultimately took. He and South African officials also saw Cabora Bassa as more than an economic and developmental project. The attraction of more than a million white settlers, the opportunity to encourage South African business investment and enterprise northward, the industrial ramifications, and the strategic implications all augured well for South Africa's outward-looking policy. Coupled with these supplementary ad-

15. *Rand Daily Mail,* December 29, 1970.

16. *Sunday Times,* Johannesburg, April 4, 1971, Business Times section, p. 5.

17. See, for example, *The Times,* Blantyre, September 4, 1969, p.9, and *Rhodesia Herald,* Salisbury, September 4, 1969, pp. 1, 10.

vantages, here was an ideal opportunity to implicate the Western powers in the maintenance of the status quo in southern Africa. Thus the intrusive powers in Europe and America, through the extension of governmental credits and investments, and through the participation of their private banks and industries, would become in effect committed partners in continued Portuguese rule and ipso facto defenders of white presence and rule in southern Africa. The successful bidder was the South African-French-German consortium. The British-Italian and the American-French groups were unsuccessful but, significantly, no less intent on participating. So, in one way or another, various companies and to some extent the governments in all the major Western countries have expressed interest in participating in a project that cannot help but strengthen white rule in southern Africa. This assuredly must bring comfort to white southern African governments. At present, nevertheless, South Africa's stake in the project is almost two-thirds of the total capitalization.

KARIBA

The only major hydroelectric facility that contributes to cooperative interaction between otherwise hostile or uncooperative regional states is at the Kariba Dam, financed and built chiefly by Great Britain. From its first conception and planning in the 1950s, the Kariba project was thwart with political overtones. Northern Rhodesia (now Zambia) preferred that the facility be located nearer to the Copperbelt it was designed to service, and favored a site on the Kafue River. Southern Rhodesia favored Kariba for strategic reasons. Somehow, by the persuasion and threats of Lord Malvern, and because of the establishment of the Federation of Rhodesia and Nyasaland, the Copperbelt mining companies abandoned their preference for Kafue. By 1960 the £80,000,000 scheme was producing electricity. It was not by accident that the power station was built on the south (Rhodesian) bank of the Zambezi. Clearly Southern Rhodesian groups were influential in the British decision on the location. Although it is ostensibly jointly owned and operated by Rhodesia and Zambia, the Rhodesians have within their power the means to destroy the Zambian economy. When Zambia became independent in 1964, copper supplied 92 percent of the country's exports, 53 percent of the total government revenue, and 47 percent of the net domestic product.[18] Continued operation of the copper mines is absolutely central to the Zambian economy. More than 80 percent of Zambia's electricity is consumed by the copper industry, and as late as 1968 almost 80 percent of Zambia's electrical power was supplied by Kariba.[19] Thus, a Rhodesian flick of a switch could not only plunge Lusaka and the Copperbelt into darkness, but could silence the pumps that clear water out of the mines. The mines might then flood in between 48 and 72 hours, and the great asset of the country would be destroyed.

It is small wonder that considerations regarding control of the Kariba facility conditioned much of the contingency planning and military speculation leading up to and subsequent to the Rhodesian UDI. It is equally clear why the Zambian government has, since independence, striven to achieve a self-sufficiency in the production of electrical power. It decided early to develop the Kafue site. Although the World Bank refused to finance the Kafue scheme, preferring instead to support the Kariba II (north bank) scheme with Great Britain guaranteeing the loan, the government did find Yugoslavian financing. Kafue entered into production in 1972. Construction on Kariba II has begun. The north bank project, when completed, along with Kafue and several smaller schemes, should meet Zambia's power requirements into the 1980s.

Rhodesian leaders have threatened to sever the flow of current to Zambia in retaliation for Zambia's alleged support of guerilla operations. But Zambia insists that Great Britain is responsible for the operation of the dam complex. Thus Rhodesian restraint has not been a function of good will for Zambia. Rather Rhodesia rightly fears that interference with Zambia's share of Kariba power would, more than any other act short of invasion, precipitate British military intervention. Not

18. Hall, *The High Price*, p. 88.

19. Legum and Drysdale, eds., *Africa Contemporary Record, 1969–1970*, p. B246.

only would such a Rhodesian act violate an international treaty (with the World Bank) of which Great Britain is the guarantor, but equally compelling, the British interests in the Copperbelt would suffer irreparable damage, as would British financial and industrial institutions dependent on a continuing flow of Zambian copper. So the ability to deny Zambia electrical power is, nevertheless, neutralized by an equal fear that the continued existence of the independent Rhodesian state might be threatened.

KUNENE

The other hydroelectric projects have created less publicity and far less controversy. They are, however, equally important in the anticipated economic unity of the region. In January 1969 Portugal and South Africa agreed to collaborate in a complex hydroelectric, irrigation, and economic development scheme on the Kunene River dividing Angola and South West Africa. Agreements worked out in 1965 by the Portuguese, the South West African government (represented by the Odendaal Commission), and the Industrial Development Corporation of South Africa (represented by the aforementioned Dr. van Eck) launched the earlier stages of planning and finance. Eventually the power grids of the two territories will be integrated completely. Some six combined hydroelectric facilities are to be constructed on the river and the first station at Calaque is expected to begin supplying power by 1976. The Kunene project is also being planned as a settlement region for up to a half million immigrants, but there is little chance that large-scale settlement will occur. Financing (jointly by the two governments) and construction of the facilities and consumption of Kunene power is to be less multinational than in the case of Cabora Bassa. But for a different reason the Kunene scheme evokes external speculation. It does, after all, involve the controversial territory of South West Africa and could precipitate some international, perhaps UN resistance at some later date.

OXBOW

Of similarly narrow scope is the proposed Oxbow Dam across the Orange River in Lesotho, where it is called the Malibamatso River. South Africa has agreed in principle to purchase water if the scheme is completed. A feasibility study financed by the UN Development Program has been completed and technical discussions involving the World Bank, South Africa's Department of Water Affairs, and the Lesotho government's Oxbow Steering Committee are proceeding. Financing has not been assured and the scheme is a far distance from realization. Given the practically complete economic dependence of Lesotho on her surrounding neighbor, and noting South Africa's need for water resources, the completion of the Oxbow project might correct, though only slightly, the prevailing asymmetry.

In the area of hydroelectric and other water development projects there are several additional potential and planned international schemes. Although they will not alter present interaction patterns measurably, they may by and large reflect the expanding and interlocking character of the white southern African economies. As importantly, they provide a multiplicity of contact points by which the economic configuration of the region overflows into the realm of international politics.

In the late 1950s and early 1960s South Africa and Portugal were progressively excluded (i.e., they were suspended or expelled, or they withdrew) from numerous international organizations, many of which provided functional economic linkages with the rest of the continent. These included UNESCO, the Commonwealth, the Committee for Technical Cooperation in Africa, the Scientific Council for Africa, the Economic Commission for Africa, the International Labor Organization, the International Telecommunications Union, the Congress of the Universal Postal Union (not the Union itself), the Food and Agriculture Organization, and the International Civil Aviation Organization. South African delegates could not attend any international conference of universal scope without the issue of their participation or South Africa's membership being raised. From this position of isolation South Africa has sought, by a series of bilateral arrangements and by the establishment of some multilateral functional ties, to expand its influence and contact among regional states. The conference on regional tourism that was held in Malawi in 1970 (governments represented were Lesotho, Mauritius, Malawi, Portugal, South Africa, and Swaziland) is an example of the latter type.[20] The planned integration of the electric power systems of Swaziland and South Africa illustrates the former.[21] The hydroelectric schemes discussed above and the various joint transport undertakings to be dealt with further on add to the functional government-to-government network.

Private Business Relationships

Far more long-standing and probably more significant than the inter-governmental contacts in southern Africa are those among private firms or between private firms and governmental bodies. Although South Africa is a capital importing country, by 1967 it was estimated that South African private investment in southern Africa had reached $910 million.[22] It has increased considerably since then. The overwhelming proportion of this investment is in the copper mines of Zambia and in the mines and farms of Rhodesia.[23] A recent tendency has been for South African capital to move also into Angola, Botswana, Malawi, and Mozambique. A wholly government-owned subsidiary, the aforementioned Industrial Development Corporation of South Africa (IDC), has been instrumental in encouraging regional investment. In May 1965, for example, the IDC announced that long-term multimillion-dollar loans had been made available to South African companies for the construction of a sugar mill in Mozambique and another in Malawi.[24] In July 1965, Portugal in a decree law that guaranteed the repatriation of profits and capital helped to clear the path for increased foreign investment in its overseas territories, although industries for the

20. *ARB* (Econ.), VII, 1756B–C, August 31, 1970.
21. Ibid., pp. 1785C–86A, September 30, 1970. *The Star*, August 22, p. 17.
22. Rhoodie, *The Third Africa*, p. 146, citing the South Africa Foundation, *Tempo*, April 1967. A December 1956 estimate of $280 million in direct investments indicates the speed of investment growth; see H. R. P. A. Kotzenberg, "Africa and the South African Economy," in SABRA, *South Africa in the African Continent*, p. 113.
23. See Hall, *The High Price*, pp. 86–92.
24. Rhoodie, *The Third Africa*, p. 147.

exploitation of natural resources (excluding minerals) were specifically closed to the domination of foreign capital. The decree law has had the effect of stimulating extensive prospecting and economic activity in Angola and Mozambique.

South African firms have bid successfully on governmental projects in Zambia and Malawi, among others. They have made direct investments regionally. They have joined partnerships and consortiums with firms in the territories in which they invest. They have exported their products. They have established subsidiaries throughout the region. By and large, however, South African capital investments in Africa tend to be concentrated in white-controlled territories. The little South African capital that does get into black Africa is most frequently found in mineral extraction and not in industry, which black governments would prefer to develop. This also has the added advantage, for South Africa, of utilizing skilled white technicians (and hence imparting a racist pattern of labor relations), purchasing South African products and industrial equipment, and reinforcing the core of the white southern African subsystem. It is this sort of enterprise that does not necessarily receive publicity—as, for example, does Malawi's decision to exchange diplomats with the Republic of South Africa—but which has the cumulative effect of creating patterns of interaction that are no less characteristic of South Africa's outward-looking policy. They serve to knit more closely the territories involved and in this way to encourage governments to interact in order to protect and promote further investment. In short, it is this field of private economic activity that represents the submerged, less public, but no less intensive instrument of the outward policy.

Transport Routes

In part, inter-state business patterns in southern Africa are determined by the transport facilities, the principal lines of which had already been established by the 1930s.[25] Indeed, from

25. See Frank Brandenburg, "Transport Systems and Their External Relations," in Abshire and Samuels, eds., *Portuguese Africa*, pp. 320–44; especially pp. 334–44 and the useful footnotes.

1889 to 1906 interterritorial relations in southern Africa were largely pursued by means of negotiations, compromises, agreements, and disagreements over railway routes and rates, and customs tariffs. The Union of South Africa was itself partly conceived as a political solution to these recurrent problems. Colonial governmental controls and a series of international agreements affected the division of traffic. Later developments, such as the independence of Malawi and Zambia, the breakup of the Federation of Rhodesia and Nyasaland, and the Rhodesian UDI, have threatened to alter these patterns.[26] Until the Rhodesian UDI in 1965, the predominant flow from as far north as the Zambia-Katanga Copperbelt was southward and coastward toward Rhodesia, South Africa, Angola, and Mozambique. Copper and other minerals are the most important source of traffic and revenue for the regional rail network. The landlocked situation of Zambia, Malawi, Rhodesia, Botswana, Lesotho, and Swaziland virtually dictated their continued dependence upon routes and ports under white control. Although that is still the predominant direction of inter-state shipments, the construction of the Tan-Zam railway should alter this pattern significantly. The extent of Zambian dependence on white-controlled routes can be seen from the data for 1967 (table 5). The completion in September 1968 of the pipeline from the oil refinery at the port of Dar es Salaam to Ndola changed this picture somewhat. All of Zambia's petroleum needs (except for a small amount of special lubricants) are now supplied by the pipeline, which carries about 17 percent of Zambia's imports (by weight). Formerly, most of this arrived by rail and road from Rhodesia. Likewise, as much as 40 percent of the Katanga copper trade moves over the Benguela railway and another 30 percent over Rhodesia Railways to Beira or Lourenço Marques. Malawi is also entirely dependent upon rail connections to Mozambique and road routes through Mozambique and Rhodesia. (See map 1.)

Locational advantages provide Angola and Mozambique with strategic political leverage in dealing with their neighbors. Although the Benguela railway is a great profit-making enterprise

26. Haefele and Steinberg, *Government Controls on Transport.*

TABLE 5
ZAMBIA EXTERNAL TRANSPORT PATTERNS, 1967
(In percentages of totals)

Route	*By tonnage* Exports	Imports	*By value* Exports	Imports
Angola—by rail to Lobito	11.8	4.0	20.3	17.3
Congo—by road and rail to Boma and Matadi	7.8	0.2	1.0	0.2
Malawi—by road and rail to Beira	0.9	3.9	1.2	1.8
Rhodesia—by rail through Mozambique ports	48.7	58.9	41.5	29.6
South Africa—by rail	12.6	15.8	5.6	27.0
Tanzania—by road through Tanzanian ports	17.1	12.2	30.2	12.1
Other routes (via Kenya, South West Africa, and Botswana)	1.1	5.0	0.2	12.0

SOURCE: Data is from the first nine months of 1967 and is taken from the Computor Print Outs, September ledger, Central Statistical Office, Lusaka.

in Angola, it is 90 percent British-owned, and charges on goods carried between the Copperbelt and the port of Lobito provide only a small fraction of Angola's income. In Mozambique, income derived from transit trade with neighboring states is markedly more important, so much so that some economists have characterized the monetary sector of the economy as an economy of ports and railroads. These dependences that have existed for years become more acute when an independent black state realizes that it must maintain correct relations with white-governed neighbors in order to develop its economy.[27] For Lesotho and Swaziland there are simply no transport alternatives. For Botswana and Zambia there are perceived though economically unattractive alternatives. For Malawi, although alternatives exist, the easier and more profitable course is to recognize

27. See, for example, the incident involving Beira dockworkers' refusing to handle Zambian goods. *The Star*, March 20, 1971, p. 5; June 19, p. 1; and August 14, p. 15. Also the 50 percent surcharge unilaterally imposed by Rhodesia on low-rated Zambian rail traffic using the Rhodesian railway system. *ARB* (Econ.), VIII, 1926C–27A, February 28, 1971.

Map 1. Principal Railway Routes, Southern Africa

limitations, work within the prevailing constraints, and deemphasize political considerations. It is to the more recent changes in southern Africa's transport linkages that we now turn, for they reflect and symbolize the foreign policy directions envisioned by various heads of government.

Events in the last decade have changed transport patterns measurably. The dissolution of the Federation of Rhodesia and Nyasaland in 1963 led to an agreement between the governments of Rhodesia, Malawi, and Zambia relating to Rhodesia Railways. Ownership passed to a joint authority of the three governments. But Zambia, preparing for independence, began to search about for substitute routes for the transshipment of her copper. The Rhodesian UDI in 1965 was the catalyst for an earnest exploration of alternatives. Such earnestness led to a Zambian decision in April 1966 to refuse to transfer currency to Rhodesia for payment of copper shipment expenses. It was not until the summer of 1966 that Zambian traffic was resumed on the railway and a means was found to transfer funds to Rhodesian accounts without violating the letter of sanctions resolutions. Alternative routes had been tried meanwhile. A temporary airlift of petroleum products, the disastrous "Hell Run" over the Great North Road to Dar es Salaam, road transport to Malawi and thence by rail to Beira, the unreliable Congolese "Route Nationale," and the Benguela railway were employed. None proved entirely satisfactory.[28] Plans went ahead for the pipeline from Dar es Salaam (Italian financed), improvement of the Great North Road (United States and World Bank financed), and the Tan-Zam railway (Chinese built and financed).[29]

The most publicized and most politically pregnant transport development is the Tan-Zam railway, currently under construction.[30] There is little point detailing here the history of the various proposals for such a project, or the economic discussions that ensued. Suffice it to say that repeated feasibility surveys rejected the proposed 1,100-mile route as economically unsound. Nevertheless, President Kaunda was convinced of the necessity,

28. Hall, *The High Price*, pp. 161–77; Sutcliffe, "Zambia and the Strains of UDI," *The World Today*, XXIII (1967), 506–11; Ostrander, "Zambia and the Aftermath of Rhodesian UDI," *African Forum*, II (1967), 50–65; St. Jorre, "Zambia's Economy," *Africa Report*, XII (December 1967), 36–39.

29. The pipeline as well as the other routes are still vulnerable to sabotage. See, for example, *East African Standard*, Nairobi, December 27, 1969, p. 1.

30. A fairly thorough history and discussion of the political issues of the project appears in Curran, "Communist China in Black Africa," which has a particularly useful bibliography. See also Corsi, "The Tan-Zam Rail Project."

primarily political, of such a major line northward. He never thought of the project primarily in terms of economic viability. As he put it before UDI: "This railway is a political necessity. Even after Rhodesia wins majority rule, there will still be Mozambique and South Africa between us and the sea."[31] As early as March 1963, Kaunda sent a then close confidante, Simon Kapwepwe, to Dar es Salaam to discuss the possibility of the new railway.[32] From this initiative the modern history of the line began. Various Western surveys and Western mining interests sought to discourage the project, and the search for Western financial backing was fruitless. Into this frustrating vacuum stepped the Chinese Peoples' Republic. Its first offer of help, in February 1965, was more completely tendered in June 1965 when Premier Chou En-lai visited Dar es Salaam. Within a few weeks after his conversations with President Nyerere a Chinese survey team was in the field.[33] The Chinese were not invited into Zambia. President Kaunda preferred Western backing and still sought it. He was further encouraged in 1966 when a joint British-Canadian survey team (Sir Maxwell Stamp and Associates) maintained that the project was feasible and might be economically sound provided that all Zambia's copper was shipped over the line and Zambia's level of imports through Dar es Salaam was increased. Approaches were then made to the United States, Great Britain, France, and Japan, and to various international funding agencies, to little avail. At this point Kaunda became reconciled to Chinese-Tanzanian-Zambia collaboration. A firm tripartite agreement was signed in September 1967 that led to the July 1970 agreement on the conditions of finance and construction. The exact terms of the agreement do not interest us here. What does interest us is the obvious effect the railway will have in reorienting Zambian shipping and trade patterns, and the tremendous costs that it entails for all three partners, an open testimony to the intensity of political commitment toward majority rule in southern Africa and economic independence for black Africa, against the white-ruled states.

31. As quoted in Hall, *The High Price*, p. 211.
32. Ibid., p. 212.
33. Ibid., pp. 212–15.

The construction of the pipeline and the railway, coupled with the Mulungushi reforms of April 1968, which sought to "Zambianize" the economy, and the nationalizations of 1969 and 1970, especially the 51 percent takeover of the copper mines, have ostensibly been designed to enable the Zambian government, instead of foreign nationals and white southern African governments, to control the pace and direction of Zambian economic development and foreign policy. Zambian officials feel that these moves have provided Zambia greater latitude in shaping its future. They do this, however, at some short-run costs, both socioeconomic and political.

It has been calculated that of the three alternative new routes open to the Zambians, the Tan-Zam link would be by far the highest in economic costs.[34] Moreover, there are the problems of rail-gauge differences, port inadequacies at Dar es Salaam, vulnerability of the route to sabotage, and the greater distance of Dar es Salaam from the European and American markets for Zambia's copper, compared with other ports. Almost 65 percent of Zambian exports (in value) is destined for West Europe or the United States.[35] About 21 percent goes to Japan. So Zambia would have to search for greater trade with eastern markets in order to take full advantage of its northward moves up the east coast of Africa. There is also the important possibility that the route can eventually be extended southward into Botswana, in the heart of white-ruled southern Africa, thereby adding a strategic as well as an economic dimension.

A potentially greater problem for President Kaunda grows out of the reorientation of Zambia's economic life because of the look to the north. The already discontented Lozi and Tonga peoples of the Western Province will be even more disadvan-

34. "Economic Costs of Zambia's Alternative Rail Routes" (see Bibliography, Unpublished Papers). The author of this anonymous paper, apparently produced in Lusaka in 1969, has been associated with the *Economist* Intelligence Unit. The three estimates are (in kwacha per ton) 23.75 for Tan-Zam, 16.40 for Benguela (bypassing the Congo) and 14.15 for Malawi-Mozambique (Nacala). Commercial costs could be 40 to 50 percent higher than the estimated economic costs.

35. Zambia, *Monthly Digest of Statistics*, May–June 1968, as cited in Kaplan et al., *Area Handbook for Zambia*, p. 376.

taged and economically bypassed in favor of the Bemba and other residents of the Eastern and Northern provinces through which the line will run. The Portuguese, Rhodesians, and South Africans have not been averse to exploiting this dissatisfaction.[36] So (without even mentioning the more controversial impact of the association with China and the Chinese workers), the reorientation of Zambia's trade and transport routes, the restructuring of her domestic economy, and the attendant foreign policy options and ramifications render the Tan-Zam project a most vital and important factor in the international politics of the region.

The Congo, as well, plagued by disruptions in the early 1960s, and frustrated by the basic lack of competitiveness of its combination rail-barge "route national," has decided to modernize and complete a rail line from Katanga to the port of Banana. Dissatisfied by her dependence upon the Benguela line for the export of copper, the Congo has invited tenders on the construction of a rail link between Kinshasa and Port Franqui, where the present Katanga rail line ends. An Anglo-Belgian-Japanese consortium may be on the verge of winning the $238,000,000 contract.[37] Should the Katanga-Zambian copper be divided between these two routes, neither would be economically viable.

Although construction of these routes would serve to move the Congo and Zambia out of the orbit of white-controlled transport routes, other regional transport projects would have the opposite effect of reinforcing black economies southward. The Portuguese, for example, have been attempting to convince the Zambians to commit more of their copper to the Benguela route. In return, the Portuguese have undertaken to build the Cubal Variant, a 91-mile stretch near the coast that, because of steep grades, has been a bottleneck. The new stretch, to cost approximately $24 million and scheduled to be completed in

36. Caplan, "Zambia, Barotseland, and the Liberation of Southern Africa," *Africa Today*, XV (August–September 1969), 13–17.

37. *The Star*, October 10, 1970, p. 12. The Japanese government has offered about $80 million in aid for construction of a bridge across the Congo and the railway to connect Matadi with Port Banana. *Economist*, 239 (April 17, 1971), 82.

1973, should double the capacity of the line. An even more significant proposal was presented to President Kaunda early in 1969. The president of the Benguela Railway proposed then to bypass Katanga and thereby link the Copperbelt directly to Lobito via the underdeveloped North-Western Province of Zambia. But even though this cutoff would cost only $45 million, it still would pass through Portuguese-held territory, precisely what Kaunda seeks to avoid. Numerous incidents since 1966 have demonstrated to Zambia that this route is not entirely reliable.[38]

Malawi has clearly opted to improve her transport connections with the white South. In August 1970 a 63-mile link between the Malawi Railways line and the Mozambique town of Nova Freixo became operational. This relieves Malawi of her dependence upon the congested port of Beira. The construction was by a consortium of South African firms and was financed by a £6.4 million soft-loan from the quasi-public South African Industrial Development Corporation. It is hoped by officials that the new line will expedite the development of the central and northern regions of Malawi.[39] For the route to be entirely profitable, however, Malawi must earn haulage fees on Zambian exports. Futile efforts have been made to induce the Zambians to build their rail line to the Malawi border at Fort Jameson. The Malawians would then construct a 133-mile line from Salima (their rail terminus) to the Zambian border.[40] The Zambians have firmly rejected such a proposal, since it would still make them dependent on a Portuguese-controlled route. So far FRELIMO has been unable or else has not chosen to disrupt shipments on the Portuguese section of the Nacala line. The latter is probably the case. There has been some speculation that FRELIMO and Dr. Banda had arrived at an "agreement" that would protect the route, provided Malawi did not

38. Anglin, "Confrontation in Southern Africa," *International Journal*, XXV (1970), 507–13.

39. "Impact of the Nacala Link Upon the Economy of Malawi" (see Bibliography, Unpublished Papers). This paper was written by someone associated with the *Economist* Intelligence Unit.

40. *ARB* (Econ.), VII, 1829C, October 31, 1970. *Guardian*, February 23, 1973, p. 4.

vigorously harass refugees from Mozambique and FRELIMO operatives. This, however, has never been confirmed.

In road construction, as well, the Malawi government looks to the white South. Both the Portuguese and the South African governments have advanced loans to tar the present gravel road between Blantyre and Salisbury. The Portuguese will advance loan capital to tar the part from Blantyre to the Mozambique border at Zobue and the South Africans will cover the remainder through Mozambique and Rhodesia.[41] This loan is believed to be the first advanced by Portugal to an independent black African state. Likewise, the Malawian government seeks to integrate its transport network into the new developments at Cabora Bassa.

Additional planned rail, road, and port expansions further integrate the white states and their weaker black neighbors and contribute to already prevailing patterns. A few representative examples could illustrate this point. An agreement on construction of a railway between Mozambique and Swaziland was signed in February 1970, and surveys and talks on a South Africa-Swaziland link have been undertaken.[42] A 220-mile pipeline from Moambo in Mozambique to Johannesburg is being constructed to supply natural gas to the Witwatersrand. The total cost of about $140 million is to be borne by the Mozambique Gulf Oil Company and partly by long-term loans raised mostly by commercial banks in the RSA.[43] Portugal and South Africa had been planning to join in the construction of a large ship repair yard at the port of Narinda in Madagascar. A delegation of Malagasy officials, including the minister of transportation, were in Lisbon in February 1971. But since the Malagasy military coup the chances that this sort of trilateral collaboration may be undertaken have been diminished.[44] Even internal South African railway expansion—for example, the new line from the eastern Transvaal to the planned port at Richard's Bay

41. Ibid., p. 1787B, September 30, 1970.
42. Ibid., p. 1688B–C, May 31, 1970, and p. 1657C, April 30. See also the discussion of Botswana's transport situation and the proposed new Rhodesia-South Africa rail link farther on in this chapter.
43. Rhoodie, *The Third Africa,* p. 188.
44. *The Star,* March 6, 1971, p. 19.

—may in the future provide Rhodesia and Botswana with their most feasible bulk export harbor.[45] Other than the Tan-Zam railway (which could eventually be extended into Botswana), the pipeline from the Copperbelt to Dar es Salaam, the improvements on the Great North Road, and the proposed completion of an all-rail "route national" in the Congo, almost all the planned and recent international transport developments in southern Africa have had the effect of reinforcing a pattern that is to the advantage of the white South and the political disadvantage of the black states in the region.

Labor Supply and Migration

The developed regions of southern Africa have been for years a magnet to ambitious African laborers who have sought to move beyond a subsistence agricultural existence. These patterns of labor migration have been toward white and away from black southern Africa, except for the attraction of Zambia's rail line and her Copperbelt cities. (See table 6.)

One other complication in this general pattern of migration is the massive movement of refugees from Portuguese Africa (and to a lesser extent from Rhodesia, South West and South Africa, and the Congo). This is, of course, not a form of migratory labor, but rather is the flight from political repression and unrest. The refugee problem and its ramifications will be discussed more completely in Chapter 6. For now, we will concentrate on the effects of migration, particularly migratory labor, on the regional states as both "exporters" and "importers" of manpower. (See map 2.)

No state has been more profoundly affected by migration than Lesotho. It is generally estimated that at least 43 percent of the adult male population of the country is employed in South Africa. During 1970 the number of Basuto laborers employed by the gold mines which are members of the Chamber of Mines of South Africa averaged 62,576 per month. These men are recruited by private organizations—principally WENELA, the Witwatersrand Native Labour Association—operating

45. Ibid., March 13, 1971, p. 17.

Table 6

Total Foreign-Born African Residents

Country of origin	*Les*	*Bot*	*Swazi*	*Zam*	*Mal*	*Con*	*Tan*	*Moz*	*Ang*	*Rho*	*RSA*	*SWA*	*Total*
Les	..	....	.....	.....	......	......	.....	...	..	......	117,000[6]	.....	117,000
Bot	..	....	.....	.....	......	......	.....	...	..	1,000[5]	59,000[5]	.....	60,000
Swazi	..	....	.....	.....	......	......	.....	...	..	......	39,000[5]	.....	39,000
Zam	..	....	.....	.....	22,000[6]	15,000[9]	.....	...	..	44,480[70]	16,000	.....	97,480
Mal	..	....	.....	45,000[7]	......	......	10,000[7]	400	..	163,330[70]	80,000[7]	.....	298,730
Con	..	....	.....	300[9]	......	......	2,000[71]	...	..	......	.....	.....	900
Tan	..	....	.....	.....	11,000[6]	......	.....	...	..	......	.....	.....	11,000
Moz	..	....	5,600[2]	5,000[71]	206,000[6]	......	55,000[71]	...	..	109,030[70]	161,000[5]	.....	515,630
Ang	..	3,800[71]	.....	10,000[71]	......	400,000[71]	.....	...	..	8,000[5]	11,000[5]	10,000	416,000
Rho	..	....	.....	6,800[5]	34,000[6]	......	300[9]	...	..	......	27,000[4]	.....	68,100
RSA	..	300[9]	14,000[2]	500[9]	9,000[6]	......	300[9]	...	..	......	......	.....	24,100
SWA	..	300[9]	.....	400[9]	......	......	100[9]	...	..	......	2,000	.....	2,800
Total	–	4,400	19,600	68,000	282,000	415,000	67,700	400	–	325,840	512,000	10,000	1,650,740

Superior figures indicate year ([2] = 1962, [5] = 1965). Figures without these are approximations based on generalized information.

Sources: Data for this table have been drawn from numerous and diverse sources, chief among them: *HCR Bulletin*, no. 7. July–August–September 1969, p. 9; *Marches Tropicaux*, no. 1268, October 16, 1971; William A. Hance, *Population, Migration, and Urbanization in Africa* (New York and London: Columbia University Press, 1970); Malawi, *Ministry of Labour, Report 1963–1967* (Zomba: Government Printer, 1969); Rhodesia, Ministry of Finance, *Economic Survey of Rhodesia, 1970* (Salisbury: Government Printer, April 1970); and J. A. Lombard et al., *The Concept of Economic Co-operation in Southern Africa* (Pretoria: Econburo, Pty., Ltd., 1969), table II.

Note: Although some of the data date from 1962, 1964, and 1965, it is likely that they have not changed greatly in these specific cases. The most important changes in the past decade have chiefly to do with refugees and with labor migration into Rhodesia. In these cases relatively up-to-date figures are available.

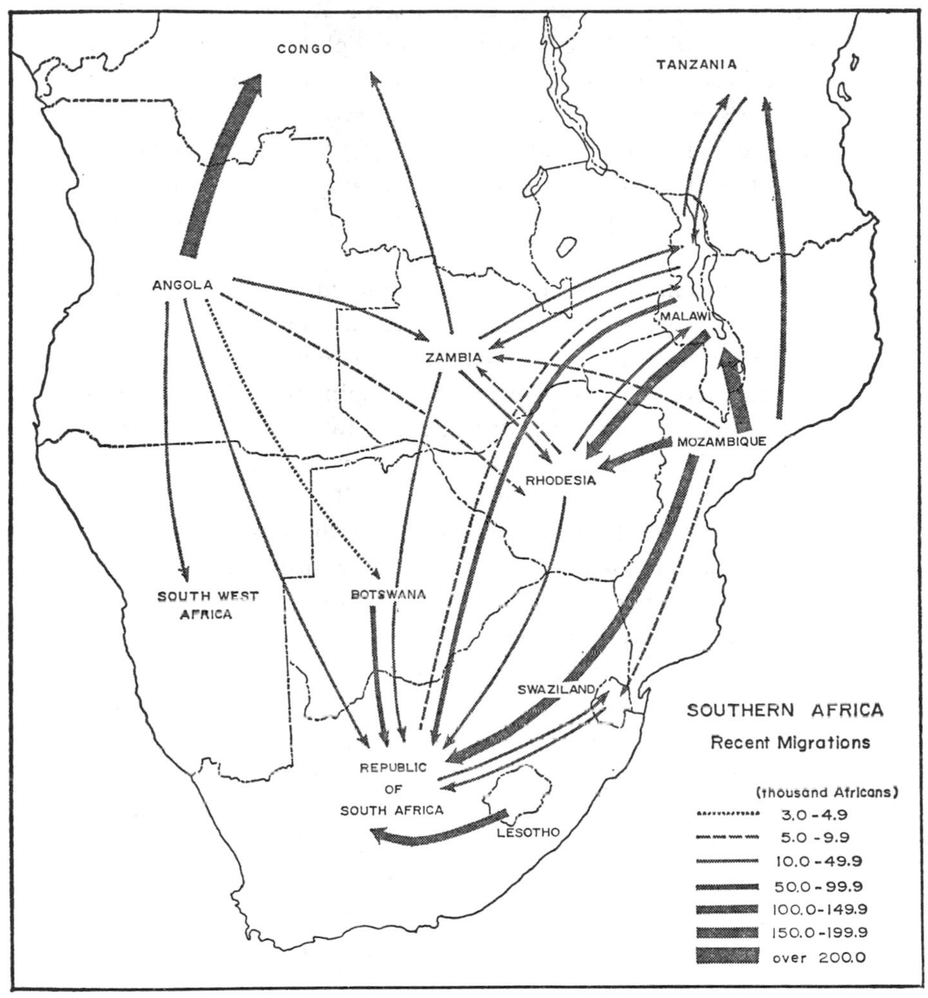

Map 2. Migration of Foreign Africans

in and with the assistance and cooperation of the Lesotho government. Their wages, remittances, and deferred pay are sent to Lesotho by the employers' organization and by the workers.[46]

46. Spence, *Lesotho*, p. 64. For comparative over-time data see *Basutoland 1956 Population Census*, table IV, p. 73, and *1966 Population Census of Lesotho*, table 1. Also *Standard Bank Review*, no. 630, September 1971, p. 18. General coverage of this subject is in Breytenbach,

In 1965–66 the sum amounted to some R4,395,000 out of a total Lesotho GNP of R39,244,200 or slightly over 11 percent. More impressively, this income is approximately equal to the country's exports and, combined with recruiting fees and taxes paid to the Lesotho authorities (R178,570) and the revenue from the customs and excise (R1,636,500), it renders the Lesotho economy and governmental revenues highly dependent on South Africa.[47]

Botswana has similar though less pronounced conditions. (See table 7.) Fully 20 percent of the adult male population is working in South Africa at any given time. These men tend to concentrate, more so than the Basuto, in mine work.[48] They provide the chief source of cash wages for Botswana. In 1960 they brought about R712,000 into the Bechuanaland economy. By 1967 that figure had risen to R1,097,976. This labor contributes 10.6 percent of the total value of Botswana's exports.[49] More than 60 percent of Botswana's cash labor force is employed in South Africa at any given time. This figure, however, has been dropping steadily from the high of some 70 percent in 1950.

Swaziland likewise reflects this general pattern. In 1962 some 9,400 men (28 percent of the African male labor force) and 800 women were employed in South Africa.[50] By 1966 this figure had dropped to 6,700 in a total work force of 36,200 (about 18 percent).[51] In 1962 migrant workers injected R400,000 in deferred pay and family allowances into the Swaziland economy, and about R450,000 in the value of goods and money brought home when contracts were fulfilled. A supplemental R28,000 of tax money was deducted from mine workers' pay and paid

---

Vreemde Bantoewerkers in Suid-Afrika en Rhodesië, issued by the Africa Institute, 1971.

47. Ward, "Economic Independence for Lesotho?" *JMAS,* V (1967), 355–68. The figure for remittances is approximately the same for 1970. *Standard Bank Review,* no. 633, December 1971, p. 16.

48. Munger, *Bechuanaland,* pp. 39–41, 116.

49. Botswana, Information Services, *Fact Sheet,* p. 8. See Botswana, Central Statistical Office, *Statistical Abstract: 1969,* table 26, p. 32, for over-time data (1965–68) on recruits and deferred payments and remittances.

50. Halpern, *South Africa's Hostages,* p. 384.

51. British Information Services, *Swaziland,* p. 34.

TABLE 7
BOTSWANA LABOR FORCE, 1950–65

Type of employment	*1950*	*1955*	*1960*	*1965*
Domestic-wage labor force	7,500	10,000	13,000	24,913
On contract to South African mines	14,500	15,000	22,500	32,319
Other employment in South Africa	3,700	2,000	4,000	8,000

SOURCES: The 1950–60 data are from Munger, Bechuanaland, p. 116; 1965 data from *Republic of Botswana—Fact Sheet* (December 1968), pp. 9–10, and British Information Services, *Botswana* (London: HMSO, 1966), p. 26.

directly to the Swaziland government. So, close to R1,000,000 was added to the economy that year.

Two other countries rely heavily on the export of labor to South Africa and Rhodesia. About 80,000 Malawian laborers are in South Africa. About 46,000 are contracted to WENELA and another 34,000 are "free flow." A labor agreement between Malawi and South Africa in 1967 sought to "legitimize" the free-flow laborers. The purpose was to provide them with documents so that their presence would not be in violation of South African immigration laws. A more efficient system of transport, tax, and pay remittance was established, contract problems were cleared up, and the two governments became more directly and jointly interlinked in administering the migratory labor process. It is estimated that a further 110,000 Malawian men are in Rhodesia (mostly on farms and mines), but this is a far less formal process. A quasi-governmental recruiting agency, the Rhodesian African Labour Supply Commission, with a head office in Salisbury, accounts for only about 3,000 laborers a year. In 1969 remittances into Malawi by or on behalf of migrant workers yielded £3,457,704. About 83 percent came from South Africa, 10 percent from Rhodesia, and slightly over 6 percent from the 20,000 men in Zambia.[52] WENELA alone remitted over £2 million into Malawi. Since Malawi's 1969 exports were only £22 million, the returns from migrant labor represented a substantial source of foreign exchange. Moreover, Malawi politicians cannot help but be conscious of the potential domestic

52. See Malawi, Department of Information, *Malawi 1969*, p. 99; Malawi, *Ministry of Labour, Report 1963–1967*, pp. 4, 18–42.

ramifications should relations with South Africa or Rhodesia become strained and these then unemployed laborers be dumped on the Malawi labor market. It should be noted, in contrast, that in 1966 Zambia ordered WENELA to close its offices in the country. There, however, recruitment was on a much smaller scale (in absolute as well as relative terms). Side effects were minimal, except in Barotseland.[53]

Mozambique is an exporter of large numbers of laborers. For example, there has been a largely unrecorded permanent emigration to the tea plantations of southern Malawi. Perhaps as many as 380,000 Lonwe-speaking people settled there before 1945.[54] Since they now regard Malawi as home and remit practically no funds to Mozambique, their political importance in terms of international relations is conjectural. By far the more important flow is to the mines of South Africa and the farms and mines of Rhodesia. According to 1963 data, 119,871 Mozambique-born laborers were registered as contract workers in Rhodesia. Their numbers have declined steadily since the breakup of the federation in 1963. The number of immigrants into Rhodesia from Mozambique was reduced from 55,000 in 1957 to 12,400 in 1962 and to as low a figure as 4,300 in 1967.[55]

Approximately 87,560 Mozambique migrants went to South Africa in 1965, raising the estimated total of Mozambicans in South Africa to 161,000. The majority were male laborers who were employed in the mines of the Witwatersrand and Natal. A current agreement (signed in 1901 and updated in 1928) with the South African government provides a private organization of mining employers, the Witwatersrand Native Labour Association (WNLA as it is known in Mozambique, and by other abbreviated names in other countries), with the exclusive right to contract for not more than 100,000 workers per year, all from the area of Mozambique south of the 22d parallel. By terms of this agreement, South Africa agrees to ship at least 47.5 percent of the exports from and the imports to the Transvaal through

53. Kaplan et al., *Area Handbook for Zambia,* p. 226.
54. Abshire and Samuels, eds., *Portuguese Africa,* p. 174.
55. Hance, *Population, Migration, and Urbanization,* p. 157.

the port of Lourenço Marques, and WNLA pays the Mozambique government a head fee for each recruit, whose wages are paid to the Mozambique authorities who in turn deduct taxes and convert the rest into Portuguese currency. In this way the Mozambique labor force in South Africa remits some $10,360,000 in cash and goods to Mozambique every year.[56] Nevertheless, according to one source this accounts for only 2 percent of the total annual provincial income.[57] This seems to be a rather low estimate of its importance when one considers that, in 1963, of the approximately 882,000 persons employed in the wage economy of Mozambique 271,804 (about 30 percent) were registered as contract workers in Rhodesia and South Africa.[58] Moreover, these men are relatively better paid than their counterparts within Mozambique and are transferring to Mozambique valuable and convertible South African funds. The fact remains, however, that the export of labor is far less vital for the Mozambique economy than it was even a decade ago.

So far, the focus has been on labor-exporting territories. If we reverse the coin, it might be useful to see the extent to which the two major labor-importing countries, Rhodesia and South Africa, rely upon foreign labor and the effect it has on their economies. According to the 1961 Rhodesian census of Africans, 11.3 percent of the 3.6 million Africans were born outside Rhodesia; 54 percent of these were living in European farming areas and 40 percent in urban areas. Malawi accounted for almost half of the foreigners. Of the 555,000 Africans in paid employment, 50 percent were foreigners coming from Malawi (42.2 percent), Mozambique (38.5 percent), and Zambia (16.1 percent). With the breakup of the federation and the 1965 UDI, fewer and fewer foreign Africans entered Rhodesia. Zambians and Mozambicans especially declined in numbers.[59] The years since 1959 have seen a net migration of foreign African men averaging 8,900 per year. It is still estimated that there are over

56. *South African Journal of Economics*, March 1967, p. 52, as cited in Rhoodie, *The Third Africa*, p. 184.
57. Abshire and Samuels, eds., *Portuguese Africa*, p. 173.
58. Herrick et al., *Area Handbook for Mozambique*, p. 261.
59. Hance, *Population, Migration, and Urbanization*, p. 157.

200,000 aliens in employment, but this is less than a third of the total number of Africans now employed.[60] High local unemployment and the relatively depressed economic conditions on the tribal trust lands serve to cushion the impact of declining numbers of migrant laborers from neighboring territories. Consequently, Rhodesia still possesses a potentially powerful lever in its threat to expel foreign labor to recalcitrant or uncooperative neighboring states—notably Malawi or Zambia. That threat was sufficiently credible that in 1966 and 1967 the Malawi Ministry of Labor sought to make contingency preparations for such a possibility. Those who come by agency contract are relatively easy to locate and police, and thereby pose little problem for the government.

With regard to South Africa, the impact of foreign-born labor is generally less important. Alien laborers constitute only about 10 percent of the total economically active African population, estimated at about 4,586,000.[61] It is when we examine the distribution of these alien laborers throughout the economy that we realize that in some respects alien laborers do play an important role in South Africa. A large proportion of aliens are employed in the mining industry. Some 89 percent of the 636,000 mineworkers are African, and, particularly in gold mining, a high proportion are Africans from outside South Africa. For example, of the 372,000 Africans in gold mining, only 116,000 (31 percent) were recruited in South Africa. The rest came from foreign territories (23 percent from Lesotho, Botswana, and Swaziland; 21 percent from tropical Africa, mostly Malawi; and 24 percent from the east coast).[62] Thus 69 percent of Africans working in the gold mines are from outside the republic.

By and large, most of these laborers are recruited by the South African Chamber of Mines' labor recruiting branches, WENELA (Malawi), WNLA (Mozambique), or the South West Africa Native Labour Association (SWANLA), or by various Ministries of Labour in African states. The fairly standardized

60. Rhodesia, *Economic Survey of Rhodesia, 1969*, pp. 23, 7, and 24.
61. RSA, Assembly, *Hansard*, April 2, 1968, col. 3208.
62. Data from a report of the Government Mining Engineer, *The Star*, September 26, 1970, p. 3.

contracts are for eighteen months or two years. The contracting organization sees that contract laborers are examined, immunized, documented, and transported to their place of work. It assures that their taxes are paid, that a set proportion (60 percent after the first six months) of their pay is deferred (to be paid when they return to their home territory), and that at least part of their pay is remitted to relatives at home. While in South Africa (without their families) they are housed, fed, and paid (minimum basic wage for Malawians is around 55 U.S. cents per day), and their lives are regulated by their employers and by governmental officials. Malawi, Lesotho, Botswana, and Mozambique maintain labor offices in Johannesburg to oversee this process and assure compliance with the labor agreement. Around half of the mineworkers extend their contracts because of sufficiently escalating pay scales for men with experience.[63]

We are not concerned here with the causes of labor migration.[64] Rather, we are interested in the impact of these patterns on regional international relations. With regard to the exporters of migratory labor, at least three major effects can be noted. First, the export of labor serves to relieve population pressures on the land, to keep down the level of domestic unemployment, and in general to serve as an outlet for economic expectations that the government and the local economy are unable to fulfill. As a result, it can be suggested, domestic levels of discontent are reduced, and thus the likelihood of internal unrest and possibly political instability is diminished. Second, the export of labor can be a significant source of foreign exchange, a lucrative source of governmental revenue, a plus factor in the gross national product, and hence, superficially at least, a positive contribution to the level of economic productivity. Third, the export of labor may in the long run have an effect counter to that noted in the short run. It tends, by removing the healthiest, most economically ambitious element of the African population from the country, to retard the extent

63. Interviews, MAL–48, MAL–49, MAL–50, Blantyre and Limbe, September 1 and 2, 1969; Herrick et al., *Area Handbook for Mozambique*, pp. 263–64.

64. See Hance, *Population, Migration, and Urbanization*, pp. 161–204.

of locally generated economic activity. So the chances for self-generated reform of the economy are diminished in two ways. (1) The relief of domestic pressure, prompting governmental initiatives to rectify an unacceptable situation, lessens the chances for reform. (2) The removal of those most likely to take private initiative and to show entrepreneurial spirit (at a local level) deadens local economic growth. Thus, a distorted population structure that is high on children, females, and the very old puts an abnormal drain on the institutions of government and the economy, without possessing the attributes for persuading the government to make structural changes.

Among the importing countries we can discern six important effects. (1) Cheap imported labor serves to depress the economic conditions of the domestic labor force of South Africa. Though to a Batswana or a Mozambican the wages paid by the South African mines, especially if they come in the form of deferred payments on his return home, may seem like a rather impressive reward for his physical labor, these wages are not sufficient for him to achieve a reasonable standard of living in South Africa, even for Africans. Cheap foreign labor competes with domestic manpower and thus weakens the bargaining power of local African laborers. (2) By importing male labor, the South African authorities need not wrestle with the problem of a man's family seeking to leave their Bantu homelands and relocate nearer their breadwinner in designated white areas. This simple fact eliminates a plethora of social and ultimately vexing political issues that the authorities would rather ignore or deal with without social conscience. (3) By importing foreigners, the overall problem of policing and supervising of their lives is lessened—they are, in effect, prisoners of the compound. Their entire lives under contract circulate around the compound and the mine. The factor of deferred pay and the liaison with their own home government are generally adequate levers to assure compliance with the directives of the employers and the authorities. (4) Because of the aforementioned factors, the implementation of apartheid and separate development is facilitated. (5) The fact that hundreds of thousands of foreign Africans are seeking to enter the RSA provides the South African information service with a powerful propaganda point in their running debate with opponents. (6) Internationally, the implied and perceived political instrument attending the possibility of the expulsion of expatriate migrant labor has proven to be a useful weapon in dealing with neighboring states. Those states most amenable to South Africa's pressures and blandishments are those that supply labor to the RSA. This is not to say that they are amenable because of the fact that they supply labor. Rather, that fact is just one more among others placing constraints on foreign policy independence. For governments inclined to be skittish about their dealings with economically stronger neighbors, the export of labor serves to make foreign policy caution seem all the more realistic and prudent.

Economic Assistance

So far, intra-regional economic assistance has not had a marked effect on regional international relations. Its importance has been primarily symbolic, as evidence of a deeper underlying commitment to cooperation in common international policy goals. Cooperation, however, can be interpreted many ways, not the least likely of which might be that cooperation equals the ability to make the other party see things your way or at least to act as if it sees things your way. Before dealing with intra-regional economic assistance, it would first be helpful to outline very briefly the forms and extent of extra-regional developmental assistance. In this way we can put the intra-regional assistance in perspective.

The black states in the region were formerly the colonial wards of Great Britain, and today, as then, Britain is an important source of economic assistance to them. In the case of the former HCT's and Malawi, Britain is the chief financial crutch. For example, 59 percent of Botswana's budgetary revenue in fiscal 1968/69 was supplied by Britain in the form of grants-in-aid and payments from the Overseas Aid Scheme. In addition, various other forms of development assistance (loans, "topping up" funds for expatriate salaries, technical assistance) have been made available through the Ministry of Overseas

Development. The fiscal 1969/70 estimates for Swaziland place revenues at R11,221,000 and British assistance at R5,453,000.[65] It is this economic vulnerability and dependence that continues to make British assistance so vital to the governments in question. Only in the case of Zambia has the relative importance of British assistance been lessened.

In the case of the former HCT's and Malawi, a substantial proportion of assistance is devoted to balancing the budget and providing for services and operating costs. Little of it goes toward long-range economic development and capital expenditure. Even British provision of additional and improved welfare services, though it may free other funds for development projects, is only peripherally related ultimately to freeing their respective economies from frustrating and embarrassing annual deficits. Such frustration and embarrassment have led the Malawi government to announce in 1971 that in two years' time it would no longer request nor need British budgetary aid.[66] The use of the word "need" does not, however, refer to financial requirements, but rather to a political desire to reduce British influence in Malawi.

Probably the most radical realignment of relations between Britain and a regional black state involves Zambia. Precipitated by the Rhodesian UDI and the British response thereto, President Kaunda was reluctantly brought to the realization that Britain was unwilling to pay the price necessary to cushion Zambia's losses from UDI sanctions.[67] Despite an abiding faith that British Prime Minister Harold Wilson would not fail Zambia, it became increasingly evident that Zambia would suffer most heavily, and practically alone, from UDI sanctions. Wilson was able to use the Rhodesian issue for domestic partisan purposes, while President Kaunda found himself weakened domestically. Zambia sustained tremendous financial punishment during the first few years of sanctions. Early in 1968,

65. Legum and Drysdale, eds., *Africa Contemporary Record—1969–1970*, p. B325; see also pp. B260, B268.
66. *The Star*, March 20, 1971, p. 13.
67. The general course of British-Zambian relations is carefully discussed in Hall, *The High Price*, pp. 121–77, on which I have drawn in this brief account.

Kaunda claimed that sanctions had up to that point cost Zambia £35 million. It became imperative to prevent this loss of hard-earned capital. In February 1967 Britain agreed to supply support costs amounting to £13,850,000—a figure which was justly regarded as inadequate since Zambia was bearing the losses on a policy that Britain had always insisted was a direct British responsibility. Moreover, some £5 million of this sum was allocated outside Zambia. Part of the agreement was that support cost funds should never be referred to as conventional "aid." This the British Ministry of Overseas Development promptly violated, to the further dissatisfaction of Zambia.

It is clear that Britain no longer enjoys its former preferred position in Zambian official circles. The Zambians have found other friends, among them Italy and the Chinese Peoples' Republic. Just as the UDI led to the severing of long-standing economic links between Britain and Rhodesia and etched stronger ones between Rhodesia and South Africa and Portuguese Africa, so it has diversified Zambia's extra-continental as well as continental relations.

A second important source of bilateral assistance for economic development might have been the United States. In fact, however, U.S. assistance has been marginal, compared with the British share. The black southern African states have not been designated "emphasis countries"; that is, bilateral assistance is no longer extended to them. New United States assistance officially can only take the form of assistance to regional projects involving several recipient states together, or assistance tendered in cooperation with international assistance institutions or in collaboration with other donor countries. Thus current U.S. bilateral assistance to Botswana, Lesotho, and Swaziland is residual, and consists only of Peace Corps volunteers, some agricultural assistance under Public Law 480 (sometimes called the "Food for Peace" program), and some minor self-help projects. Bilateral U.S. assistance to Malawi, since termination of the Peace Corps program at the request of the Malawi government, is concentrated in the areas of education and rural development, and this is being phased out.

In 1968 the U.S. Agency for International Development

(AID) opened a regional office for southern Africa in Lusaka. This office has sought to develop regional and multi-donor programs, and to terminate the remaining bilateral technical assistance projects, especially those in Zambia. The AID still must convince recipient governments of the efficacy of the regional approach. Recipients are inclined to see this as an abandonment of black southern Africa. Nevertheless, four region-wide projects, costing nearly $1 million, have gotten under way and additional proposals are being considered.

The pretentious geographical scope of the U.S. regional assistance program in southern Africa cannot hide the meager amounts allotted for these states. Though the United States has yet to be tapped for its fullest potential in developmental assistance, there are slim prospects for increased aid in the next few years. It is difficult not to conclude that the United States and Europe, except for Britain and Italy, have abandoned the weaker black states to the economic hegemony of the white South. Regional black states (except for Zambia) are in no position to bring about a modification of that apparent orientation.

By and large, economic assistance from one regional state to another means South African assistance. The only Portuguese economic assistance to a black state ever is a loan to Malawi to tar a road from Blantyre to the Mozambique border.[68] There had been talk of the Portuguese joining with the South Africans in building a large ship repair yard at Narinda in Madagascar, but this turned out to be a private undertaking rather than a governmental one.[69] In August 1970 the Rhodesian House of Assembly voted a R$1 million loan to an unnamed country. It is likely that this loan, if in fact this is what it is, is for a neighboring African government. But the minister of foreign affairs told the house that if the recipient were identified Rhodesia would "immediately forfeit the confidence of that Government, which will not tolerate any discussion of its identity or its affairs in this House."[70] Except for these two and possibly three proj-

68. *ARB* (Econ.), VII, 787B, September 30, 1970.

69. *The Star*, March 6, 1971, p. 19.

70. As quoted in September 12, 1970, issues, p. 1, of *Rhodesia Herald* and *The Star*.

ects, the field of assistance is abandoned to the RSA, which alone among regional states has made available some technical and economic resources in the form of loans and assistance for purposes of fulfilling foreign policy objectives.

Rather than discuss specific South African aid projects or their impacts on recipient states and governments, it would be more helpful to outline the principles, purposes, forms, and extent of South Africa's technical and economic assistance abroad and to look for patterns by which such assistance has been extended.[71] In general one can see two basic purposes underlying South Africa's assistance policy—to assure the republic's long-range regional security by establishing and expanding cooperative and perceived mutually beneficial relationships, and to contribute to its economic growth and prosperity by orienting regional economic structures southward and encouraging South African private business to move into the surrounding countries. In a sense, its rationale is founded on the basic rationale of the outward policy itself: South Africa seeks to create in neighboring states a vested interest in the republic's continued existence and prosperity. The often quoted remark of the South African industrialist Anton Rupert, regarding the former High Commission Territories, exemplifies the mentality of this economic linkage: "If they do not eat, we do not sleep."[72] In other words, declining or even constant standards of living in nearby black states inevitably create the conditions for political unrest that are translatable into policies hostile to South Africa and its internal order. And if neighboring economies can be lifted above subsistence levels, it is assumed, greater contiguity of interests will be self-evident since South Africa will be the logical market for their commodities and they, in turn, will buy the products of South Africa. This reasoning is subject to numerous questions that cannot be treated here.[73] Suffice to say that these views are widely believed among many segments

71. For a discussion of the above points (from a pro-South African government viewpoint) and a country-by-country breakdown in some detail see Leistner, *South Africa's Development Aid to African States.*

72. *The Star,* October 29, 1966.

73. On these issues see Morgenthau, "Political Theory of Foreign Aid," *American Political Science Review,* LVI (1962), 301–9, and

of the dominant white communities in the RSA. An optimism thereby pervades the *verligte* mentality that may be unwarranted, at least in the long run.

The stated principles that shape South Africa's assistance policies are relatively simple. They claim that "non-interference" in the domestic affairs of the parties must prevail, but this has, heretofore, been unidirectional and narrowly defined. As with the South African response to dialogue, other parties are to refrain from public efforts to influence South Africa's racial structures. But the very act of tendering assistance, no matter how technical and no matter how far it is ostensibly removed from politics, has some interference effect on the domestic affairs of recipient societies, particularly with the deep ideological and racial overtones pervading regional affairs. The character of the economic and technical assistance thus far tendered by South Africa clearly serves to reinforce the governments to which it has been offered, and in each case the recipient government has been one whose presence and continuation in power would be helpful to the RSA. The terms of assistance have not so much demanded that new policies be undertaken (hence the claim that no strings are attached) by the recipient government, or that new values be created or that new elite groups be established, but rather that existing norms, elites, and trends in recipient countries be encouraged and strengthened. Although it would be difficult to document a causal link between the foreign policies of the recipients and the directions of aid, the fact is that assistance by regional white states functions to maintain and expand the southern African sub-system. A second principle is that the potential recipient must request assistance specifically. According to a former head of the Africa Division in South Africa's Department of Foreign Affairs, "We do not peddle our preparedness to assist." In his view, the new states of Africa are sensitive. To approach them in this direct fashion permits the inference that they do not know how to run their own affairs. Rather, he said, "We simply tell them, 'If

Baldwin, "Foreign Aid, Intervention, and Influence," *World Politics*, XXI (1969), 425–47.

you think we can help you, will you let us know?' "[74] The third, fourth, and fifth principles emanate from South Africa's own status as an importer of investment capital. Thus the stress is on technical rather than financial assistance, and loans rather than grants. Moreover, South Africa regards its assistance programs as supplementary to and not in competition with assistance provided by the larger and more industrialized countries of Europe and North America. Even so, one can easily sense an underlying desire on the part of South Africa to displace the United Kingdom as the chief patron, as it were, of the Banda government and other governments in the region.[75] The wisdom and the prospects for success of such a policy are doubted by some South African officials.

So the forms that South Africa's assistance takes are fairly clear—loans in preference to grants, technical and personnel rather than financial assistance, the encouragement and expedition of private investments and loans in preference to scarce governmental outlays, and, finally, the creation of infrastructural projects that will integrate regional economies and that will orient black economies southward and expand trading relationships with the RSA.

Bearing in mind these professed guidelines, it should be made clear that the extent of South African assistance is not great and, so far, has been highly concentrated in a few countries. In 1972 the total extent of financial assistance was approximately R171 million to five states: Malawi, Madagascar, Swaziland, Lesotho, and Portugal.[76] The largest single South African government-financed project has been a loan of R8 million to Malawi to finance the first phase of building a new capital at Lilongwe. The quasi-public Industrial Development Corporation granted R20 million in credits to the Portuguese government for the Cabora

74. Interview SA–17, Pretoria, August 9, 1969.
75. Interviews MAL–51, 53, 54, 55, Blantyre, August 28–September 4, 1969.
76. *Facts and Reports*, Amsterdam, vol. II, item 253, March 4, 1972. There have also been reports that South Africa was financing an airport in Gabon and financially assisting the Ivory Coast, but they have been denied.

Bassa project. Other large financial assistance projects include a loan of R5 million (March 1965) to Rhodesia to finance a number of capital development projects dealing with railway and hydroelectric infrastructures, the private financing of the R11 million rail link between Baleka (in Malawi) and Nova Freixo in Mozambique, and a loan of R2.32 million to the Malagasy government for infrastructural developments around the proposed Nossi Bé tourist area—a project that the military government of Madagascar canceled after it assumed power in 1972.[77]

Technical assistance has been concentrated in Lesotho, Swaziland, and Malawi. These programs, which usually involve the secondment of South African governmental officials to the recipient country and the supply of special equipment, have proven most effective. Occasionally, the African Division will try to locate a private South African to undertake specialized work abroad on a term contract, and it will pay or "top up" his salary. In Malawi, for example, South African personnel have been highly placed in the Department of Information, the Malawi Development Corporation, the Malawi Broadcasting Company, the Post Office, the Department of Planning, the Office of Tourism, the Capital City Development Corporation, and the Medical Office. There have been a number of special short-term visits of technical personnel as well. Both Malawian and South African officials have expressed satisfaction with the arrangements thus far. One well-placed South African official directing a Malawi government office candidly put it this way: "My loyalty is to South Africa and to our Prime Minister. I want to make a success of this job because I must answer to my Prime Minister, and he told me to make a success of it." Only in this way, he continued, would South Africa–Malawi relations expand and bear fruit. So in his mind, there was less a conflict of loyalties than if a private citizen of another country had been hired on a contract basis. In short, he perceived a perfect similarity of interests between the two governments.[78]

77. Leistner, *South Africa's Development Aid,* pp. 11–30; *ARB* (Econ.), VII, 1868C–70A, December 31, 1970.
78. Interview, MAL–53, Blantyre, September 3, 1969.

So far, at least, South Africa's programs have been selective, carefully administered, and apparently effective. Even though funds have been limited, South Africa has reaped impressive benefits in symbolic and propaganda terms. An expansion of assistance largely awaits the willingness of more African states to deal with South Africa openly. At least as it is currently conceived and executed, there is a good deal of room for the expansion of South Africa's programs—in intensity, scope, and direction.

Conclusion

To summarize the findings of this chapter, the primary economic fact in the region is the dominant position of South Africa, and next, and more generally, the economic power of the white-governed states over their by-and-large landlocked black neighbors. We can see this in data on gross domestic product, in the character of the various economies, in the directions of trade, in the flows of migratory labor, and in shipping, communications, and transport patterns. Not content with its preferred position, South Africa is pursuing in regional economic relations an "outward policy" which complements, indeed propels, the republic's regional diplomatic and strategic offensives. In neo-Leninist terms, South Africa, because of its relatively advanced capitalist structure and the need to secure markets for excess production, projects for finance capital, and sources of raw materials for manufacturing industries, must inevitably embark on an imperialist foreign policy. It remains to be seen whether this mode of analysis pertains. Certainly it would be some time before we could expect to see the bourgeoisification of South Africa's internal proletariat—the nonwhite labor supply. Nevertheless, elements of Lenin's model come to mind when surveying this data in gross terms and they suggest an explanation for the outward policy emerging from South Africa's imposing economic strength and resiliency.

But despite what could be described as white southern Africa's economic hegemony, greater economic integration has not led to institutional expressions of these patterns. The Customs

Union is one such organization, but it is more than sixty years old, by no means an outgrowth of the outward policy. If anything, and with some exceptions, organizations involving both white states and black states have been dismantled, owing to their political sensitivity. Efforts are being made by black-governed states to etch out new patterns, more palatable politically and, because they provide economic and political alternatives, more helpful in providing negotiating leverage. These states, chief among them Botswana and Zambia, want nothing to do with a South African-inspired "co-prosperity sphere," by whatever name. For essentially similar reasons they would be wary of any entangling arrangements, and very likely would be even in the event that black governments were established where white minority governments now are entrenched.

Part of the "outward" economic policy has been an expanded functional interaction with regional neighbors. But the most extensive projects, Cabora Bassa and Kunene, have involved other white regimes. So far, at least, financial and technical aid, and cooperation with black governments, have been limited in scope, concentrated, and highly symbolic. Conversely, the massive Tan-Zam railway project involves two black states. Only with Oxbow and at a much earlier stage Kariba was there any interracial cooperation. In both of these cases, the extent of white-black exchange is marginal, since project planning and execution involved primarily white officials and technicians.

Today gigantic efforts are being made to redress infrastructural imbalances, particularly by Botswana, Tanzania, Zaïre, and Zambia. Lesotho and Swaziland have little in the way of alternatives in this regard. Given no change of regime in the white South, these projected changes in the economic infrastructure, once completed, can be expected to have a radical effect on regional trade and transport patterns. But until the economies of the black states are radically changed there appears to be little long-run relief from the dependences growing out of labor migrations to the white states.

Unfortunately, much of what can be said about the relationship between economic dependence and political manipulation must be speculative. In the absence of hard data on actual negotiations and motives, it becomes conjectural just what these economic patterns mean. That they do mean something for the political affairs of the region seems undeniable. Meanwhile we must be content to explore tentatively and more generally the realm of influence in the economic-political sphere.

We are concerned here with the potential and actual use of economic power in international interaction. Unfortunately, influence is extraordinarily difficult to trace empirically. We have seen in the preceding sections that established trade and transport patterns and economic investments are far more important in the influence process than economic assistance and the more formal device of the bilateral treaty. Even racial similarities on occasion may be transcended by economic patterns. Thus Angola is somewhat removed from the economic pull of South Africa, while Zambia and Malawi are not. Trade tends to create dependences in weaker countries upon particular goods and products received from economically stronger ones. Once the dependence is established and perceived as such by the government of the weaker state, the door is opened to increased political influence. This does not necessarily mean that it will be exercised, but the channels for expanded influence are, at least, evident.

In the southern African context we can see superficially that white regimes have most of the economic advantages. The black states are landlocked. They lack capital, trained labor forces, and in some cases easily exploitable resources. Their economies are in each case based upon a single commodity, and they are almost exclusively primary producers and subsistence agriculture economies. In many instances they are surrounded or practically surrounded by white-governed territories. In the center of the white African stage is the dominant industrial might of the Republic of South Africa. This situation, manifesting the essential imbalances in the region, is a primary source of regional tension and conflict. Asymmetrical economic relationships cannot help but lead to the temptation to assert unequal political relationships. Economically stronger states tend to seek directly to bring their economic superiority to bear on political problems, and in so doing they cause tension and conflict. Even when these states are not blatantly penetrative, the weaker ones may be hypersensitive to political pressures and thus perceive political pressure to have been exercised when, in fact, it was not. The fear that economic penetration may overflow into political affairs is a perceptual condition. A state submits to control, adjusts to pressure, or resists on the basis of its perception of threat. Different statesmen and different societies may react differently to the proximity of an economically dominant neighbor. Nevertheless, it is evident that white southern Africa is inordinantly more powerful, economically, than the black southern African states and this fact precipitates tensions, real or imagined, that underlie many international issues.

Despite this asymmetry, white southern Africa is not united and the RSA is not monolithic. Geographical isolation from European affairs may have been a military blessing for southern Africa, but it was an economic liability. Because of this, and in spite of it, each of the white-governed states is still economically vulnerable, and their economies are in many ways Europe-oriented, particularly those of Portuguese Africa. Thus it is not altogether impossible to imagine situations in which the white South could become more "dependent" on its black neighbors. For as white southern Africa establishes a growing network of economic links with black Africa two things occur: (1) there is a multiplication of the levers by which pressure can be applied by one state upon another, and (2) these contact points in many ways eliminate the need to apply direct pressure since these interlocking economic relationships serve to bring a perceived mutual coincidence of interests. The likelihood of policy divergence of two states so economically intertwined is diminished. Thus their value, utility, or preference systems are more likely to converge and their policies thereby be complementary. Nevertheless it is unlikely that attempts to influence will be eschewed. Even if the stronger state feels that the asymmetrical position makes it virtually impossible for the weaker state not to do as the stronger might wish in foreign affairs, the stronger one will tend to seek insurance against the possibility of error in its prediction. There is never absolute certainty that state *A* will behave as state *B* has predicted. So there is always a built-in incentive to try to influence.

Asymmetries notwithstanding, international influence and leverage can hardly be a one-way affair. Every point of penetration is also a counter pressure point. In any dyad of states, the very reality of international interaction means inter-influence, no matter how small. But in fact the international system and the regional system do not form a dyad or a multitude of dyads. We are sometimes seduced, for analytical purposes, into seeing international relations in dyadic terms. The fact is that at any given time, all states are influencing all others, directly or indirectly, merely by sharing the same spatial, temporal, and sociopolitical environment.[79] It is extremely difficult for any state to trade or deal with another without this interaction having some impact upon third parties. Thus when Malawi accepts a loan from South Africa, this has a direct effect on blacks in South Africa and upon black states elsewhere on the continent. As Singer (note 79) says, "the system is characterized not only by reciprocity but by multiple reciprocity." What the dominant regional powers seek to do is to create a situation where the systemic factor (a combination of factors external to the state to be influenced) is predominant. In the southern African situation such a situation inherently favors white Southern Africa and particularly the RSA.

The economic instruments available for intra-regional influence are many. But if we are concerned primarily with the politics of international economics, essentially the ends in mind are simple—to modify the behavior of another state or to reinforce that state's behavior if it is considered to be fundamentally in tune with that of the influencer. To these ends, essentially two approaches are employed, one positive and the other negative, the promise of reward on the one hand, and the threat of punishment on the other. Carried to their logical conclusions, these become policies of actual reward for compliance and punishment for noncompliance. In general, implied threats and promises are more common. This being the case, the credibility

79. Singer, "Inter-Nation Influence," *American Political Science Review*, LVII (1963), 420–30.

of any possible fulfillment becomes all important. And because so much of the economic leverage is implicit, the perception of constraint or latitude guides ultimate policy choice. Even when the range of choice open to officials may, objectively speaking, be severely limited, some choice nevertheless underlies their decisions, even if it is merely that of acquiescing in the limitations of the external and internal environments. The "psychological environment" thereby becomes more important than the "operational environment" in which the officials function.[80] But although the psychological environment contributes directly to the decisions arrived at and the policies pursued, the outcome of the actual policies, their successes or failures, are in the last analysis a function of the operational environment. From the presentation of the data in this chapter it should be clear that the operational economic environment is, at present, heavily weighted in favor of white Southern Africa, and trends seem to be reinforcing this imbalance. This is the socioeconomic milieu in which those regional black statesmen determined to assert their independence of the white South and those anxious to redress the inequities in the region and within the white states must function.

80. Harold and Margaret Sprout, "Environmental Factors in the Study of International Politics," *Journal of Conflict Resolution,* I (1957), 309–28.

3

The Political and Diplomatic Networks

Too much discussion means a quarrel.
—*Ivory Coast*

Formal and informal political contacts between states are far more extensive and complex than some might realize. Astoundingly varied opportunities are made available to or are sought out by southern African statesmen seeking to make contact or negotiate with other states. These include formal and permanent diplomatic representation, quasi-diplomatic contact, and contacts while attending meetings of international governmental organizations such as the United Nations, the British Commonwealth, the Organization of African Unity, and the Conferences of the East and Central African Heads of State and Government. In this chapter this diversity of avenues is described and analyzed in order to lend clarity to a complicated picture of rather intense if not always open activity.

Bilateral Diplomacy

FORMALIZED REPRESENTATION

The compilation of one set of data relating to formal diplomatic representation enables us to sketch quite easily a first schematic illustration of this sort of contact in the southern African sub-system. A crude though vivid reflection of the emerging overall patterns is apparent in the network of diplomatic recognition and representation pursued by independent states. When they are charted, certain patterns become evident that merit analysis. Figure 1 represents the diplomatic relations and contacts in 1969–71.

A first glance reveals the existence of two distinct though perhaps fluid poles, and the presence of a number of regional actors who function around both or neither of these. The northern pole consists of the Congo (Kinshasa), Tanzania, and Zambia, though the latter does at least look southward in a cooperative fashion as evidenced by its intention to establish permanent ambassadorial-level diplomatic relations with Lesotho and its exchange of high commissioners with Botswana (1966) and with Malawi (1970). The other pole includes South Africa, Rhodesia and Portugal, plus black-governed Malawi. Diplomatically, the reputedly pivotal role of Malawi is obvious.

Before October 1966, when the Congolese government severed diplomatic relations with Portugal, the "clarity" of this polar pattern was somewhat blurred. In the early 1960s the Kinshasa government was the only independent black African state to have diplomatic relations with Portugal. As a result, however, of accusations that Portugal was permitting foreign mercenaries to use Angola as a base of operations against the Congo, a mob attacked and damaged the Portuguese Embassy in Kinshasa, and the Portuguese chargé d'affaires was abducted and injured. Two weeks later, in reaction to Portuguese protests, relations were severed and the Embassy was closed. Since then, Portuguese interests in the Congo have been taken care of by the Spanish Embassy, where Portuguese diplomats function. In addition, relations between Malawi and Portugal have been upgraded, a Portuguese ambassador replacing a chargé d'affaires in Malawi in 1969 and the Malawian high commissioner in London becoming, in addition, the ambassador to Portugal in 1967. Finally, a full Malawian Embassy was established in Lisbon late in 1969. The Portuguese have maintained an Embassy in Swaziland since that country's independence in 1968,

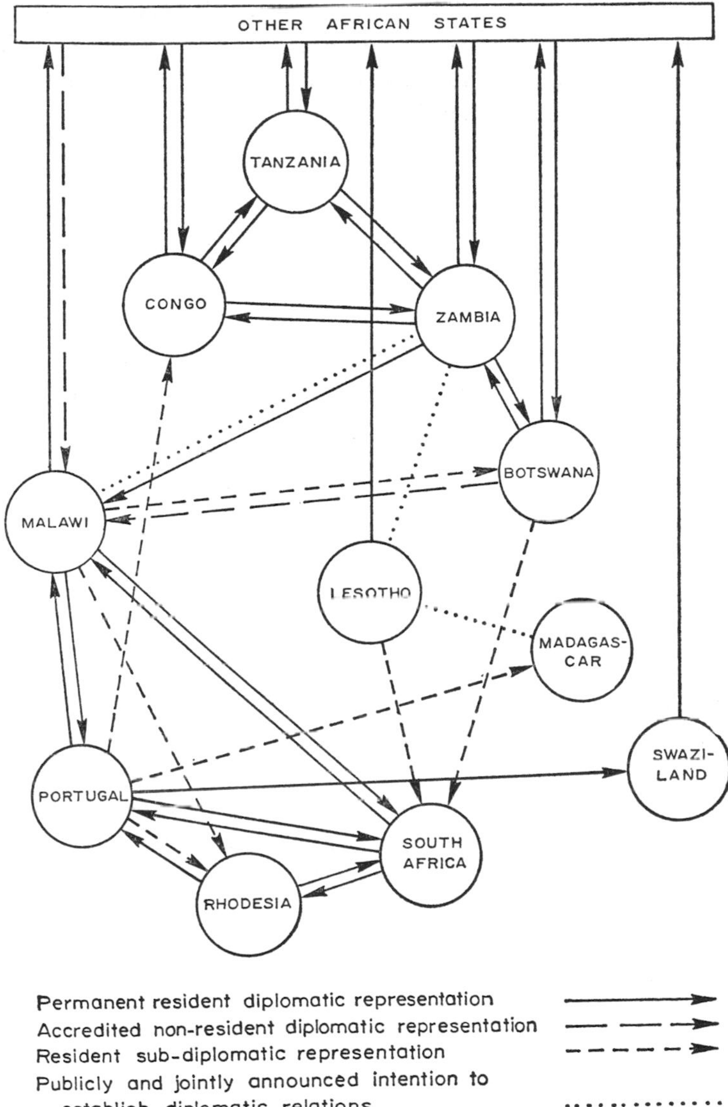

Figure 1. Formal diplomatic representation, 1969–71.

and a Portuguese official is attached to the German Embassy in Madagascar. Portugal also claims to maintain diplomatic relations with Lesotho and Botswana, but this has not been confirmed.

Two linkages that would have complicated this pattern were almost established. First, there was a time when Kenneth Kaunda felt that Zambia could maintain friendly relations with the Republic of South Africa. To this end, at least twice before Zambian independence and the Rhodesian UDI, he suggested that an independent Zambia would be prepared to establish diplomatic relations with South Africa provided a black Zambian diplomat would be accorded the same treatment in South Africa as other emissaries from abroad.[1] Despite his reported professions of sincerity, it was believed in South African governmental circles that Kaunda's proposal was largely electoral propaganda to persuade white voters in Zambia that his United National Independence Party had shed its extremism. The South Africans felt that a serious offer, which they claimed they favored in principle, would have come through direct or indirect representations to the government and not in the form of a public speech. No official reaction from South Africa resulted, and no further Zambian offer was publicly forthcoming.

The second linkage also involves Zambia and a white southern African government. Immediately after the Rhodesian UDI, the Zambian government commenced efforts to find alternative shipping routes. A British military airlift of oil and copper between Beira and Ndola was considered. But it needed both Portuguese and Zambian approval. At about the same time Portugal was seeking permission to establish a consulate in Lusaka. Negotiations were unsuccessful in both cases.[2]

Too much should not be read into these configurations and abortive relations. Decisions to establish formal relations with other states do not always reflect the political and ideological orientation of a state. Rather they are a function of many factors, some of which are largely deterministic. First, initial diplomatic relations are often historically determined. Newly independent states have been inclined to establish relations with the former metropole first, and then to seek other ties afterward.

1. *ARB*, I, 3A, February 15, 1964, and 53A, April 1964.
2. Anglin, "Confrontation in Southern Africa," *International Journal*, XXV (1970), 508.

Second, the question of geographical location limits the range of choice. Since states usually have more economic and routinized dealings with neighboring states than they do with countries farther away, it stands to reason that one would generally establish relations with neighboring states early. Third, it is also a matter of economics. An embassy abroad is an expensive proposition. Unless there is an absolute and recognizable need for permanent representation, why should a poor state undertake such an expenditure? In addition, the availability of sufficient trained personnel must be considered. However, a decision may also be reached because of certain economic advantages that may accrue to the weaker partner, either in the form of a reward for the establishment of relations in the first instance, or as opportunities for financial and technical assistance and trade relations open up more readily to the state with on-the-spot representation. Finally, it can be a function of preference, too. A state may seek to exchange diplomatic representatives with another state as a gesture of good will and in an effort to improve and expand relations between the two countries. Particularly since the states of black southern Africa are so economically wanting, it would not be wise to assume that decisions regarding diplomatic representation are solely expressions of ideological and political preference.

QUASI-DIPLOMATIC LINKS

To an important degree figure 1 fails to indicate the extent of the diplomatic involvement of the former High Commission Territories with South Africa. None of these states have, as yet, formalized their diplomatic contacts with the Republic of South Africa although each has since independence expressed an interest in exchanging diplomatic representatives. In May 1972 it was announced that Lesotho and South Africa had agreed to have reciprocal consular representation. But the chief instrument for official contact has been the quasi-diplomatic linkages which are maintained in two ways—through the existence of a few joint functional bodies (most notably the customs union), and by the utilization of the Africa Division within the South African Department of Foreign Affairs for regularizing diplomatic contact. As a subdivision within a South African governmental department the Africa Division was never intended to serve as a diplomatic medium. Yet, in fact, it has been employed as a sort of clearinghouse through which the RSA, Botswana, Lesotho and Swaziland can maintain relatively constant contact. One high-level South African diplomat has said that never in all his diplomatic experience had he seen a more efficient contact between states than through the Africa Division.[3] Thus by means of telephone neurons and unpublicized visits black states are able to conduct regular business with a pariah state, and thereby avoid the more acute stigma of formalized association as evinced by overt diplomatic exchange. Physical presence is not the only evidence of diplomatic contact. Nonetheless, rumors abound about imminent diplomatic exchanges between the republic and the former HCT's. Obviously, this means has built-in limitations from the viewpoint of the black states. But so does open diplomacy. And the volume of business between the RSA and the former HCT's necessitates some regularized procedures. One could expect more formalized diplomatic procedures to be established first at the consular level and then, perhaps, beyond.

One can also see that the former HCT's and Malawi, by virtue of their scaled-down diplomatic structures, have sought to maintain a formal presence in the black North, as well as in the Organization of African Unity. Swaziland and Lesotho have representation based in Nairobi, and Botswana has representation in Ethiopia, accredited in each case to several heads of state.

SUB-DIPLOMATIC REPRESENTATION

For a further elaboration of these patterns and for perhaps a slightly different perspective on the issue one is obliged to note the existence of official "sub-diplomatic" representation throughout the region, the pattern of official visits between relevant governmental officers, and the activities of "unofficial" irregular contacts between various governments. At present

3. *Rand Daily Mail*, April 29 and May 5, 1972; Interview RSA–17, Pretoria, August 9, 1969.

there are at least six offices operating in the region that may attempt to represent the interests of one state in another outside normal diplomatic channels. These offices are functioning, or have functioned, in some instances in lieu of diplomatic personnel. They provide many of the services that diplomats usually handle without enjoying and in most instances without seeking formal diplomatic status. In other cases they continue to exist even when diplomatic links have been formalized. The variety of forms that these offices might take can be seen by the following illustrations.

Malawi, for example, at present maintains three such offices. In 1967 the "Malawi Government Office" was established in Gaberones, Botswana, to deal with Malawi laborers' problems and probably to offset the growing influence of Zambian diplomatic representation there.[4] The officer, a Malawian African, also distributes literature (mostly speeches by Dr. Banda) and tourist information. A far more active and larger operation takes place at Malawi House in Salisbury.[5] The present "Malawian Government Representative" is a British citizen with long experience in various Malawian and Nyasaland ministries. This office was established before World War II and has always been headed by a European. It is without formal diplomatic standing and it deals mostly with labor issues, but matters of trade, immigration, customs, information, and tourism occupy a good part of its time. The significance of the official presence of a black-governed state in post-UDI Rhodesia cannot be ignored. The "Malawi Government Representative" in Johannesburg fills an office which existed long before diplomatic relations were established in 1967, dealing mostly with the problems of Malawian laborers in South Africa. There is, of course, no need for him to perform quasi-diplomatic functions now that formal diplomatic representatives have been accredited.

Lesotho and (since July 1971) Botswana also maintain "Government Representatives" in the Johannesburg area. Their tasks again are limited to labor, tax, and welfare issues involving their citizens, and other clerical concerns, the diplomatic

4. Interview BOT–28, Gaberone, August 13, 1969.
5. Interview RHO–39, Salisbury, August 26, 1969.

and political matters being dealt with by techniques discussed in the preceding section. Earlier, the labor section of the British consulate-general in Johannesburg handled these matters. Swaziland's affairs have been handled by the Lesotho Labour Agency.

Before Rhodesia was declared a republic in March 1970, Portugal was represented in Salisbury by a consul-general accredited to the Queen. Under pressure from the British government Portugal on May 9, 1970, transferred its consul-general. But under a deputy the mission has remained open for "business as usual." In that fashion, the Portuguese have effectively sidestepped the British demands.[6] South Africa is the only country with official diplomatic representation in Salisbury, and its officer in charge is accredited at the foreign ministry level and not to the head of state. Rhodesia's republican constitution, therefore, does not directly affect its status.

Another "sub-diplomatic" office emerged from unilateral Rhodesian measures when the Zambian government, after the UDI in 1965, became anxious to explore and expedite alternative transport routes to handle the outflow of copper and the inflow of petrol.[7] Early in 1966 a "Zambian Government Liaison Officer" was appointed to coordinate such efforts in Malawi. He was responsible directly to the secretary-general of the cabinet in the president's office. This officer, a European, operated out of Blantyre. There is no longer any need for this officer, however, since the early uneasiness about transport routes has been essentially alleviated, and a Zambian High Commission was ultimately established in November 1970.

OFFICIAL VISITS

Figure 2 attempts to illustrate the complex pattern of official visits within the region in the years 1966 to 1970.[8] It becomes obvious that Malawi, South Africa, and Zambia are the most

6. *ARB*, VII, 1761A–B, June 15, 1970. In April 1971 an acting consul-general arrived in Salisbury to take up duties; *ARB*, VIII, 2084C, May 15, 1971.
7. Interview MAL–46, Blantyre, August 29, 1969.
8. A recent study using state visits as a source of data (and generally illustrating that visits cannot be equated with influence) is Steven J.

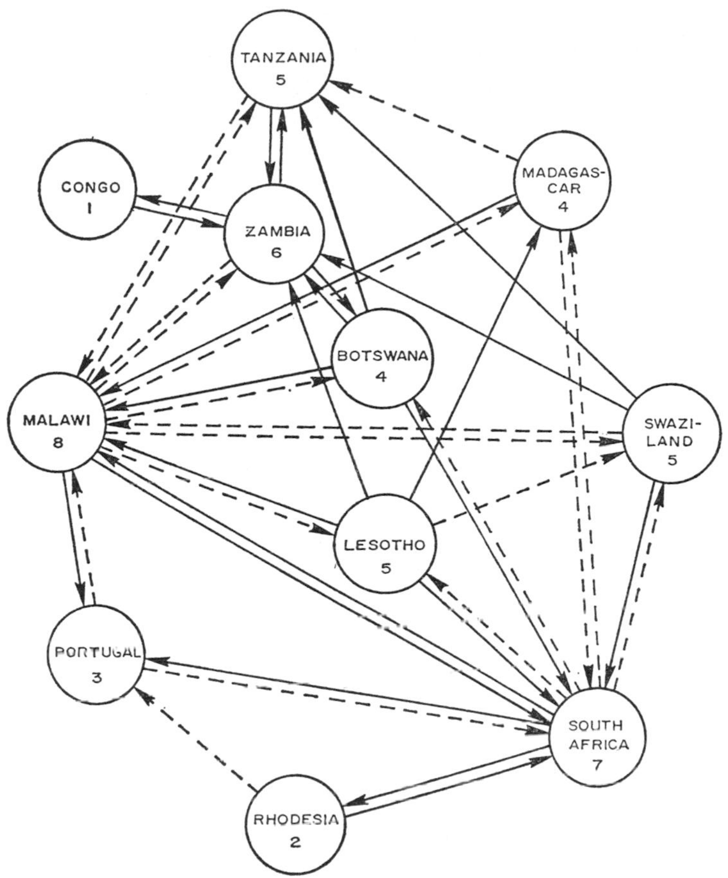

Figure 2. Intra-regional diplomatic visits, 1966–71. (Does not include visits to attend meetings of international organizations.)

active states, having visiting relationships with 8, 7, and 6 regional states, respectively.

Brams, "The Structure of Influence Relationships in the International System," in Rosenau, ed., *International Politics and Foreign Policy*, pp. 583–99.

Malawi again appears to fulfill its self-proclaimed pivotal role, as do, on a smaller scale, the former HCT's. The extent of Zambian activity southward comes as something of a surprise, particularly in the efforts to prevent a total abandonment of the black southern African states by the black North. Zambia, committed to a united front of black states against white racism, apparently is unwilling to write off altogether the former HCT's and Malawi and in this respect is a fence mender within independent black Africa rather than a bridge builder between white and black Africa.

IRREGULAR CONTACTS

The extent of irregular diplomatic and quasi-diplomatic contact among regional states is difficult to gauge since efforts are frequently made to conceal such activities. Direct, although irregular, discussions have taken place usually in response to specific issues. Occasionally black-governed states have found it necessary to deal directly with the white South. For example, after Rhodesia's UDI the Central African railways and airways ceased operations as single entities and became three separate railways and three airlines. Bargaining over the distribution of joint assets was a slow and frustrating endeavor for Zambia, since the Rhodesians made sure that at UDI they held a disproportionately large share of the companies' movable assets. In other instances, South Africa and Malawi have negotiated major trade and labor agreements. The former HCT's in 1969 together renegotiated the customs and excise agreement with the RSA.

Similarly, post-UDI conditions necessitated Zambian-Portuguese negotiations. Though Zambia is embarrassed by this necessity and finds permanent relationships unacceptable, it does regard ad hoc arrangements as necessary. For example, in February 1966 Zambia and Portugal concluded an agreement regarding the rail and port facilities in Mozambique. Bilateral meetings in London, New York, and Lusaka led to a general agreement in June 1968 "to promote peace and to work towards mutual cooperation within permissable limits." This related to promises by each government to diminish the use of its territories for armed incursions against the other. Growing out of this, at least three high-level Portuguese missions have visited Zambia to investigate Zambian claims on the spot. Although Zambia denies the existence of such a body, Portugal would like the "Mixed Luso-Zambian Commission" for inspection to be established on a permanent rather than an ad hoc basis. In 1971 a senior Zambian envoy, Mainza Chona, adviser to President Kaunda, visited Lisbon secretly to clarify certain issues relating to the kidnaping of six Portuguese technicians by the insurgent Comité Revolucionário de Moçambique (COREMO). The Zambian high commissioner and the Portuguese ambassador to Malawi also conferred on this issue.[9] Despite such instances of limited cooperation, Zambia has refused to regularize these and similar proceedings and has sought to avoid further functional, economic or diplomatic collaboration with Portugal.[10]

The use of intermediaries (from within or outside the region) is common. Some successful examples include Malawi's mediation of disputes between Zambia and Portugal, stemming from the arrest of Portuguese soldiers in Zambian territory and Zambian nationals in Mozambique;[11] and the "Swiss device" of July 1966 that enabled Zambia to pay for copper shipments through Rhodesia after Zambia had, at first, upheld the currency restrictions imposed on Rhodesia.[12] These are the sorts of issues in which the "bridge builders" insist they can render a service.

The use of sub-state instrumentalities has also been employed, generally sub rosa, in regional relationships. South Africa in particular, in exploring openings for its outward policy, has utilized a variety of "unofficial" contacts. Since economic linkages are so vital a part of its African policy, South Africa as-

9. *The Star*, March 27, 1971, p. 3.
10. See the excellent treatment of these subjects in Anglin, "Confrontation in Southern Africa," *International Journal*, XXV (1970), 497–517.
11. See *ARB*, VI, 1537A, October 15, 1969; *Malawi High Commission Newsletter* (London), II, 1–3, April 28, 1972; and pp. 130–31, below.
12. Hall, *The High Price*, pp. 165–66. In another crisis regarding Zambian payments for Rhodesian coal, Prime Minister Verwoerd of South Africa publicly offered to send coal to Zambia. Zambia did not respond. *Cape Times*, Cape Town, January 27, 1966.

sumes that businessmen can provide expanded contacts. The role of Harry Oppenheimer—the chairman of the Anglo-American Corporation, which has mining interests in Zambia—is potentially crucial despite his lack of identification with the Nationalist Party in the RSA.[13] By encouraging South African businessmen to secure British passports to ease their transit through black Africa, the RSA has facilitated contacts. Some South African citizens are eligible for British passports, according to United Kingdom law, but according to South African citizenship law they are not. In these cases the Department of Foreign Affairs can arrange for them to possess "dual passports." The South African government has also been alert to direct but unofficial contacts with officials from black Africa by means of the numerous professional and personalized relationships involving South African citizens.[14] Such contacts have flowered through the years, particularly before the achievement of independence to the north.

Throughout black southern Africa there have been, and still are, even in Zambia, South African and British citizens close to the levers of power. These expatriates are regularly employed by both sides as intermediaries for contact and exchange. Zambia utilizes two or three Europeans, personally close to President Kaunda, who deal indirectly with white-ruled governments.

Perhaps the most celebrated instance of such political interaction was disclosed in April 1971 when Prime Minister Vorster, in uncharacteristic fashion, told the House of Assembly that irregular and secret contacts between South Africa and Zambia had been taking place since 1968.[15] According to Vorster, South Africa had sent out "feelers" to Zambia as early as 1965. The first sign of success allegedly came in April 1968, when a Zambian envoy arrived in South Africa bearing a long critical

13. See Munger, *Notes on the Formation of South African Foreign Policy*, pp. 62–63. For one opinion of the extent of Anglo-American operations see Nkrumah, *Neo-Colonialism*, pp. 110–61.
14. See the speculation on the role of Sir Richard Luyt and his association with President Kaunda in Hall, *The High Price*, pp. 29–30.
15. RSA, Assembly, *Hansard*, April 21, 1971, cols. 4928–48; *The Star*, April 24, 1971, pp. 1–2.

letter from President Kaunda. An exchange of acrimonious letters took place, after which Kaunda is said to have suggested a meeting between himself and Vorster. Meanwhile the prime minister arranged to send a personal envoy to Zambia in May 1968, but this contact was apparently delayed until June because of a hostile speech by Kaunda (during a visit to Botswana) and Kaunda's hurried assurances (according to Vorster) not to take the speech too seriously. The Kaunda-Vorster correspondence was discontinued in August 1968. After persistent requests from South Africa, Kaunda received another South African envoy at Lusaka in February 1969 and there it was suggested that the two heads of government should meet in November. That meeting never materialized. Secret contacts were maintained throughout 1970 and early 1971 at the time of Vorster's disclosure.

The Zambians have admitted that Kaunda wrote three letters to Vorster and that Vorster sent one. The texts were made public by the Zambian minister of information. In addition they acknowledge four visits by emissaries of Vorster, but claim that at no time had Zambia requested that an envoy of Dr. Kaunda be received in Pretoria.[16] The South Africans appear to have taken and maintained the initiative in seeking high-level meetings.

The political motivation of Vorster's disclosure is still very much a matter of speculation. But it does illustrate the extent of secret contact that goes unnoticed (or unmentioned) by the press and political observers, including one fairly informal meeting with Vorster's emissary while Kaunda was in Munich and at least three visits by Vorster's emissaries to Zambia. Some of this contact bridges the racial and ideological divisions in the region; indeed, that may be an important reason why it is clandestine.

For black governments, inter-racial contacts must be limited since black citizens in white-ruled southern Africa do not enjoy

16. *Zambia Daily Mail*, April 23 and 24, 1971; *Times of Zambia*, April 23 and 24; *The Star*, May 1, p. 6; Zambian High Commission, *Details of Exchanges*. On the effects of the disclosures see "Dialogue: The View from Lusaka," *Africa Confidential*, XII, 4–5, May 14, 1971.

the access to influential people as do the white southern Africans in the black-ruled states. The white-dominated societies are too closed for this sort of contact. There are, however, ways to evade this limitation. The Malagasy government, anxious to explore the possibilities for expanded economic contacts with the RSA, for this purpose in October 1968 appointed a longtime French resident of South Africa who, in close concert with the planning adviser to the South African prime minister, initiated preliminary consultations that culminated in the loan agreement of 1970 between the Malagasy government and the RSA.[17] In the future, however, racial limitations may be slightly changed as white business interests open more direct business relationships with private black businessmen from black Africa. "Honorary white" status may be granted to black clients visiting South Africa. In the case of Madagascar, South African exporters had, before the military coup, begun to develop "third-party" arrangements through Madagascar to evade the African boycott on goods produced in South Africa. In these fashions the RSA gets, according to its value structure, the best of both worlds: it continues to preserve a rigidly segregated social order and at the same time is enabled to extend its influence more broadly throughout the region.

International Governmental Organizations

It has been demonstrated that ties with international governmental organizations provide most nations with far greater access to the outside world than do bilateral diplomatic relations.[18] Despite a moderately high correlation between diplomatic exchanges and international governmental organizational affiliations, the qualitatively different channels for contact provided by shared membership in the international governmental organizations is worth exploring.

17. "Link Between Two Lands," *News/Check*, IX (January 1971), 30; *Rand Daily Mail*, June 16, 1971. The reference is to Pierre-Jerome Ullmann. This loan agreement apparently was canceled by the Madagascar military government in June 1972. *Observer*, June 25, 1972, p. 4.

18. Alger and Brams, "Patterns of Representation," *World Politics*, XIX (1967), 646–63.

THE UNITED NATIONS AS ARENA FOR CONTACT AND CONFLICT.

The United Nations provides a unique high-level forum in which all of the independent states of southern Africa—except for Rhodesia, whose independence has not been formally recognized—are members. Angola and Mozambique are ostensibly represented as "part" of Portugal, and Namibia (South West Africa) has been since 1966 officially the responsibility of the UN itself although there is no UN presence in that territory owing to the terms of a League of Nations mandate. Thus all regional state entities other than Rhodesia are represented in one way or another at the UN.

There is no way of knowing precisely how much the regional member states have taken advantage of the various formal and informal avenues of exchange within the UN organization. In the proceedings of the General Assembly, the Security Council, and the various committees, the black states are usually arrayed on one side in regional questions and Portugal and South Africa on the other. Precisely because such proceedings are directed against the white-governed states and are direct challenges to the legitimacy (with regard to the UN charter and the more amorphous and encompassing norms of "international opinion") of their internal policies and, in the case of Rhodesia and Portugal, their very existence on the continent, the questions are raised in categorical and hence conflictive terms. And because questions of human rights and the character of modern nation-states are so vital and emotion-laden they have taken precedence over less contentious issues such as regional economic and social cooperation.

The purpose of this section is not to review an already well-documented record of hostile resolutions and intended ad hoc ostracism of the RSA, Rhodesia, and, to a lesser extent, Portugal.[19] Rather some interpretive efforts will be made to place such relationships in a larger perspective.

In the early days of black African independence an almost optimistic atmosphere pervaded the corridors of the UN head-

19. For general background see Leiss, ed., *Apartheid and the United Nations Collective Measures*; Pratt, "African Reactions to the Rho-

quarters, or so one would think if he talked solely with black African delegates. UN membership was the badge of international legal equality and each new session of the General Assembly brought new black African members and hence inflated their voting strength in that body. An African caucusing group seemed to be increasingly determined to speak with a single voice and to use that unity for transforming the UN into an organization primarily concerned for ultimate emancipation and decolonization of the continent, and for the twin objectives of economic development and human dignity for men of color.[20] But the cautious euphoria of the early 1960s was soon dashed on the rocks of repeated Congo crises and the Rhodesian issue. It was the former issue that divided African states openly. It was the latter, plus the inconsequentiality of repeated and progressively firmer resolutions aimed at the RSA, that led some African statesmen to frustration and, ultimately, to disenchantment with the UN as a viable instrument for their policy objectives. Even the overwhelming majorities they mounted, which often included all of the great and "super" powers, were to little avail. They learned after much hope and effort that the UN might serve as a sounding board for their aspirations and policy pronouncements, but that it would be a long time before the UN supplied the muscle and structure to turn aspiration and resolution into reality.

With a growing disillusionment with the UN among black statesmen came a parallel growth of optimism among some South African diplomats. Not that they felt that the UN and its related organs would ever do their bidding. Rather they seemed to take a new perspective on this international organiza-

---

desian Crisis," *International Journal,* XXI (1966) 186–98; Cefkin, "The Rhodesian Question at the United Nations," *International Organization,* XXII (1968), 649-69; Mudge, "Domestic Policies and UN Activities," ibid., XXI (1967), 55–78; George Martelli, "The Issues Internationalized," in Abshire and Samuels, eds., *Portuguese Africa,* pp. 367–88.

20. Hovet, *Africa in the United Nations*; Mazrui, "The United Nations and Some African Political Attitudes," *International Organization,* XVIII (1964), 499–520.

tion. They had, after all, been expelled from many of the specialized and technical agencies spawned by the UN (ILO, FAO, and so on), but no direct steps had been taken to force South Africa out of the organization itself.

Outside the UN chambers, however, calls for South Africa's expulsion have been common. The most important example appears in the April 1969 "Manifesto on Southern Africa," signed at Lusaka by representatives of thirteen African states.[21] Perhaps it was with the Manifesto in mind that the foreign minister of Kenya suggested to the 25th General Assembly that South Africa's continued membership in the UN "should be seriously reviewed." More likely he sought to dispel speculation that Kenya was drifting closer to the Malawian position and opening more trade links with the RSA. Whatever the reasons, it was somewhat surprising that there was no immediate sign that other African states would join in this effort to debar South Africa.[22] What followed, however, was the next nearest thing. By a vote of 60 to 42 with 12 abstentions, the Assembly adopted a resolution sponsored by the African group that would withhold recognition of the credentials of the South African delegation. By a ruling of the Assembly president, which was implicitly accepted by the Assembly, South Africa's rights and privileges of membership during the remainder of the session were not canceled. The Assembly, in other words, expressed the strongest possible condemnation of South Africa's policies short of suspension of membership. This action was repeated in the 26th General Assembly by a vote of 60 to 36, with 22 abstentions.[23]

Resolutions have called for stronger and stronger measures against the RSA, but failure of enforcement and compliance have enabled the South Africans to live with the UN. From 1948 on, the Nationalist Party governments had been isolationist at the UN. They had consistently insisted on a strict interpretation of Article 2, paragraph 7, of the Charter, and, rather than discuss the issues as they arose, they tended to invoke what they

21. See the final section of this chapter and Appendix 2.
22. *The Star*, September 26, 1970, p. 5.
23. Ibid., November 14, 1970, p. 1, and December 24, 1971, p. 14.

regarded as relevant charter provisions and treat matters as closed.

But the South West Africa issue was considerably different. This territory, while continuing under RSA administration, had an admittedly international status.[24] Yet various UN efforts to persuade South Africa to submit voluntarily to international demands led nowhere. Therefore, in 1960 Ethiopia and Liberia, on behalf of the African members of the UN, instituted contentious proceedings before the International Court of Justice at The Hague. By terms of Article 7 of the League of Nations mandate, in the event of a dispute between members of the league and the mandatory that could not be settled by negotiation, the ICJ was to have jurisdiction. South Africa participated in the preliminary proceedings by raising a series of jurisdictional objections which ultimately were rejected by the court by a narrow vote of 8 to 7 in 1962. What this meant, simply put, was that South Africa was forced now to argue the case on its merits. The legal team representing the RSA was carefully assembled and was told to abandon the old defensive posture and to "work as if you are going to win."[25] The South African presentation was a tedious, detailed, and point-by-point contention over each issue raised. Both parties attempted to document their positions carefully, and this led to a long litigation. More importantly, by a vote of 8–7 in July 1966, the ICJ technically ruled that Ethiopia and Liberia lacked sufficient legal interest to obtain a judgment regarding their contentions that South Africa was violating the mandate.[26] Despite the narrowness of the vote and the pettiness of the ICJ's findings, the South African government was elated. In its eyes, it had directly contested the facts in the case and had "won." In the words of one official of the South African Department of Foreign

24. ICJ documents for the cases discussed below are *South West Africa Cases, Preliminary Objections, Judgment, I.C.J. Reports 1962*; *South West Africa Cases, Second Phase, Judgment, I.C.J. Reports 1966*; *Legal Consequences of the Continued Presence of South Africa in Namibia, Advisory Opinion of 21 June 1971.*

25. Interview, RSA–19, Pretoria, August 9, 1969.

26. See the discussion in Falk, *The Status of Law in International Society*, pp. 126–73 and 378–402.

Affairs, this decision gave the republic a new "confidence." It had broken down the "laager complex" and encouraged South Africa to put forward its position with greater vigor.[27] According to a former member of the South African permanent mission to the UN, the experience gained by preparing South Africa's case before the ICJ has had a profound effect on the way the Nationalist government now reacts to overseas opposition, even at the UN. Where, in the past, accusations about various South African policies were tersely denied or even ignored, the Department of Foreign Affairs has, in the past four or five years, been replying in detail.[28] Perhaps this is reading too much into a singular event, but it was about this time that "outward" tendencies within the government were in need of reinforcement. The "non-decision" in the South West Africa case provided at least this much—it encouraged and perhaps accelerated tendencies already set in motion.

Despite that misplaced "confidence," in June 1971 an advisory opinion requested by the Security Council held that the continued presence of South Africa in Namibia was illegal (13 to 2) and that UN members were under obligation to recognize the illegality of that presence and the invalidity of South Africa's acts on behalf of or concerning Namibia (11 to 4). Henceforth member states must refrain from any acts and dealings with the South African government that would imply recognition of or lend support to such presence and administration. There is still some question as to what this judgment means, in that advisory opinions are given in the form of an answer to questions raised and do not, of themselves, give rise to the need for enforcement. Nevertheless this particular judgment does respond to a question on the matter of enforcement of a UN decision already taken, and hence is something stronger than an authoritative statement of the international law on the point at issue.

27. Interview, RSA–18, Pretoria, August 9, 1969.
28. For example, the department's *South West Africa: South Africa Reply to the Secretary-General of the United Nations,* issued in September 1969. See also Barratt, "South Africa and the United Nations," SAIIA *Newsletter,* no. 1, February 1969, pp. 22–39.

South African authorities have not lost their optimism about reaching a satisfactory modus vivendi, from their perspective. Continued confidence was reflected in the 1972 visit of UN Secretary-General Kurt Waldheim to South Africa and Namibia, in his discussions with Prime Minister Vorster and others there, and in the South African offer to permit a UN official to be sent to Pretoria or Windhoek to help with continuing consultations.

A recent by-product of South Africa's more ambitious African policy has been a willingness on the part of some black neighbors to take positions at the UN in opposition to the Afro-Asian states and in effective support of the RSA. It began on October 27, 1966, when the General Assembly, in response to the angry reaction of the Afro-Asian world to the 1966 ICJ judgment on South West Africa, adopted a resolution terminating South Africa's League of Nations mandate and declaring that the RSA had no other right to administer the territory, which "henceforth . . . comes under the direct responsibility of the United Nations."[29] This resolution was adopted by a vote of 118 to 2 (Portugal and South Africa), with three abstentions (France, Malawi, and the United Kingdom). While Botswana and Lesotho strategically absented themselves from the voting, more importantly the RSA had found in Malawi a black ally in Africa, willing to stand up and be counted. Until this time, black Africa had presented a consistently united front voting against the southern white governments. The abstention, in this case, was more significant than a simple abstention might otherwise indicate. It not only was a break in the united front, but it provided a rationale for continued Malawian rejection of the preferences of the OAU caucus and encouraged other black African states to abandon African solidarity. The following year Botswana joined Malawi in abstaining on the South West Africa vote and other states ultimately followed their lead.

This pattern was repeated again on December 12, 1966, when the 21st General Assembly adopted (70 to 13, with 22 absten-

29. UN, General Assembly, *Official Records,* 21st sess., Supp. 16 (A/6316), Res. 2145, October 27, 1966.

tions) a resolution which, inter alia, recommended that the Security Council make it obligatory for all states to sever diplomatic and economic relations with Portugal.[30] Again South Africa and Portugal voted against and Malawi abstained, and Botswana and Lesotho were absent. A few days later another resolution—declaring that the continuation of colonial rule threatened international peace and security, and that apartheid constituted a crime against humanity, and urging all states to provide assistance to the national liberation movements in colonial territories—prompted another Malawi abstention.[31] Malawi abstained at least twice more on regional political issues before the Assembly.

The 22d General Assembly, in 1967, saw a continuation and extension of this example. Botswana and Lesotho were able to join Tanzania and Zambia in stands against Portuguese colonial rule and Rhodesia, but Malawi had become a reliable abstainer on regional issues. On the virtually unanimous resolution condemning the "illegal arrest, deportation, and trial" of 37 South West Africans under South Africa's Terrorism Act of 1967 there were 110 votes to 2 (Portugal and South Africa) and only one abstention (Malawi).[32] Malawi, out of step with all the world but Portugal and the RSA, insisted in explanation that the UN must take a realistic approach that would encourage negotiations between contending positions. Botswana joined Malawi in abstaining on a resolution that established a UN Council for Namibia that was to serve as the administering agency in the Territory.[33] The 28 abstainers included both the communist bloc and the Western powers, but a second state had been chipped away from the African group. On all other occasions, however, Malawi was alone among black states in failing to vote with the African group.

In 1968 and 1969 Malawi continued to abstain on regional questions. On one occasion, in the voting on a resolution calling for South African authorities to withdraw from Namibia, Bots-

30. Ibid., Res. 2184, December 12, 1966.
31. Ibid., Res. 2202, December 16, 1966.
32. Ibid., 22d sess., Supp. 16 (A/6716), Res. 2324, December 16, 1967.
33. Ibid., 5th special sess., Supp. 1 (A/6657), Res. 2248, May 19, 1967.

wana abstained again, arguing that South Africa was the de facto administering power and should be engaged in negotiations to facilitate the ultimate self-determination and independence of the people of Namibia.[34] Botswana, Gabon, the Ivory Coast, Lesotho, Malawi, and Swaziland were all, at one time or another, to register abstentions on regional issues in 1969.[35] The Ivory Coast, in fact, by late 1969 had become a fairly regular abstainer on southern African questions. To a certain extent among African member states, the South African and Portuguese governments were not as alone in the General Assembly as they had been in the early 1960s. Some black African states were reluctant to join the overwhelming majority of members in all resolutions aimed at the white South.

Although for years there has been a strong feeling in South Africa that the republic ought to abandon the UN, the government has not taken steps to renounce its membership. Its view has been that South Africa would continue as a member for as long as it was deemed in the country's interest to do so. The government sees the utility of using the UN as a platform to counter critical resolutions and statements, and has done so with increasing frequency since 1966. Moreover, the opportunities to deal informally with regional and other African states that are facilitated by UN membership are not ignored. South Africa has occasionally indicated disapproval of specific UN actions by withholding portions of its annual contribution by prorating the costs of such activities, but otherwise indications are that the government seems convinced that the so-called outward policy is beginning to make foreign affairs at the UN easier.[36] Simply put, South Africa is slightly less uncomfortable at the UN than was the case a decade ago. Although the resolu-

34. Ibid., 23d sess., Supp. 18 (A/7218), Res. 2403, December 16, 1968.
35. See, for example, ibid., 24th sess., Supp. 30 (A/7630), Res. 2508, November 21, 1969. All six abstained when the General Assembly called upon the United Kingdom to use force, if necessary, to put an immediate end to minority government in Rhodesia.
36. Foreign Minister Dr. Hilgard Muller contended on his return from the 25th General Assembly that his address drew the largest audience (including black delegates) of any he had seen for a South African speech in years. He has attended the UN for at least eight years. *The Star*, October 17, 1970, p. 1.

tions passed in the UN are increasingly shrill and call for more active steps against the white South, there is little question that the outward-looking policy, by reason of the repeated professions of South African willingness to cooperate with black states and the growing network of linkages, has enabled those who deal openly with South Africa to rationalize their involvement by public declaration. For states that economically are unable to find suitable alternatives to South African linkages, the outward policy has provided encouragement and public buttressing they would otherwise have lacked. In the UN they are only slightly more constrained to take the South African position than in their actual bilateral and regional dealings with white neighbors. There has been a slight, perhaps insignificant, but nonetheless discernable trend in the past decade at the UN from a clear-cut black-white dichotomy among regional states at the General Assembly toward some erosion in the black front. South Africa reads this as endorsement of her putatively new posture.

THE COMMONWEALTH'S CHANGING ROLE

The past twenty years have witnessed a change not only in the composition of the Commonwealth, but a change in the relationship of members to the United Kingdom and to the body itself. The Commonwealth is being transformed both in conception and in purpose and process. Professor Ali A. Mazrui sets the transition date at 1960, and there is little reason to quarrel with this.[37] With the inclusion of India, Pakistan, and Ghana the Commonwealth became a multiracial institution. But it was with the entry of Nigeria in late 1960 that the racial balance shifted. A further stage was reached by the end of 1964 when black states constituted an absolute majority of Commonwealth members. With the changing nature of membership, not only in racial, but in economic and cultural terms, the newer members sought to use the Commonwealth to fulfill some of their ideals and aspirations in international affairs. And

37. Mazrui, *Anglo-African Commonwealth*, pp. 1–8, 27–41. The effects of this transition are discussed in Jeeves, "The Problem of South Africa," *International Journal*, XXVI (1971), 418–32.

their intent and interest in changing the external environment led, accordingly, to a decline in Britain's own control over Commonwealth affairs. Not that British influence was destroyed; rather, it was now to be shared. It is perhaps too strong to say as does Professor Mazrui that this constitutes the African "conquest" of the Commonwealth, but clearly two centers of power were emerging in this loose organization, one at London and the other in Africa. The newer members found that by exerting influence on Britain, the Commonwealth's most influential member, they could thereby shape and influence the Commonwealth itself.

Their first major effort in this direction arose over the issue of the membership of South Africa. In the early Commonwealth, the Union of South Africa had been instrumental in diffusing power on the basis of the sovereign equality of all member states. The British had agreed to this in deference to Afrikaner nationalism. Nevertheless, the Nationalist governments of South Africa resisted the accession of black African states to the Commonwealth. It was the entry of Ghana that not only upset South African officials but stood as testimony to a continuing decline in South African influence within the Commonwealth. The 1960 referendum that led to the establishment of a republic on May 31, 1961, became the vehicle for South Africa's expulsion from the Commonwealth. Technically, Dr. Verwoerd withdrew South Africa's request to continue membership. In reality, however, it was his unwillingness to depart from South Africa's racial policies or to compromise his stance at the March 1961 Prime Ministers' Conference, in addition to the pressure directed at Britain by black African members and potential members that precipitated South Africa's "withdrawal." Ghana threatened to leave the organization by declaring: "It is either South Africa or Ghana–Commonwealth must decide."[38] Julius Nyerere of the yet-to-be-independent Tanganyika stated that his country would not apply for membership if South Africa remained a member.[39] It had been es-

38. As quoted in Mazrui, p. 33.
39. His complete statement is in *The Observer*, London, March 12, 1961.

tablished at the prime ministers' conference the preceding year that on attaining republican status, South Africa must "ask for the consent of the other Commonwealth governments." After a few days at the 1961 conference, Dr. Verwoerd realized that his application to continue membership would be most embarrassingly denied if he persisted in pressing it, so he chose to withdraw the application. By law South Africa was not expelled but rather voluntarily withdrew from the Commonwealth. In fact however, the black states forced South Africa to this decision.[40]

The successful campaign encouraged African members to be more assertive at Commonwealth sessions. Particularly, the British handling of the Rhodesian issue and the Heath government's decision to sell arms to South Africa prompted repeated threats that they would leave the organization or sever diplomatic relations with Britain. Yet actual withdrawal was never attempted, and as a result the threat has lost some of its credibility. When Ghana and Tanzania in December 1965 severed diplomatic relations with Britain, in compliance with a recommendation of the OAU Council of Ministers meeting of December 5, they continued to participate in Commonwealth affairs. President Nyerere explained that the Commonwealth was a multi-national organization, not solely a British one.[41] It is a short step from this position to the stand taken by some, although not most, African members in response to the 1970 announcement by the new Conservative government that it intended to sell certain types of arms to the RSA. Some offered new threats to withdraw from the Commonwealth in addition to threatening to sever diplomatic relations with Britain. But Prime Minister Busia of Ghana even suggested that if Commonwealth members were unable to persuade the British government to drop the idea, and arms were sold against the advice of a majority of the members, the *British government* should feel compelled to withdraw from the Commonwealth: "There are agreed principles among the Commonwealth member na-

40. See Miller, "South Africa's Departure," *Journal of Commonwealth Political Studies*, I (November 1961), 56–74, and Vandenbosch, *South Africa and the World*, pp. 174–88.
41. *The Observer*, December 12, 1965.

tions and if one member acts against these principles it should withdraw. It certainly gives up its claims of moral leadership."[42] This outcome would, however, have the effect of destroying the Commonwealth, since Britain would probably take the old dominions with her, and, with political ties severed, economic and financial linkages probably would wither if not be immediately dismantled.

The threat to remove the United Kingdom from the Commonwealth is the culmination of the evolution of that body. Initiative within the Commonwealth is in new hands. The Commonwealth's regular conferences of Heads of Government have, since 1964, permitted the African members to shape, in large part, the agendas. The conference as a medium gives an advantage to the position with the most numerous representation. Sovereign equality as a principle of representation has led easily to the emergence of the dominant issue of racial equality in Commonwealth political deliberations. Thus the Commonwealth is now an association by which the African members seek to influence Britain, and not the other way around as it was probably conceived in London when the African states first gained their independence.

But the African members are by no means unified on these vital issues. One cannot really speak, today, of a Commonwealth bloc, or even a bloc of African members. With states like Malawi, Lesotho, and possibly others unwilling to pressure Britain to take more militant, vigorous, and active policies aimed at the white South, and with Britain's entry into the European Common Market, it is anybody's guess what will become of the Commonwealth, and exactly what meaning one can attach to Commonwealth linkages.

THE ORGANIZATION OF AFRICAN UNITY—COOPERATION AND CACOPHONY

The break in the unified black front that occurred at the UN and among Commonwealth members has surfaced even in the

42. *The Star,* November 14, 1970, p. 15. See also *ARB,* VII, 1824A–26C, August 15, 1970. A discussion of African diplomacy on this issue is in Gruhn, *British Arms Sales to South Africa.*

OAU, that organization intended to be most representative of black unity. Every independent black state in Africa belongs to and, to some extent, participates in OAU affairs, but by no means all member states agree with and actively support organizational policies.

Two issues involving southern African questions seem to be reflective of a general division among southern African members of the OAU. They are also reflective of what could be called the "dual strategy" of the OAU on those questions. On the one hand there is outright acceptance of the need to use force against Portugal and the Republic of South Africa. The African Liberation Committee (ALC) was to be the coordinating agency of the OAU in this strategy.[43] The second strategy centered around the Rhodesian question. Here the OAU sought, at first, to encourage African members of the Commonwealth to pressure the British government to deal more firmly and, if necessary, forcefully with the white rebellion.[44] It might be helpful here to concentrate on the internal OAU political issues that shape international affairs in the region.

Perhaps the organization with the greatest promise for bringing black African states together to facilitate the liberation of the indigenous peoples of southern Africa is the OAU. This potentiality adds to the tragedy of division within its ranks. Philosophically speaking, if independent black Africa is unable to speak with a single voice, how can the OAU and its ALC possibly demand and secure acceptance of the principle of unity among liberation movements from a single territory or from the entire region? Among member states there have been varying degrees of commitment to the liberation struggle, and serious doubts have been raised about the efficacy of that struggle, or at least about the form that struggle has taken.

At the center of the stormy debate has been Malawi. As early as the July 1964 Conference of Heads of State and Government,

43. Wallerstein, *Africa—The Politics of Unity*, pp. 152–75.

44. The ALC's role in the liberation of southern Africa is dealt with in some detail in Chapter 6, below. OAU treatment of the Rhodesian question is outlined carefully and insightfully in Tandon, "The Organization of African Unity," in Rotberg and Mazrui, eds., *Protest and Power in Black Africa*, pp. 1153–83; see esp. pp. 1164–72.

at Cairo, President Banda was out of step with the OAU. There he was reluctant to support the OAU recommendation for a complete economic and diplomatic break with South Africa and the Portuguese territories in Africa.

In contrast, both Tanzania and Zambia have been active and influential members of the OAU. Their delegates regularly participate and assume leadership roles in the OAU's committees and commissions, particularly in the ALC. For domestic Malawian reasons, and for reasons of ideological consistency in Tanzania and Zambia, relations between Malawi on the one hand and her black-governed neighbors on the other have been less than friendly.[45] These strained relations reached a dangerous level when, at the 1965 Conference of Heads of State and Government, at Accra, President Nyerere publicly accused Malawi of treasonous activity with regard to the liberation of southern Africa. Earlier it had been proposed by the OAU Council of Ministers that Malawi should become a member of the ALC. To this President Nyerere firmly stated:

> Malawi is in collusion with the Portuguese in Mozambique to sabotage the work of the Liberation Committee and if admitted into membership Tanzania would find it difficult to continue as a member of that Committee knowing as she does that Malawi, in collaboration with Portugal, is sabotaging the work of liberation.[46]

Eventually the Malawian application was withdrawn, but the effect of this public humiliation was to force President Banda further out of the operations of the OAU and in the direction of greater cooperation with his southern neighbors. Previously there had been ample evidence of Malawi's deviations from OAU policies.[47] Since then Malawi has been frequently excoriated at OAU sessions for failing to support the ALC's po-

45. See the final section of this chapter and Chapter 4 below.
46. *The Nationalist*, Dar es Salaam, October 27, 1965. See also the 1971 effort to expel Malawi from the Conference of Heads of State and Government of East and Central Africa. This was led by the Tanzanian delegation and is described in the next section of this chapter.
47. Exile opposition forces have attempted to document this contention in Bwanausi et al., *Dr. Banda's Malawi*, esp. pp. 16–21.

litical and military strategies. Periodically some leader or group demands Malawi's expulsion.[48] Throughout the middle and late 1960's Malawi and particularly President Banda refused to attend certain meetings, and when attending Malawi often opposed or expressed reservations about proposed and adopted resolutions, especially regarding southern Africa and the Middle East. Malawi has, of late, spoken out derisively at the OAU about ALC and liberation movement activity, possibly because more and more member states have themselves concurred in questioning the wisdom of OAU policies. At a Council of Ministers meeting in February–March 1970, Malawi was one among seven that expressed reservations about and abstained from voting on a resolution calling for Britain to use force against the Rhodesian government.[49] At the August 1970 ministerial meetings in Addis Ababa the "reservations" device was used again as it was at the Conference of Heads of State and Government meeting the following month. On a resolution that opposed, inter alia, the sale of arms to South Africa and condemned specifically France, West Germany, and Britain, ten member states expressed reservations and eight abstained.[50] On a three-part draft resolution dealing with Portuguese territories, Rhodesia, and Namibia, seventeen member states registered reservations. Dissent has become commonplace, even on issues that earlier were the bread-and-butter questions that assured a façade of continental solidarity. Malawi has been the leader of those who have opted to reject the philosophical basis for OAU dicta in dealing with the white South.

Less consistently removed from, but still in frequent opposition to, expressed OAU policy regarding South Africa (though less so regarding the other white governments) have been Bot-

48. See, for example, *Daily Graphic*, Accra, as quoted in *ARB*, VII, 1747B–C, June 15, 1970, and a Pan-Africanist Congress circular at the OAU summit in Addis Ababa, as quoted in *The Star*, September 5, 1970, p. 3.

49. *ARB*, VII, 1691C–92A, April 15, 1970. The others were Botswana, Congo (Kinshasa), the Ivory Coast, Madagascar, Niger, and Tunisia.

50. *ARB*, VII, p. 1833B, September 15, 1970, and "Solidarity at Addis Ababa," *West Africa*, no. 2779, p. 1047, September 12, 1970. Abstainers were Dahomey, Gabon, the Ivory Coast, Lesotho, Madagascar, Malawi, Niger, and Rwanda. *ARB*, VII, 1859A–61C, October 15, 1970.

swana, Lesotho, and Swaziland. Lesotho's Chief Jonathan has accused the OAU of basing its decisions on sentiment and emotion. Such decisions, he argues, cannot be implemented. Moreover, he feels that the OAU does not understand and thus deliberately distorts Lesotho's relationship with the RSA. He has invited the OAU to come and see for themselves. "In effect," he has said, "they [the OAU] want to Cubanise us at our own expense. This I will not allow."[51] Botswana and Swaziland are less outspoken in their criticism of the OAU. Nonetheless, they perceive their interests differently from the majority of OAU members and vote accordingly. Botswana has directly requested the OAU to prevent Zimbabwe nationalists from traversing Botswana territory, since they jeopardize continued businesslike relations with the Rhodesian authorities. By and large, in the case of the former HCT's, the OAU and its members seem to be more sympathetic to the motives for the former HCT's caution, and more willing to refrain from open criticism of them, than to the positions taken by Malawi.

Unfortunately, thus, the OAU has been unable to assure cooperation with and unity among her southern African member states. Even solidarity among extra-regional actors is eroding. To some extent, the OAU by constantly posing questions about southern African affairs is serving as an arena for alienating Malawi even further from the mainstream of African attitudes and policies. That alienation was most apparent at the 1972 OAU summit meeting in Rabat, Morocco. Malawi was the only member of the OAU to boycott the meeting. Considering that the chief issue under consideration was the liberation struggle, a unity was displayed that had been lacking at earlier meetings. For instance, all 41 attending members unanimously agreed to increase their contributions to the ALC by 50 percent in 1972. Malawi once again is the odd man out. Malawi, for a while, had to some extent successfully made inroads into that mainstream, or at least exploited already existent conservative tendencies in some black African governments. In the past two or three years the thrust of African solidarity on southern African questions had become blunted, frustrated, and even, indeed,

51. *The Star*, May 30, 1970, p. 6.

divided. The entry into the OAU of the southern African black states had itself contributed to this diffusion. Perhaps a new solidarity may be emerging.

THE CONFERENCES OF HEADS OF STATE AND GOVERNMENT OF EAST AND CENTRAL AFRICA AND THE LUSAKA MANIFESTO

Since March 1966 the governments of East and Central Africa have held meetings to attempt to encourage better regional relations and to coordinate their policies, particularly with regard to southern African questions. Four of the states under consideration in this study—Congo (Kinshasa), Malawi, Tanzania, and Zambia—have participated in this group and its meetings. Table 8 indicates the extent of their participation and the nature of the group's activities.

On the surface, the Conferences of Heads of State and Government of East and Central Africa would be an ideal means for unifying independent black Africa behind the liberation movements. The conference group is smaller and less diverse than the OAU, and it does not include the states of black southern Africa whose governments are more sensitive to South African pressures and hence reluctant to advocate violent solutions to regional problems. By and large, this commitment is reflected annually in the final communiqués of its meetings.

A most complete and consistent policy position with regard to southern Africa is embodied in the group's April 1969 communiqué, generally called the "Lusaka Manifesto" (see Appendix 2 for text). That position can be summarized as follows. The states concerned accept the belief that all men have an equal right to human dignity and respect, and a duty to participate, as equal members of the society, in their own government. Although they recognize that implementation may be imperfect, and that transitional arrangements may be necessary to achieve individual equality from a condition of group inequality, there must be a commitment to these principles in order to secure a basis for peace and justice in the world. Thus they feel a fundamental hostility toward the colonialism and racial discrimination currently practiced in some states of southern Africa. By rejecting racialism, they thereby express their hostility to the

TABLE 8
SUMMIT CONFERENCES OF HEADS OF STATE AND GOVERNMENT OF EAST AND CENTRAL AFRICAN STATES

Date	*Place*	*Southern African Delegates*	*Chief Issues*
March 31–April 2, 1966	Nairobi	Pres. Nyerere, Pres. Kaunda, Pres. Mobutu, Malawi's Minister of Transport and Communications John Msonthi	Rhodesia, liberation of southern Africa, refugees, and border incidents
February 12–14, 1967	Kinshasa	Pres. Kaunda, Pres. Mobutu, Tanzania's 2d Vice-Pres. Rashidi Kawawa, Malawi absent	Rhodesia, liberation of southern Africa, aggression of white regimes, implementation of group decisions
December 15–16, 1967	Kampala	Pres. Kaunda, Pres. Nyerere, Pres. Mobutu, Malawi absent	Mercenaries, economic and technical cooperation, security
May 13–15, 1968	Dar es Salaam	Pres.Kaunda, Pres. Nyerere, Malawi's Minister of State for External Affairs Alex M. Nyasulu, Congo's minister	Nigeria, southern Africa, attempted coup in Congo (Brazzaville)
April 14–16, 1969	Lusaka	Pres. Kaunda, Pres. Nyerere, Malawi's Minister of State Nyasulu, Congo's minister	Liberation of southern Africa (Lusaka Manifesto), Nigeria
January 26–28, 1970	Khartoum	Pres. Kaunda, Tanzania's minister, Malawi's Minister of Agriculture Richard Chidzanja, Congo's minister	Aid to liberation movements, regional cooperation, Middle East
October 18–19, 1971	Mogadishu	Pres. Nyerere, Zambia's Vice-Pres. Mark Chona, a Malawi Ambassador, Congolese delegation	Malawi membership, southern Africa (Mogadishu declaration), Middle East
September 7–9, 1972	Dar es Salaam	Pres. Nyerere Pres. Kaunda Zaire's minister Malawi's minister	Support for armed liberation struggle, Middle East

SOURCE: *Africa Research Bulletin*, vols. III–IX (1966–72).

governments of those states, not because they are controlled by whites, but because they are and seek to perpetuate minority rule in pursuance of doctrines of human inequality. One clause (no. 8) specifies: "We believe that all the peoples who have made their homes in the countries of Southern Africa are Africans, regardless of the colour of their skins; and we would oppose a racialist majority government which adopted a philosophy of deliberate and permanent discrimination between its citizens on grounds of racial origin." This being the case, they specifically reject what they call "reverse racialism," "African imperialism," and boundary alterations in the region. There is to be no compromise with these fundamental positions. Whether or not violence is employed to achieve their institutionalization in southern Africa depends upon the extent to which peaceful methods of struggle succeed. It is, after all, "violence against human dignity" that they oppose. Thus the possibility of continuing the struggle through peaceful means varies from country to country. The manifesto then goes on (nos. 13–24) to outline a different strategy for each territory.

But this position, no matter how reasoned and conciliatory it might have appeared to other black states, was unsatisfactory to Malawi. On returning home Malawi's chief delegate expressed reservations about the final communiqué in both substantive and procedural terms.[52] Malawi's alienation was further evidenced at subsequent meetings of the group. One example was a preparatory meeting of East and Central African foreign ministers in January 1970. This meeting was called to hammer out a final communiqué to present to the sixth Conference of Heads of States and Government, at Khartoum. Since the governments of Portugal and South Africa had not accepted enthusiastically the essence of the Lusaka Manifesto, the ministerial delegates felt that white Africa had "closed the door to the possibility of a peaceful solution."[53] The Malawian delegation denounced this draft and also angrily disassociated itself from a

52. *ARB*, VI, 1372A–B, May 15, 1969.

53. *ARB*, VII, 1631A–C, February 15, 1970. Cf. the favorable reference by the minister of foreign affairs in RSA, Assembly, *Hansard*, May 7, 1969, cols. 5450–51; also his remarks quoted in *ARB*, VI, 1543A–B, November 15, 1969.

message of praise sent to the government of Sweden for ordering firms in that country to withdraw from the Cabora Bassa hydroelectric project in Mozambique. The Malawians disclosed that they made last-minute efforts to alter the tone of the communiqué, as well as some of its specific points. In the end, the Malawian chief delegate could merely state that he considered peaceful ways to be the answer and that Malawi would continue to deal regularly with Mozambique and to participate in the Cabora Bassa scheme.[54] Reportedly, because of this position, Malawi's status in the group was called into question. However, the chairman of the meeting—Moto Nkama, Zambia's minister of state for foreign affairs—later discounted such reports, explaining that the criterion for membership was merely independence within the region.[55] The Khartoum Conference later confirmed this abandonment of dialogue: the ground rules of the Lusaka Manifesto were not acceptable to white Africa.

At the seventh conference (1971) in Mogadishu, Somalia, the Tanzanian delegation sought to have Malawi expelled from the meetings and from the conference organization itself. This effort was thwarted by the Kenyan delegation who argued that the matter had not been on the agenda and was outside that meeting's terms of reference. Nevertheless, there seemed to be a feeling, as the Congo (Brazzaville) delegation put it without mentioning Malawi by name, that South African spies were present at the meeting and that they should be ejected.[56]

On the broader issue of how to deal with the white-governed states, a "Mogadishu Declaration" was adopted which again rejected the idea of dialogue and stated that because South Africa had rejected the Lusaka Manifesto black Africa must now commit itself to the violent overthrow of apartheid by increasing its aid to the liberation movements. Thus the more accommodating tone of Lusaka was superseded by an unbending stance at Khartoum and Mogadishu. Malawi, Burundi, the Central

54. *The Star*, January 10, 1970, p. 1.
55. *ARB*, VII, 1631B–C, February 15, 1970.
56. *ARB*, VIII, 2247–49B, November 15, 1971; *The Star*, October 23, 1971, p. 4.

Africa Republic, and Kenya expressed reservations as to the wording of the declaration.

The primary announced purpose of the East and Central African grouping has been to draw together the states in the region, to encourage greater cooperation in their developmental efforts, and to deal in common with mutual problems and the vital issues of southern Africa. With the exception of Malawi, the participants have been relatively successful in maintaining regional unity. The Lusaka Manifesto on southern Africa was carefully reasoned and extremely well written. It projected a favorable image of their struggle to the outside world and forced Western governments to admit the merits of their case and their position. Even the South African foreign minister was moved to respond, unofficially, that there was much in the document with which South Africa agreed. The fact that it led to no further dialogue with the RSA is no fault of those who drafted it.

The patterns of diplomatic and political networks that have emerged in southern Africa over the past half-dozen years have been complex. Diplomatically there has been a high level of activity. Malawi, South Africa, and Zambia are perhaps the most active states in this respect. There has also been a surprisingly high level of exchange across racial lines, particularly in secretive diplomatic contact, and even in formal, governmental terms. The following chapter will focus upon these patterns. International organizational activities, however, have tended largely to isolate the white governments and their black collaborators, and consequently have served to reinforce those committed to the liberation of white southern Africa and to intensify contacts among black African states. Thus the two facets of activity, diplomatic and organizational, do not necessarily overlap and reinforce, but rather confront one another with, to some extent, counter configurations.

4
The Bridge Builders

He who begins a conversation, does not foresee the end. —*Mauritania*

We have seen in Chapter 1 that there are divisions in southern Africa along racial lines, and, even more certainly along lines of professed racial or cultural policy. Nevertheless, those divisions are by no means firm in their political-diplomatic aspects and even less so in economic ones. There are at least five black states in the region who deal openly (to one degree or another) with white southern Africa, and who purport to be willing to serve as bridges between white and black Africa. It is to the foreign policies of these states that we now turn.

Why Build Bridges?

What is meant by "bridge building" in this chapter is not simply the act of serving to stimulate contact between white and black Africa. If that were the case then Zambia's provision of transit camps for guerrilla fighters heading southward would be bridge building. Or, to reverse the coin, if Malawi were to provide a military airport for South African armed forces, this would be a "bridge" function. But such arrangements cannot illustrate "bridge building," owing to their hostile and unidirectional character. Bridge building, for our purposes, refers to activities carried on by black states in southern Africa with the object of seeking to expand proper, if not friendly, dialogue and perhaps relations between, at present, distrustful poles of white and black Africa.

In many respects a decision by a black government to attempt to bridge a gap between the two groups of states is a recognition of geopolitical and economic realities and an effort to make the best of an unfavorable situation. There may be, as has been discussed in Chapter 1, a conviction on the part of such a government that the encouragement of dialogue with white southern Africa is the sensible approach to dealing with a racially repulsive and economically unacceptable status quo there. I attempted to posit earlier that such a line of argument is a rationalization for a policy that the bridge builder would rather have avoided, had his perception of alternatives been sufficiently attractive. The fact is that these southern African states that have undertaken the role of professed mediators have perceived few alternative courses open to them. Their position in most cases is not advanced on the basis of principle or dedication to an abstract concept of "peaceful coexistence," a phrase they use repeatedly. Rather, they openly admit that with them it is a matter of survival. "Having survived for 150 years," a Lesotho diplomat put it, "we have no intention to commit national suicide through bravado."[1] Sir Seretse Khama of Botswana prefers the term "prudence."[2] Whatever the phraseology, black Africa's bridge builders have felt compelled to deal with the white South largely because of the geographically proximate and economically dominant RSA, or because of the geographical advantages (for instance, ports) of Mozambique and Angola. But one suspects that their racial sympathies if not their ideological ones lie with the black North. Hence the role of bridge builder strikes them as the obvious viable alternative.

The influence of such economic and geographical—that is, systemic—variables depends, at heart, on how statesmen per-

1. Kotsokoane, "Lesotho and Her Neighbours," *International Affairs*, LXVIII (1969), 138.
2. "A Policy of Prudence," *Africa Report*, XI (October 1966), 19–20.

ceive and interpret them. In the case of Lesotho and Swaziland, and slightly less of Botswana, systemic features external to the states are so imposing that no head of government could help but place primary emphasis on them. This would probably hold true regardless of partisan, class, racial, ideological or idiosyncratic factors. Regardless of who is in power in Pretoria and regardless of South Africa's policies, the primary determinant of foreign policy in the former HCT's would probably be systemic. Farther north, and particularly in Malawi, where the presence of the white South (except for Mozambique) is not so pervasive, a greater element of choice could enter into foreign policy decisions. Thus the element of constraint felt in the external system is a function of perception as well as reality. Two governments, confronted by essentially the same external conditions, might respond in entirely contradictory ways. One statesman, seeing his state's economy penetrated by external forces and being nearly surrounded by a strong and potentially hostile neighbor, may choose to adapt to the situation. He may perceive that his state lacks the capacity to resist, alter, or deflect the demands of the environment. Rather than bargain, he will acquiesce, maybe even to the extent of altering his state's internal political structure to please his neighbor's government. Another statesman, confronting essentially the same conditions, may reason that the situation is intolerable and decide that his government, while avoiding a precipitous confrontation with the powerful neighbor, must take all steps possible to sever those constraining linkages. The tendency in the black southern African states is to approach the former course rather than the latter.

In addition to these reasons for opting for a policy of adapting to the situation, there is another strongly compelling motivation. There are short-run material benefits to be gained by dealing with the ostracized side in a confrontation of this sort —in this case, with the racist white governments. This is especially so when the ostracized side is economically and technically more powerful, and willing to pay for what it seeks—in this case, the benefits of breaking out of the crude cordon by which it would be denied access to independent black Africa. In Cape Town there is a statue of Cecil Rhodes beckoning northward with upraised arm. The inscription on the pedestal reads: "Your hinterland is there." The industrial and financial magnates of present-day South Africa, along with its increasingly confident and regionally conscious Nationalist government, have taken this message to heart and have sought, in the past few years, to become more directly involved in black Africa. Playing on these desires and growing out of his own inability to resist the economic pressures and blandishments of the white South, an official in neighboring black Africa may reason that a policy of collaboration need not compromise his own racial principles and policies domestically, and that such a policy may in fact materially benefit his own people and in the long run provide his state with the wherewithal to become economically as well as legally independent. Historically, many important states have based their entire foreign policy for extended periods on acting as middlemen or honest brokers between sides in major, ostensibly unbridgeable, confrontations.

But there are tremendous difficulties facing any black African government that envisions for itself this role. The issues that divide black and white Africa are deep and emotional. Because of their racial content they envelop the whole world in some degree. It would be difficult for even the most powerful third party to bring both sides together. To be successful a mediator must not be identified with one side or the other. Moreover, each side must be anxious for a settlement. It would be helpful, as well, if the prospective mediator were sufficiently powerful to exercise some bargaining leverage over both contending sides. A large segment of black Africa is not in the least interested in a permanent modus vivendi with white southern Africa if such an arrangement recognizes and legitimizes the continuation of minority rule and racial discrimination and exploitation there. On the other hand, though the white-governed states are anxious to reach regional accommodation with their black neighbors, that accommodation involves little compromise on the part of South Africa, the keystone of the white south. The

South African government has consistently maintained that any acceptable modus must include an acceptance of the principle of noninterference in the domestic affairs—including, in its own case, racial policies—of other countries. This is precisely the principle that most black African leaders reject as unsatisfactory, owing to the tolerance of racism that it requires. Even though individual black governments might come for one reason or another to deal with the white South on the basis of this principle, by doing so they would almost automatically forfeit any possibility of acting as linkages between the bulk of black Africa and the white-ruled South. The fact is that if bridges are to be built, each side must be convinced of the other's sincerity and skill. Given emotional issues, the conviction that a government is sincere often is reached by the actor dealing with that government only after it openly identifies with him. But by identifying with him the government automatically may write off the possibility of its being regarded as sincere by the opposite side. So the element of trust becomes an important ingredient in the diplomatic mix. For a black government that would deal openly with white racist states, that element of trust could only be achieved if the rest of black Africa realized that such dealings were an absolute necessity, could not be avoided, and were consciously held to a minimum.

In their role of bridge builders, the rhetorical style of Dr. Banda of Malawi and Chief Jonathan of Lesotho makes a difficult task all the more so. Their lecturing to black Africans about the folly of an unaccommodating approach to the white South only further convinces black Africa that they are collaborators, sell-outs, or puppets. Their tendency to lecture does not sit easily with black Africa. The *Times of Zambia*, commenting on an announcement that Zambia would establish diplomatic relations with Malawi, quoted "informed sources" as saying that Zambia's main aim was to attempt to influence Dr. Banda to be less vocal in his support for white governments. In its view Zambia sought to influence Malawi not to cease dealing with racist governments but to cease broadcasting its heresy. Zambia sought, thus, to bring Malawi more into the

African bloc at the UN and the OAU.[3] To exploit or exacerbate the sensitivities of either side is not to build bridges.

The geographical factor is also pertinent to the success of such an endeavor. Those states that are economically and geopolitically the "captives" of white-governed territories are accorded a greater measure of tolerance, and even indulgence, by black Africa. If such a state should be regarded as a "hostage," the rest of black Africa might expect merely that its government make some efforts to decrease its economic dependence on white neighbors, that it continue to pay lip service to principles of racial equality and majority rule, that it at least refrain from open criticism of black Africa's revolutionary efforts or open approval of white responses, and that it not collaborate with white governments by denying asylum or transit permission to political refugees from the white South. If bridges are to be built, such states may be well placed to build them, especially if black Africa is convinced that they deal with the white South out of necessity rather than by choice.

Botswana is geographically better situated than Lesotho or Swaziland to maintain linkages with the black North, being strategically important for both sides. It thus has some leverage to bargain. First, Botswana shares a common border with Zambia. To be sure, there is some legal question about the extent of such a border. In 1970 the existence of a common border was denied by the South Africans although they had permitted direct ferry crossings for decades. Finally, late in that year, they formally conceded a right of way across the Zambezi based on eighty years of established usage. Botswana in turn agreed not to construct a bridge at the point of contact, Kazangula.[4] This border, then, prompts Botswana and Zambian officials to perceive policy opportunities otherwise absent.

3. *ARB*, VII, 1862B–C (October 15, 1970).

4. See *The Star*, April 18, 1970, pp. 5, 7, 10, and 11; *ARB* (Econ.), VII, 1640C–41A–B (April 30, 1970), 1668C–69A (May 31), and 1839C–40A (November 30). The South African position is based on documents reprinted in *Africa Institute Bulletin*, VIII (1970), 196–97. A careful survey of the legal issues is Craig, "Zambia-Botswana Road Link," *Zambia and the World*, pp. 25–32.

The second strategic consideration is the railway link between South Africa and Rhodesia. Botswana's economic lifeline has been the railway that runs from Bulawayo in Rhodesia through Francistown, Gaberone, and Lobatse on the eastern edge of Botswana and thence to Mafeking and eventually to Johannesburg.[5] As further evidence of Botswana's vulnerability, this line is owned and managed by Rhodesian Railways, despite post-UDI sanctions. This is, moreover, the only rail link between South Africa and Rhodesia. From time to time there has been discussion in both South Africa and Rhodesia about the merits of building a connecting line along the sixty miles between Beit Bridge and West Nicholson or along some alternative route in order to bypass the Botswana line, a frightening prospect for the Botswana economy. In May 1971 Rhodesia announced its decision to construct the new rail link with South Africa, and it was anticipated that the project would be completed in 1973.[6] Although no responsible Botswana official has suggested using the railway to bargain for better relations with the white South, this is a future possibility, especially when the road from Francistown to Zambia is a reality or if Botswana should utilize the threat to extend the Tan-Zam railway link into Botswana.

A third strategic possibility involves the use of Botswana as a vestibule—either as the most accessible route for guerrilla fighters or regular military units from the north against Rhodesia, South West Africa or the RSA, or as the RSA's window on independent black Africa. Both sides are cognizant of Botswana's potential role, and Botswana is careful to maintain correct relations with both sides.

It can be seen that although the potentialities for linkages are there, tremendous obstacles must be surmounted. After exam-

5. Discussion of the issues regarding this railway appears in Munger, *Bechuanaland*, pp. 95–99, and Smit, "Botswana Railway Line," *Africa Institute Bulletin*, VII (1970), 272–80.

6. A representative debate is treated in *Rhodesia Herald*, August 23 and September 4 and 5, 1969. According to 1971 reports, Prime Minister Smith believes a direct Rhodesia–South Africa link will be needed by 1975 and that the preferred route would take about eighteen months to build. *The Star*, March 13, p. 17, and May 29, p. 13. A detailed report is in *ARB* (Econ.), VIII, 2037C–38B (June 31, 1971).

ining in some detail the actual links that have been forged, we will be better equipped to look at the total effects of these efforts, from the standpoint of regional international relations.

The Actual Links Between Black and White Southern Africa

Since the white South is more powerful economically and militarily, we usually assume that black states that deal with white southern Africa are "involved," or are showing an increasing "commitment" to a continuation of white rule in the region. Although this might not necessarily be so, we should attempt to outline the ways in which those governments that seek the role of intermediary have developed contacts with both sides in the contest and how they have sought to use these two-way links to improve their own intra-systemic positions. The types of relationships include, in probable reverse order of political importance, trade, sympathetic policy pronouncement, diplomatic contact, similar votes at international gatherings, aid, and military collaboration. The diplomatic picture and the economic (trade and aid) relationships have already been dealt with (chap. 3). Rather than restate them, it would be helpful to explore those aspects of the links that reflect directly on the brokerage role so actively sought.

MALAWI

Perhaps no statesman has more actively sought the position of intermediary than Malawi's president, Dr. Banda. In its thrust and trend, however, his foreign policy posture has been conciliatory toward the white South, and as a result his status and credibility in black Africa have suffered. Even before Malawi's independence, Banda in February 1962 paid an official visit to Lisbon, met Premier Salazar, and held secret talks with the Portuguese minister of foreign affairs. Again, in 1963 on the eve of independence, he invited Winston Field (then prime minister of Rhodesia and leader of the rightist party that succeeded Sir Roy Welensky in Salisbury) to Malawi, where secret talks were held. Hence his southward orientation has a long history. The crowning achievement was the 1967 act of exchanging diplomatic representatives with the RSA, the effect of which was compounded by vituperative lectures to African leaders who criticized him and whom he referred to as "snarling hyenas and jackals." When boundary disputes flared up with Zambia and Tanzania, the Zambians became, inter alia, "turners and cobblers," and Dr. Nyerere a "jellyfish." This is not the language of a conciliator or an intermediary. Three other actions served particularly to anger black African nationalists—Prime Minister Vorster's May 1970 visit to Malawi, Banda's much publicized tour of South Africa the following year, and the presence of a South African military attaché in Blantyre-Limbe. Vorster's visit and the visit by Banda led many to accuse Malawi not only of foolishness, but of serving as an ally of South Africa. Malawi, said a ZANU editorial, was being turned into "a Bantustan in a greater racist Commonwealth and common market."[7]

The military attaché has aroused even more loathing in the hearts of African officials. Not only is there speculation that South Africa agreed to provide logistical support to Malawi forces in the event of external attack on Malawi, but there is further concern that South Africa may be seeking an advanced military air base in Malawi. Rumors abound that Malawi and South Africa have already reached secret agreement on the use of Malawi as a South African military base. Denials have failed to dispel fears.[8] The speculation was not stilled when the South African minister of health, mines, and planning was quoted as saying: "It will mean much if an airfield or an airport is built

7. These events and others are recounted, with an insider's knowledge and commitment, in Chipembere, "Malawi's Growing Links with South Africa," *Africa Today*, XVIII (April 1971), 27–47, esp. 33–36. See also *Zimbabwe News*, V (May 1970), 6–7; the ANC–London *Spotlight on South Africa*, VIII, 5, 10, June 8, 1970; *ARB*, VII, 1750A–51C, June 15, 1970, and VIII, 2189C–92C (September 15, 1971). The speeches by Banda and Vorster on the occasion of the visit are available in Malawi, Department of Information, *Pioneers in Inter-African Relations*. For a recent diatribe against the "African Judas" see Duma Nokwe, "Banda Belly-Crawls to Vorster," *Sechaba*, V (October 1971), 2.

8. *East African Standard*, December 20, 1968, p. 1; *The Star*, May 23, 1970, p. 1, and May 22, 1971, p. 14.

in Malawi which could also be used by military aircraft."[9] This caused a minor flap in the South African government amid repeated government insistence that negotiations on this subject had not been opened. Nevertheless, a high-level military officer has been assigned to the mission in Malawi, and Malawi is increasingly regarded by her black neighbors as a "projection of South Africa into free Africa." During the 1971–72 escalation of the FRELIMO offensive in Tete Province, Banda requested and received material South African military assistance to help secure his southern border and to neutralize FRELIMO fighters on Malawian territory.[10] It looks as if the RSA is prepared to respond when Banda sounds the Macedonian cry.

These three illustrative and flamboyant associations with the white South have rendered Dr. Banda's standing in black Africa doubtful, and thus his ability to function as middle man is weakened. We have already seen the extent to which Malawi has been ostracized in intra-African bodies such as the OAU and the Conferences of Heads of State and Government of East and Central Africa. Bilateral relations with its black neighbors have been at least as tortuous, although they show signs of improvement.

Take the case of Tanzania-Malawi relations. There has been a measure of conflict between President Nyerere and President Banda since their pre-independence contacts in the Pan-African Freedom Movement of East, Central and Southern Africa in 1959. The clash became virulent after 1964 when a number of Malawian cabinet ministers who had either resigned or been sacked by Banda were given asylum in Tanzania. This in itself would not be sufficient to strain relations between the two neighbors. However, President Banda became convinced that Tanzania went too far in its hospitality to former Ministers Chipembere, Chirwa, and Chisiza. He then attacked Tanzania in the ruling Malawi Congress Party (MCP) newspaper, the *Malawi News*, by means of an editorial headed "Tanzania Involved in Invasion of Malawi," wherein he accused Tanzania of

9. As quoted in *Rand Daily Mail*, March 30, 1970.
10. Angola Committee, *Facts and Reports*, vol. I, items 1430, 1485, and 1502–5 (December 11 and 25, 1971).

training and financially assisting exiled Malawians who were intent on overthrowing him. Banda has repeatedly claimed that he can prove his case and in each instance President Nyerere and others have denied the charges.[11] The 1965 OAU incident described in Chapter 3 made already bad relations even worse.

In May 1967 Nyerere enraged Banda by declaring that Tanzania did not recognize the "artificial" boundary between Tanzania and Malawi which follows the shoreline of Lake Malawi. The Tanzanian government informed the Malawian government of its attitude and stated it would continue to recognize the original boundary which passes through the middle of the lake. The British had changed it upon the establishment of the now defunct Federation of Rhodesia and Nyasaland. But it is President Nyerere's position that since Tanzania was a UN Trust Territory, the British had no right to do this without the permission of the Trusteeship Council. Banda flatly rejected the claim and the matter thus stands today.[12]

The crucial fact is that there are three deep issues dividing Tanzania and Malawi: President Banda's continuing diplomatic, political, and economic cooperation with the white South and his criticisms of the liberation movements from the North and their sponsors; Tanzania's boundary claim on Malawian territory; and Tanzania's asylum and possible assistance to Banda's chief political enemies.

Similarly the animosities between Presidents Banda and Kaunda and hence between Malawi and Zambia are many faceted. When Banda returned to Africa in 1958, Kaunda regarded him as a heroic African nationalist. But a personal slight in 1963 and a series of accusations by Banda regarding alleged Zambian complicity with Tanzania in assisting Malawian revo-

11. *East African Standard,* October 19, November 2, and December 23, 1964, and June 15 and 16, 1965; *Tanganyika Standard,* Dar es Salaam, December 22 and 31, 1964. See also *Africa Report,* XII (March 1967), 27. Malawian insurgents were allegedly recruited in Tanzania by Chisiza, taken to Zambia for training, and then sent into Malawi from the Fort Jameson district of Zambia. *ARB,* IV, 887A–B, November 15, 1967, and 903A–B, December 15.

12. *ARB,* IV, 775A (June 15, 1967), 794B (July 15), and 817A–B (August 15).

lutionaries led to strains. As Banda expanded contacts with South Africa and Portugal, Zambia openly questioned his wisdom. Banda lashed back at Zambia by telling the Malawian Parliament: "As for my critics in neighbouring countries, I treat them with utter contempt, because they are physical and moral cowards and hypocrites. . . . While they are decrying South Africa, they are doing so on stomachs full of South African beef, mutton and pork. . . . They are doing so while allowing South African financiers and industrialists to invest heavily in their mines, industries and agriculture."[13] Malawi's unwillingness to participate actively in sanctions against Rhodesia also enrages Zambians, who have borne the brunt of the campaign—to the tune of approximately $47 million per year.

The low point was reached probably in September 1968 when President Banda laid claim for Malawi to four districts of Zambia equal in size to his country's present territory.[14] This claim temporarily disrupted hesitant steps toward the exchange of diplomatic representatives, but the territorial claim was not allowed to escalate. Banda, sensing that the loss of support and good will in black Africa might ultimately weaken his overall foreign policy, began in 1968 and 1969 to attempt to mend his fences. At the 1969 annual convention of the MCP he announced that Malawi's relations with her black neighbors had been improved. Ministerial delegations had been exchanged with Zambia, and Malawian ministers had been well received in Tanzania.[15] Further improvement followed as Zambia's first acting high commissioner left to take up his post in Blantyre on November 20, 1970.[16] Nevertheless, the cordiality marking Malawi's relations with the white South is absent in its dealings with black neighbors, Tanzania and Zambia. There have been occasional gestures in the direction of good will between the two states and Malawi, but invariably they have not been totally successful because of Banda's consuming fear of internal op-

13. Banda, *Agreements with South Africa and Portugal,* p. 9.
14. Banda, *Opening of the Lilongwe Convention, September 16, 1968,* pp. 38–39. See also *ARB,* V, 1178B–C, October 15, 1968.
15. Banda, *Opening Address to the MCP Convention, September 1st, 1969,* pp. 21–24.
16. *ARB,* VII, 1924C, December 15, 1970.

position and his conviction that his most dangerous enemies not only are organizing against him from sanctuaries in Tanzania and Zambia, but are doing so with the cooperation, assistance, and encouragement of these governments. For their part, Tanzania and Zambia cannot bring themselves to be magnanimous with a man they regard as a traitor to Black Africa. The pride of three key heads of state is at stake as well.

To join the majority condemning the white South would be out of character for President Banda. In his estimation, most African leaders have been "unrealistic" in their attitudes and policies toward the South. This has been reflected in Malawi's diplomatic estrangement from the North. For example, in 1966 Malawi declared the UAR ambassador in Blantyre and his staff persona non grata, and Ghana was asked to close its High Commission in Malawi when Banda ordered the withdrawal of the Malawian High Commission in Accra.[17] Banda has repeatedly called for closer economic and cultural links between white and black Africa. But by taking this position he knows full well that he will be regarded as "the most unpopular man in Africa."[18] The resultant policies, however, follow logically from his public pronouncements. Malawi has been drifting ever closer to complete identification with the external policies of the southern sub-system.

This posture, then, complicates Malawi's self-proclaimed role as intermediary. Nevertheless, President Banda and other Malawian officials have repeatedly stated that they are prepared to mediate between black and white Africa if a dialogue can be initiated. They have also urged other black states to follow their example. For example, Banda has offered Malawi as a neutral venue for British and Rhodesian political leaders to settle their differences.[19] Malawians see another way in which Malawi could serve as a bridge, directly beneficial both to itself and to South Africa. Malawi has sought to encourage South African industrialists to establish factories there, using the argument that products carrying the "Made in Malawi" label

17. *Africa Diary,* VI, 2767, March 7–13, 1966.
18. Banda's own label, as quoted in *ARB,* IV, 773C, June 15, 1967.
19. *The Star,* July 4, 1970, p. 8.

would enable South African industry to have an outlet in black Africa that might otherwise be closed to them.

Offers to serve as a broker or agent do not, however, constitute policy fulfillment. Malawi has also, in actual policy, served and is serving several "bridge" functions. It has served as host for regional conferences and celebrations bringing together officials of white and black governments. More importantly, in the wake of border incursions by the Portuguese in pursuit of guerrilla fighters, Zambian authorities in June 1969 arrested two Portuguese soldiers, who were convicted and sentenced by a Lusaka magistrate. The sentence was quashed by the High Court of Zambia. Since the High Court was composed of Europeans, tensions were heated. President Kaunda later issued restriction orders against the detainees. In response the Portuguese detained three Zambians for an alleged border infringement. At this point President Banda intervened to obtain the release and exchange of the detainees. He worked quickly and circumspectly, and did not publicize his role. In this ad hoc effort, the role of intermediary was well performed.[20]

A more continuous bridge function grows out of the fact that Malawi is the only black-governed state having formal diplomatic relations with the Republic of South Africa and one of only two having such relations with Portugal. When officials of other black states want to visit Botswana, Lesotho, or Swaziland for governmental purposes, they work through the Malawian Ministry of External Affairs. The ministry in turn deals directly with the South African chargé (now ambassador) in Malawi, who then arranges inconspicuous passage through South Africa.[21] One might suspect that the reverse process, the unpublicized entry of South African officials into black states, might be expedited in this manner, though this may not be entirely necessary. While the extent to which this linkage is employed is un-

20. *ARB*, VI, 1479C–81C, August 15, 1969, and 1537A, October 15; *The Star*, May 8, 1971, p. 13. A similar episode in 1972 is mentioned in *Malawi High Commission Newsletter* (London), II, no. 5 (April 28, 1972), 1–3.

21. Interview MAL–55, Blantyre, September 4, 1969. For a discussion of "contacts" between diplomats of black and white Africa in Blantyre see *The Star*, April 10, 1971, p. 10.

clear, we do know that the South African Department of Foreign Affairs claims to have arranged passage for dozens of black African officials through Jan Smuts Airport annually. Malawi's "bridge" functions are thereby marginally performed without undue publicity.

South African commentators seem to be optimistic about the long-range impact of President Banda, who they have called "the white hope," "the South's key," and "the greatest asset South Africa has in black Africa." South African officials, however, are unwilling to indicate that they see Malawi as a "wedge," or as an instrument for leaping the cordon in Africa. Nevertheless, they are quite willing to commend Banda for what they call his realism and common sense. This praise for his foreign policy comes from politicians and officials of all three major South African political parties, and from African officers from the Bantu homelands, too.[22] But nowhere is praise more effusive than among the verligte press corps. Unsigned articles in *News/Check* have described Banda as a "bridge" toward expanded South African relations. In one instance *News/Check* saw President Jomo Kenyatta of Kenya as the "bridgehead," the target that would lend "respectability" to dealing with South Africa. In another instance the establishment of diplomatic relations between Malawi and Zambia was regarded as a move in the direction of lending acceptability to Banda's associations with the RSA.[23] One suspects that his relations with President Tsiranana of the Malagasy Republic may have been the model such a viewpoint had in mind. In a sense, by being the first to deal openly with the RSA, Malawi's example enabled others so inclined to join in. During his visit to Malawi in 1969, Tsiranana began vigorously to speak out for the first time in

22. See, for example, the statements by Chief Buthelezi, chief executive officer of the Zululand Territorial Authority, in *The Star*, June 20, 1970, and *The Times*, July 7, 1972, p. 6, and the diverse reactions after President Banda's visit to South Africa, ibid., August 21, 1971, pp. 1–2.

23. "Banda Could Be the South's Key," *News/Check*, IX, 17, September 18, 1970, and "White Hope," ibid., p. 15, October 2, 1970. See also articles in *The Star*, by Robin Drew, July 11, 1970, p. 13, and July 25, p. 11; and by Guy Dickson, "This Man is the Key to African Accord," June 19, 1971, p. 11.

favor of dialogue, and hesitant steps toward contact between his government and the RSA were initiated. It is unlikely, however, that Banda can win over either Kenya or Zambia to dealing cordially and openly with South Africa. They are both too committed to opposing South Africa, and too independent politically from the white South, despite recognizable economic relationships. If further breakthroughs are made by South Africa in her outward-looking policy, which is likely, they will probably not be a product of Malawian intercession.

LESOTHO

Chief Leabua Jonathan, the prime minister of Lesotho, finds himself in a position similar to that of Dr. Banda.[24] He has suggested that his country could serve as a bridge for a dialogue between the Republic of South Africa and independent black states. He has also offered to approach the South African government "in the spirit of the Lusaka Manifesto" if black Africa as a unit or the great powers will give him some encouragement.[25] But encouragement has not been forthcoming; there has been only tepid concurrence from statesmen who themselves have made similar offers and have gained disdain from the rest of black Africa.

For this response, however, he has only himself to blame. Chief Jonathan has become too closely identified with South Africa. On a number of issues, Lesotho policy could be regarded as an extension of South African foreign policy. He has said, for example, that should the necessity arise he would be prepared to cooperate with South Africa to eradicate communism and to bring about the cessation of "terrorism." In numerous statements Chief Jonathan has repeatedly ridiculed nationalists to the north, and particularly their approaches to dealing with the issue of southern Africa. At the UN and the

24. Historical background for these relationships appears in Glass, *South African Policy towards Basutoland.* Internal sociopolitical conditions that affect foreign policy are dealt with in Frank, *The Basutoland National Party,* esp. pp. 16–29, and Weisfelder, *Defining National Purpose in Lesotho.*

25. *The Star,* October 24, 1970, p. 5, and October 31, p. 5; *Sunday Times,* May 23, 1971, p. 1.

OAU Lesotho has lined up with Malawi in opposing efforts to boycott, isolate, and violently destroy white-minority rule. He has referred to "disgruntled Pan-Africanists" of the OAU as "extremists," called their advocacy of force "childish" and a "waste of money," and labeled "economic war" against South Africa "ignorant."[26] Chief Jonathan has thereby violated two cardinal rules for any potential intermediary—to refrain from criticism of the parties, and to avoid identity with either one.

There is, likewise, an economic relationship that renders Lesotho independence tenuous. Post-independence economic arrangements have not altered that situation.[27] One might conclude that, given the general geographic and economic situation of the country, no measure of economic progress could yield true freedom of foreign policy behavior for Lesotho. As Chief Jonathan put it: "Our geographical position in regard to South Africa is a permanent feature of our fate." On this foundation, he is intent on continuing close and friendly relations with South Africa.[28] And the South African government, in turn, strongly supports him. When, after apparent defeat in Lesotho's first general election (January 27, 1970) since independence, Chief Jonathan declared a state of emergency and arrested opposition Basutoland Congress Party (BCP) leaders, South African officials expressed sympathy with and encouragement and support for Chief Jonathan's actions. Prime Minister Vorster told his House of Assembly that the government's attitude was exactly the same as its attitude toward Rhodesia: "We are continuing as if nothing has happened." He commented that it was an undeniable fact that the BCP leader was a "Peking communist."[29] In his opinion, Chief Jonathan was in effective control, so relations would continue as in the past. But the guise of noninterference was not entirely convincing when it

26. *ARB,* V, 974A, March 15, 1968; *Africa Diary,* no. 26, pp. 3452–53, June 25–July 1, 1967; *The Star,* daily edition, August 16, 1969, p. 3, and June 13, 1970, p. 3.

27. See Leistner, *South Africa's Development Aid,* pp. 11–19, for an account that supports the South African government but is nonetheless a useful compilation of data otherwise hard to accumulate.

28. *The Star,* December 20, 1969, p. 6. See also Chief Jonathan, *Address at the First Anniversary Pitso, 4th October, 1967,* pp. 7–8.

29. *The Star,* February 7, 1970, p. 1.

became evident that South African legal advisers had urged Chief Jonathan to assume control and that "effective control" was a product of Lesotho's efficient paramilitary Police Mobile Unit, which received financial aid from South Africa and was responsible for the suppression of the incipient guerrilla movement that festered immediately after the elections.[30] South African support in this crisis was more than verbal, though frequent professions of neutrality and noninterference were issued.

Chief Jonathan had long made it clear that he would not tolerate "destructive" criticism of his policy of good-neighborliness toward South Africa. In his estimation criticism amounted to subversion.[31] He was referring to BCP statements that Lesotho under Chief Jonathan was a victim of "unchecked interference" in its domestic affairs, and thus a "puppet" of South Africa.[32] Clearly, South Africa would be anxious to maintain Chief Jonathan's government.

There had all along been doubts about Chief Jonathan's independence. Suppressive behavior in Lesotho only served to convince African nationalists that the government in Maseru was suspect and a prisoner of Pretoria. His nationalist credentials in question, Chief Jonathan in 1970 launched a round of diplomatic activity aimed at black Africa. Before the year was out, a four-man delegation visited ten African states to explain the Lesotho takeover. Another mission went to Madagascar, Malawi, Mauritius, and Swaziland. Chief Jonathan himself attended the OAU summit in Addis Ababa and the UN General Assembly and visited Ghana and Nigeria. Lesotho was represented at the conference of nonaligned nations in Lusaka. Cultural agreements were signed with Ghana and Nigeria, and the heads of government of Ghana, Nigeria, and Zambia accepted invitations to visit Lesotho.[33] Later in 1971 Chief Jonathan made an official visit to Madagascar, where plans were laid for exchanging diplomatic representatives. The two governments

30. *Sunday Times*, April 26, 1970.
31. *ARB*, V, 1143B–C, September 15, 1968, and 1177A, October 15.
32. Ibid., IV, 930B, January 15, 1968.
33. *The Star*, August 15, 1970, p. 11; October 10, p. 12; October 17, p. 11.

agreed to form a joint commission to study methods for the creation of a regional organization of African countries that favor a dialogue with South Africa, yet would not allow themselves to be an "ideological tool" for any bloc. Since then the Tsiranana government has been overthrown (see below) and Chief Jonathan has himself cooled toward South Africa. In addition, Chief Jonathan's ruling party, the Basotho National Party, had even before the election promised to open negotiations with South Africa for the return of "conquered" territory in the Orange Free State. But such activities and statements have not made Lesotho "respectable" in the eyes of nationalists to the north. And without this minimal respectability, any desire to serve as intermediary between black and white Africa must be deferred.

BOTSWANA

Far better situated to play the role of "bridge builder" is Botswana.[34] We have already examined Botswana's options growing out of at least not total encirclement by white-dominated territories. We have also pointed out the importance of the Botswana railway. Moreover, Sir Seretse Khama, the president, has demonstrated a political skill that has enabled him to be at once independent of South Africa and yet unwilling to precipitate a direct confrontation. He is flanked by opposition parties on the right and left—one calling for a more aggressive stand against apartheid and the other urging closer ties with South Africa and Rhodesia. So he occupies the middle in domestic politics as well as in international politics. In his estimation Botswana is well equipped to bring about a rapprochement between the white South and the black North.

Botswana has managed, in the process, to convince other black African states that it is indeed independent of South Africa. The country has refused repeated offers from South Africa to finance a new road between Gaberone and Lobatse. An aide to the president put it this way: "We don't think it

34. On Botswana's foreign policy see Dale's unpublished "Botswana's Post-Independence Relations with South Africa" and his *The Racial Component of Botswana's Foreign Policy*.

would be good for our reputation with other African countries to be going hat in hand to an apartheid government. We care very much about our reputation."[35] What little aid that has been extended by South Africa has been in the fields of animal husbandry, health, and education.[36] At other times Botswana has demonstrated that proximity to South Africa has not meant intimidation. For example, it established diplomatic relations with Czechoslovakia in 1967 and the USSR in 1970. This means that the Czechoslovak and Russian ambassadors in Lusaka visit Botswana periodically. Botswana is the only former HCT to maintain diplomatic relations with a communist government. The South African reaction to Botswana-USSR relations has been less than favorable. One Afrikaans newspaper called the Russian mission in Botswana a potential "base for subversive activities" and another called it "a Russian listening Post" on South Africa's borders.[37] But the fact is that Botswana did not feel constrained in its options.

Likewise, Botswana's officials have been adamant in their insistence on the existence of a common boundary with Zambia. Initial South African objections and protests rejecting the joint border were dealt with frontally. Consequently a US-financed road will be constructed to the Zambesi River border point, a pontoon ferry service will be operated there, and, to the satisfaction of South African authorities, assurance has been given that no bridge will be constructed on the border. Again Botswana did not submit to South African pressures and earned, in the end, a neat compromise.[38] Botswana thus has a good record as an "independent" African state, worthy of the support and understanding of the states to the north.

Conversely, Botswana has consistently rejected any activity that might lead to violence in southern Africa. President Khama has said that any violence would weaken black governments more than it would weaken minority regimes. He did not con-

35. As quoted in *NYT*, September 25, 1969, p. 8.
36. See Leistner, *South Africa's Development Aid*, p. 26.
37. As quoted in *The Star*, March 21, 1970, p. 7, and April 11, p. 4.
38. *The Star*, April 18, 1970, pp. 5, 7, and June 6, p. 8; *ARB* (Econ.), VII, 1640C–41B (April 30, 1970), 1756C–57A (August 31), 1786A–B (September 30), and 1839C–40A (November 30).

demn those who resort to violence when all other paths were closed, he was careful to add.[39] Regulations dealing with the activities of political refugees in Botswana are tight and, as much as Botswana's small police force can assure, honestly enforced. Within the framework of his anti-violent philosophy, the president opposes the sale of arms to South Africa. He is also against any Western military involvement with countries that deny self-determination to their majority populations, feeling that it might lead to a great-power conflict in southern Africa similar to the wars in the Middle East and Vietnam.[40]

Besides the important substantive policy differences between Botswana on one hand and Lesotho and Malawi on the other, there are major stylistic differences. President Khama is not inclined to lecture and deride his fellow African politicians as is Dr. Banda or Chief Jonathan. His attempts at bringing the black and white governments together have not been particularly active or impressive, but he has laid a firm groundwork for trust on both sides, and thus shows more promise as a broker than other regional statesmen who would like the assignment.

SWAZILAND

The prime minister of Swaziland, Prince Makhosini Dhlamini, in contrast to the heads of government of Malawi, Lesotho, and Botswana, has not actively sought the role of intermediary.[41] Instead he has been content to attempt to pursue cordial relations with all parties. By and large, however, the dictates of geography predominate. Swaziland's relations with South Africa and Portugal appear to have priority. Economic linkages are already intimate and continue to be expanded. Prince Dhlamini has opposed the use of force against South Africa, and has even subscribed to the term "terrorist," pre-

39. *The Star,* December 19, 1970, p. 7. His statement on "peaceful means" is quoted in the issue of April 10, 1971, p. 11.
40. *ARB,* VII, 1883A, October 15, 1970; *The Star,* December 19, 1970, p. 7.
41. For more detail see Potholm, "Transaction Flows and Policy Formation: The Limits of Choice for Swaziland in the Southern African Complex," in Dale and Potholm, eds., *Southern Africa in Perspective* (forthcoming).

ferred by the white governments, for those who use it. In his words: "We hate any form of terrorism and anything of this kind will be dealt with very sternly in Swaziland." If Swaziland should be attacked by guerrilla forces or if guerrillas used Swaziland as a route to attack South Africa, "South Africa would come to our aid."[42] It is this sort of talk that prompts opposition leader Dr. Ambrose Zwane of the Ngwane National Liberatory Congress to claim that Swaziland has been abandoned to the "Herrenvolk hegemony of Pretoria."[43] What to Prince Dhlamini is a "realistic working relationship" with Pretoria, is, to Dr. Zwane, "Pretoria's pull."

Nevertheless, efforts to assert a modicum of independence from White African ties have been made. Principles of majority rule and nonracialism are accepted, and repeatedly the government has stated that Swaziland "belongs to Africa" and needs the good will of Africa. Significantly, the extradition treaty concluded with South Africa in September 1968 specifically excluded political refugees seeking asylum in or transit through Swaziland.[44] Swaziland has accused the United Kingdom of a sell-out on Rhodesia, and also has opposed the British sale of arms to South Africa. Further links with Africa to the north are sought. A trade agreement with Zambia has been signed. A trade delegation that visited East Africa in 1969 expressed interest in associate membership in the East African Community. Prime Minister Dhlamini has even offered assurances that no items of South African origin would be reexported to East Africa.

In sum, these relationships suggest that the Swaziland government wants to live peacefully with all her neighbors, immediate and afar. It is not intently anxious or especially well placed, at this point at least, to mediate or bring together contending parties. Nevertheless, speculation persists that Swaziland, because of a relative silence on key issues, may yet be inclined to expedite dialogue between the two camps.[45]

42. *The Star*, daily edition, April 8, 1968.
43. *ARB*, V, 1181–82C, October 15, 1968.
44. Ibid., pp. 1175C–76A.
45. *The Star*, April 24, 1971, p. 12.

MALAGASY REPUBLIC (MADAGASCAR)

In the case of the Malagasy Republic's foreign policy, before the 1972 military coup, the bridge function had been especially emphasized, including an occasional reference to the theme of dialogue. Dialogue seemed to be the decoration that was offered to render the package of closer economic association with South Africa more acceptable to black Africans conditioned to reject out of hand the ideology of white racism. To be sure, Malagasy officials unequivocally condemn racial segregation. But, as they put it, it is better to chip away at the corner of apartheid (implicitly and explicitly affirming that doing business with South Africa contributes to this) than to offer "useless threats." In this vein, Malagasy governmental figures could criticize President Kaunda, an opponent of "dialogue and contact" as they conceive it, for trading with South Africa.[46]

In many respects, growing Malagasy relations with South Africa could be viewed outside the African context. The relationships were essentially economic in nature, and the political contacts that surfaced were of the sort designed to expedite economic contact: Madagascar was seeking to broaden its economic partnerships and to free itself from increasingly stagnant French patronage. Particularly after the retirement and death of General De Gaulle, President Tsiranana sought to "mondialize" Malagasy trade and aid patterns. So far, other Western and industrial powers had not been much attracted to expanding ties or extending developmental aid and investment in Madagascar. South Africa, anxious to break down its isolation and expand especially business contacts abroad, seemed to be the logical source for what Madagascar wanted. The difficult issue of race and apartheid was overcome by President Banda's example and persuasive powers and by economic exigencies and temptations; the political and ideological ramifications were played down. Despite some internal misgivings, even within Tsiranana's cabinet, the policy flourished.[47] It led to rumors of

46. For example, ibid., November 28, 1970, p. 9.

47. Ibid., and also January 16, 1971, p. 5; *ARB*, VI, 1576A, December 15, 1969.

possible diplomatic links, talk of strategic use of Madagascar's ports to combat the "Russian threat" in the Indian Ocean and the establishment of a permanent joint commission to further cooperation, and suggestions that the South Africans might like to expand fruitful Malagasy ties as steppingstones into French-speaking Africa by way of Afro-Malagasy and Mauritius Joint Organization (OCAMM). Much as Malagasy officials might have liked to gainsay the political and strategic implications of their economic and functional involvement with South Africa, the fact was that these relationships were viewed in South Africa and in black Africa as politically portentous.[48] Both Madagascar's desire to be free of overweening French economic and cultural influence and the government's deepening alarm about "threats to security" from efflorescent Chinese and Russian interest in southern Africa and the Indian Ocean made more palatable the formation of linkages with South Africa. But even if the new military government should be so inclined, the extent to which Madagascar can furnish South Africa with entrée into OCAMM political circles is marginal. Rather, if such entrée is to be opened, it will be expedited by other statesmen, perhaps President Félix Houphouet-Boigny of the Ivory Coast, or even by Bantustan leaders posturing as "independent statesmen."

HOUPHOUET-BOIGNY AND DIALOGUE WITH SOUTH AFRICA

It is not altogether unexpected that a state removed from the southern African sub-system and from South Africa's economic hegemony should produce a call for dialogue that has generated the loudest response and perhaps the most favorable reactions among sister African governments. Since the initial impact of Malawi's exchange of diplomatic representatives with the RSA quieted, there has been a feeling in Pretoria that little is to be gained by formalizing diplomatic links with neighboring black governments that are widely recognized as being "captives," geographically or economically, of the republic. Rather, so thinking seems to indicate, a real breakthrough in the outward

48. For example, Wulf Nussey, "Madagascar Far From Developed," *The Star*, November 28, 1970, p. 15; *News/Check*, IX, 15, November 13, 1970.

policy can be gained by establishing deeper ties with either (1) states that, though in the southern African area, are regarded as undeniably independent and African nationalist—such as Zambia, Tanzania, or Zaïre, or (2) states that are entirely outside the South African sphere geographically and economically, even though ideologically there might be some question of their commitment to radical Pan-African goals—Gabon, Ghana, the Ivory Coast, and Kenya being those most frequently mentioned. In this way, it is thought that South African policy can outflank militant black states in the region and deny them a unified and reliable foundation to the north.

Such a breakthrough, or at least the possibility of one, was provided by President Houphouet-Boigny of the Ivory Coast when he told an Abidjan press conference in November 1970 that the time had come for Africans to take reality into account and "to prepare seriously for a summit" that would lay the basis for a better future for Africa. Rejecting force as a solution to the problem of apartheid, he said: "The only invasion of South Africa that I would like to see should be that of African diplomats."[49] To this end, he proposed that his government would make contact with all African heads of state individually to define his country's viewpoint and to ensure that the dialogue with South Africa would not be unilaterally initiated by the Ivory Coast. The South Africans welcomed the gesture.[50]

Such an offer should have come as no surprise to the world. Two and a half years earlier, at a February 1968 press conference, Ivory Coast's foreign minister had urged African states to seek a dialogue with South Africa.[51] Such a dialogue, it was suggested, was necessary, to make the South Africans understand "their mistakes" and to show them that their "abominable

49. *Le Monde*, November 6, 1970. He expanded on his views at a four-hour press conference in May 1971. See "Ivory Coast: President's News Conference," *West Africa*, no. 2813, p. 554, May 14, 1971, and *ARB*, VIII, 2064A–65A, May 15, 1971.
50. *ARB*, VII, 1921C–22A, December 15, 1970; *The Star*, November 7, 1970, p. 10; *News/Check*, IX, 5, November 13, 1970; *South African Digest*, November 13, 1970, p. 1.
51. *ARB*, V, 1000A–B, April 15, 1968.

doctrine" of apartheid was wrong. But it was just such a reference to South African domestic policies that led South African governmental sources to say that they would refuse such a dialogue if this meant discussing the policy of "separate development." Though they appreciated the motives of the Ivory Coast minister, and they had said that they would like to have friendly relations with independent African states, they insisted that the sort of cordial relations they had with Malawi and Lesotho were based upon strict adherence to the principle of noninterference in each other's internal affairs. It is likely that in the intervening period, this opening gambit was taken up by the two parties. Certainly the central role of A. B. F. Burger—the former head of the Africa Division in the South African Department of Foreign Affairs and since August 1969 the RSA ambassador to France—should not be underestimated. Most likely he has worked in concert with Jacques Foccart, President Georges Pompidou's adviser for Afro-Malagasy affairs, and Maurichot Beaupré, a Frenchman who is a top technical aide to President Houphouet-Boigny. It is reliably rumored that the funeral of General De Gaulle provided the excuse and venue for much of the preliminary work. Significantly, when Houphouet-Boigny made his appeal for a summit in 1970 no such reference was made to altering the racial structure within South Africa.

Public governmental reactions within black Africa were mixed. Figure 3, using the analogy of the rugby match, depicts the heated and involved debate that ran through Africa in 1970 and 1971 on the issue of dialogue with South Africa. Many of Africa's more vocal political personalities are lined up on either side of the issue in this South African political cartoon. The majority of governments opposed, but a significant minority favored, dialogue. Among those who initially approved of the proposed dialogue were the presidents of Dahomey, Gabon, Ghana, Lesotho, Malawi, and Niger, and senior government officials in Madagascar and Sierra Leone. In one form or another they seemed to favor wider discussions about talks with South Africa. A good many states, however, equivocated or remained silent, thus providing encouragement to those who openly ad-

Figure 3. The dialogue question. This political cartoon appeared at the time of the 1971 summit conference of the Organization of African Unity. From *The Star,* Johannesburg, weekly air edition, June 19, 1971, p. 1. Reproduced with the permission of the editor, *The Star.*

vocated dialogue. Most of the other African states distant from South African influence opposed the Ivory Coast initiative.[52] There is, however, a great deal of speculation as to just how many governments may join in Houphouet's repeated offers. Tactically, Houphouet seems inclined to use the OCAMM as the organizational core of his thrust. If he can persuade a majority of the OCAMM members to endorse his initiatives, he may be able to confront the OAU and request a continent-wide official discussion. However, the best that could be achieved at the January 1971 OCAMM summit conference was a statement in the summit communiqué that the meeting had "taken note" of communications from the Ivory Coast and Madagascar delegations on the question of the proposed dialogue with South Africa. Since then the issue has not officially been advanced. This was not an impressive showing, considering that the

52. Ibid., VII, 1922A–24B, December 15, 1970; *The Star,* November 14, 1970, pp. 2, 8; *Zimbabwe News,* V (November 1970), 13–15. On later Ivory Coast initiatives see *ARB,* VIII, 2063C–66B, May 15, 1971.

French government welcomed and may have added its voice and pressure to Houphouet's policy. Thus, in no event is a majority of OAU member-states likely to join the call for dialogue in the near future, and the issue may be one that could weaken, if not deeply divide, that body.

There were a number of reasons for Houphouet's optimism regarding his appeal for dialogue.[53] Houphouet personally and the Ivory Coast along with him have grown steadily in prestige in French-speaking Africa and especially within the OCAMM. The country's economic successes over the past decade have been superficially impressive, in comparative terms, and close relations between the Ivory Coast and France, together with the latter's expanding economic links with South Africa, may have provided the impetus. Likewise, South African trade with Franco-phonic Africa is growing, and is organized in large part by French brokers operating out of Gabon, the Ivory Coast, and Madagascar. It is not new for Houphouet to clash with OAU positions. Add to this his close personal relations with the then President of Ghana, Dr. Kofi Busia, and we can see why South African commentators were optimistic that even if Houphouet could not convince a majority of black African governments to bargain directly with South Africa, a sufficient number might be identified, division within OAU ranks would divert energies and attentions, and a certain legitimacy would accrue to those who now dealt openly or privately with the republic. Even a "failing" effort might yield "positive" results for South Africa and, perhaps, for an Ivory Coast intent on opening relations anyway. Nevertheless, this initiative, supplied by a nonregional actor, stirred up intense diplomatic activity as no similar move by a regional black government has, including the Malawian-South African diplomatic exchange. It may be that no regional actor is in a position to serve in this capacity. Too many patterns and opinions have been etched into the minds of other partici-

53. A fairly detailed explanation of his policy was released in Paris in January 1971. See *The Star*, January 9, p. 1, and *Africa Confidential*, XII, 1–5, May 14, 1971. The most complete statement of a position opposing dialogue is Tanzania, Ministry of Information and Broadcasting, *Why We Will Not Negotiate*. Kenya's position was expressed in *East African Standard*, December 17, 1971, p. 8.

pants to enable them to accept the leadership of one whose interests are too evidently with one side or the other. The intrusive or peripheral actor may still be best situated to affect major issues of sub-systemic affairs.

At present only five black African governments, those of Botswana, Gabon, the Ivory Coast, Lesotho, and Malawi, are actively and openly seeking to pursue policies that can be described as "bridge building" in the sense of supplying a political linkage between two hostile camps, a linkage that both sides may utilize easily to expand relations with the other and to deal with contentious issues that heretofore have engendered or reflected enmity and hostility. Both Botswana and Lesotho may be abandoning this position in order to assert their independence of Pretoria. President Khama maintains that Botswana abides by the provisions of the Lusaka Manifesto and that he is thereby opposed to "unconditional dialogue." To be sure, a few other states have endorsed the policy of dialogue, but the extent of their commitment to an intermediary role has yet to be demonstrated. This does not necessarily mean that these five have been successful in their endeavors. Malawi, for example, has cultivated links with white southern Africa without markedly improving its ties with black Africa. Recently Malawi has sought to place its relations with neighboring black governments on a more cordial footing, and this has not been easy. As a bridge, particularly as a two-way bridge, Malawi is relatively unused. President Banda's style has not facilitated this. But style alone is not the answer. Perhaps the assignment itself is too imposing, too sensitive, to admit of easy solution. Perhaps the objective and subjective conditions leading to a détente do not exist in the present state of sub-systemic and continental relations.

The South African bargaining attitude in the "dialogue about dialogue" has not been particularly conciliatory. In a sense, it has advocated the mere establishment of contact in return for which black Africa agrees not to meddle in "internal" South African affairs.[54] This in itself was not enough to reduce tensions or intrusive pressures. Dialogue implies a give and

54. See Vorster's statement in *The Star*, March 20, 1971, p. 2.

take, and what the South Africans propose to give is insufficient to satisfy most black governments. To be sure, by expanding contacts South Africa can offer black Africa certain short-range economic attractions (technical and financial assistance and trade). Even in this field its assets are limited. Clearly, South Africa must go further, must provide manifest demonstration that it is moving to deal with domestic racial inequities in an imaginative and truly just way. So far that step has not been taken. The few adjustments in petty apartheid that have facilitated diplomatic and business contact with black, non-South-African Africans do not represent adequate change to most black Africans. So the pattern of the outward policy toward black Africa has been little more than a sort of "rand diplomacy." Only minor breakthroughs can be achieved by money means. A tangible demonstration of good faith in racial policy has not, so far, been forthcoming. Such a course, one Nationalist intellectual put it, need not be regarded as a loss of face or a concession to outside interference.[55] In this regard, Prime Minister Vorster's statement in March 1971 that in any dialogue the subject of separate development could be "discussed," and that "as a matter of course" it would be, can be regarded as a first, albeit marginal, gesture in this direction. In his view, "for the moment" he is not concerned with the motives of the people who want to talk to him.[56] But still these questions may be premature. The process merely reached the early stage of "talks about talks," and even this has practically died.

The proposed solution to the profound conflict situation in southern Africa that has been advanced by each of these aspiring intermediaries (we cannot justifiably call them third parties in that they have, in the eyes of one side or the other, or of both sides, been too closely identified with the opposite side) has made minimal demands on South Africa. They merely seek to open more and more lines of contact and communication be-

55. Otto Krause, "Dialogue Means a Give and Take," *News/Check*, IX, 6, December 1970. President Houphouet's similar reservations were noted in *The Star*, May 1, 1971, pp. 1, 5.

56. The press conference transcript is printed in *The Star*, April 3, 1971, pp. 12–13. See also the editorial on p. 11.

tween contending sides. The assumption is that as contacts expand, so will the quality and cordiality of those contacts improve. This may be an unwarranted assumption. The "bridge builders" propose to facilitate and encourage that contact by providing good offices, or by simply assigning greater respectability to those elements on either side that wish to open contacts or expand nascent ones. In many respects, they do so because they have themselves already opened contact with white-ruled Africa, and they feel that by providing already established channels of intercourse they may be able to enhance their own status and exploit those relationships by providing conduits or bridges. Bridge builders perhaps envisage a toll that they might ultimately collect for services rendered. In another sense, the offer to build bridges is a camouflage or rationalization for their own highly publicized, politically sensitive, indeed dangerous, yet profitable (at least in the short run) policies.

What would be the effect of expanded contacts between black and white Africa? Do the efforts of the bridge builders blunt the unity of the thrust of African nationalism in its struggle to destroy colonialism and racism and to achieve majority rule in southern Africa? The answer to this latter question is, it appears, simply "yes." But it could be argued that a singular or unified thrust is not the best approach to white southern Africa for it prompts a unified counterthrust. It might be asked, then, do the bridge builders retard the struggle against racism and minority rule? Not necessarily, provided contacts are not widely established with many black states, for the struggle can go on fruitfully on more than one front. It has been argued in Chapter 1 that "token" approaches (not necessarily bridge building) to establish relations with South Africa, for example, will not alone serve the purpose of weakening racist regimes measurably. Indeed, the likelihood is that such contacts will strengthen the white South. But, in combination with continued and growing militancy by other black states and groups, and a deepening hostility in Western quarters, South Africa's dealings with its black neighbors pose certain dilemmas for the government and for the citizenry, especially for the Afrikaners. They force white populations to divide on key issues that heretofore have been dealt with in ideological and categorical terms. Their government's dealings with black states may force Afrikaners out of adamant, uncompromisable positions. In order to defend domestic racism, a white government may find that it must become less racist in foreign policy. And the unity of a racist population suffers when it is faced with inconsistencies and dilemmas.

Thus the struggle against racism and minority rule can, conceivably, go on simultaneously on more than one front. But, there are limits to how far this can go. Insofar as they are actually compelled to deal with their white neighbors, the black states of southern Africa—Botswana, Lesotho, Madagascar, Malawi, Swaziland, and Zambia—can pose dilemmas for white Africa. But there is an indiscernible line between contacts that can open doors or can negate consistently racist attitudes toward black Africa and others that may strengthen the white South psychologically, militarily, or economically. Moreover, to a large extent, the fact of black states dealing with the white South out of sheer necessity might be construed by an outside world—already predisposed to deal with white Southern Africa—as a rationalization for assisting the white South or for delaying efforts to apply pressure on it to revolutionize its racist social structures. If this is to be the outcome, as is suggested by the attitudes of the Nixon administration in the United States and the Heath government in Britain, then building bridges may be self-defeating.

It is necessary, however, to distinguish between the establishment of correct relationships with both sides and the role of intermediary, for the latter is far more demanding than the former. The first situation simply represents two sets of bilateral relationships with separate parties (see fig. 4, *a*). The second constitutes a trilateral arrangement that is designed, should it bear fruit, ultimately to bypass that intermediary stage (*b* in the figure)—its services no longer being necessary—and produce multilateral relationships (resembling *c*). It may be that the first stage (*a*) is necessary for the establishment of the others (*b*, *c*), but that remains to be seen. Judging from southern Africa,

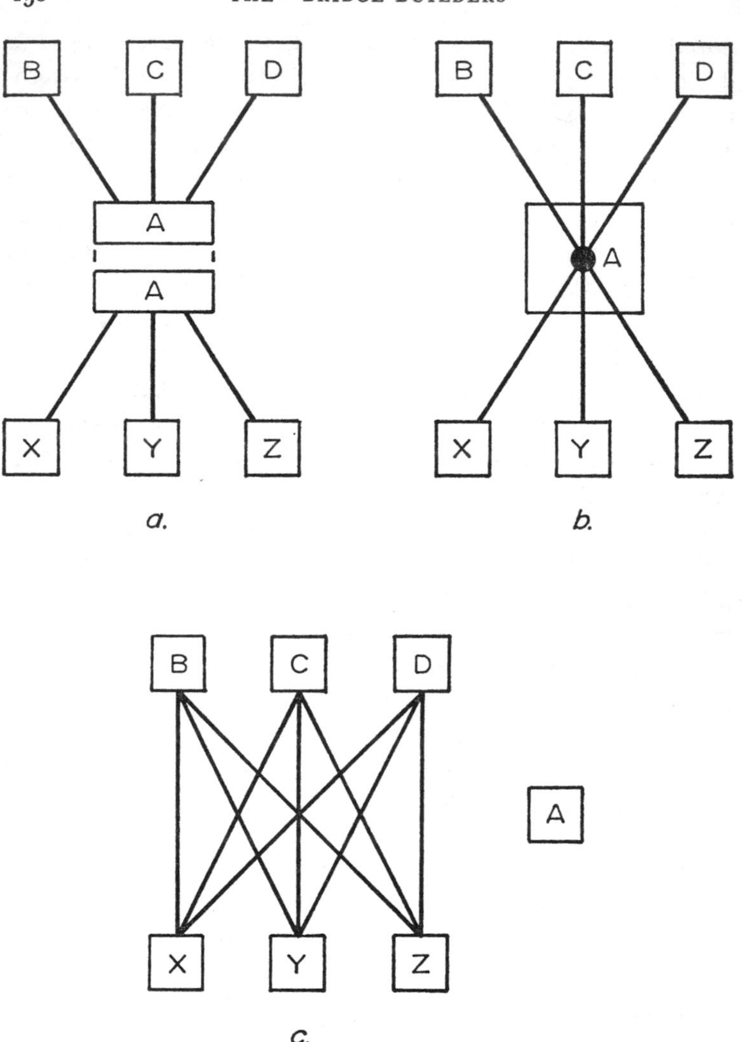

Figure 4. Some types of intermediary relationships.

it would seem that this need not be so. Rather it appears that states with little or no contact with white Africa might be less stigmatized and therefore be better situated to expedite the communicative process. Commitments and passions run so deep that, so far, the very act of calling for dialogue marks a black government, from the African nationalist perspective, as being less than trustworthy, too willing to compromise principles of the most fundamental sort. This negates the effect of the bridge builders' efforts. Until this attendant stigma is erased, the hurdles facing the bridge builders will be insurmountable.

5

Revolutionary Thought and Revolutionary Practice

The poor man and the rich man do not play together. —*Ashanti*

In this chapter our chief concern is to introduce the general subject of guerrilla warfare as it has been propounded and practiced by southern Africans. In many respects the coverage is condensed, for this is not the place for a full-blown study of the revolutionary crucible that southern Africa in fact is and will continue to be for some time.[1] Rather our fundamental purpose here is more modest—to set the stage for a fuller discussion of the variegated intra-African yet international ramifications of military affairs in the region. This chapter is, in other words, a descriptive springboard for a more systematic treatment of one facet of the international patterns to be dealt with in the following chapter. It is divided approximately in half. The first section is devoted to a discussion of the theory of guerrilla warfare espoused by leaders of the nationalist movements involved and by those officials assigned the task of combating guerrilla

1. Such an effort, as it applies to all Africa, is my *Guerrilla Struggle in Africa*. Much of the material in this and the following chapter is abstracted from that more specialized volume. It appears here with the kind permission of Grossman Publishers and the World Law Fund.

incursions into white-dominated southern Africa. The second half contains capsule descriptions of the development of the struggle in each of the target territories. There is, naturally, an emphasis on the international ramifications of these wars in the introductory descriptions contained therein. Much will be omitted since all we seek is to supply sufficient information to make Chapter 6 intelligible.

The Theory of Guerrilla Warfare in Southern Africa

There is no need to demonstrate the importance of revolutionary warfare to the prospects for political change in southern Africa. Simply by juxtaposing the vision of political utopia held by a good many blacks inside and outside southern Africa and the determination of white governments to continue their monopolies or preponderance of political and economic power it becomes painfully evident that the most obvious approach to radical change and to maintaining the status quo involves organized violence. When legitimate channels of dissent have been exhausted or are nonexistent for the blacks, the resort to force often seems justified and irresistible. Thus internal insurrection, external intervention, and coup d'état take on dramatic and profound meaning in Africa. Referring to the war in Mozambique, yet with apparent wider meaning, the late Eduardo Mondlane observed:

> People more familiar with the policies of other colonial powers have accused us of resorting to violence without cause. This is partly refuted by the fate met by every type of legal, democratic and reformist activity tried over the preceding forty years. The character of the government in Portugal itself makes a peaceful solution inherently unlikely.[2]

This view was advanced even more cogently by South West Africa People's Organization (SWAPO) leader Toivo Herman Ja Toivo at his trial when he pleaded:

2. Mondlane, *The Struggle for Mozambique*, p. 123. See also Mondlane, "Violence: Not Whether, but How Much," in Vickers, ed., *Dialogue on Violence*, pp. 34–38.

> There are some who will say that they are sympathetic with our aims, but that they condemn violence. I would answer that I am not by nature a man of violence and I believe that violence is a sin against God and my fellow men. SWAPO itself was a non-violent organization, but the South African Government is not truly interested in whether opposition is violent or non-violent. It does not wish to hear any opposition to apartheid. . . . We have found ourselves voteless in our own country and deprived of the right to meet and state our own political opinions.
>
> Is it surprising that in such times my countrymen have taken up arms? Violence is truly fearsome, but who would not defend his property and himself against a robber? And we believe that South Africa has robbed us of our country.[3]

Thus violence is seen as becoming justifiable and necessary only after other techniques proved to be fruitless and dangerous.[4] Virtually every liberation movement in southern Africa has placed responsibility for warfare on the shoulders of the government it seeks to displace. The simple fact is that their political aims are in direct opposition to those of the ruling group and cannot be reconciled. Compromise does not appear to be a live alternative when the very nature of the regime is at issue.

In table 9 there is a list of the names and abbreviations of the major revolutionary movements in the area. It also contains some basic data about these groups. This is, however, an incomplete listing of the groups that accept the necessity for violence against established white governments. Several groups that are identified exclusively with isolated acts of violence, sabotage, and terrorism have been omitted, largely because they have not achieved a level of success militarily that would enable them to be regarded as full-fledged guerrilla movements and also because the impact of their activities on regional international politics has been marginal.

In addition to the issue of violence discussed above and in Chapter 1, black African thinking about guerrilla warfare pre-

3. Toivo, *Statement*, p. 4.
4. For the evolution of this attitude among South African nationalists see Spence and Thomas, *South Africa's Defense*, pp. 5–13. A different explanation for the utilization of armed revolutionary warfare can be found in *Sechaba*, III (July 1969), 16–23, and "From Gandhi to Mandela," ibid. (May 1969), pp. 10–12.

TABLE 9
PRINCIPAL SOUTHERN AFRICAN REVOLUTIONARY MOVEMENTS

A. Political and Military Wings	
Angola	GRAE/FLNA (Governo Revolucionário de Angola no Exílio/Frente Nacional de Libertação de Angola); military wing, ELNA (Exército de Libertação Nacional de Angola) MPLA (Movimento Popular de Libertação de Angola); military wing, APLA (Armée Popular de Libertação de Angola) UNITA (União Nacional para a Independência Total de Angola)
Mozambique	FRELIMO (Frente de Libertação de Moçambique) COREMO (Comité Revolucionário de Moçambique)
Rhodesia	ZANU (Zimbabwe African National Union); military wing, ZANLA (Zimbabwe African National Liberation Army) ZAPU (Zimbabwe African People's Union) FROLIZI (Front for the Liberation of Zimbabwe), an ostensible unity movement composed of some supporters of ZANU and some of ZAPU
South Africa	PAC (Pan-Africanist Congress) ANC (African National Congress) Numerous smaller movements: Poqo, Umkonto we Sizwe, African Resistance Movement, "The Hill Movement," Unity Movement of South Africa (UMSA), etc.
South West Africa	SWAPO (South West Africa People's Organization); military wing, Namibia Liberation Army

This is by no means a complete listing of all groups accepting the necessity of violence against established governments and regimes. Several groups that are identified exclusively with isolated acts of violence, sabotage, and terrorism have been omitted, largely because they have not achieved a level of success (militarily) to be regarded as full-fledged guerrilla movements and also because the impact of their activities on regional international politics has been marginal.

B. Basic Data

Movement	*President*	*Date Military campaign officially launched*	*Number of armed fighters in target territory in 1971*
GRAE/FLNA	Holden Roberto	March 15, 1961	3,000–8,000
MPLA	Dr. Agostinho Neto	February 6, 1961	5,000–7,000
UNITA	Dr. Jonas Savimbi	February–March, 1966	1,000–1,500
FRELIMO	Presidential Commission[a]	September 25, 1964	6,000–8,000
COREMO	Paulo Gumane	October 24, 1965	250–300
ZANU	Rev. Ndabaningi Sithole[b] Herbert Chitepo (chairman)	April 29, 1966	200–300
ZAPU	Joshua Nkomo[b] James Chikerema[c]	August 13, 1967	250–500
PAC	Potlako K. Leballo[c]	Unknown	Unknown
ANC	Oliver R. Tambo[c]	December 16, 1961	Unknown
SWAPO	Samuel Nujoma	August 26, 1966	100–150

[a]Consisting of Marcelino dos Santos and Samora Marchel. [b]Imprisoned or detained. [c]Acting president.

sents other major themes, which might be identified as reliance upon the peasantry, political-military interaction, and the protracted war. Such categories do not include a discussion of choices of tactics and techniques, most of which are situationally defined and differ little from guerrilla practice elsewhere in the world, except insofar as they are limited by material and manpower considerations.

RELIANCE UPON THE PEASANTRY

It seems almost axiomatic that a movement that functions in a continent where probably 90 percent of the population is rural and that seeks to achieve durable political power at the nation-state level should concentrate on building a following among the peasantry. Moreover, there are practical reasons for this preference. Success of guerrilla movements depends on numerous factors, not the least of which are the presence of felt relative deprivation and the inability of the ruling power to deter or repress organized expression of deprivation that takes violent forms. Generally speaking, relative deprivation in the southern African countryside has been greater than in the urban centers.[5] People in small towns and villages are not unaware of economic conditions elsewhere in the territory. Their hopes and aspirations are intense and high. On the other hand, the established white governments, each representing an identifiable minority, are incapable of convincingly establishing the legitimacy of their rule, particularly in urban centers where political awareness is most evident. Central government power is greatest in the capitals, but government support among the African population is most in doubt there. Those who seek to organize a revolutionary movement at present seem inclined to concentrate in areas where relative deprivation is high and the effectiveness of the instruments of deterrence and repression are low: in short, where the government is most vulnerable. The countryside is the logical arena.

There are at least two additional reasons that prompt such strategic considerations. One has been the repressive effectiveness of counterrevolutionary operations in population centers during the initial, usually organizational stages of the movement, especially in South Africa. The lesson is not lost on those who have survived and fled into exile or into the bush. To be sure, the vast cities of South Africa afford some measure of anonymity and secrecy, but networks of informants jeopardize revolutionary activities. The second reason for greater reliance upon the countryside is particularly apparent in the cases of the movements aimed at Angola and Mozambique, where so much depends upon an adequate supply of refugees for recruitment, information, and support. In Angola the Bakongo and in Mozambique the Makonde, each with significant population segments across the borders in the Congo (Kinshasa) and Tanzania, quite naturally have served, respectively, as core groups for the GRAE and for FRELIMO. Neither was an urbanized people in the territories they fled. Reliance upon them practically pre-

5. For example: AlRoy, "Insurgency in the Countryside," *Antioch Review*, XXVI (1966), 149–57, and, Mbeki, *South Africa*, esp. pp. 65–94.

cluded an urban-based struggle, at least in its opening stages. Even bearing in mind these points, it would be possible to argue that guerrilla movements in southern Africa, particularly in Rhodesia and South Africa, show greater urban proclivities than elsewhere on the continent.[6]

To be sure, the "rural" and "urban" designations employed by scholars distort the social realities of Africa. The norms that most guerrilla leaders hold might be regarded as "modern," and are often shared with those who have drifted to the cities. Still, the African sectors of cities in southern Africa, particularly outside South Africa, are what might be called (with a few exceptions) first-generation neighborhoods; that is, the greater part of their populations migrated to them. Moreover, there is evidence that these urban populations are in constant flux, as earlier migrants return to the countryside and new migrants take their places. To some extent neighborhood segregation in white southern Africa is actually encouraged and decreed by policies of the white governments. Life styles and thought patterns change with physical relocation, but village thought patterns still affect daily behavior. So it can be argued that the analytical "rural and urban" dichotomy is a misleading one in the African context. Still, on the basis of the locational genesis, organizational concentration, origin of supporters, scene of conflict, and ideological appeal, it may be defensible to regard the more successful southern African guerrilla movements as manifestly peasant-rural movements even though the dominant leadership element is drawn initially from intellectual-urban groups.

Certain characteristics of black African society pose distinctive and knotty problems that guerrilla leaders in other con-

6. Recent ANC materials concentrate on the need to trigger guerrilla warfare in the countryside: see the broadside "These Men Are Our Brothers, Our Sons," distributed illegally in Cape Town, Port Elizabeth, East London, and Johannesburg in November 1969 and reproduced in *Sechaba,* IV (January 1970), 1, 3, and 5. A more complete discussion of this theme appears in my *Guerrilla Struggle in Africa,* pp. 56–59, and in Spence and Thomas, *South Africa's Defense,* pp. 14–19.

tinents do not have to face. First are a number of issues growing out of ethnic heterogeneity. One factor contributing to the success of some non-African guerrilla movements is a widespread sense of national identity. The presence of identifiable outsiders focuses discontent against a common enemy. In Africa, although anti-foreign motivations are a significant source of guerrilla strength, the designation "foreigner" often has a more parochial association. Loyalties and horizons are narrower. The guerrilla leaders can attempt to widen them, and in some instances have done so. In other cases the leaders themselves have narrow vision. In order to find a catalyst capable of causing the initial eruption, they may exploit local grievances and may sharpen traditional local animosities.

Even when the enemy is clearly identifiable (for instance, as an alien, racially distinct colonizer or permanent minority), political involvement in high-risk struggle demands a heightened sense of loyalty and sacrifice uncommon in territory-wide movements in southern Africa. Localized symbols may increase the intensity of loyalties, but they automatically compress the territorial extent of the appeal. When a movement based on local symbols extends beyond its ethnic territorial base, the guerrilla fighters take on the complexion of hostile occupiers rather than a liberating force. These problems are particularly acute for the revolutionary groups focusing on Angola, Mozambique, and Rhodesia. Even if symbols are widened and a coalition of ethnic forces can be constructed, charges of ethnic favoritism often lead to the alienation of elements otherwise inclined to support the movement.

African guerrilla reliance on rural populations grows out of the exigencies of their respective situations rather than out of an intellectualized dedication to theoretical constructs. What is clear, however, is that southern Africa's revolutionary leaders, especially in Portuguese territories, are becoming increasingly aware of the revolutionary potential of what had once been regarded as a politically retarded and quiescent countryside. The real conflict of attitudes comes over the political-military relationships that inevitably arise in any such movement.

PATTERNS OF POLITICAL-MILITARY INTERACTION

The goals of revolutionary struggle, whether they be a "war of liberation" against a colonial power or a violent conflict to destroy an indigenous, nominally independent government, involve the necessity both to assert military superiority in the field and to establish and maintain political order in any territories that are taken over. A viable theory of guerrilla warfare, therefore, should include both military and political components. The ultimate goal is political power. The instruments are both persuasive and coercive. Guerrilla tactics enable an apparently weaker revolutionary force to combat an apparently greater military power. Such tactics depend upon popular support to supply the decisive advantage regarding intelligence which can, in its turn, enable an "inferior" military force to choose the locale and time of battle, rely upon surprise, concentrate forces, escape, and demoralize the enemy.

The most important disputes that arise over the issue of political-military interaction revolve around the matter of priorities and how to initiate the struggle. One school of thought and action argues that emphasis must be placed on establishing a reliable popular base in order to facilitate successful military operations. The other persuasion contends that a vanguard of dedicated guerrilla fighters can with a few well-planned military attacks actually precipitate a revolutionary response from the people despite the people's initial lack of political involvement. Seldom are the positions this categorical. Regardless of general preferences, both sides realize that political support and military success are both essential to a dynamic movement. Even within a single movement, thinking on both sides of the issue is apparent. Indeed, individual leaders vacillate on this question. So what we are dealing with here is a somewhat artificial and largely analytical distinction.

Emphasis on the political arm is the traditional Marxist-Leninist position, although acceptance of this view does not necessarily make one a communist. Communist revolutionary thought has long held that revolution is impossible without a "revolutionary situation." The people must be aware of their deprivation, conscious of their class status, convinced that violent revolution is the only possible remedy and that the revolution can succeed if supplied with the proper leadership and organization. The ANC of South Africa, as late as 1967, maintained that a revolutionary situation did not exist in South Africa at that time. The ANC nevertheless agreed that a revolutionary situation was the "essential precondition" for an insurrection. By 1969, ANC spokesmen took the position that South Africa was becoming ripe for revolution.[7]

From this viewpoint, a premium is placed on pre-insurrection political education and organization. Revolutionary leaders must make the masses conscious of their relative condition and, more importantly, convince them that guerrilla warfare can improve their lives. The Reverend Uria Simango, who for a time was one of the triumvirate that assumed FRELIMO leadership after the assassination of Eduardo Mondlane, once was asked what had been FRELIMO's most important victories. He replied that there were three: first, the formation of a liberation movement; second, "the unity of our educated and uneducated people"; and third, "the emergence of nationalism." "With these three victories the real fight began."[8] First political education and organization, then the fight began. According to Mondlane, every area of Mozambique had a FRELIMO team working clandestinely to train leaders and provide civic education to enable the people to understand how they relate to the overall revolutionary strategy.[9] Whether this was or still is the case should not trouble us here. The point is that this priority was established in FRELIMO doctrine.

In contrast, Régis Debray's contribution to guerrilla thought, based upon his Latin American experience and his association with Che Guevara, is inspired by the military doctrines of

7. See Joe Matthews, "Forward to a People's Democratic Republic of South Africa," *Sechaba*, vol. I, September 1967. A more current exposition of ANC strategy can be found in *Sechaba*, III (July 1969), 19–20, and in Matthews, "The Development of the South African Revolution," ibid., December 1969, pp. 5–8.

8. As quoted in Nkoana, "The Struggle for the Liberation of Southern Africa, Part II," *Africa and the World*, IV (January 1968), 16.

9. Kitchen, "Conversation with Eduardo Mondlane," *Africa Report*, XII (November 1967), 49.

Maoism (as opposed to its political side). Debray argues that guerrilla contact with the civil population must be kept to a minimum. Rather than swimming like fish in the water of the peasantry (as Mao has put it), the guerrilla must be self-reliant. The movement must be structured so that the people are not aware of the fighters' day-to-day activities. Political propaganda is unnecessary to win over a quiescent populace. The very act of fighting on behalf of the people's interests serves political purposes. First of all, it gives visible evidence that the ruling group is not invulnerable. The longer the fighting continues, whether or not military "victories" are registered, the better become the chances of convincing the peasantry that guerrilla warfare can win. Second, fighting is catalytic. It sets in motion a set of actions and reactions that increase political consciousness, grievance, economic dislocation, and governmental repression: just what the guerrillas want. Unwittingly the government, in a sense, takes over the responsibility of educating and radicalizing the masses. Third, successful guerrilla operations may liberate enough territory to create an internal base area. This has the important propaganda effect of denying the government forces access to a segment of the population while providing the guerrillas free access to it. A liberated area that is properly organized gives other peasants an object lesson as to what life might be like in a "free" country. But this course poses many risks, for if the war is begun too soon and is squelched, a negative object lesson has been registered, making future efforts more difficult.

By and large, southern African guerrilla movements pay lip service to the politics-first persuasion, although their behavior indicates that they may prefer—or, alternatively, may feel that conditions demand—the second position. Each leader, anyway, seems aware of the political ramifications of successful military performance. The mix is complicated, often implicit, and generally pragmatic, depending on the situation.

Organizationally, southern African revolutionary movements manifest this dualism. Problems of coordinating political and military endeavors are immense. Generally what exists is a central political organization (either a central committee or a government in exile) that operates outside the target territory and purportedly directs both the political activities and the war effort. The military arm manages daily tactical affairs in the target areas, often including political education and organization in occupied and contested areas. This dual military-political role epitomizes the problems of coordination. The political arm must maintain supervision of and assert ultimate control over potentially independent sources of power, but even within the military wing divisions arise. Once territory is occupied, these internecine clashes may be exacerbated. A strong party that can assert its dominance over the guerrilla army is needed.

Crucial for what a guerrilla movement can accomplish is how it manages the territory it occupies. Several southern African guerrilla leaders have dealt publicly with this question, some (Mondlane, for example) more fully than others. Indications are that FRELIMO has best prepared for eventual political concerns. In its "liberated areas" effective programs of formal and political education are being established. A rudimentary economic system and a formalized legal structure are being instituted. Rather than follow a preconceived doctrine propounded while out of power, leaders have evolved a series of pragmatic responses based on experience.

THE PROTRACTED WAR

The Chinese and Algerian wars have made an indelible imprint on southern African guerrilla thinking in other ways besides those noted above. Increasingly, leaders realize that the struggle is not easy, that wars will be protracted, and, indeed, that guerrilla forces can use time to their own advantage. The level of comprehension of and dedication to the time variable does not appear to be as advanced in Africa as in Asia, but it is becoming more and more important in southern African guerrilla planning. Indeed, in the early stages some movements displayed a staggering naïveté about the time factor. With regard to Angola, for example, Marcum points out that at the outbreak of hostilities in 1961 there was little to suggest that the nationalist leadership either expected or had a strategy for sustained military action.[10]

Later nationalist views in Angola seem more soundly rooted in reality. One regional guerrilla commander has said: "This is a war of the will. It took the Algerians seven years before the French gave in. We are just as determined." Another stated: "We will never be able to match the Portuguese man for man. But we can make a lot of trouble until the politicians find a settlement. And we can wait. Time is our best friend."[11] A young FRELIMO official reckoned that he would spend most of his life in the struggle.[12] Mondlane evidenced an awareness of time in the military-political sense. The same can be said of various South African and Zimbabwian revolutionaries. Contrarily, the SWAPO president, Sam Nujoma, stated in 1970 that the liberation struggle in southern Africa was approaching its climax and that the "final showdown" was "much nearer than is imagined."[13]

An awareness of military time also presumes a knowledge of certain tactical as well as strategic realities. First of all is the realization that guerrilla warfare is only a preliminary stage, albeit an important one, on the road to the use of other military techniques.[14] Second, leaders must understand the virtues of extending the struggle while keeping the level of military confrontation low, in order to wear down the enemy psychologically as well as physically. Third is a comprehension of the value of fighting experience, particularly as regards the planning of each attack and also for assessing when it is necessary to move into larger-scale warfare. Finally, of course, comes the hard lesson of self-reliance: that one cannot depend upon outsiders to sustain the war, despite the obvious importance of help from

10. Marcum, *The Angolan Revolution*, pp. 145–46.
11. *NYT*, West Coast edition, December 13, 1963, and August 25, 1962.
12. Ibid., October 7, 1969, p. 16.
13. *Namibia News* (SWAPO-London), III (January–March 1970), 3.
14. For example, Mondlane, "Our Chances: An Interview," *The New African*, IV (1965), 104–5, and Liberation Support Movement, *Daniel Chipenda, Interview*, pp. 4 and 7–8.

abroad. Building up the reserves and skills necessary to "do it yourself" is a long-term process. Additionally, political considerations relating to forging a common national consciousness in the shared experiences of extended military struggle are not to be ignored. Mondlane explained: "The fact that the war will be drawn out in this way may in the long run be an advantage to our ultimate development. For war is an extreme of political action, which tends to bring about social change more rapidly than any other instrument. . . . This is why we can view the long war ahead of us with reasonable calm."[15] At heart, he was pointing to the crux of the utility of guerrilla warfare as a *political strategy* as distinct from a military strategy or tactic. Increasingly, after some initial sobering experiences, African guerrillas have come to understand the possibilities and problems of protracted war.

When it comes to guerrilla strategy, by and large, southern Africa's revolutionary leaders are temperamentally pragmatic rather than doctrinaire. In general, Southern African theories of guerrilla warfare are truncated, disjointed, unrefined, eclectic, nebulous, and situationally specific, but these qualities are understandable, given the nature and spread of guerrilla warfare in Africa. Southern African theories of guerrilla strategy have yet to be written. Even Mondlane's book is not a full-fledged theoretical tract. The author was too flexible for that. Nevertheless, the need for a "correct and clear ideology" is openly admitted. With the struggle in progress, leaders have not spent the time systematizing their ideas. Moreover, their ideas are in flux, based on an expanding and kaleidoscopic body of experiences. There is no reason to doubt that in the future some southern African revolutionary will refine and reduce his thought into an identifiably African theory of guerrilla warfare.

COUNTER-GUERRILLA THINKING IN SOUTHERN AFRICA

Professional soldiers and government officials charged with destroying guerrilla movements in southern Africa have read and thought as much about this form of warfare as have revolutionary leaders themselves. Portuguese, Rhodesian, and South

15. *The Struggle for Mozambique*, pp. 219–20.

African soldiers and police get at least as much training in counterinsurgency tactics and operations as do African revolutionaries in guerrilla practices. And there is some evidence that some of their leaders have read Mao Tse-tung as carefully, too. But evidence also indicates that only selected officers have access to the works of Mao and other communist thinkers. For example, in 1971 it was discovered that a list of "recommended" books that had been issued to South African Citizen Force trainees contained four "banned" books. These included both Mao and Guevara on guerrilla warfare. Thus, though the trainees are studying "unconventional warfare," they are not permitted to read its classics. Only Permanent Force officers are given access to banned books, and then such books can only be consulted at the Defense Headquarters library.[16]

Whereas the principal thrust of revolutionary ideology is toward nationalism, self-determination, and independence, leaders in white southern Africa fancy themselves as "bulwarks" against the domination of the African continent by "alien" powers.[17] They talk repeatedly about defending Western civilization and Christianity against the incursions of communist Russian and Chinese influence, not only in their conceptualization of guerrilla warfare in southern Africa, but in their view of world politics in general. As they see it, the defense of southern Africa is crucial in the total defense of the Western world. Take, for example, the conception of world politics expressed by the Rhodesian prime minister, Ian Smith: "Africa is the key continent. Who controls Africa in the next decade will control the balance of power between East and West in the next

16. *The Star*, January 16, 1971, p. 8.
17. Again, the ANC tends to see itself in global rather than regional terms, but this may be largely a function of its identification with Marxism-Leninism and the Soviet Union; see *Sechaba*, vol. III (July 1969). This global perspective is also evident among the various combinations of revolutionary movements of different territories—for instance, ZAPU–ANC and CONCP (see pp. 219–21). Note also the final resolution of the Mobilization Committee of the "International Conference in Support of the Peoples of Portuguese Colonies and Southern Africa," Khartoum, January 18–20, 1969, reprinted in *Namibia News*, II (April–June 1969), 6–10.

century."[18] Without southern Africa the West is seen as being strangled to death by communist control of critical resources and the sea lanes to Asia. To a large extent this is warmed-over Mackinder, a geopolitical attitude in fairly simplistic terms. A domino theory of southern African international politics is popular, particularly among the Rhodesians, who have an inflated impression of the importance of their position. The Rhodesian secretary for external affairs put it this way: "If we go, Mozambique can't hold out for six months; the others would fall in order."[19] But this perspective has an almost mirror image among those seeking revolutionary change in southern Africa. Discussing the geopolitical future of southern Africa, Emile Apollus of the UN's Council for Namibia, has stated: "If there is any validity to the domino theory anywhere, it is in Southern Africa. And here the weak link is the Smith regime in Zimbabwe."[20] Ironically, there seems to be a strange agreement among regional protagonists on certain strategic considerations. These attitudes are also increasingly apparent in the military journals of the southern African defense forces. The pages of *Kommando*, the official magazine of the South African Defense Force, and *Assegai*, the magazine of the Rhodesian army, reflect not only a growing dedication to the problems of counter-guerrilla activities in southern Africa but also an awareness of the importance of the study of guerrilla and counter-guerrilla activities elsewhere.

The Portuguese have had far more practical experience fighting revolutionary nationalists than the South Africans and

18. As quoted in *Rhodesian Commentary*, Salisbury V (April 1971), 3.

19. Interview, RHO–37, Salisbury, August 25, 1969. See also the propaganda pamphlets published in Salisbury by the Ministry of Information, Immigration and Tourism: *Rhodesia in the Context of Africa* (1966); *Red for Danger* (1967); and *Zambezi—Red Frontier* (1968). Apparently, many South Africans accept this view. For an instance see the letter to the editor in *The Star* (issue of November 21, 1970, p. 14) by R. H. Mason, the national president of the South Africa-Rhodesia Association, which had launched a nationwide "Anti-Terrorist Fund" to aid Rhodesia "in its magnificent struggle against world aggression."

20. As quoted in *News/Check*, IX, 12, October 2, 1970.

Rhodesians. Special counterinsurgency training was instituted in 1961, and increased reliance has been placed upon training officers in counterinsurgency techniques at United States military schools. The present Portuguese military commander in chief in Mozambique is reportedly the author of a volume on the strategy and tactics of guerrilla warfare.[21] Psychological campaigns and resettlement schemes designed to win over the peasantry have been attempted, but to little avail. As a district governor in Angola put it: "This is a war for population, not for territory."[22] At least this much the revolutionaries and the Portuguese agree upon: guerrilla struggle is as much a political contest as a military one.

South African fears of a popular uprising or of externally based incursions have been heightened by hostilities in surrounding territories. South Africa has come to see itself in the context of Africa—not in isolation. Interest in the wars in Mozambique and Angola has been intense, and the decision to assist the Rhodesians with men and materials is obvious testimony to its sense of concern and its inclination to look at guerrilla warfare in southern Africa regionally rather than territorially. As Cape Town's *Die Burger* said some years ago: "It must be obvious that an underground war that recognizes no borders also necessitates underground defence." The Johannesburg *Sunday Times* likewise stressed the need for a complete policy to deal with insurgents:

> South Africa will perhaps have to go deeply and professionally into this business, for no games are being played by the other side. . . . One aim should probably be to deprive the revolutionary of his sense of security once he has left South Africa. For that the South African defence will have to develop long and skillfull arms in the knowledge that when the life of a nation is involved unorthodox methods have always been orthodox.[23]

21. Biographical sketch of General Kaulza de Arriaga in *Rhodesia Herald*, August 29, 1969, p. 13; see also *The Star*, October 17, 1970, p. 12.
22. *NYT*, August 6, 1969, p. 3. See also Wheeler, "The Portuguese Army in Angola," *JMAS*, VII (1969), 425–39, esp. 431–37.
23. These two 1963 quotations are cited in Halpern, *South Africa's Hostages*, p. 49. The chairman of the Nationalist Party's foreign affairs group in Parliament went further when he suggested that the govern-

The activities of its operatives in London, Lusaka, Dar es Salaam, and elsewhere attest to South Africa's determination to wage preventive and disruptive underground warfare.

As these statements imply, South Africa sees the need to develop a superior intelligence system. Going further, officials are threatening preemptive strikes against countries harboring guerrilla forces. Both Prime Minister Vorster and Minister of Defence P. W. Botha have warned that countries that continue to support revolutionaries against South Africa might themselves be the targets for raids aimed at destroying guerrilla bases in the manner of Israel's response to guerrilla provocations launched from Jordanian territory.[24] Perhaps South Africa may not be seriously considering so direct a course at present but the statements must make Zambia aware that it may be a target of massive violence.

A nationwide survey has indicated that the chief fear for the future among South African whites concerns "black terrorists from neighboring states."[25] The question posed and the results were:

> Here is a list of factors that people have mentioned to us. Which one of these factors or problems do you personally think is the greatest threat to South Africa's future?

	Percent
Population explosion	6
Soil erosion	10
An uprising of the Bantu population	12
Drought	27
Black terrorists from neighbouring states	40
None of these	6
Total	101

---

ment should allow foreign Africans to use RSA territory to launch guerrilla attacks against their own black governments. *The Star*, May 6, 1972, p. 6.

24. Vorster's Rustenburg speech, *ARB*, IV, 891B, November 15, 1967, and Botha to the House of Assembly, April 5, 1968, as reported in *ARB*, V, 1047C–48A, May 15, 1968. See also *Rand Daily Mail*, April 4, 1968. See also the Rhodesian warning to Zambia of "consequences" if it did not curb the activities of guerrillas operating from its territory. *Guardian*, September 6, 1972, p. 4.

25. *Rand Daily Mail*, August 18, 1969, p. 17.

In this case more than half of the white population interviewed was alarmed about the possibility of some form of violent revolutionary activity by blacks.

This greater attention to guerrilla warfare has grown out of and also contributed to the publication in South Africa of numerous popular novels, books, and articles on the subject, and even of a small manual of guerrilla warfare that advocates the establishment of a defensive guerrilla network if outside powers should intervene in the region.[26] The South African government seeks to manipulate this widespread popular interest, turning it from an element of fear to a potential source of strength and white unity.

The Pattern of Guerrilla Struggle

GUERRILLA WAR IN ANGOLA

The Angolan guerrilla war has been in progress since March 15, 1961.[27] But preparations for that initial uprising and a few spontaneous and planned incidents and outbreaks preceded the actual fighting by many months, and brought the revolutionary movement into contact with the Congolese government as well as the Congolese government into conflict with Portugal. From 1958 to 1960 the União das Populações de Angola (Union of Peoples of Angola, UPA), under the leadership of Holden Roberto, set up headquarters in the Congo and began to or-

26. A representative novel, Chapman's *The Infiltrators,* deals with guerrillas who pass from Zambia through northern Botswana and into Rhodesia. Popular treatments include: Harrigan, *Defence against Total Attack*; Teixeira, *The Fabric of Terror*; Venter, *The Terror Fighters*; and, Morris, *Terrorism.* The South African press is regularly filled with reports and feature articles about guerrilla wars in Africa. See, for example, the piece by Venter, "Ten More Years of Terrorism?" in *News/Check,* IX, 12–15, September 4, 1970. The manual referred to is Orpen, *Total Defence.*

27. A more complete bibliography on this war appears in my *Guerrilla Struggle in Africa,* p. 91. The definitive treatment of the genesis of the war is Marcum, *The Angolan Revolution.* Relatively recent, pro-MPLA, accounts are Davidson, "Angola in the Tenth Year," *African Affairs,* LXX (January 1971), 37–49, and also his *In the Eye of the Storm.* On the effects of the war on the civilian population see Bender, "The Limits of Counterinsurgency," *Comparative Politics,* IV (1972), 331–60.

ganize a political underground capable of functioning inside Angola. By mid-1960 the UPA had established offices in Matadi, Leopoldville, and Elizabethville in the Congo as well as centers in the interior of Angola. Military training was first provided by a Tunisian officer serving in the Congo.

After the initial outbreak of hostilities in Luanda the theater of battle was largely confined by the Portuguese forces to an area of northern Angola approximately 150 miles wide and 200 miles deep. It was to be a war of attrition. The chief task of the nationalists was to secure help from outside Angola and to build up a military force capable of combating the Portuguese offensive as well as a political cadre able to mobilize the populace in the countryside.

It was only natural that they should turn to the Congo. Angolan nationalism first expressed itself among the Bakongo, a group that numbers some 1,000,000 in the Congo and 500,000 in Angola. During the first five years of the rebellion the bulk of the fighting was confined to northwestern Angola where the Bakongo are concentrated. And the Portuguese, although they could not hope to wipe out the rebels completely because of the latter's passage into and out of the Congo, were able to concentrate their forces in the region and to contain the war. (See map 3.)

One year after the opening of hostilities, Lisbon radio admitted that Portuguese forces were unable "to completely close the frontier."[28] Indeed so thoroughly had they failed that by 1967 more than 300,000 Angolan refugees were to cross that frontier on their way to asylum in the Congo. Congolese assistance to the nationalists added to Portuguese counterinsurgency problems. As if to rub salt in Portugal's wounds, the Congolese government blatantly announced in August 1962 that it was giving aid to the Angolan rebels, and what is more that it had "donated" to them a guerrilla training base at Kinkuzu near Thysville. The recruits were even wearing hand-me-down Congolese army uniforms and using weapons supplied by the Adoula government. The new recruits were trained

28. As quoted in Marcum and Lowenstein, "Force: Its Thrust and Prognosis," in Davis and Baker, eds., *Southern Africa in Transition*, p. 252.

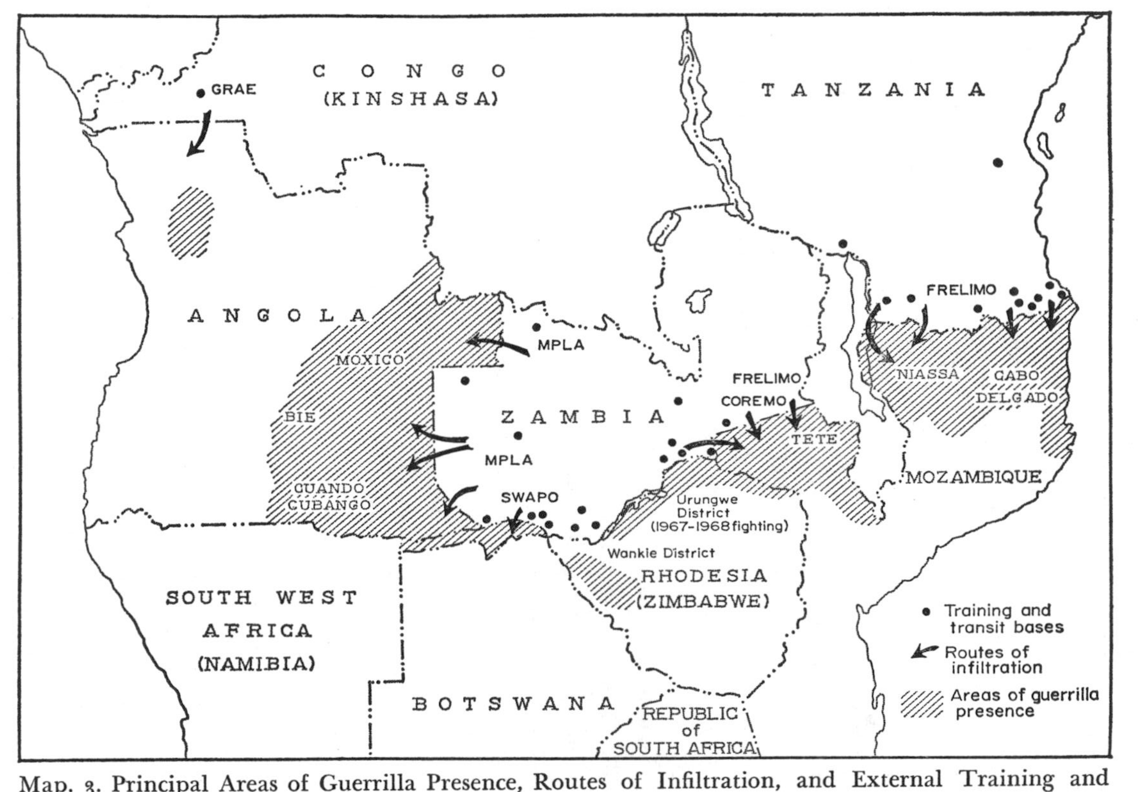

Map. 3. Principal Areas of Guerrilla Presence, Routes of Infiltration, and External Training and Transit Bases

by Angolan officers who had received their in-combat training in Algeria.[29]

For a while it looked as if Portugal might move to break off diplomatic relations with the Congo. The Congolese brusquely rejected a formal Portuguese request for an explanation by frankly admitting collaboration with the rebels. Portugal's overseas minister, acting as if his alternatives were limited, merely responded by criticizing the "privileged sanctuary" in the Congo and by hinting that Portugal might ask its military forces to pursue fleeing raiders into the Congo and destroy their bases.[30]

It was not long, however, before the Portuguese secured the means by which they could pressure the Congolese government. As the Congolese secessionist province of Katanga fell to UN and central government forces early in 1963, hundreds of Katangese gendarmes and a few mercenaries in the employ of Moise Tshombe fled into Angola where the Portuguese provided them with shelter and food. Despite repeated Congolese protests, one high Portuguese official reasoned: "The Congo is openly providing a military base for operations against us. Morally we are certainly justified in maintaining mercenaries and gendarmes on our soil."[31] By summer 1964 more than 2,000 Katangese gendarmes were encamped in Angola. Although the Portuguese repeatedly assured the world that the gendarmes and mercenaries were unarmed and would not be permitted to return to the Congo, Colonel Jean Schramm, who headed the small group of mercenaries there (as he did at Bakavu in 1967 and later in Rwanda) promised his men that they would march on Katanga when the UN forces left.

In 1963 the Congolese government and the OAU granted de jure recognition to the Governo Revoluciónario de Angola no Exílo (Government of the Angolan Republic in Exile, GRAE), an act that under international law Portugal could interpret as hostile. It became quite clear that Congolese assistance to the rebels kept the war smoldering.

29. *AD*, II, 741, September 8–14, 1962. Recruits at that time numbered 1,300. *The Times*, London, November 26, 1962.
30. *AD*, II, 799, October 13–19, 1962.
31. Ibid., June 6–12, 1964, p. 1788.

The year 1964 marked a turning point in the struggle. In July, Moïse Tshombe came to power in Leopoldville and almost immediately the GRAE found it more difficult to conduct business in the Congo. Tshombe did not attempt to suppress Angolan revolutionaries. Rather he sought to suffocate them. GRAE received less cooperation from the authorities, its military activities on the border were more constricted, and this in turn led to greater political struggle within and among the nationalist movements. Personal, ideological, and ethnic differences became more pronounced and this took its toll on the fighting effectiveness of the insurgents.

This was just as well for Tshombe, for he wanted to make his peace with the Portuguese without losing too much influence in his own country and among his fellow Africans.[32] It was not until Tshombe's removal in October 1965 that the rebellion regained its momentum and the Congolese border became penetrable once more.

The rebellion had become immobilized by the internal unrest in the Congo coupled with the sheer weight and concentration of Portuguese military power. A new effort and perhaps a new front were needed. In 1966 and 1967 they were supplied. A raiding party from Dr. Agostinho Neto's Movimento Popular de Libertação de Angola (Peoples' Liberation Movement of Angola, MPLA) attacked Portuguese forces in Cabinda, north of the Congo River. They had been "experimenting" there as early as 1963–64. Holden Roberto's forces revitalized the war in the northwest. Then Angola was invaded across the Zambian and Katangese frontiers. There was even a lively flare-up around Luanda itself. The border, once more, thanks to sympathetic Congolese and Zambian governments, had been allowed to become an instrument for guerrilla warfare, and for the first time, Portugal was forced to disperse its troops.

Vigorous pursuit of insurgents across Zambian and Congolese borders became a tactic more frequently employed by the Portuguese. In 1967 two additional charges leveled against the

32. There were even reports in June 1965 (which Tshombe promptly denied) that he had secretly met with President Salazar in Lisbon. *AD*, V, 2399, July 3–9, 1965.

Portuguese by the Congolese government reflected tensions along the border. In June the Portuguese and Spanish were accused of a plot to sabotage the Congolese economy by destroying the electrical and railway lines running through Katanga. The unsuccessful saboteurs allegedly entered Katanga through Angola.[33] A more bizarre report was made public in November, when two groups of armed white mercenaries (from 100 to 200 in all) allegedly entered Katanga near the railway line. They stole trucks and drove to a railway station where they commandeered a train and headed toward Lubumbashi. About 150 miles along the line they came into contact with Congolese army units, and although apparently no fighting occurred, the mercenaries retreated back into Angola.[34] Portugal denied that these mercenaries had come from Angola. But it did concede that 75 of them had taken refuge in Angola after leaving the Congo.

The flare-ups of these two years led to a break in diplomatic relations between Portugal and the Congo (October 1966), and to Congolese complaints being filed against Portugal in the UN Security Council on two separate occasions (September–October 1966 and November 1967). Border incidents had increased in intensity and expanded territorially along the border.

Although the chief desire of Angolan nationalists is to end colonial rule in Angola, there is no evidence that the post-1966 attacks have been orchestrated by a coordinated leadership. On the contrary, at least three different organizations are involved. The GRAE carries the brunt of the fighting in the northwest. The MPLA is responsible for the fronts in Cabinda and along the eastern frontier with Katanga and Zambia. UNITA, based in Zambia and the eastern Congo, has been marginally successful along the rail line to Lobito.

But no progress has been made to resolve long-standing conflict among Angolan nationalists, and this has led to diminished military performance. OAU-ALC conciliation commissions produced nothing. Segments of the army in the other Congo

33. *ARB*, IV, 800A, July 15, 1967.
34. *AD*, VII, 3717–19, December 24 and 31, 1967. See also *The Times*, London, March 12, 1968, p. 6.

(Brazzaville) became increasingly wary of MPLA activities and associates (particularly a number of Cubans and Chinese) who seemed to be too deeply involved in the country's domestic politics. After the mid-1968 military coup in Brazzaville the MPLA found its welcome tarnished and moved its main administrative headquarters to Lusaka, virtually abandoning the Cabinda front. Today, the only truly viable guerrilla offensive is in Moxico and Cuando Cubango, west of the Zambian border, with extensions into the central provinces of Malange and Bié. This is MPLA country. The GRAE-UPA triangle in the northwest (northeast of Nambuangongo) has shrunken under Portuguese pressure and is little more than a defensive operation of symbolic significance. At present the war could be described as militarily stalemated, although all parties insist that they are making political progress.

GUERRILLA WAR IN MOZAMBIQUE

The Mozambican war for independence commenced on September 24, 1964, when guerrilla units that had crossed the Ruvuma River between Tanzania and Mozambique attacked Portuguese military installations.[35] However, in the case of Mozambique, actual military operations were preceded by years of planning and organization by the Frente de Libertação de Moçambique, a coalition of nationalist parties in exile, put together in 1962. Dr. Eduardo Mondlane, the first leader of FRELIMO, had worked hard to secure unity in the movement (still not totally unified) and was able to gain the support of the OAU at its Addis Ababa meeting in May 1963. Then began the difficult tasks of political and military organization inside Mozambique, the training of recruits outside the country, and the securing of funds from abroad. Careful preparation paid dividends. Although the Portuguese had since 1961 expected an assault from Mozambican nationalists in Tanzania, they were unable to uncover FRELIMO's military cadres in the

35. So far the literature on the war in Mozambique is limited. Perhaps the most detailed account, and a rather fair history, is Mondlane's book *The Struggle for Mozambique*.

Cabo Delgado, Niassa, and Tete provinces. Unaware of the details of FRELIMO's military plans, the Portuguese decided to defend the 500-mile Ruvuma River frontier, a physically demanding assignment. They concentrated on training volunteers, constructing landing strips and roads, and modernizing their armed forces in the region. But still the initiation of hostilities caught them off guard.

After almost a decade of fighting the war had not been going especially well for the nationalists until Cabora Bassa became an inspirational target (see map 3). In 1966 the guerrilla general staff moved part of its headquarters from Tanzania to Mozambique. Later its field operations were widened, although it has been forced to reduce its operations in Cabo Delgado Province somewhat in order to concentrate on its symbolic target, the Cabora Bassa project, in Tete Province. A rival nationalist body, the Comité Revolucionário de Moçambique (Revolutionary Committee of Mozambique, COREMO), makes its presence felt by periodic probes into Tete, too. An estimated 4,000 to 8,500 guerrillas have managed to engage and harass at least 45,000 Portuguese troops, and to stir considerable apprehension among Rhodesian and Malawian authorities who are concerned about the security of their transport routes.

The first Portuguese reaction to the outbreak of fighting in 1964 was to retaliate with full fury. They razed rebel-held villages, burned crops, and sought to isolate the rebels from the populace. Eventually, the Portuguese attempted to create a no man's land along the Ruvuma River by clearing out villagers on the Mozambique side of the frontier (some 250,000 were moved), burning their dwellings and fields, and relocating them into 150 fortified villages.[36] The result was to precipitate an exodus to Tanzania, mostly of the Makonde people who live on both sides of the river (about 120,000 in Tanzania and 80,000 in Mozambique). By 1971, refugee totals had risen to 55,000 in Tanzania and 5,000 in Zambia.

Portugal and Tanzania have been brought to the brink of hostilities over the mutual boundary. Tanzania has hardly

36. *AD*, VII, 3238, January 28–February 3, 1967.

sought to avoid a clash.[37] Although accusations and counteraccusations have come from top government officials on both sides, the Tanzanian government has taken the further step of allowing military training camps for guerrillas to be constructed in the southern frontier area, where no fewer than nine separate training bases have been reported. The Portuguese claim to have evidence that instructors from the Chinese People's Republic are operating at four of the bases.[38]

As early as 1965, the Portuguese foreign minister, Alberto Franco Nogueira, commented that Portugal might undertake "legitimate retaliation" against countries which allowed "terrorist" bases to be established along their frontiers with its territory. "There is now a new doctrine of legitimate retaliation," he said. "We are taking a very good note of this new doctrine."[39] Since then, numerous incidents within Tanzanian territory have appeared to lend some substance to his warning, with Tanzania charging repeated violations of its airspace by Portuguese military and civilian reconnaissance planes. Antiaircraft guns have fired on the violators but no hits have been reported.

Malawi has become increasingly enmeshed in Portugal's counterinsurgency operations, in response to refugee and FRELIMO movements on Malawian territory, a product of the stepped up fighting in Tete. On Lake Malawi (Nyasa), Malawian patrol boats have been under the command of Portuguese naval officers to watch over FRELIMO activities. Fearing FRELIMO troop movements into Malawi, the Banda government has also solicited military assistance from South Africa.[40]

In early 1969 two events occurred that might have shattered lesser nationalist movements. Dr. Mondlane, who had stood

37. The chief concession Tanzania made to Portugal's international sensitivities was to request of FRELIMO that it stop bringing Portuguese prisoners over the border for detention in Tanzania. During 1966 this amounted to fewer than 20 prisoners. *East African Standard,* December 30, 1966, and *Africa Report,* XII (February 1967), 23.

38. *AD,* VII, 3238, January 28–February 3, 1967.

39. *The Nationalist,* May 11, 1965.

40. *Southern Africa,* IV (October 1971) 8, and *Daily Telegraph,* London, December 3, 1971.

virtually alone as FRELIMO's leader since its 1962 creation, was killed by a bomb in Dar es Salaam on February 3. The initial and long-range impact has been staggering. A few weeks earlier the deputy military commander of the FRELIMO forces, Samuel Kankonbe, had been assassinated in southern Tanzania. FRELIMO might have disintegrated in a leadership crisis based on ideological-ethnic-personal divisions. For years there has been talk of dissatisfaction among Makonde militants. Some Makonde members, whose people bear the burden of the battle in Mozambique, raided FRELIMO headquarters in Dar es Salaam at least twice in 1968, sending some officials to the hospital with knife wounds. Then in March 1969 Chief Lazaro Kavandame, a sixty-five-year-old FRELIMO officer and the most prominent political leader of the Makonde, defected to the Portuguese. He claimed that FRELIMO had been using the Makonde as cannon fodder.[41]

Despite some significant setbacks, FRELIMO survived. The central committee reorganized the leadership structure by abolishing the office of president and electing three men to serve as a "Council of the presidency." The council was composed of Marcelino dos Santos, the Reverend Uria Simango (who served as the coordinator in Dar es Salaam and has since joined COREMO), and Samora Machel (chief commander of the FRELIMO military forces in Mozambique and possibly the strongest of the three). However, the new collegial leadership has had its problems. Morale has suffered, and field effectiveness with it. Accusations of tribal and regional favoritism and personal animosity have contributed to defection and military weakness. The Makonde and Nyanja (bordering Malawi), who heretofore supplied the bulk of FRELIMO fighters, have become less committed because of their leaders' taking issue with FRELIMO's top echelon, comprising mainly southerners from the Ronga and Shangaan tribes. Geopolitically, since the Makonde and Nyanja peoples come from northern border areas, it was to be expected that they would be among the first refugees and hence among the fighters. But if one were from these

41. *ARB*, VI, 1389B–90B, May 15, 1969, and *Africa Confidential*, XII 5–6, May 1, 1971.

groups, it would be easy to assume that FRELIMO's leaders were exploiting them. The leadership, for its part, has continued to insist that the movement is national in scope and appeal.

Despite efforts of President Nyerere and the OAU's Liberation Committee, the three-man council of the presidency broke up. Currently the leadership is shared by Samora Machel as secretary of defense and commander of the army and Marcelino dos Santos as secretary for external affairs. The immediate result of this development was a slowdown if not an actual surrender of initiative to the Portuguese in Cabo Delgado. However, in the past two years the movement has regained momentum, especially in Tete Province around Cabora Bassa.

ZIMBABWE LIBERATION ACTIVITIES

Although open and violent internal resistance to the Smith government in Rhodesia had not been absent, for the first years after the UDI internal African opposition, by and large, lacked organization and coordination.[42] It had essentially taken the form of spontaneous and sporadic outbursts with little promise of long-range effect. This type of resistance to minority rule had been an outgrowth of the tortuous history of the African nationalist struggle in that country. By the time of the Rhodesian UDI, the two nationalist liberation movements—the Zimbabwe African People's Union (ZAPU) and Zimbabwe African National Union (ZANU)—were in serious and open conflict with one another. This situation changed little in the intervening years, notwithstanding the purported 1971 decision to form a unified movement, the Front for the Liberation of Zimbabwe (FROLIZI), and the internal activities of the African Nationalist Council in opposition to the terms of the proposed settlement between the Smith government and the United Kingdom. But even lacking a centralized common organization, the

42. Among the few accounts of these operations is Rake, "Black Guerrillas in Rhodesia," *Africa Report*, XIII (December 1968), 23–25. Particularly useful for the international ramifications is Mlambo, *Rhodesia*.

opposition to the 1971 settlement proposals and the response to the Pearce Commission indicate the depth and intensity of opposition to the Smith government.

The effectiveness of ZANU and ZAPU guerrilla fighters has been marginal. Before 1969 they had managed to infiltrate a few hundred guerrillas into Rhodesia, but apparently had sent few until 1972. In their divided state the two movements posed chiefly a symbolic and harrassing challenge to the Rhodesian forces (reinforced by up to 3,000 South African soldiers and police). The guerrilla campaigns began in August 1967, when apparently joint forces composed of ANC of South Africa) and ZAPU fighters crossed into Rhodesia from Zambia in a group and then split into several units fighting in three seperate areas. They were engaged by Rhodesian and South African forces, and most were killed or captured, or were obliged to flee into Botswana, where some were apprehended and imprisoned. Infiltrations were resumed in March 1968 and were scarcely more successful. They largely followed the same pattern, although in these incursions the nationalists appeared to be better armed and trained than before. Later "heavy" infiltration took place in July–August 1968 and again in late 1972 and 1973. It is noteworthy, that the scale of the fighting is small, compared with that in the Portuguese territories, where thousands of rebels are in the field.

Why have the Zimbabwe nationalists so little to show for their efforts? By far the most important reason has been the internecine battles for control going on within and among the various nationalist movements. Because of this competition, they have found it virtually impossible to organize within Rhodesia and thus lack an indispensable ingredient for effective warfare. Contributing to this organizational difficulty, of course, has been the efficient informant network built up by the Rhodesian and South African police (working in both Rhodesia and Zambia), which has freely exploited ZANU-ZAPU animosities. Another explanation can be adduced from the geographical character of the boundaries. Rhodesia has Botswana, South Africa, and Mozambique as neighbors on three sides. Its most vulnerable flank is the 495-mile border with Zambia. Thus the Rhodesian and South African security forces can be relatively concentrated. Moreover, running the length of this border is the Zambezi River (and in part, Lake Kariba), a formidable barrier in its own right. Even so, military analysts question whether the border-patrol system devised by Rhodesian security officials can prevent infiltration. Another difficulty for the Zimbabwean nationalists is the knotty dilemma that Zambia faces in dealing with them. Zambia is doubtless sympathetic with their aims. Both ZANU and ZAPU have offices in Lusaka (and also in Dar es Salaam). Both have used Zambian radio to whip up support, although the broadcasts are jammed by Rhodesian authorities. But President Kaunda is fearful that the Smith government or South Africa may retaliate economically and militarily, and is unwilling to have Zambia turned into another Congo. For example, in late 1971 there were some land-mine incidents in the Caprivi strip, in which there were casualties among South African forces. Officially, Zambia denies harboring Zimbabwe nationalists. Its territory serves primarily as a transmission belt and jumping-off place for guerilla fighters coming from training in Tanzania and bound for Rhodesia, Angola, and points south.

Rhodesian authorities, who have been secretive about the extent of the violence and the policies taken to combat it, are edgy about a possible escalation. The minister for law and order has said: "If we relaxed our guard for a moment, gangs would again cross the Zambezi to continue their acts of murder and violence and sabotage."[43] The result is that measures have been taken to strengthen the Rhodesian security forces and to increase cooperation with South African forces. Although small-scale infiltration has been usual, and there were no major incursions in 1969, group penetration has once again been attempted since 1970. Still the incipient guerrilla war in Rhodesia has been militarily unimpressive. In respect to relationships across the border, however, the UDI and its repercussions have

43. As quoted in Legum, "Guerrilla Warfare and African Liberation Movements," *Africa Today*, XIV (August 1967), 6.

served to orient Rhodesia southward and to force Zambia to search out alternative economic patterns and military support while giving assistance, albeit cautious assistance, to the Zimbabwe nationalists.

REVOLUTIONARY NATIONALISM AND NAMIBIA

Militarily, the impact of guerrilla activities upon South West Africa has been negligible. Some limited fighting has been triggered by South African security forces that either stumbled upon infiltrating guerrillas or sought out guerrilla operatives. Attacks by guerrillas, though rare and militarily inconsequential, have nevertheless their symbolic importance—as the first concerted blows within South Africa's immediate defense perimeter—and thus have significance as political gestures (in the Debrayian sense) for inhabitants of South West Africa, for the immobilized United Nations, and for all the world to see.

The South West Africa People's Organization (the only active liberation movement operative directly within the territory) regards August 26, 1966, as the opening of the "final stage" of its liberation struggle. Its organization, however, dates back to the Ovamboland People's Organization, formed in 1959 and transformed into SWAPO in 1960. Its leaders, for their organizing efforts, were penalized by being rusticated in Ovamboland by the authorities. Sam Nujoma fled the country in 1961 to set up operations in Dar es Salaam. In limited concert with SWAPO leaders within South West Africa, he began to recruit guerrilla trainees.[44] Spirited out of South West Africa in small groups, the recruits were moved through Botswana, where the SWAPO office in Francistown expedited their passage to the Kongwa camp in Tanzania, and thence were fanned out to various training camps in other African states (Ghana, Algeria, and Egypt) and in communist states (Russia, the Chinese People's Republic, and North Korea).

44. See Dale, "South African Counterinsurgency Operations in South West Africa," unpublished paper presented to the African Studies Association, Los Angeles, October 16–19, 1968, pp. 8–10; Dale, "Ovamboland," *Africa Report*, XIV (February 1969), 16–23; and Horrell, *South-West Africa*.

SWAPO men began returning to Ovamboland after September 1965. They established a training and base camp at Ongulumbashe which for several months went undetected. On August 26, 1966, South African police, after having the camp under surveillance for several days, launched an attack, killing two guerrillas and arresting nine. The subsequent guerrilla operations have been isolated and ineffective.

Still, the importance of the guerrilla operations as a catalyst must not be underestimated. SWAPO claims that these operations and the South African countermeasures have led to the flight of some 4,000 refugees to Zambia and some others to Botswana. Further, in late 1971 and early 1972 some bands of the Ovambo people "invaded" Angola from South West Africa and destroyed fences, claiming territory up to the Kunene River. The incident brought South African police and Portuguese troops to the area.[45]

The location of nationalist actions in Namibia and the composition of the nationalist participants, predominantly if not exclusively Ovambo, must also be considered. Ovambos form the largest single population group in the territory, estimated at 270,000 in 1966 and representing 45 percent of the total. Ovamboland is strategically situated for guerrilla struggles. The border with Angola makes it accessible to support and supply from abroad, and it is a densely forested region (unlike most of South West Africa), with good cover for guerrilla activities. A final consideration is that for years Ovamboland has been relatively divorced from the rest of the territory's economic life.

Ovambos nevertheless, as migrant laborers, play an important part in the economy. They provide about 70 percent of the labor for the modern industries in the southern, "white" part of the territory and some 90 percent of its miners. Their influence was felt in December 1971 when an illegal, largely spontaneous strike among Ovambo workers in Walvis Bay spread to the work force at the Tsumeb mine, the largest base metal mine in South West Africa, and from there throughout

45. *Namibia News*, II (April–June 1969), 4–5, and *Facts and Reports*, II, item 101, February 3, 1972.

the territory. Altogether about 23,000 Ovambos walked off their jobs. They were protesting the contract labor system run by the South West Africa Native Labour Association.[46] The strike posed a number of knotty problems for the government. Special police were flown in from South Africa and a large number of African policemen were reported to have been dismissed for being sympathetic to the strikers. About 10,000 Ovambos voluntarily returned to Ovamboland. Ultimately the South African Ministry of Bantu Administration was forced to negotiate with the strikers and the tribal authorities. Without detailing the issues and the negotiations, suffice to say that the strikers demanded greater freedom of movement within the territory, freedom to choose their own employers, and freedom to change work without retaliation from their employer. They wished to have their families with them at their work places and to receive higher wages. The government's concessions were in many ways a watered-down version of the old system, with shorter contract periods, improved pay, the possibility of accommodation for families, and the right to change jobs. SWANLA, the old contracting agency, was eliminated, and the authorities in the homelands were empowered to establish employment agencies to perform many of its services for employers.

After the agreement was announced, protests and disturbances continued. Clashes between Ovambos and police, together with the Angolan border incident, indicate that a new stage of nationalist activity has been started, more popular, more spontaneous, and less identified with militant forces outside the territory. Internal unrest has supplanted infiltration as the chief source of insecurity for the white regime.

Despite ethnic homogeneity, there is by no means ideological or political agreement on the course which ought to be taken. In response to the Odendaal Commission report (1964) and following the non-decision of the International Court of Justice in July 1966, the South African prime minister offered to

46. "Namibia: The Ovambo Challenge to South Africa," *Africa Bureau Fact Sheet 18*, February 1972, supplement to *X-Ray*, vol. II (February 1972).

Ovamboland a form of carefully monitored self-government. Hand-picked Ovambo leaders accepted the offer, and in the process requested the South African government to help in combating guerrilla nationalists operating in Ovamboland.

Another nationalist group, the South West Africa National Union (SWANU), was formed before SWAPO (in 1959), but it has been unable to gain either internal or external support. Generally identified with the less numerous Herero peoples (approximately 40,000) of the eastern part of the territory, its primary source of assistance is the Chinese Peoples' Republic. The OAU initially supported both movements, and under ALC pressure their leaders agreed to form the South West African National Liberation Front (SWANLIF), with headquarters in Dar es Salaam. This failed to be more than a paper union, and after SWANU became even less active, the ALC in 1965 threw its support behind SWAPO. Today SWANU is practically dead.

SWAPO still maintains party operations within South West Africa, although clearly overt activities are severely circumscribed. External SWAPO leaders, with provisional headquarters in Dar es Salaam, three other offices in Africa, (Lusaka, Cairo, and Algiers),[47] and three elsewhere (New York, London, and Helsinki), have also entered into the struggle. They have managed to infiltrate, recruit, and train a few men within South West Africa and to politicize many followers there. They have also convinced the OAU of the sole legitimacy of their movement in the territory and they have solicited and secured assistance from the ALC and from bilateral sources, principally the Soviet Union. And they, in cooperation with Zambia and the MPLA, have opened a front against the most formidable security force in southern Africa, no small accomplishment notwithstanding their still modest beginnings. This, if it can be coordinated with widespread discontent among laborers in South West Africa, may be the most likely pattern for political change there.

47. There have been, at other times, offices in Leopoldville, Accra, and Francistown.

REVOLUTIONARY AFRICAN NATIONALISM AND SOUTH AFRICA

In 1971 it was reported that 13 policemen had been killed and 3,699 injured while on active duty "against terrorists threatening South Africa's borders during the past two years."[48] It was not made clear in the report whether these included South African losses outside the republic (in Rhodesia, South West Africa, Mozambique, and Angola). Even so, it would be difficult to maintain that guerrilla warfare has begun in South Africa.[49] Although it could be argued that black Africans in the RSA are more politically attentive, as a group, than those elsewhere in southern Africa, the nature of the ruling white government and the Africans' own strategic and tactical errors have served to dissipate what following they once boasted, and to force into exile, execution, or prison many of the best leaders. The terror and sabotage campaigns from 1961 to 1964 represent the most intense form of organized anti-systemic violence that has appeared.

By and large, African nationalist organizations had eschewed violence before the tragic Sharpeville shootings of 1960. But the Sharpeville experience, compounded by the ruthless and unbending suppression of any form of non-white nationalist expression, seemed to teach the African nationalists that peaceful opposition was fruitless and that legitimate channels for substantial change were denied their people. Apartheid was intransigent. Its proponents were willing to employ any means to defend it. Revolutionaries reasoned that they would have to be willing to use any means to destroy it. The question remained: when and how would violence be expressed, and who would supply leadership and structure to the cause?

48. *The Star,* daily edition, March 13, 1971.
49. There is a wealth of important primary materials on African protest and revolutionary movements in South Africa, and they have served as the source for a number of solid analytical works that have been invaluable for my study: Carter, *The Politics of Inequality*; Feit, *African Opposition in South Africa*; Feit, *South Africa*; Feit, *Urban Revolt in South Africa*; Kuper, *Passive Resistance in South Africa*; and Mbeki, *South Africa.* Mbeki is an ANC leader currently imprisoned in South Africa.

Initially violence assumed a variety of forms. Groups earlier committed to nonviolent protest spawned secret movements working for the violent overthrow of the government. Umkonto we Sizwe (Spear of the Nation) went into action for the first time on December 16, 1961. It had been created a month earlier by African National Congress militants. It had recruited and trained men in explosive techniques and launched a coordinated sabotage campaign throughout the republic. Sabotage seemed to its leaders the sensible approach, given the imbalance of forces and the ends sought. Nelson Mandela, an ANC leader and one of the founders of Umkonto, felt that there were four alternative courses: sabotage, guerrilla warfare, terrorism, and open revolution. Despite the choice of sabotage because it "offered the best hope for future race relations" and "did not involve loss of life," the movement provided for guerrilla training and planning. Umkonto was effectively smashed by the arrest of seventeen top leaders at Rivonia in July 1963 and their subsequent trial and imprisonment. Smaller sabotage groups were even less active, and it soon became clear that, in the context, sabotage was not an effective instrument for revolutionary change.

Terrorism—the calculated use of brutal and ritualistic violence aimed at persons—was taken up by numerous smaller groups, chief among them was "Poqo," which was vaguely linked to the Pan-Africanist Congress (PAC). It is more than likely that Poqo was formed in 1962 by a breakaway group of PAC members. The PAC had sought repeatedly to assert its control over Poqo, with little success.

Even more concentrated and potentially more revolutionary in impact was the peasant uprising in Pondoland (the Transkei) in 1960. Aimed primarily at the system of Bantu Authorities, the violence was carefully directed against the property and persons of black officials and supporters identified with the Pretoria government. These black officials were an extension of the white government in Pretoria, and as such they represented a form of indirect rule along colonial lines. Councillors, headmen, and chiefs found their lives and property threatened, and assassinations were widespread. The movement established "mountain committees" to challenge the Bantu Authorities and their puppets, the traditional chiefs, and to direct the program to ostracize or if need be punish collaborators. By October 1961, thirty Pondos had been sentenced to death for their part in the unrest. In the years following the end of World War II various smaller and less well-organized resistance movements sprouted —in Witzieshoek, on the border of Basutoland; in Marico, south of Bechuanaland; in Sekhukhuneland, in the northwest Transvaal; in Zululand; and throughout the Transkei. All were forcefully suppressed.

Sabotage and terrorism, as well as open revolutionary protest, have so far been counterproductive in South Africa. Organization was weak, solidarity doubtful, competition among movements self-defeating. Acts of violence were generally uncoordinated, and these provided the government with further grounds for intensifying its repression of still legitimate dissent and for carrying out a thorough elimination of potential African leaders inside the republic. The government is generally confident that revolutionary African nationalism has been practically suppressed. Rather than alarm about an internal uprising, its current fears relate to the infiltration of nationalists from sanctuaries in independent black states. Nevertheless, the government must be somewhat alarmed by the ease with which the ANC underground inside South Africa exploded a series of "pamphlet bombs" in several cities in August 1970, and by the increasingly critical outspokenness of Bantustan officials and urban African leaders regarding apartheid, separate development, and other aspects of government policy.[50] Despite adversity, the potential for coordinated violence is high.

Outside the republic, planning and training and fighting continues, although at a very depressed level. The PAC has been ineffectual and badly divided in Dar es Salaam and Lusaka, but the ANC has struck up an apparently mutually acceptable alliance with ZAPU. Together their fighters have penetrated

50. Numerous South African newspaper reports of the "bombs" are reproduced in *Spotlight on South Africa* (ANC, London), vol. VIII, August 21, 1970) ; *Rand Daily Mail*, June 14 and August 3, 8, 11, and 28, 1971; and *The Star*, January 29, 1972, p. 12.

Rhodesia and engaged both the Rhodesian and South African military and police. They have made little effort to move men into South Africa since about 1969. The movement is not ready to strike within the republic. But guerrilla warfare is now the chosen medium, and preparation, mostly verbal, goes on.

We are ready now to plunge into the task set out in the opening paragraph of this chapter—to explore the multiple patterns of intra-African relationships growing out of the revolutionary struggles in southern Africa. After examining the various sources and effects of external assistance for nationalist movements, and especially the critical role of host states, we shall deal with the issue of external support for white governments. Then we shall analyze the balance sheet of traditional components of military power, touching upon the impact organized violence has had upon these components. A final section covers the matter of military "alliances" established by the revolutionary movements of various countries and the fairly high measure of regional military planning and cooperation developed in white southern Africa.

6

Lifelines and Tensions: The International Relations of Guerrilla Warfare

When spider webs unite, they can tie up a lion.
—*Ethiopia*

Although at heart a guerrilla war is won or lost by the ability of the revolutionary group to win over the population of the target area, evidence indicates that, particularly before and in the initial stages of the fighting, guerrilla movements are dependent also upon support from outside. In many respects this is largely a matter of resources.[1] Both the incumbents and the insurgents have resources that extend beyond the frontiers of the fighting zones. The incumbent government has alliances and other political associations that can be tapped for military, economic, and technical aid. Normal legal, commercial and economic relationships and the supply of weapons from abroad also contribute to their defense. But to the insurgents, external relationships are even more crucial. A larger proportion of their material resources are supplied by other countries, resources, moreover, that once secured cannot easily be denied

1. Modelski, "The International Relations of Internal Wars," in Rosenau, ed., *International Aspects of Civil Strife*, pp. 14–44.

them without intense pressure on the governments providing the assistance. Without foreign assistance insurgents would have practically no tangible assets or safe sanctuary in battle, and, as symbols of hope and support, and as refuges in the event of final defeat, the friendly outside countries perform a psychologically invigorating role as well. However, as the geographical base of the war expands within the target, the importance of external resources diminishes and the revolutionary movement becomes more able to sustain itself than before.[2]

External Sources of Support

Material and financial assistance. Communist countries supply the bulk of the financial and material assistance to southern Africa's revolutionary movements and guerrilla forces. (See table 10.) Exactly how much is difficult to say in absolute and proportional terms. It is likely that of those five movements represented in guerrilla fighting in Angola and Mozambique, all but one (GRAE) secure more aid from communist countries than any other source. This generalization applies to the South African, Namibian, and Zimbabwian parties as well. Since May 1968 there has been a significant increase in assistance from the Chinese People's Republic, and the fundamental competition in assistance is increasingly between spheres in the communist world—China and the Soviet Union—rather than between communist and noncommunist sources.[3] The movements heavily dependent on Chinese aid are SWANU, the União Nacional para a Independência Total de Angola (UNITA), and COREMO, with PAC, ZANU, and FRELIMO also drawing on

2. For example, as the fighting in Mozambique expanded, FRELIMO established a base area which it controlled and administered. Where five years before virtually all revolutionary fighters were trained outside the target territory, today FRELIMO claims that some 80 per cent are trained internally. Space in military terms is more than square mileage. For discussion of this see my *Guerrilla Struggle in Africa*, pp. 44–45.

3. Whitaker, "The Liberation of Portuguese-Held Africa," paper prepared for African Studies Association meeting, Montreal, October 15–18, 1969; Patrick Keatley, articles in *Manchester Guardian Weekly*, July 24 and 31, August 7 and 14, 1969.

	Angola			Mozambique		Rhodesia		South Africa		South West Africa	
	GRAE/FLNA	*MPLA*	*UNITA*	*FRELIMO*	*COREMO*	*ZANU*	*ZAPU*	*PAC*	*ANC*	*SWAPO*	*SWANU*
Principal headquarters	Kinshasa	Lusaka[a]	Int.[b]	Dar es Salaam	Lusaka	Lusaka	Lusaka	Dar es Salaam	Morogoro	Dar es Salaam	Dar es Salaam[c]
Supplementary headquarters	——	Brazzaville Dar es Salaam	Lusaka Cairo	——	——	Dar es Salaam	Dar es Salaam	Lusaka	Dar es Salaam Lusaka	Lusaka	
Principal sanctuary	Congo-K	Zambia	Zambia	Tanzania	Zambia	Zambia	Zambia	Zambia	Zambia	Zambia	
Secondary sanctuaries	Zambia	Congo-B	——	Zambia	——	Tanzania	Tanzania	Tanzania	Tanzania	Tanzania	
Principal training grounds	Congo-K	Int.[b]	Int.[b]	Int.[b]	Int.[b]	Tanzania	Tanzania	Tanzania	Tanzania	Tanzania	
Supplementary training grounds	Algeria Tunisia	Congo-B Algeria CPR Morocco Ghana[c]	CPR	Tanzania Algeria	CPR	Ghana[c] CPR	CPR Cuba USSR Korea Algeria	CPR	USSR CPR Ethiopia Cuba	Int.[b] Algeria UAR CPR USSR	
Sources of funds and materials (in probable order of importance)	Congo-K Non-Af.[d] Af. bilat.[e] Refugees	USSR Non-Af.[d] OAU CPR	CPR Non-Af.[d] Af. bilat.[e]	USSR CPR West. p.[f] OAU Non-Af.[d]	CPR Zambia Non-Af.[d] Af. bilat.[e] West. p.[f]	CPR OAU	USSR OAU	CPR OAU	USSR OAU CPR	USSR OAU	CPR
Recognized by OAU	Y (de jure)	Y	N	Y	N	Y	Y	Y	Y	N	N
"Khartoum Alliance"[g]	N	Y	N	Y	N	N	Y	N	Y	Y	N
CONCP Member[h]	N	Y	N	Y	N	N	A[i]	N	A[i]	A[i]	N
"Congo Alliance"[g]	Y	N	N	N	Y	Y	N	Y	N	N	N
Other intra-African affiliations	——	——	——	——	——	——	ZAPU-ANC Alliance		ZAPU-ANC Alliance	——	——

SOURCES: Paul M. Whitaker, "The Liberation of Portuguese-Held Africa," typescript, paper prepared for the meeting of the African Studies Association, Montreal, October 15–18, 1969; John Day, *International Nationalism* (London, 1967); *Africa Research Bulletin*, 1965–71.

Congo–K=Congo (Kinshasa). Congo–B=Congo (Brazzaville). CPR=Chinese People's Republic. OAU=Organization of African Unity. Y=yes. N=no.

[a]Although top MPLA leaders reside in Lusaka, since March 1969 the MPLA claims to have moved its headquarters inside Angola. [b]Int.=Internal (inside target territory). [c]Formerly. [d]Non-Af.=Non-African bilateral. [e]Af. bilat=African bilateral, [f]West. p=Western private. [g]See chap. 6. [h]CONCP=Conferência das Organizações Nacionalistas dos Colónias Portuguesas. [i]A=associate membership.

the Chinese. The chief recipients of Russian assistance are MPLA, ANC, ZAPU, FRELIMO, and SWAPO. Direct bilateral aid from the West is practically nonexistent and tends to stigmatize any movement it seeks to support. The only other assistance that could in some measure offset the concentration of communist sources comes from the Organization of African Unity itself, and of course from the host countries themselves.

THE AFRICAN LIBERATION COMMITTEE

Various nationalist parties in colonial and white-dominated Africa have for years felt like second-class citizens in their relationships with the governments of independent black African states.[4] Because of their desire for juridical recognition and acceptance, assistance from brother African peoples, and treatment as equals, they took the initiative at Addis Ababa in May 1963.[5] During the summit conference at which the OAU was formed the liberation movements, in a joint memorandum to the heads of state, urged the creation of an "African Liberation Bureau" to raise the status of their movements. Although their request was never honored, the OAU established the African Liberation Committee in 1963 to coordinate aid and to grant legitimacy of a sort to acceptable revolutionary movements. The imprecise criteria for recognition applied by the ALC seem to relate to: (1) demonstrated success in the field; (2) willingness "to co-ordinate efforts by establishing common action fronts"; and (3) political and ideological reliability. The first criterion is probably the most important although it has been loosely applied to include not only military success but a broadly based

4. Background information for this section was drawn from Wallerstein, *Africa—The Politics of Unity*, pp. 152–75.

5. The forerunner of this was the Coordinating Freedom Council of the Pan-African Freedom Movement of East and Central Africa (PAFMECA—since 1962 the Pan-African Freedom Movement of Eastern, Central and Southern Africa, PAFMECSA). The council administered a "Freedom fund," but each exile movement could expect little more than about £1,000 per year. Still the principle of collective responsibility for the liberation of southern Africa was accepted by independent African states. Cox, *Pan-Africanism in Practice*, esp. pp. 45–50, and Glickman, "Where Exiles Plan—And Wait," *Africa Report*, VIII (July 1963), 4.

popular following, particularly in territories where fighting has been either limited or nonexistent. This policy gives a distinct advantage to movements that have already been able to attract outside support or have initiated hostilities, or both. Thus the overall impact of Russian and Chinese assistance is magnified since an OAU endorsement is likely to follow demonstrated military capability or promise.

The ALC, moreover, has sought to establish itself as the coordinating organ for assistance both from independent African states and from outside the continent. Thus far, it has not been altogether successful in this aim.

In 1964 the OAU established a special fund into which each member state must pay an annual levy computed on the basis of a UN scale that accounts for factors such as gross national product, trade, and per capita income. In theory, approximately $2.1 million should be contributed into this fund annually. In reality, only three African states are paid up in full: Tanzania, Uganda, and Zambia. Some states have never made a payment. The total unpaid levy amounts to around $7 million. In 1970 only twelve states paid their contributions and receipts were less than $1 million. It is this financial weakness that makes the ALC ineffectual.[6] Its annual budget of approximately $1.7 million represents about a tenth of the total value of assistance received by revolutionary movements, if one includes the costs of training recruits and supporting refugees (most of whom are helped by agencies not directly related to revolutionary parties).[7]

The result is that at most of the ALC's meetings a recurrent theme has been the lack of money and active military and political support for the ALC from African states themselves. Moreover, the parent body, the OAU, has set up various committees

6. From a Guardian News Service report in *The Star*, March 6, 1971, p. 13; see also E. M. Rhoodie, "Luke-Warm Liberation," *To the Point*, Johannesburg, I, 51–52, February 12, 1972. This inability to collect assessed contributions did not prevent the OAU members from unanimously (Malawi was absent) deciding at the 1972 Rabat heads of government meeting to increase their contributions to the ALC by 50 percent in 1972. *Observer*, June 18, 1972, p. 7.

7. *Manchester Guardian Weekly*, July 24, 1969, p. 14.

to investigate the ALC—its status, effectiveness, management of funds, and future prospects for success. These committees have foundered for lack of cooperation from OAU member states.

To some extent the ALC has delegated its own responsibility to countries that border on target territories. These "host" countries thus administer assistance to the nationalist movements that apply for their protection. In this way host governments can perhaps protect themselves against revolutionary visitors who might seek to precipitate an outright engagement between the host and the target government. Most host countries are seated in the ALC. This membership and the ALC's delegation of responsibility gives them a measure of leverage to prevent or reduce the internal and international tension and jeopardy they risk by their role. But since many external suppliers and supporters choose to aid the nationalist movement directly and others have been wary of allowing the ALC to manage their funds and reap the political dividends, the ALC has suffered in prestige and effectiveness.[8] In fact, then, this devolution of responsibility merely represents the legitimization of the existing central role of host governments. The ALC has given nothing away that it actually controlled.

The matter of OAU recognition is of capital importance. Only recognized movements and parties are eligible for ALC aid. Naturally political influence will be exerted upon such a decision. Criteria are applied unevenly. In some territories Mozambique and Namibia) only one movement has been recognized and assisted, and in others (Zimbabwe and Angola) multiple acceptance prevails, although in reality assistance has been concentrated.

Lately, ALC policy seems to have favored parties of a radical activist persuasion. More than 50 percent of special fund monies goes to the movements in Portuguese Africa. Parties with closer links with the West have been stigmatized and the distribution of OAU support seems to reflect this. The reasons are not hard to find. The changing make-up of the ALC since its inception in 1963 indicates a drift toward more militant anti-Western gov-

8. See the speech by Sékou Touré quoted in *ARB*, V, 944B–45A, February 15, 1968.

ernments. The original nine members were the present states of Algeria, Ethiopia, Guinea, Nigeria, Senegal, Tanzania, Uganda, the United African Republic, and Zaïre. Two others were added in 1965, Somalia and Zambia. Senegal's participation has diminished since 1966 when its candidate party—the Frente de Luta pela Independência Nacional da Guiné, FLING—was completely bypassed by the ALC. Nigeria, plagued by internal civil war, reduced its involvement in the ALC, too. Thus the revolutionary-minded members gained the upper hand in ALC deliberations and recognition policies bear this out. Continued Russian support and expanded Chinese commitment also enabled the more radical nationalist parties to assert themselves in the target territories and in refugee concentrations (where the potential for winning recruits is greatest). Those parties without Russian backing have been unable to gain comparable support in the West or among radical African states. What has happened since 1965 has been an increasing confluence of OAU–ALC and Russian assistance. Parties heavily reliant upon Chinese or Western assistance, or both, have had to function without ALC support. With or without ALC support, parties find that it is the continued cooperation and endorsement of the host government that ultimately enables them to function.

GUERRILLA TRAINING

Formal instruction in guerrilla strategy and tactics has been the most fruitful medium for transmittal of various doctrines of guerrilla warfare. Virtually every major guerrilla movement in Africa in the 1960s has sent a few select recruits to China, Cuba, the Soviet Union, North Korea, and other communist or revolutionary countries for intensive instruction. The courses in China have been of varying duration and content; by and large, however, the curriculum has focused less on political theory than on tactical and technical matters. The men trained abroad have returned to Africa to serve primarily as instructors themselves, so the overall impact of foreign training is amplified. The Cubans have also sought to spread their doctrine of peasant revolution. "Scholarship" students are trained at the Cuban Academies of Marxism, Leninism, Agitation and Guerrilla Warfare, but Cuban efforts have not been as extensive as those of China.

Many potential guerrillas are reached by Chinese and Cuban instructors operating directly in Africa. The Chinese have worked in at least three countries—Congo (Brazzaville), Ghana, and Tanzania—and the Cubans in possibly as many.[9] In the early 1960s Russian instructors also were present. The students have come from practically all the countries in black Africa, in many of which there is no open warfare and with which the host governments have ostensibly correct relations.

The curricular emphasis is on military technique and tactical planning. The primary concern is to prepare technically competent fighters, not guerrilla thinkers and strategists. But the doctrinal message is never deep below the surface. President Kaunda of Zambia expressed a common opinion when he stated:

> The only people who will teach young Africans to handle dangerous weapons are in the Eastern camp. How can we expect that they will learn to use these weapons without learning the ideology as well? When they come back we can expect not only a racial war in Africa, but an ideological one too.[10]

Most of Africa's guerrillas, however, have been trained in Africa by Africans, usually by their fellow nationals and usually in the target country. FRELIMO claims that 80 percent of its fighters are trained within Mozambique. A similar claim is made for UNITA and MPLA fighters in Angola and SWAPO recruits in Ovamboland, although it is doubtful in the SWAPO case. Nevertheless, during the initial stages of a guerrilla war, the availability of a contiguous sanctuary, or at least a noncontiguous host country that can supply training facilities and assistance, seems crucial. At least ten African states have willingly supplied training sites for contiguous and sometimes distant revolutionary movements. Probably more men have been

9. *The Times*, March 12 and 24, 1968; *ARB*, V, 1211C–12A, November 15, 1968; 1212A; *NYT*, November 21, 1966; and Ghana, Ministry of Information, *Nkrumah's Subversion in Africa*, pp. 6–27, 56–59, 67–69.
10. As quoted in *The Times*, March 12, 1968.

trained in Algeria, the two Congos, and Tanzania than in other countries.

It is significant that, given their choice, African guerrilla leaders apparently prefer to call upon Algeria to assist them in training their recruits. The reasons are fairly clear and practical. Algeria is, of course, the only African nation to win independence from a determined colonial power in a protracted guerrilla war. There is little stigma attached to association with another revolutionary African country, and association would not jeopardize potential or actual assistance and support from either the East or the West, or from any country within the communist camp. This can be said of few other sources of instruction, including some other African states. Algerians themselves are eager to cooperate with other anticolonial movements, particularly those of the Portuguese colonies.

Host Countries: Pivotal and Endangered

Host countries often perform yeoman and manifold services on behalf of the parties and persons they entertain. Moreover, they undertake tremendous risks by their actions, risks of a domestic as well as an international sort. Essentially there are two types of persons the host country must deal with—first, the political exile who has fled or been expelled from the target country because of his involvement in political causes there; and second, the refugee who has fled, usually along with many others, the repression or general unrest in or near the fighting zones. Although embittered and dissatisfied with his condition he is not necessarily a revolutionary. It is the task of the political exile to focus the refugee's potential for revolutionary action into goal-directed revolutionary behavior. Both types of guests pose challenges for the host government. Professor Marcum has dealt thoroughly with the exile condition, especially from the individual, psychological perspective.[11] There is no need to restate his findings here. Our concentration will be on the re-

11. In his "The Exile Condition," in Dale and Potholm, eds., *Southern Africa in Perspective*.

lations of the host state and its guests, and we shall deal with the exile element only insofar as it provides the leadership skills to politicize and harness the potentially revolutionary refugees.

THE REFUGEE PROBLEM

Black refugees from the fighting zones or from political repression have come to host countries in Africa in numbers which few of these countries are prepared to entertain.[12] The extent of the influx can be seen in table 11.

The Congo (Kinshasa) has been the most inundated, receiving Angolan refugees estimated to number between 300,000 and 600,000. During the first five years of the war in Angola the bulk of the fighting was confined to northwestern Angola, inhabited by the Bakongo. About a million Bakongo also live across the border in the Congo. Despite this massive migration, many Bakongo have found homes among their ethnic brothers. To some extent, although on a much smaller scale, the same conditions applied to the Makonde on either side of the Ruvuma River border between Mozambique and Tanzania, and the people on the Angola-Zambia border. But this arrangement brings with it as many problems as it resolves, particularly administrative problems. Few African states have the resources to support temporarily unproductive populations. Sometimes the refugees resist resettlement since they feel their immigrant status will be only temporary. Although several international groups have been active among refugees in southern Africa—notably the UN High Commission for Refugees, the Oxford Famine Relief Committee, the International Labor Organization, the Lutheran World Federation, the League of Red Cross Societies, the World Food Program, the Food and Agriculture Organization, and the World Council of Churches—invariably the host governments have been burdened with most of the expenses. In countries where public resources are scarce and a good deal of domestic politics revolves around the issues of distributing those scarce resources, refugee services create an issue with deep domestic political ramifications. There are also dis-

12. See Hamrell, ed., *Refugee Problems in Africa*, esp. chapters by Cato Aall, pp. 26–44, and Margaret Legum, pp. 54–64.

TABLE 11

REFUGEES FROM SOUTHERN AFRICA: MAJOR HOST COUNTRIES AND SOURCES

Host and source	*1964*	*1965*	*1966*	*1967*	*1968*	*1969*	*1971*
CONGO:							
Angola	225,000	250,000	270,000	300,000	350,000	370,000	400,000
Other	62,000	36,000	47,000	57,000	64,000	94,500	89,000
TANZANIA:							
Mozambique	–	10,000	12,000	19,000	25,000	31,000	55,000
Congo	–	1,700	3,000	800	650	600	2,000
Other	12,000	13,300	13,500	13,500	14,150	14,000	14,500
ZAMBIA:							
Angola	–	–	100	3,800	6,200	8,000	10,000
Mozambique	–	–	5,000	1,800	2,750	3,000	5,000
Congo	–	–	–	–	925	300	–
Other	–	–	–	–	865	1,700	1,500
BOTSWANA:							
Angola	–	–	–	–	–	3,500	3,800
Other	–	–	–	–	–	300	225

SOURCES: Data are not easy to locate and invariably are estimates. Figures of the UN High Commission for Refugees tend to be conservative. Those for 1964–67 are UNHCR data as reproduced in Sven Hamrell, ed., *Refugee Problems in Africa* (Uppsala, 1967), pp. 14–15, 25. The 1968 data are from UN, General Assembly, Executive Committee of the High Commissioner's Programme, 19th session, *Report on UNHCR Operations in 1967*, A/AC. 96/390, April 30, 1968. Those for 1969 are from *HCR Bulletin*, no. 7, July–August–September 1969, p. 9. Those for 1971 were provided by the HCR and are from *Marches Tropicaux*, no. 1268, October 16, 1971.

putes that crop up between local indigenous inhabitants and the newcomers. Administrative difficulties only add to the problems of the host governments.

The case of Tanzania is illustrative. For years a tolerant, "open door" policy prevailed. Practically any refugees were admitted if they were politically acceptable. The Tanzanian government supplied the bulk of them with camps and facilities, and others were to be integrated into local agrarian populations. But as the extent of the burden became known, the Tanzanian government placed increasing responsibility for refugee administration upon the various nationalist movements of the territory of emigration. Entry is now limited to those individuals for whom the nationalist movements will accept responsibility. Refugees have even been expelled when their affiliation with recognized nationalist movements was challenged.

Zambia as well has abandoned its original policy of fairly free entry. With the increasing inflow of thousands of refugees, the Zambian government became more selective, granting only transit rights to those for whom Zambia is not the first country of asylum (for example, South Africans), and their movement in Zambia is restricted. A Refugee (Control) Bill passed in 1970 further tightened administrative control over the entry, movement, and political-military activities of refugees.[13]

One of the reasons for tightening regulations is that refugees serve as the focus for political, organizational, and propaganda campaigns both by the nationalist-revolutionary movements and by the home states. The latter may seek to persuade refugees to return to the target territory, using official offers of amnesty, radio broadcasts, and pamphleting—sometimes by air drop; but these efforts have not been particularly successful.[14] Target governments have also sought to place informants among refugees.

The nationalist-revolutionary movements are even more in-

13. *ARB*, VII, 1779B–C, July 15, 1970; *The Star*, July 4, 1970, p. 3; Anglin, "Confrontation in Southern Africa," *International Journal*, XXV (1970), 506–7.

14. See, for example, reports of Portuguese planes dropping leaflets on refugee settlements in Tanzania urging refugees to return to Mozambique. *East African Standard*, December 2, 1966, and April 15 and September 21, 1967.

tently interested in establishing links with, if not actual direction of, the relationships between refugees and the host government. In the early struggles of such a movement, refugees are its chief source of recruits and, to a lesser extent, of funds and information. Moreover, since refugee administration attracts additional funds from abroad, a hand in administering and servicing refugees may afford nationalists the opportunity to siphon off funds for personal or group use. Even more important, however, is the special problem that arises where two or more nationalist movements function within a host country. Competition can become fierce as they vie with one another for the allegiance of the refugees. The competition in Congo between the Serviço de Assistência dos Refugiados de Angola (Angolan Refugees' Assistance Service, SARA), an affiliate of UPA/GRAE, and the Corpo Voluntário Angolano de Assistência dos Refugiados (Angolan Volunteer Group for Assistance of Refugees, CVAAR), associated with MPLA, was of critical importance for their access to potential recruits and followers.[15] Even more disruptive has been the physical struggle in Zambia between the ZAPU and ZANU organizations. Occasional reports have appeared of press-ganging among refugees from Rhodesia in the African townships of Lusaka. At one point Zambian authorities expelled 52 refugee Zambabwians to Tanzania.[16] Zambia became particularly alarmed with the strongarm methods used in search of potential guerrillas, particularly when ZAPU and ZANU preyed upon Zambian citizens. Tanzania also has seen threats, fights, and assassinations between competing nationalist movements and within them as well.

REFUGEES AND EXILES AS LINKAGE GROUPS

The concept of "linkage group" might be useful in explicating the complex of emerging relationships. Karl W. Deutsch regards linkage groups as critical in the flow of communications between a political system and the environment in which it

15. Marcum, *The Angolan Revolution*, pp. 305–6.
16. *Daily Nation*, Nairobi, October 16, 1968. The actual nature of Zambian assistance to guerrilla movements is outlined in Anglin, op. cit., pp. 504–7.

functions.[17] He sees a linkage group as being within a single political system. It is the transmission belt through which outside forces may penetrate the internal system. In many respects refugee groups and exile politicians might be regarded as linkage groups, but some structural modifications of the simplified Deutschian model are in order. Although they are spatially within the political system of the host government, they are not really of that system, particularly if one concentrates as does Deutsch on communications patterns and the measures of influence exercised by and upon the linkage group. That the host government can influence activities of the exiles and refugees is obvious, but host governments and refugees-exiles alike regard this situation as a temporary symbiotic relationship, especially insofar as the revolutionaries can serve as an instrument of the host country's foreign policy. In the early stages of many revolutionary wars what appear to exist are two sections of each linkage group, one external (resident in a host territory) and one internal (functioning within the target territory), and both functioning as linkage groups and in direct contact with one another.

Each linkage group is bombarded with messages and pressures from diverse sources—the host government, the target government, competing nationalist movements, and various international refugee organizations. There is a myriad of flow patterns affecting these linkage groups. Unfortunately our level of reliable and comparative data does not permit us to operationalize this model and subject it to thorough scrutiny. Nevertheless, such a schema sheds light on the patterns of contact, some of which have been heretofore overlooked or regarded as unimportant.

To continue the description of relationships, what the host and the internal-external nationalists would like is eventually to see the external refugees return to their homelands. Such refugees would join with the refugees inside the target territory

17. "External Influences on the Internal Behavior of States," in Farrell, ed., *Approaches to Comparative and International Politics*, pp. 5–26.

and thereby augment the nationalist movement. With guerrilla victories in the field the internal refugees led by the nationalists inside would be expected to grow in number and ultimately assume governmental authority in the target. Meanwhile the cordial relationships between the host government and the visiting nationalists would continue. The internal-external nationalists become the organizational expression and vanguard of this movement. Thus, external refugees can be viewed by the host as an instrument of its foreign policy. And the host in turn can be viewed by the nationalists and refugees as a vehicle for the fulfillment of their policy goals. Problems emerge when policy preferences of the nationalists and refugees begin to conflict with those favored by the host. Host countries are not usually friendly with the government of the target territory. But they do wish to be able to control the pattern and pace of relationships. Here then we come upon the issue of autonomy and control of nationalist movements.

THE QUESTION OF CONTROL

Among other things, the revolutionary nationalists are interested in creating fighting forces capable of defeating those of the target government. As such, nationalist movements represent concentrations of organized, trained, and armed men—concentrations that could become a problem in internal security for the host government. In addition to the normal difficulties posed by outsiders in one's territory there are a number of special problems that emerge because of the size and nature of forces and their training and orientation toward guerrilla warfare. In the first instance, they might directly confront the host government with demands the host government might find contrary to its perceived interests, as the Arab guerrillas did in Lebanon and Jordan. In the second instance, segments might break away from the dominant nationalist revolutionary leadership and wage warfare against their compatriots in the territory of the host government. A third possible problem is that members of the revolutionary movement might become disillusioned and sell their weapons to dissident elements of the local population of the host territory, thereby facilitating civil war, as when eastern Congolese rebel refugees sold weapons to southern Sudanese fighters in 1964–65, and when the Somali shiftas who had been fighting on the borders of Kenya and Ethiopia sold weapons to Turkana border raiders along the Kenya-Uganda frontier in 1966–67. Fourth, revolutionary forces might be so effective as to provoke the forces of the target territory to retaliate directly or indirectly against objectives within the host country, thereby precipitating a confrontation between host and target forces. All of these possibilities are contingencies of which the host governments are aware.

The seriousness of the problems is affected, of course, by the relative strengths of the fighting forces. The revolutionary nationalist army may be as large in size as that of the host territory (see tables 9 (*b*) and 12). In Tanzania, for example, the army has 10,000 men, and FRELIMO alone claims a fighting force of up to 8,500. To be sure, most of these men are not in Tanzania at any one time, but they could be in the event that fighting were to break out with host forces.[18] In addition, Tanzania serves as a training ground for several hundred guerrilla fighters from other movements in camps (such as Bagamoyo, Kongwa, and Morogoro) in the north. Their presence can add complications. Zambia's difficulties are slightly different, since the Zambian force of some 4,500 men must be widely deployed to defend not only the border with Rhodesia but also those areas along the borders with Angola and Mozambique where incidents have occurred. Although combined guerrilla forces within Zambia probably do not equal those of the national army, their distribution could leave Zambia vulnerable to the sorts of unrest mentioned above. The Congo (Kinshasa) has some 45,000 men in its armed forces, and should have no difficulty in controlling guest nationalists, but the country's peculiar political problems of internal disintegration and secession and the unfortunate history of its national army tempt conjecture about its ability to control nationalist forces, especially since GRAE's own fol-

18. See *ARB*, VII, 1785C–86A, July 15, 1970, for an account of a plot aimed at overthrowing the Nyerere government and ostensibly to involve PAC fighters. Also *NYT*, July 19, 1970, p. 12.

lowing is so highly concentrated among the politically conscious and strategically located Bakongo.

Understandably, host governments have been sensitive to these issues and have sought noncoercive means to regularize the situation. They have by no means neglected the training, force levels, weaponry, or deployment of their armies. But their chief instruments have been their favorable political and ideological relationships with nationalist movements and their function as coordinators and channels for assistance to the movements from abroad. The movements are thereby dependent on host governments for continued effectiveness, particularly in the early stages when the host is most vulnerable because of the presence of large numbers of guerrillas. A few unfavorable key decisions by host governments could be even more debilitating to the nationalist movements than physical suppression by the host government or a display of force.

EXTERNAL DANGERS

Through its initial willingness to receive refugees and to entertain and support nationalist movements, a host government becomes an obvious and sometimes vulnerable object for retaliatory action by the target government. Reprisal might take numerous forms, from outright declaration of war and physical invasion to more subtle incursive and subversive techniques, or there might be no reaction at all. Target governments have sought to play upon the evident sense of insecurity of host governments and thereby intimidate them and persuade them to limit, withhold, or withdraw support from nationalist guerrilla movements.

Warnings have been subtle as well as ostentatiously open. All three target governments have used them. As was noted earlier, Portuguese Foreign Minister Nogueira has alluded to a doctrine of "legitimate retaliation" growing out of the establishment of guerrilla bases in southern Tanzania. The most blatant threat by a top official of the white South was made by South Africa's Prime Minister Vorster in October 1967: "If you [Zambia] want to try violence," he told a Nationalist Party rally at Rustenburg, "as you have advised other States in

Africa, we will hit you so hard that you will never forget it."[19] Defence Minister P. W. Botha warned African states that a continuation of their assistance to rebel groups could provoke a South African counterstrike at guerrilla camps like the action by Israel against Jordan-based guerrilla attacks. South African army and air force officers have been notably impressed by the Israeli attacks in the 1967 war and by the Israeli doctrine of "anticipatory counter-attack."[20] The Israeli analogy is a popular one in South Africa, not just for tactical military purposes, but from a Biblical and ideological perspective and as an argument for South African policy in the face of its systematic isolation.

But threat alone does not constitute policy. What, in fact, has actually been done in retaliation? Tanzania and Zambia have reported overflights of their air space by Portuguese, Rhodesian, and South African planes—not just light aircraft for spotting and leaflet drops, but modified Canberras on photographic missions. Zambian authorities also have reported bombing and strafing attacks by Portuguese jet fighters against Zambian villages suspected of harboring guerrilla infiltrators. In December 1968 the *Times of Zambia* reported that Portugal had offered to pay compensation for damage to Zambian life and property. The newspaper claimed that the Portuguese, through successful representations by Zambia to Portugal at the UN, had been satisfied "beyond doubt" that their forces were responsible for six separate incidents. Within two days the Portuguese Ministry of Foreign Affairs stated that this report was not correct. While confirming the indemnity payments, the Portuguese claimed that the incidents had taken place on the borders and had been provoked by "terrorists" which the governments of Zambia permitted in its territory. At any rate, reports of air raids have persisted.[21]

19. As reported in *ARB*, IV, 891B, November 15, 1967. See also the statement by Ian Smith quoted in *The Star*, February 14, 1970, p. 4.
20. See the account of an address by General Mordechai Hod, commander of the Israeli air force, to the officers of the Air Force College, Voortrekkerhoogte, and their reactions to it. *Sunday Express*, Johannesburg, September 10, 1967.
21. *The Times of Zambia* account of December 6, 1968 and the Portu-

In response, both Tanzania and Zambia have sought to reinforce their air defenses. Tanzania has acquired surface-to-air missiles of Chinese manufacture and Russian "Sam" design. These missiles are thought to be capable of hitting aircraft at altitudes up to 50,000 feet, but are not practicable for use against low-flying Portuguese planes.[22] Zambia began in 1968 to negotiate with the British Aircraft Corporation for the purchase of Rapier, Bloodhound, or Thunderbird missiles. Largely impressed by arguments that the high-altitude missiles demanded large, highly skilled ground crews which would be expensive to maintain, the Zambians ultimately decided on the Rapier, a mobile weapon effective up to 10,000 feet.[23] The contract was subsequently suspended by Zambia until British arms policy toward South Africa should be clarified to its satisfaction.

Ground incursions by armed forces from Rhodesia, Angola, Mozambique, and South West Africa, usually in pursuit of retreating guerrilla units, have been common, particularly onto Zambian and Congolese soil. The Ruvuma River border of Tanzania renders such incursions a blatant violation of an obvious demarcation. There have been reports also of unexplained bombings in Tanzanian villages at night and of firings across the river.[24] All this has led to deployments of the armed and police forces of host governments. The Portuguese have sought to enlist border officials of at least two host countries—Malawi and the Congo (and Katanga during its declared independence)—to collaborate by either arresting or harrassing infiltrators and refugees, and by tipping off the Portuguese officials about suspected incursions.[25] Vorster's surprise

guese denial are reported in *ARB*, V, 1276A–B, January 15, 1969. According to the foreign minister of Zambia, 25 air violations by the Portuguese alone between May 18, 1966, and June 30, 1969. *ARB*, VI, 1478B–C, August 15, 1969.

22. *East African Standard*, February 12, 1968.

23. See Hall, *The High Price*, pp. 186–88; *Rhodesia Herald*, August 20 and 21, 1969; *Sunday Times*, Johannesburg, August 31, 1969.

24. Representative cases can be found in *ARB*: VI, 1305A, February 15, 1969, and V, 1251A, December 15, 1968, and 1275C, January 15, 1969.

25. Marcum, *The Angolan Revolution*, pp. 234–35, 297–98.

announcements and then denial of South African hot pursuit into Zambia in 1971 sparked a complaint to the UN.[26] There have been reports of kidnapings and illegal arrests of suspected guerrillas by white southern African police within black-governed territory. The international ramifications of such cases—for example, the Ramotse arrest in Botswana—merit future detailed exploration.[27] The confusion and insecurity along certain parts of the borders between host and target territories has led to heightened tensions and to threatening, but by no means major, troop concentrations. It has not led as yet to massive interventions.

The effect of such military pressure upon the governments of host countries is hard to assess. It has not led to any withdrawal of open support for nationalist movements, although the target governments have other means at their disposal, particularly vis-à-vis Zambia and, to a lesser extent, the Congo. Since economic questions have been dealt with in Chapter 2, one example of economic pressure should be illustrative. Zambia is heavily dependent on land transport to export its copper. The Benguela Railway via the Congo and Angola to the port of Lobito is one important route especially since the Rhodesian UDI, and Zambian officials want to free Zambia from an inordinate dependence upon the other rail route through Rhodesia to Beira in Mozambique. In March 1967, UNITA guerrillas operating out of Zambia managed to cut the Benguela Railway despite a Zambian directive to cease attacks on this vital link. Tanganyika Concessions Limited, an essentially British-owned holding company which owns some 90 percent of the railway, then pressured the Portuguese to demand that Zambia clamp down on Angolan nationalists operating out of Zambia. For three days through traffic on the line was disrupted, giving the governments of both Zambia and the Congo (which also uses the line for shipments from Katanga) a chance to see what the consequences would be if Portugal carried out its threats to close the line. The Zambians responded by refusing to renew the residence permit of UNITA leader Jonas Savimbi, who

26. *ARB*, VIII, 2252A–53B, November 15, 1971.
27. See *Spotlight on South Africa*, VIII, 1, September 14, 1970.

moved to Cairo. Savimbi's departure, however, can additionally be attributed to his involvement in Zambian domestic political intrigues.[28] Since then UNITA's effectiveness has been limited. Understandably, Zambia is sensitive to economic pressure from white-dominated governments, and there is no dearth of instruments by which this pressure can be exerted, at least until a politically more reliable rail link is available.

The perils, of course, are not all one-sided. Each party—the host government and the nationalist movement—uses the other constantly. The guerrillas have been, in effect, an instrument for host countries' foreign policies. The foreign policy aims of some host governments are manifestly interventionist. Policy statements urge the destruction of white-dominated governments by force. But resources and possible risks and retaliations dictate caution. Thus, the presence of willing fighters, to the extent that their policy aims coincide with those of the host governments, enable the host to substitute a more defensible sort of activity—assistance and encouragement for peoples struggling to attain self-determination—for one of doubtful legality as well as wisdom—direct military intervention against more powerful states.[29]

Revolutionary nationalists afford the host government a weapon for covert, informal attack against ideologically hostile neighbors without committing the host's own troops to battle outside its boundaries. And host politicians' stock as bona fide revolu-

28. Whitaker, op. cit. (in n. 3 above), pp. 17–18, sheds light on this facet of the incident.

Davidson argues that Savimbi's expulsion was in 1968 and resulted from his breaking of the Zambian ban on organizing refugees and partly on suspicion of Savimbi's alleged associations with the U.S. Central Intelligence Agency. See "Angola in the Tenth Year," *African Affairs*, LXX (January 1971), 43–44. See also Anglin, op. cit. (in n. 13 above), pp. 510–13.

29. Intervention is used here in the sense suggested in Rosenau, "Intervention as a Scientific Concept," *Journal of Conflict Resolution*, XIII (1969), 149–71. This narrow usage involves "convention-breaking" behavior which is "authority-oriented"—that is, the behavior of one international actor toward another whenever the behavior "constitutes a sharp break with then-existing forms *and* whenever it is directed at changing or preserving the structure of political authority in the target society" (p. 161).

tionary nationalists can soar as well. These sorts of symbiotic ties have long been utilized by the Great Powers in similar circumstances.[30] The presence of refugees and guerrillas gives the host governments a measure of access and choice otherwise difficult to secure. Moreover, it creates debts and obligations that may, in the future, be advantageous. The coincidence of goals between guerrilla forces and host governments may be fortuitous, but it enables the host government to conduct a more active foreign policy with respect to white-dominated southern Africa, a policy that otherwise would have been primarily passive (boycotts, statements, votes at the UN, resolutions, and other efforts to isolate, politically, economically, and diplomatically, the target governments).

External Support for White Governments

The question of external support is considerably more important for the nationalist movements than for the white governments of southern Africa. Without a host country and material and financial assistance few nationalists would be able to function at any level of effectiveness. In contrast, the problem for the white government is not financial—it can find funds for defense expenditures—but political. Thus, in the strict sense, it is incorrect to describe arms and war material deals, except those that have been made between Portugal, Rhodesia, and South Africa, as assistance or aid. Rather, these governments must convince foreign governments to permit arms manufacturers to sell to them. Although a license permitting arms exports to South Africa or Portugal may greatly help those countries, it is not foreign assistance as the term is generally used.

The Republic of South Africa has been able to secure war materials, though some measure of duplicity has been needed. In 1963 a resolution of the UN Security Council called for a total embargo on the sale of arms, ammunition, and military vehicles to the RSA, with which the United States, Canada,

30. See Scott, "Internal Violence as an Instrument of Cold Warfare," in Rosenau, ed., *International Aspects of Civil Strife*, pp. 154–69.

Switzerland, and West Germany complied. Britain and France claimed the right to sell arms provided these were "not suitable for dealing with internal troubles." Thus a producing state may unilaterally determine that a particular class of weapons are primarily for defense against external enemies. It then goes ahead and licenses the sale. Is the ANC of South Africa, then, an external enemy? If we accept the position of the South African minister of police that not a single "terrorist" is at large in the republic, then any arms sale to the RSA would be legitimate since all its enemies are, ipso facto, external. At any rate, these are virtually meaningless distinctions since South Africa is practically self-sufficient in the manufacture of the less sophisticated weapons of counterinsurgency.

More complex and expensive weapon systems, however, are supplied from abroad. Since the UN resolution, for example, submarines and aircraft have been purchased by the RSA in France. A "Cactus" air defense system based on ground-to-air missiles has been developed in South Africa in concert with France. Britain, although eliminated as a principal supplier of weapons, has sold parts for them to South Africa. Obviously, the embargo can be evaded with impunity. Moreover, South Africa undertook a major renewal and expansion of heavy equipment from 1960 to 1964, and thereby diminished the impact of the UN action, which came too late to be effective. Only when one considers strategic materials such as oil can one justifiably talk about South African vulnerability.

Far more significant is Portugal's NATO association.[31] Without this, Portugal would be militarily incapable of sustaining the level of military operations it conducts in Africa. Armaments which it has acquired as a member of NATO have been used in Africa. Portugal's NATO partners insist that these weapons are to be used exclusively for defense in the North Atlantic area, but the provisions to that effect in the NATO treaty have been difficult to apply. Moreover, although it is

31. Fairly complete coverage of this issue can be found in Bosgra and van Krimpen, *Portugal and NATO*, a pamphlet which carefully documents the importance of this relationship and concludes that NATO members and NATO as an organization are crucial accessories to the Portuguese military campaigns in Africa.

clear that weapons acquired by virtue of Portugal's NATO membership are used in Africa, Portugal's main benefit from such armaments is that its domestic-European military requirements are assured, and consequently its own less impressive resources are freed for full use in Africa. A second benefit related to the first is that through NATO membership Portugal more easily can purchase weapons from manufacturers in NATO countries: Norway has refused to make any such sales to Portugal, but all other member states permit sales, usually seeking to extract a promise that the weapons will not be used outside the treaty area. Portugal maintains that their use is only for defensive purposes "within Portuguese territory," on the grounds that its African possessions are "overseas territories," not colonies, and thus an integral part of Portugal.

Further financial benefits come to Portugal under the cost-sharing formula whereby each NATO country pays what it can afford in meeting the costs of the NATO infrastructure. For Portugal this amounts to only 0.28 percent of the total. But since a number of NATO installations are in Portugal, an estimated $6 million in NATO funds is spent there annually. To this is added the $10 million per year pumped into the Portuguese economy by the United States armed forces, mostly through the Azores base, where approximately $500 million was spent for construction in 1959–65.[32] The 1971 treaty which extends use of the base facilities in the Azores makes even greater American assistance to the Portuguese likely. West Germany, France, and the United States are the chief sources of military supplies for Portugal. Their pooled knowledge of and experience with guerrilla warfare and modern weapons has been transmitted to Portuguese officers and military planners as well.

Both Portugal and South Africa have expended considerable energy trying to convince NATO military men that the most

32. There are summary discussions of U.S.-Portuguese military relations in Marcum, *The Angolan Revolution*, pp. 182–87, 272–77; Marcum, "The United States and Portuguese Africa," paper presented at the African Studies Association meeing, Denver, November 3–6, 1971; Diamond and Fouquet, "Portugal and the United States," *Africa Report*, XV (May 1970), 15–17, and Davidson, "Arms and the Portuguese," ibid., pp. 10–11.

vulnerable flank of NATO is the South Atlantic and particularly southern Africa. Playing upon Britain's withdrawal of forces from east of Suez as creating a vacuum that the Soviet Union and especially the Soviet naval forces seek to fill, both countries have pushed for the creation of a South Atlantic treaty organization which would be a part of NATO or would be coordinated with it. Whether or not NATO governments like the idea, South Africa regards itself as part of an organization to defend western European civilization against communist and racial incursion. In South African eyes it is just a matter of time before NATO recognizes South Africa's strategic importance and comes to respect and support its defensive contribution.[33]

Traditional Components of Military Power and Revolutionary Innovation

It is quite clear from a comparative lineup of the military forces and matériel available to the states of southern Africa that the white-dominated South has a considerable advantage in regular force levels. (See table 12.)[34] What is more, the imbalance is growing. To take the most important example, South Africa's defense estimates showed an eightfold increase from 1960 to 1970, and have mounted further since then:[35]

33. The South African position is well served by various military institutions in the West. See Royal United Services Institute for Defense Studies, *The Cape Route* (1970) and the same Institute's *The Security of the Southern Oceans—Southern Africa the Key* (1972). President Kaunda's appraisal of South Africa's defense relationship with NATO was expressed in a broadcast on December 11, 1969, and quoted at length in *Spotlight on South Africa*, VIII, 3–4, January 12, 1970.

34. For an excellent description and discussion of this matter see Anglin, "The International Arms Traffic," in *Working Papers*, pp. 7–37.

35. The amounts are in rands (1R=US $1.40) and are from Vernon McKay, "Southern Africa and Its Implications for American Foreign Policy," in Hance, ed., *Southern Africa and the United States*, pp. 12–15; two Institute for Strategic Studies reports, *The Military Balance, 1970–1971*, p. 52, and *The Military Balance, 1971–1972*, p. 38; and *The Star*, April 1, 1972, p. 2. Commentaries on South Africa's military buildup are in Legum and Legum, *South Africa*, pp. 204–12, and Minty, *South Africa's Defence Strategy*.

TABLE 12
APPROXIMATE MILITARY FORCE LEVELS, 1970–71

Country or territory	*Regular army*	*Full-trained reserves*	*Air force*	*Navy*	*Police*	*Police Reserves*	*Armed Militia*
Botswana	None	None	None	None	1,000	None	None
Congo (Kinshasa)	45,000	None	850	150	20,800	n.a.	n.a.
Lesotho	None	None	None	None	1,325	None	None
Malawi	1,150	n.a.	n.a.	n.a	3,000	n.a.	n.a.
Swaziland	None	None	None	None	700	None	None
Tanzania	10,000	4,000	500	600	8,500	n.a.	n.a.
Zambia	4,500	1,000	1,000	n.a.	6,250	1,600	n.a.
Angola	60,000	n.a.	3,000	3,500	5,500	n.a.	15,000
Mozambique	45,000	n.a.	2,700	3,500	1,500	n.a.	7,000
Rhodesia	3,400	8,000	1,200	n.a.	6,400	28,500	n.a.
South Africa	32,000[a]	23,000	8,000	4,250	34,437	20,000	78,000

SOURCES: Richard Booth, *The Armed Forces of African States, 1970* (London, 1970); Institute for Strategic Studies, *The Military Balance, 1971–1972* (London, 1971); and numerous other reports.

[a]Includes citizen force under training at any given time.

n.a. = not available.

1960/61	R 43,591,000	1966/67	R 255,850,000
1961/62	71,550,000	1968/69	253,000,000
1962/63	119,775,000	1969/70	271,600,000
1963/64	157,111,000	1970/71	257,100,000
1964/65	210,000,000	1971/72	316,500,000 (budgeted)
1965/66	230,000,000	1972/73	344,040,000 (budgeted)

In April 1969 the minister of defence stated in a white paper that over the next five years nearly R1,647 million would be spent on defense.[36] By contrast, in the five years from 1962/63 to 1966/67, years of major reorganization and the search for self-sufficiency in armaments, slightly more than half of that amount was expended. The standing armed forces (the army, air force, and navy) had been steadily augmented, from 7,721 in 1961 to 18,000 in 1971. Comparable increases have occurred in practically every branch of the regular and reserve security forces.

Moreover, South Africa is consciously trying to make its military forces self-sufficient by developing the economic infrastructure and the defense industries to maintain them, even under conditions of psychological siege. As a response to the international campaign for an arms embargo, research on new weapons manufacture was instituted, not without significant success. In May 1968, Parliament passed legislation to enable the government to establish a state-owned armaments industry, Armaments Development and Production Corporation of South Africa (ARMSCOR), with a share capital of more than R100 million. There have been rapid increases in budget provisions for the manufacture of munitions and weapons.[37] Belgian FN rifles (under special license), small planes, ammunitions of various calibers, radio and service equipment, mortars, and armored cars are now being manufactured in South Africa. Even more sophisticated weaponry is being tested and manufactured, including rockets, and systems purchased abroad are

36 *The Star* (daily edition), April 26, 1969.

37. From R368,000 in 1960–61 to R51,102,000 in 1965–66. McKay, in Hance, ed., *Southern Africa and the United States*, p. 14. See also *The Star*, February 14, 1970, p. 5, noting the government's decision to take over "the full technical responsibility" for a major privately-owned munitions plant.

being placed into operation.[38] Oil refining and steel production in the republic have expanded tremendously since 1960. In short, South Africa is coming to regard itself as a potential arsenal for the rest of southern Africa, including black-governed states. In contrast, the debilitating economic problems related to development with only scarce resources make such an augmentation of force levels almost impossible for the black states to the north.

In some respects the same developmental problems apply to Portuguese military expansion.[39] By 1968 defense expenditures were swallowing almost 50 percent of the total regular budget of Portugal, and the proportion has continued at or around this level. For a country as poor as Portugal this is a tremendous outlay. Still, Mozambique and Angola are potentially valuable territorial assets. Their economic possibilities are just beginning to be appreciated in Lisbon, Pretoria, New York, London, and elsewhere. For economic reasons, among others, Lisbon thinks they are worth fighting for. Whether or not the effort can be sustained at present or even accelerated rates is conjectural. Some commentators argue that the wars have stimulated economic expansion and reform in the long-stagnant colonies. At least one Portuguese businessman is reported to have said: "We really should build a monument to the terrorists. If it weren't for them we wouldn't have any development at all."[40] Nevertheless, any rational economist must conclude that this is an inefficient way to stimulate long-range development, and the result, as in Vietnam, is a distorted economy, by no means prepared for sustained growth.

38. For example, *Sunday Times*, Johannesburg, August 3, 1969, pp. 8–9. As early as 1965 the defence minister somewhat exaggeratedly boasted that South Africa was not only self-sufficient in the production of armaments for an "African" war, but could also supply all the neighboring states with weapons and even export certain arms to Western Europe. Rhoodie, *The Third Africa*, p. 196.
39. Information for these paragraphs was gleaned from Wheeler, "The Portuguese Army in Angola," *JMAS*, VII (1969), 425–39, and from Herrick et al., *Area Handbook for Angola*, pp. 375–90, and *Area Handbook for Mozambique*, pp. 287–313.
40. Quoted in "The Skirmishes Aren't the Real War," *Economist*, January 25, 1969, pp. 37–38.

The overall imbalance in force levels and military matériel between the black-governed states and those of white southern Africa is compounded by the inexperience of the black states' soldiers and officers, and by those states' immense problems of communication, logistics, and supply and their lack of support services. Moreover, the loyalty of their military men is, at least, subject to debate. Against this, the white-governed states have relatively modern equipment and weapons, and their generally mobilizable reserve forces (except in the Portuguese territories, where paramilitary civilian "volunteers" and African militia units are of questionable reliability) could perhaps multiply field forces four or five times.

The Military "Alliances"

COOPERATION AMONG AFRICAN NATIONALISTS

Within the Pretoria-Lisbon-Salisbury axis there seems to be evidence of a good deal more military cooperation between partners than in the North. Despite the entreaties of men like Kwame Nkrumah that Africa or the OAU should establish a functional, unified military force, nothing of this sort has emerged. The OAU's Liberation Committee has sought to pressure various movements and states to coordinate and cooperate in their common endeavors, but results are meager. There is also an OAU Military Commission, and conferences of "military experts" are conducted periodically to the same effect. The military coordination that has taken place has come essentially from the nationalist movements themselves. Since the summer of 1967, ZAPU-ANC forces have worked together in organizing incursions into Rhodesia. But this cooperation may have, in the short run, been counterproductive, since it has provided the South African government with a rationale for *open* collaboration with Rhodesian security forces. The South Africans would have joined in anyway, but the circumstances provided a way to represent their efforts to the outside world as legitimate. There have also been reports of joint COREMO-PAC infiltration routes through Mozambique and MPLA-SWAPO cooperation in Angola, but so far these have been on such a small scale as to be little more than symbolic.[41] On the other hand, some infiltrating insurgents have been faced by the hostility of some black governments. Lesotho, notably, has actually suggested that it is prepared to cooperate with South Africa to eradicate "communism" and "terrorism."[42] Some other states have tightened regulations on their activities (for example, Botswana, Malawi, and Swaziland). Further, field competition between groups (as in the case of the MPLA and GRAE) occasionally reaches violent proportions.

Nevertheless, "alliances" of a sort have been attempted, although the measure of actual military planning and cooperation undertaken is a matter of speculation. Mostly they have grown up in exile and their existence has not been reflected in the field. Examples of these are the Conferência das Organizações Nacionalistas dos Colónias Portuguesas (Conference of Nationalist Organizations of the Portuguese Colonies, CONCP), the "Khartoum Alliance," and the "Congo Alliance." (See table 10 for memberships of these organizations.) These amorphous groups have arisen largely because of the immobilism of the OAU's ALC, and as bargaining units vis-à-vis the ALC, which was initially assigned the responsibility for the coordination of strategies. The nationalists found themselves being victimized by the political disputes among the independent states of Africa. The ALC members as well as other OAU members and the host countries were unable and unwilling to defer their own intra-African squabbles in order to assist the liberation of their brothers to the south. Realizing this, certain nationalist movements (on the basis of one movement per country—after all, they too had many petty as well as profound divisions that prevented all-out coordination) pooled their leverage to facilitate their struggle.[43] The oldest and most effective coalition has

41. See *ARB*, V, 1102A–B, July 15, 1968, and "Communist-Backed Southern Africa Terrorist Onslaught," *Africa Institute Bulletin*, VI (June 1968), 130–48.
42. *ARB*, V, 974A, March 15, 1968.
43. For a brief discussion of these points see Marcum, "The Exile Condition," in Dale and Potholm, eds., *Southern Africa in Perspective*, and Marcum, "Three Revolutions," *Africa Report*, XII (November 1967), 9–22.

been the CONCP, formally established in December 1961. In 1967 CONCP parties linked up with the incipient ZAPU-ANC alliance, and in concert with SWAPO, participated in the Khartoum conference of January 1969. The resulting "alliance" is functionally and organizationally loose, but at least the idea of the necessity for regional coordination is implanted.

As a reaction to this coalition, an anti-CONCP combination emerged, first in 1963–64 and again in 1967, with the encouragement of the Congo (Kinshasa) and perhaps of the Chinese People's Republic. Known as the "Congo Alliance," it is an exceedingly informal combination limited to occasional consultation and based on common dependence on either Peking or Kinshasa. To regard these combinatory efforts or the various resolutions and joint declarations by other African bodies as anything approaching military alliance is, however, misleading. In striking contrast with this is the picture in the South.

WHITE REGIONAL PARTNERSHIP

Speaking in January 1968, a South African official said that South Africans truly realized that if the soldiers maintained by Portugal in Angola and Mozambique were to be withdrawn, South Africa could become involved in a "terrorist war" within weeks. He went on to say that the Portuguese territories and Rhodesia had become South Africa's first line of defense.[44] This was but one recent expression of a philosophy that has been recognized for some time.

The Defence Act of 1913 provided that South African armed forces would serve in South Africa, both inside and outside the Union of South Africa, but the effect was to restrict their service to the then High Commission Territories, South West Africa,

44. T. J. A. Gerdener, the administrator of Natal Province, speaking at a meeting to establish the fund mentioned below. *Africa Diary*, VIII, 3753, January 14–20, 1968. This viewpoint is especially widespread in Natal, where the Durban *Sunday Times* has tried to evoke sympathy for the Portuguese position. See particularly the series of feature articles by Aida Parker around Christmas 1967. See also the alarmist broadside, "What This War Means to South Africa" (n.d.), released by the the Mozambique/Angola Soldiers' Comforts Fund from postal box addresses in Cape Town and Durban.

and Southern Rhodesia. Defence Minister Oswald Pirow argued in 1939 that the purpose of the Union Defence Force was limited to helping settler communities in British Africa, should Africans revolt.[45] Since the outbreak of war in Angola, however, initial misgivings about the reliability of Portugal as an ally (a product of a sense of Anglo-Saxon superiority in South Africa) have been overcome. Although many Afrikaners still have their doubts about a too close identity with the Latin Portuguese (who are, after all, Roman Catholic, and who publicly profess multiracialism), South African officials have sought to coordinate greater military cooperation, in planning and practice, with their regional white neighbors. At first, in the early 1960s, this involved Portugal and the old Central African Federation; it now includes the Smith government of Rhodesia. Claims of an "unholy alliance" have been in the news since about 1961. Officials of Portugal, Rhodesia, and South Africa repeatedly deny the existence of any formal alliance. On one such occasion Prime Minister Vorster said: "We are good friends with both Portugal and Rhodesia, and good friends do not need a pact. Good friends know what their duty is if a neighbour's house is on fire. I assure you that whatever becomes necessary will be done."[46] It is generally believed both by whites in the region and by African nationalists that South Africa will do whatever is necessary to try to prevent revolutionary nationalists from nearing her borders. Although rumors persist, whether or not the alliance has been formalized is not crucial. In practice collaboration is extensive.

After the eruption of the war in Angola, the South African defence minister visited Lisbon, and increased collaboration soon became evident and speculation as to secret arrangements grew.[47] There was a time when the cooperation extended into

45. Spence, *Republic under Pressure*, pp. 7–8.

46. *ARB*, IV, 845C, September 15, 1967. For a similar Portuguese statement see *ARB*, VI, 1452B–C, July 15, 1969.

47. For example, *Africa Diary*, II, 557, May 19–25, 1962; *The Star*, September 29, 1962, and March 16, 1963; *Le Monde*, September 14, 1965; Ainslie, *The Unholy Alliance*; "The Council of Three," *The Times*, March 12, 1968; and the numerous reports in Angola Comité, *Facts and Reports*, 1971–72.

black Africa itself. Until 1963 both the Central African Federation and the Katangese government of Moise Tshombe took part in the arrangements.[48] The Katangese secessionists were materially assisted by the Portuguese and the South Africans, and in return the Portuguese were assisted in surveillance of the Katanga-Angola frontier, UPA offices in Elisabethville were closed and UPA officials—so leaders of the association claim—were turned over to Portuguese authorities. Current cooperation between the South African, Rhodesian, and Portuguese armed forces extends to training, consultation, and joint maneuvers and border patrols. In addition there have been frequent reports of the presence of South African military men in the fighting areas and of South African supply helicopters and even bases in the region. The three governments see their futures militarily intertwined.

Although South Africa and Rhodesia openly admit the presence of South African forces in Rhodesia, hard evidence of the extent of South African military participation is difficult to secure. The most obvious manifestation of cooperation surfaced during the August 1967 nationalist infiltration into Rhodesia.[49] Prime Minister Vorster officially confirms reports that South African "police" are assisting the Rhodesian security forces. Actually, however, the assistance is far more significant than that of police units. Before the 1967 infiltrations South African military forces had been training Rhodesian anti-guerrilla patrols in the Zambezi Valley, and these units, which included helicopters, were pressed into service, probably in August.[50] Special police were flown in to interrogate prisoners, an additional so-called police unit joined the Rhodesian forces in the Wankie area, and an armored car unit of "police" arrived in September. ZAPU estimated that approximately 500 South African men were in the field with the Rhodesian forces. Responsible esti-

48. Marcum and Lowenstein, in Davis and Baker, eds., *Southern Africa in Transition*, pp. 272–73.
49. Colin Legum in *The Observer*, August 27, 1967.
50. Ibid. Kaunda charged that South African police and army personnel had several times landed a helicopter at Katimo Mulilo on Zambia's southwestern boundary, close to the Caprivi Strip. *ARB*, IV, 891A–C, November 15, 1967.

mates range as high as 3,000 during the subsequent period. There is also some indication that South Africa attempted to disguise the extent of its involvement by painting its helicopters in Rhodesian colors and by putting some of the troops into police uniforms.[51] It would appear, therefore, that South Africa is intent on maintaining the current governments in Rhodesia, Angola, and Mozambique, even to the point of committing its military forces in their defense. It is direct assistance like this that confims the confidence of Vorster and others that functional ad hoc arrangements serve the purpose of the status quo white governments adequately and can probably do so for some time to come, barring unprecedented Northern collaboration in the future.

On the surface it would seem that most of the strategic and diplomatic advantages lie with the status quo forces of white southern Africa. Normal economic and diplomatic ties strengthen and legitimize their rule. Working "alliances" serve to provide a cooperative common military front against revolutionary forces. Status quo defense expenditures are far larger than those of the African nationalist movements and their host governments. The military forces of the white-ruled countries are larger and better trained. Their matériel is more modern and serviceable. Their economic infrastructures and sectors are better able to sustain a protracted conflict. The more the communist states assist African revolutionaries, the more the Western states and NATO—judging from past performance—will feel obliged to prop up the minority white governments. The OAU and its ALC have shown no great ability to assist revolutionary parties materially, and repeated divisions within African and guerrilla ranks only confirm their reluctance to commit scarce resources to futile struggle. Even the host governments which heretofore have risked the most in helping guerrillas and standing up to white governments, seem reluctant to give guerrillas unlimited and unrestrained access to target territories. This is not to say that hosts are not committed to a destruction of the

51. Legassick, "The Consequences of African Guerrilla Activity," paper presented to the African Studies Association, New York, November 3, 1967, pp. 3, 11.

status quo in the South. Indeed they are, and they have courageously proven their commitment by rendering assistance. But they are not unaware that they are on the battleline and that they are, in a multitude of ways, vulnerable to penetration from abroad and to subversion from within.

This chapter and the preceding one have tried to demonstrate the complexity of relationships growing out of revolutionary nationalism and, in particular, guerrilla struggle. It should be evident that in the context of revolutionary warfare it is not enough to detail the distribution of the traditional components of military power. This seems to be the case in southern Africa especially. A classical military confrontation is not likely.

Suppose that a state could field 30,000 well-armed and reasonably well-trained soldiers, 35 jet fighters, and 15 helicopters, backed by 15,000 police. Of what use would these resources be if, at the outbreak of hostilities, the social and economic fabric of the state should collapse because of a lack of popular support for the government or the war? Few if any of the black states in southern Africa could be sure of all-out support for a military undertaking of general magnitude. Most discussions of military force levels generally assume an essential stability of the political and the economic systems necessary to sustain forces in the field, but this assumption should not go unquestioned. Similarly, although it seems certain that non-African actors will participate in any general conflict between the two sides, no one can be quite sure what the alignments and the extents of various external involvements would be. Most important of all is the knowledge gained by experience since World War II that vast numbers of troops, concentrated fire power, and sophisticated equipment are not alone adequate to defeat a well-organized and determined revolutionary movement. This is not to say that revolutionary movements cannot be defeated. Classic components of military power are not to be deprecated, for they serve as useful deterrents to potential rebels or to outside forces considering the prospects of intervention. Still, modern theories of guerrilla warfare maintain that to the traditional factors of warfare must be added a new appreciation of other factors—time, space, and political ideology—which are far less quantifiable and yet may well work to the advantage of insurgent elements.

There are a number of supplementary factors that would affect, if not determine, the balance. It may be useful to put them into the equation. Among such factors are (1) the problems of national integration, (2) the vulnerability of most national economies in the region, (3) the likelihood of external, non-African intervention,[52] and (4) the overall lack of experience on both sides. Reliable and comparable data on these and various other facets of the southern African problem are difficult to secure at present, particularly given the propaganda disseminated and the inaccessibility cultivated by both sides.

We have seen how the various nationalist revolutionary movements are aware of the possibilities open to them through protracted guerrilla warfare, and how some military thinkers and planners are also alert to such possibilities. Portugal, Rhodesia, and South Africa have concentrated on training and equipping their security forces for counterinsurgency operations. The creation of a white guerrilla force is also discussed. Commandant Neil Orpen of South Africa, for example, in his book *Total Defence*, advocates that South Africa begin to build up her irregular forces and train them in commando resistance, a tactic used with success by the Boers.

It is not easy to appraise the prospects of a full-scale military confrontation in southern Africa. Many are convinced that it will come and that it will be a long and bloody struggle. Others do not expect it, feeling that hostilities will drift along at their present level of intensity—a war of attrition in a low key. Still others, such as Lesotho's prime minister and the Malawian president are convinced that the white governments, should they put their mind to it, could triumph easily and quickly.[53] The difficulty is that no matter how precise our data

52. Deutsch has suggested ways to measure the direction and extent of outside intervention and the effectiveness of particularly ruthless or terrorizing tactics. See his "External Involvement in Internal War," in Eckstein ed., *Internal War*, pp. 100–110. Unfortunately the sorts of data needed to do the computations are not available or are unreliable for the southern African cases.

53. The shortest estimate was made by Chief Jonathan, who said that

on force levels and trends in military preparedness, there are many other important variables (mostly economic and political) for which reliable data are slight or not available.

South Africa, if attacked, would take no more than six hours to overwhelm Africa. *Africa Diary*, VIII, 3736, January 1–7, 1968. President Banda was more guarded when he said that South Africa and Rhodesia could conquer Africa as far as Cairo "tomorrow" if they wished, "and the United Nations would do nothing about it, just talk, talk and talk." *ARB*, V, 1144A–B, September 15, 1968. Even if we regard these statements as absurd or even more charitably as overly dramatic they do illustrate the tendency on the part of these leaders to disparage the military capabilities of black Africa and to inflate the strength of Rhodesia and South Africa.

7

South Africa's "Outward-Looking Policy" In Africa

A cow must graze where she is tied.
—*Sierra Leone*

The focus of this study thus far has been multi-national, with concentration on the regional sub-system. But emerging from this focus has been the obvious finding that the Republic of South Africa is the keystone of the region. Because of this, it becomes necessary to consider more systematically and comprehensively South Africa's foreign policy toward her neighbors, a policy popularly known as the "outward-looking policy."[1] In its broadest sense the outward-looking policy refers to the general effort by South Africa to break out of its isolated situation in the world. Thus this policy finds expression toward Latin America, Australia, Europe, and North America, as well as toward black- and white-governed states in Africa. For our purposes we shall examine primarily the outward-looking policy toward black Africa, its most challenging, sensitive, and controversial manifestation, and secondarily at South Africa's total

1. An excellent but unfortunately brief discussion of the key issues of the outward-looking policy is Molteno, *Africa and South Africa*.

regional policy. It is this combination of subjects that shall be referred to as the outward-looking policy. And since various specific features of this policy have been discussed throughout this study, it would be helpful here to place this policy in context; to look at the background, techniques, and patterns of the outward-looking policy; to discuss the official rationales, possible causes, and domestic political considerations; and finally to speculate on how far and in what directions the policy can develop.

Background

Although the roots of the outward-looking policy go back into the history of South Africa, the term itself is of relatively recent origin. Perhaps the first use of the term "outward" in reference to foreign policy was in 1961, in the title of a pamphlet of the South African Institute of Race Relations (SAIRR): *Looking Outwards: Three South African Viewpoints*.[2] Although the authors were alarmed by the growing isolation of the Republic of South Africa following the Sharpeville incident, they did not call explicitly for an "outward-looking" foreign policy. It is practically certain that the Nationalist government, even had it been disposed to look outward at that time, would have rejected a phrase attributable to the SAIRR. A more likely predecessor to government adoption of the term came four years later in a *News/Check* article, "The Choice before South Africa—Look Inwards or Look Outward."[3] *News/Check*, a magazine published in Johannesburg from 1965 through 1970 under the editorship of Otto Krause, was identified with the young intellectual wing of the Nationalist Party, which had for years urged pragmatic, controversial policies on the government, calling for initiatives rather than responses in domestic race relations and foreign policy. Characteristically, the article in *News/Check* concluded, "Above all, in a modern world it is a

2. Friedman et al., *Looking Outwards*.
3. Much of the following discussion of the term is dependent upon the work of Barratt, "The Outward Movement in South Africa's Foreign Relations," SAIIA *Newsletter*, no. 3, August 1969, pp. 15–16.

business of looking outwards, to building contact and thriving on exchange."[4] Although the wording was not taken up immediately, Prime Minister Vorster is reported to have used the words *uitwaartse beweging* early in 1967. From about that time there has been debate over the term and its use has become commonplace, along with *verlig* (enlightened) and *verkramp* (narrow-minded), describing its proponents and opponents.[5] From the standpoint of the South African press, the *verligtes* became advocates of the outward-looking policy and the *verkramptes* resisted it. Of course, these designations are not employed solely to describe attitudes toward foreign policy. They also refer, especially with regard to the verkramptes, to a whole set of values and policy preferences affecting domestic racial and economic policies. In this chapter we shall use the terms exclusively to designate attitudes with regard to the external world, while bearing in mind their domestic antecedents and ramifications. In 1968 Vorster told a Nationalist Party congress that though he was not sure how the word "outwards" or *uitwaartse* originated, he was fully prepared to take responsibility for it. The government had accepted the term as its own.

Historically, South African and earlier Afrikaner relations with black peoples go back to the time when the Dutch East India Company and the British Government made treaties with various Bantu chiefs. At first, there was the necessity to deal with and recognize African chiefs as sovereign foreign rulers, and to make agreements with them. As the Europeans grew in numbers and power, weaker African peoples were brought under their direct control. The various Afrikaner republics in the region continued to negotiate with the stronger peoples as with foreign powers.[6] As British hegemony was asserted over the region, the African tribes came to be dealt with less as independent political entities than as wards to be "protected" or, worse, as sources of labor and occupiers of land the Europeans coveted. It

4. *News/Check*, September 1965.
5. For example, the address by Dr. H. Muller, minister of foreign affairs, at Potchefstroom University, August 31, 1967, published as *The Republic of South Africa in a Changed World*, where he uses the phrase "the outward going policy" (p. 5).
6. See Marquard, *Our Foreign Policy*, pp. 3–4.

has been said that Cecil Rhodes saw South Africa as a part of Africa, but one could argue that he saw Africa as a part of South Africa, and the latter as a part of his personal fiefdom.[7]

Once the Union of South Africa was established, in 1910, the country's relations with its African neighbors were exclusively relations with the European colonial powers, including the British Empire. These relations were not always cordial, being intimately bound up in the racial and social issues of domestic South African affairs. Politics and foreign policy were involved in a "struggle for paramountcy between the British Imperial and the South African [Afrikaner] national idealisms. . . . Between these two millstones all other considerations [were] ground to paste."[8]

It is not hard to find numerous statements by various South African officials that urge more cordial and cooperative policies toward the neighboring states and territories. But it must be remembered that during the five decades following 1910 South Africa's British Commonwealth relationship imposed limitations on foreign policies. Moreover, South African politicians tended to regard relations with neighboring Africa as relations with European colonial or European settler governments. They also made the not unwarranted assumption that eventually the High Commission Territories and South West Africa would be integrated into the Union of South Africa. Thus a sort of proprietary attitude prevailed: a culturally European state (though anxious to be independent of Europe) was looking to the eventual Europeanization (in the form of white settler control) of the entire region. Moreover, there was a tendency to see South Africa as the "natural" leader of a widened region. Indicative of this expansionist mentality was Jan C. Smuts' statement, in a passionate attack on British policy: "Then shall it be from Zambesi to Simons Bay: Africa for the Afrikaners."[9] What a strange ring those words have today. It is not without justifica-

7. On Rhodes's aspirations see Walker, *A History of South Africa*, pp. 436–56.

8. W. van Heerden, "African and South African Politics," in SABRA, *South Africa in the African Continent*, p. 126.

9. *Eene Eeuw van Onrecht* [A Century of Wrong] (Pretoria, 1899), a tract published anonymously at the time when Smuts was state at-

tion that D. F. Malan, in Parliament, once pointed to Smuts and said, "There sits C. J. Rhodes redivivus."[10] The Nationalists had often accused Smuts of being an imperialist, and even worse a British imperialist. Apologists for Smuts could contend that this was Smuts the Afrikaner nationalist speaking, not Smuts the prime minister. Thus he may have been calling for a further escape northward, an extension of the trek, not for expansion to govern more peoples. It is instructive, however, that Afrikaner leaders themselves accused Smuts of being Rhodesian at heart.

As it became more and more evident that outright expansionist and imperial aspirations would be frustrated, if by no one but the British Crown, statements regarding direct governance of the region by South Africa became less usual, and emphasis was more commonly placed upon extending other forms of South African influence more widely through the region. Particularly the theme of maintaining British colonial rule and deterring African nationalism grew in importance. When the Nationalist government first came to power in 1948 a defensiveness developed in South African foreign policy. Not that defensiveness did not underlie earlier "expansive" tendencies. Even while seeking to defend colonial rule to the north, South Africa's leaders sought to exert a wider South African independence of Great Britain and the Commonwealth, particularly

---

torney of the South African Republic, as quoted in Vandenbosch, *South Africa and the World*, pp. 6, 12. See also Smuts's appeal to build "a strong white community to hold and develop the healthy highlands stretching from Rhodesia to Kenya," in his *Africa and Some World Problems*, p. 64. For numerous similarly expansive statements regarding the High Commission Territories see Stevens, "Anglo-South African Conflict over the Proposed Incorporation of the High Commission Territories," in Dale and Potholm, eds., *Southern Africa in Perspective*. Detailed treatment of these views and policies can be found in Utete, "South Africa and Independent Africa" (Ph.D. dissertation), chap. 2.

10. Union of South Africa, Assembly, *Hansard*, XXXVII, col. 98. Cf. Rhodes's statement in 1894 that "five and twenty years hence you might find a gentleman called your Prime Minister sitting in Cape Town and controlling the whole [of southern Africa], not only to the Zambezi, but to Lake Tanganyika." Both quoted in Vandenbosch, *South Africa and the World*, pp. 57–58.

as the latter became a more multi-racial institution. But defensiveness is not necessarily introversion, despite white South Africa's preoccupation with the domestic racial issue. These sorts of fears were characterized by Prime Minister Malan's expression regarding the possibility of Britain granting independence to the HCT's. In his words, the Union could not "permit Negro States, Bantu States, to arise within our borders, States which are free and independent and which can lay down their own policy in every respect."[11] It took a while for the Nationalists to sense what was happening on "their" continent. Malan himself apparently was ill informed about the geography of black Africa and events taking place there.[12]

It was the prime ministership of J. G. Strijdom that saw the first real hint of a desire for an active rather than a reactive outward-looking policy toward black Africa. As black states approached independence, in August 1955, he evidenced an awareness of this growing reality by claiming that: "The relationship between South Africa and non-white states in Africa, with their millions of inhabitants, should be one of mutual interested parties in Africa, without hostility towards one another—a relationship of peoples and governments who recognise and respected one anothers rights of existence."[13] The evolving view was expanded in 1957 to admit the need to formalize these contacts:

> We cannot assume that the non-white countries which become independent are or must be necessarily our enemies. We shall have to move in the direction that will enable us and them to exist on a friendly basis in Africa. In the normal course of events . . . it will develop that between us and especially the countries south of the Sahara . . . points of contact will have to come and in the course of time normal and even diplomatic relations will have to come.[14]

By and large, however, South Africa's Africa policies before the 1960's were irrelevant to modern Africa. They simply failed

11. Union of South Africa, Assembly, *Hansard,* August 11, 1953, cols. 1328–29.
12. Munger, *Notes,* pp. 28, 92.
13. Speech to the Natal Nationalist Party congress, August 25, 1955, as quoted in Spence, *Republic under Pressure,* p. 70.
14. As quoted in Barratt, op. cit. (in n. 3 above), p. 19.

to come to grips with the realities of African independence. When opportunities first presented themselves, upon Ghana's gaining of independence in 1957, the practical implementation of these ideas expressed by Strijdom was not undertaken. The South African government was not prepared, temperamentally or organizationally, to change policy in the important and sensitive field of race relations by way of foreign policy. Policy pronouncement was at variance with an inflexible diplomatic style and performance. From March 1957 to October 1958 Ghana made efforts to exchange high commissioners with South Africa.[15] At independence, Prime Minister Kwame Nkrumah consulted informally with various African delegations about the possibility of convening a general conference of all African states, including South Africa. The South Africans, however, never did participate in the Accra Conference of Independent African States. The South African government had, fearing to face non-white Africa alone, made its acceptance of any invitation contingent upon the participation of the colonial powers. At the 1957 Conference of Commonwealth prime ministers Nkrumah seemed to be in agreement with South Africa's foreign minister, Eric Louw, on a number of questions, including the "danger of Communism" and the inappropriateness of the Commonwealth conference as a forum for the discussion of apartheid. They even lunched together. In 1958 Nkrumah seriously pondered the merits of sending his cabinet chief, Robert Gardiner, as high commissioner to Pretoria.[16] The issues were also hotly debated in South Africa. Louw called for patience, even though he admitted that diplomatic exchanges must come in the future.[17] In the end, it was South Africa that rebuffed Ghana. Even into 1960 and beyond, Ghana sought to maintain contacts. The Ghanaian foreign minister, Ako Adjei, had invited Louw to Ghana when they met at the 1959 UN General Assembly. But Louw ineptly precipitated the withdrawal of the

15. Much of this is drawn from Thompson, *Ghana's Foreign Policy*, pp. 28–43.
16. Munger, "New White Politics in South Africa," in Hance, ed., *Southern Africa and the United States*, p. 74.
17. Union of South Africa, Assembly, *Hansard*, June 10, 1957, cols. 7662, 7670.

invitation.[18] Henceforth Nkrumah's South African policy became less conciliatory. Exchange foundered, in the end, on South Africa's unwillingness to accept a return visit from a Ghanaian cabinet minister. The 1964 initiative toward diplomatic exchange by President Kaunda of Zambia got even wider public discussion and reached less advanced stages.[19] The tendency for South African officials to view all black African leaders as uniformly hostile to South Africa was manifested in uniformly cold and inept responses to ostensibly correct initiatives from the North.

More cordial contacts with black Africa developed out of Katanga's secession from the Congo. Though it may be argued whether Moise Tshombe was a representative of black Africa, he nevertheless was black, and in August 1961 two Katangese cabinet ministers visited Pretoria for discussions with the Verwoerd government.[20] Later, when he became prime minister of the central Congolese government, Tshombe requested and received South African medical aid and food supplies.[21]

Two other related issues contribute to the early development of the outward-looking policy. South Africa's attitudes to the High Commission Territories and their projected independence and to the evolving thought regarding Bantu homelands within South Africa and South West Africa have affected not only one another, but have been linked to foreign policy questions farther afield.

Successive South African governments had assumed that the South Africa Act gave South Africa the right to the Protectorates and that consequently the matter of the actual transfer of these territories would simply take place at its request.[22] But in

18. Thompson, *Ghana's Foreign Policy*, pp. 96–97.
19. See Utete, op. cit. (in n. 9 above), pp. 104–6.
20. Spence, *Republic under Pressure*, pp. 76–77; Munger, *Notes*, p. 96. The ministers were Gabriel Kitenge (public works) and Jean Kitwe (finance). Other visitors in the early 1960's included Minister Alphonse Massamba-Débat, later president of Congo (Brazzaville).
21. *The Star*, August 29, 1964; also *South African Digest*, August 28, 1964, pp. 1–12, and September 4, p. 3.
22. Formally, by an affirmative vote of the two houses of South Africa's parliament and by the concurrence of the British government. See Vandenbosch, *South Africa and the World*, pp. 136–45; Stevens,

1959 when Prime Minister Verwoerd announced his government's Bantustan policy, a change in protectorate policy was in order. Some members of Parliament rapidly saw the inconsistencies between a declaration that the Bantustans would ultimately be granted full independence if they were ready for it and requested it, and the existing government view that the High Commission Territories should be integrated into South Africa.[23] Nevertheless, at first the government maintained that the fates of South Africa and the HCT's were still linked and that should the HCT's come under its protection, South Africa would "free them stage by stage, just as she is now doing in the Transkei."[24] It was not until January 1964 that Dr. Verwoerd finally declared that although he felt that Great Britain, by controlling the HCT's, had acted contrary to its declared policy in the Act of Union, South Africa would have to recognize the changes of the past few years:

> We adopt the standpoint, in the light of developments over the years, that our Bantu areas should rather be led to independence as good neighbours than that we should strive to have one large common fatherland in which in the end the Bantu must rule because of his numerical superiority, as eventually happens in every democracy. Under all these circumstances the Government has adopted the realistic attitude that South Africa no longer claims the incorporation of these territories. . . . Our attitude is that they are neighbouring states with which we want to have the best possible relations for the sake of our common safety and economic interests. [We have] No motives of plunder.[25]

Note that Dr. Verwoerd referred to "our Bantu areas" in this speech and that he expressed implictly the relationship between Bantustans and policies with the soon-to-be-independent states of Botswana, Lesotho, and Swaziland. This was also an open expression of the Balkanization theory of quasi-colonial rule.

"Anglo-South African Conflict," in Dale and Potholm, eds., *Southern Africa in Perspective.*

23. Union of South Africa, Assembly, *Hansard,* May 4, 1959, cols. 5233–35.

24. Verwoerd, as quoted in Vandenbosch, *South Africa and the World,* pp. 141–42.

25. RSA, Assembly, *Hansard,* January 21, 1964, cols. 59–60.

It was in this seminal speech, as well, that the prime minister indicated that in time an outward policy would materialize, not as South Africa changed, but as independent black states came to see "reason." This, he stated, was imperative. "What we are dealing with here," he said, "is the preservation of the White man and of what is his, coupled with the recognition of the other peoples' rights."[26] It was on the following terms that South Africa was prepared to deal with black Africa:

> . . . as long as that feud [by African states against South Africa] is maintained by their leaders it is impossible for South Africa to have the relations with them which one should like to have. . . . [However,] when those states emerge from the maelstrom resulting from the mistaken course they are adopting at the moment, and once the nations of the world discover that they cannot continue pouring their funds into that bottomless pit; when they discover that they cannot continue pandering to them by giving them a vote in international bodies out of all proportion to those new states' importance or economic value—in other words, that they cannot continue allowing them to dominate the world at the United Nations, and when the older nations start opposing the irresponsible actions of these African states in all kinds of bodies, the time will arrive when African states will have to seek co-operation with other countries the normal way. I am convinced that then those countries will learn to appreciate the value of South Africa, and then the foundation will have been laid for a relationship different from the one existing at present.[27]

So the announced Bantustan policy would seem to have demanded a reorientation in foreign policy toward black Africa. It certainly would necessitate as well as represent an effort to transcend ideological objections to marginally self-governing African states. It would, moreover, present a number of opportunities for South Africa to exploit the quasi-independence of the Bantustans and their dealings with independent black states, much as Moscow has utilized the union republics in the conduct of Soviet foreign policy. The extent to which the Bantustan concept is a "new" policy, or simply a reformulation of an old one, is an important point. This would hinge on whether

26. Ibid., col. 54.
27. Ibid., cols. 56–57.

or not actual juridical independence is contemplated for the Bantu Homelands, as is claimed, and if so, just how genuinely independent they would be permitted to or could possibly be. The term "domestic colonialism" has been aptly applied to separate development.[28] The term dates back at least to 1957, when Leo Marquard, as president of the South African Institute of Race Relations spoke of "South Africa's colonial policy" toward her domestic African populations.[29] If this, indeed, is a correct characterization of the intended Bantustan policy, then the relationship between South Africa and the former HCT's could as correctly be described as neo-colonial. Certainly, the range of alternative policies open to these states is sufficiently circumscribed at present to make this designation not unwarranted. In this regard, South African columnist Anthony Delius has spoken of "Black Dubčeks of the future" developing inside separate development. Despite these points, the South African government continues to insist that separate development represents a pattern of de-colonization.[30] In reality, though the form seems altered and the juridical context new, separate development continues to embody—in an externally more palatable guise—the continuation of white dominance. Insofar as the former HCT's perceive similar unstated constraints on their foreign policies, Bantustan–Republic of South Africa structural relations would be akin to their own relations with the republic.

28. See Carter et al., *South Africa's Transkei: The Politics of Domestic Colonialism*. For a discussion of these issues see Utete, op. cit. (in n. 9 above), pp. 111–15.

29. Marquard, *South Africa's Colonial Policy*. A provocative set of policy recommendations on South Africa's relations with internal Bantu peoples and with neighboring black and white states is presented by Marquard in *A Federation of Southern Africa*.

30. Delius, "Internal Argument and External Policy," *African Affairs*, LXIX (1970), 373. For the government view see RSA, Information Service, *Progress through Separate Development*, esp. p. 23; *Die Burger*, Cape Town, January 28, 1964; and the transcript of Prime Minister Vorster's press conference, March 1971, in *The Star*, April 3, 1971, p. 13. A discussion of the foreign-policy ramifications of separate development in South West Africa appears in *X-Ray*, II (August 1972), 1–2. On the use of Bantustan leaders for foreign policy purposes see *The Times*, July 7, 1972, p. 6, and *Sunday Times*, Johannesburg, July 16, 1972, p. 2.

In a way, South Africa is juggling three separate but related balls at once. First are its relations with the former HCT's. Second is South Africa's handling of the Bantustans, particularly in the relationship between the Bantustans as a domestic political issue and Bantustans as potentially independent states. In either case the Bantustans may serve as a useful instrument of South African foreign policy. Third is the matter of South West Africa, and also of the evolution of Bantustans there. It is doubtful whether the RSA has formulated a grand and consistent strategy on these questions. But it would appear that South African governmental thinking, in broad terms, looks something like this. With regard to relations with the former HCT's, the current efforts to keep these territories divided, relatively weak, and intimately involved in the South African economy seem likely to be continued. Since South Africa seems relatively satisfied with its experiences with Botswana, Lesotho, and Swaziland, it would appear that the Bantustans in South Africa will probably be developed along similar although more controllable lines. South Africa would hope that by doing so it can continue to be the dominant regional force, and that it will thereby have a few additional "black" governments willing to deal with it and to carry its case northward. South Africa has already permitted various leaders of Bantu homelands to travel abroad and to broadcast the message of the sincerity of the RSA government and the necessity for the evolution of separate development. For instance, Chief Gatsha Buthelezi, the chief executive officer of Kwazulu (the Zulu homeland), Chief Kaiser Matanzima of the Transkei, and Chief Lucas Mangope of Boputhatswana (the Tswana homeland) have traveled widely in Europe and America, and somewhat in black Africa. Their message has been consistent—dialogue is preferable to confrontation with South Africa, separate development is a viable alternative to white dominance, and things are changing for the better in the RSA.

Although the South West Africa issue is more complicated, much the same line prevails in South African foreign policy thinking. South Africa reasons that it is now in a strong position to deal with the UN, largely because the threat of UN-RSA confrontation seems to be diminished. The West is not likely to approve of any direct confrontation with South Africa. The Soviet Union would seem to be too far removed because of its involvements elsewhere. The Chinese are not yet ready to become seriously involved. And the African states, without massive assistance from one of these centers of power, are not able to sustain any serious military challenge. Thus, the RSA would appear to be biding its time, talking with the UN, and projecting an image of reasonableness and flexibility. Meanwhile, South Africa is moving toward constitutional changes in the major South West African Bantu homelands. As these homelands approach nominal independence they would be given a choice—opt for independence or join up with any neighboring independent state. The Ovambos would be "free" to choose between independence or integration into Angola. The Okavangos could link with Botswana. The peoples on the Caprivi strip could join with Zambia. But most importantly, the legal precedent would then be established for the white homeland to opt to become attached to South Africa. By thus fragmenting South West Africa, contrary to the wishes of SWAPO nationalists or the UN General Assembly and the Security Council, who wish to see Namibia independent as a single integrated state, South Africa would continue to maintain control of the principal economic assets of the region, and it would have a new lever on regional political affairs. This is just one way in which South African policy makers may be thinking about the future of regional affairs and one that, of course, redounds to their country's benefit. There are, to be sure, many possible flaws in this reasoning, not the least of which is that black leaders, even though their territories may be economically dependent on South Africa, are subject to other, sometimes conflicting pressures. They may not always do the bidding of the RSA. But "Black Dubčeks," although they may emerge, can be dealt with provided the power imbalances can be maintained.

This is not to imply that the outward-looking policy is strictly or even primarily a function of changing policies toward the Bantu homelands. Rather, it was the confluence in the late 1950s of the coming independence of black African states, South Africa's belated perception of this eventuality, South Africa's industrial growth, the realization that the High Commission Territories would never be formally signed over to an apartheid government, and the development of the implementation of the philosophy of apartheid to its logical although not necessarily sensible conclusion that helped lead to new initiatives and responses in South Africa's policies. So, while statements calling for normalizing relations with black states were not especially new in South Africa, even by important and powerful men, actions seeking to implement them were. Until the mid-1960s the outward-looking policy was merely a set of policy declarations, formulated in a vacuum and seemingly without awareness of the full implications of the "winds of change."

Official Rationale

There are numerous motives prompting the outward-looking type of foreign policy at this time. A multiplicity of motives spawns a multiplicity of rationalizations for policy. The official rationale, however, can be seen as having five general themes, those related to (1) a growing sense of isolation, (2) the need for a dynamic approach to the status quo, (3) frustrated idealism, (4) a self-image as a regional power, particularly in economic terms, and (5) military and nonmilitary strategic considerations. Naturally, these themes are interrelated and often indistinguishable in any given statement. They are advanced here simply to show, in an artificially discrete fashion, the various lines of argument advanced to explain policy to black Africans, to white South Africans, and to the outside world.

Fundamentally, South Africa is a status quo power. Its chief desire is to maintain and reinforce the power of the white population in relation to the non-white.[31] If this is its purpose on the domestic level, it is also the short-range aim in foreign policy. Leaders repeatedly refer to an awareness of changing international conditions. Though policy does not always appear to reflect such an awareness, nevertheless, lip service is paid to the reality of change. They cite the independence of black Af-

31. See Lawrie, "South Africa's World Position," *JMAS*, II (March 1964), 41–54.

rican states, the alleged growth of communist influence in the region, the abandonment of Africa's whites by former colonial and North American powers, and the industrialization of South Africa. All of these factors and more lead to the conclusion that a dynamic defense of the status quo is in order. Otherwise isolation and growing vulnerability are the result.

South Africans have for years been perplexed by their geographical and cultural isolation from Europe. On the one hand it is regarded as a blessing in disguise. There is a widespread conviction that if left to "natural," internally managed forces, South Africa as a "white civilization" in Africa could survive and thrive. On the other hand, there is the realization that South Africa needs foreign markets, foreign capital, and a constant scientific and intellectual fertilization from abroad. Moreover, there is a perhaps misplaced optimism that if Europe and North America would listen openly to South Africans and if they would come to see for themselves, racial policies in South Africa would be understood, appreciated, and thenceforth supported.

The reality of South Africa's growing isolation in the late 1950s and early 1960s, particularly after the Sharpeville shootings of 1960, was evident to its financial, commercial, industrial, intellectual, and artistic communities. The pattern of international change, by that time, was undeniable. Many leaders, including important politicians and governmental officials, became alarmed by the long-range implications of these developments. By and large, however, policy responses led to further retrenchment and retreat. There were ex post facto rationalizations alleging that South Africa had always been ready to deal openly and cordially with the newly independent African states. Black Africans were the ones who precipitated tension, the argument went—when they saw the light, when they matured, they would turn to South Africa for friendship and assistance. The rest of the white world was accused of pandering to the shrill and illogical rhetoric of irresponsible and immature black Africans. White South Africans argued that the outward-looking policy, therefore, was nothing new. Just as some Africans had learned by experience and example, so would Europe and America. But the fact remains, despite denials, that South Africa was systematically ostracized by virtually all of the world, and that its response was one of further withdrawal and reactive threat. Not until the mid-1960s did a policy emerge that reflected a sense of South Africa's policy as counterproductive. It became clear that a modern defense of the white-dominated status quo in southern Africa demanded active, dynamic initiatives from South Africa.

This dynamism has taken two complementary and simultaneous paths—one expansive and one defensive. The expansive mode of policy sought to give policy expression to a long-held theme that runs throughout South African politics and foreign policy. That theme, briefly stated, is that the defense of South Africa begins at the Zambezi. Even the Nationalists who fought Smuts on the issue of the use of South African troops in World War II agreed that South Africa's defense perimeter extended at least to the Zambezi. Smuts wanted to and did go even farther. In his view Kenya and Tanganyika were "our northern boundaries so far as defense is concerned. . . . We cannot wait until the enemy reaches the Limpopo."[32] Crudely put, the best defense is a good offense and it is wise to erect one's defensive perimeter in someone else's territory. The expansionist Smuts set the tone for this argument. Prime Minister Vorster, at a 1971 press conference, was asked about South African forces in Rhodesia. In explanation he stated: "We decided . . . that it was best to meet them on the Zambezi and not wait until they reached the Limpopo."[33] Early South African thinking called for outright annexation or integration of northern territories. At the very least it was demanded that South Africa should be the dominant partner in any constitutional arrangements. Later amendments to these themes evidenced the more sophisticated realization that other, less direct forms of involvement might serve the same purposes. By establishing relations with neighboring African states, one minister said in 1970, the government was protecting the borders of the RSA against "terrorist incur-

32. As quoted in Vandenbosch, *South Africa and the World,* pp. 155 and 111. See also pp. 277–79, below.
33. *The Star,* April 3, 1971, p. 13.

sions." And he cited the case of Malawi as a country where "Communist-inspired terrorists" were unable to get through.[34] The idea of a South African equivalent of a Monroe Doctrine for southern Africa has been expressed although the more common view is that a "buffer" must be constructed between hostile black Africa and South Africa. The phrase "sphere of influence" repeatedly crops up, too. This spectrum of thought stresses the military component of policy and calls for greater cooperation with Portugal and Rhodesia, coupled with a more vigorous commercial and espionage contact with black Africa. It could only apply and appeal, however, to white-ruled territories and to white settlers in black-governed territories.

The anti-communist line is perhaps the most consistent one running through South African foreign policy statements in the 1960s and to date. Unending repetition has probably led to the institutionalization of forms of self-deception and delusion. Take, for example, Prime Minister Vorster's 1969 speech in which he argued for the outward-looking policy as a matter of "plain common sense." He went on: "Look at the map of Africa . . . look East and look West, and you will see that only Israel on the one hand and Kenya on the other hand are anti-Communist."[35] A fairly narrow vision has been created here. Variations stress a fear of (1) communist ideology in Africa, (2) Russian naval power in the Indian Ocean, (3) Russian and Chinese aid to "terrorist" fighters, (4) Chinese domination of Tanzania and Zambia and other black states, and (5) massive Chinese migration to Africa, the "yellow peril." But in every instance the impact of communism and the policies of communist governments are exaggerated and the abilities and desires of black Africans to resist communism are pooh-poohed or even ignored—through, one suspects, a self-created ideological myopia. It is only recently that nonmilitary responses to these alarms have been deemed sensible adjuncts to military pre-

34. Minister of Transport B. J. Schoeman in *The Star*, April 18, 1970, p. 2.

35. As quoted in *The Star*, November 15, 1969, p. 7. See as well the numerous statements by Minister of Defense P. W. Botha.

paredness and an inward focus of security, white unity, and loyalty.

No less a part of the outward-looking policy is the more defensive though not passive approach to foreign policy characterized by the combinatory themes of peaceful coexistence, mutual assistance, occasional symbolic concession, and noninterference. The carrot gains center stage, but the stick, military and economic, remains in the wings.

Stress now is laid on regional security, stability, cooperation and economic growth. For public consumption, the argument is made that South Africa is only to be primus inter pares in an unstructured regional community. After all, there is no absolute necessity to institutionalize these arrangements. The existing distribution of power and influence lies with the Republic. Why precipitate resistance to interaction by insisting on formalizing already expanding relationships?

In a somewhat related way it was felt that as the African states gained their independence, they would still need guidance and assistance in maintaining their relationships with Europe. South Africa proposed to supply that linkage. Foreign Minister Eric Louw put it this way in 1959:

> If the African states to the north are willing to accept South Africa as a fellow-African state and as a permanently "White" African state and if, in addition, they are willing to accept our cooperation in matters of common concern, then the Union of South Africa can usefully serve as a link between the Black states of Africa and the West, for the purpose of furthering our common aims and protecting the interests of our African Continent.[36]

Although the foreign minister admitted in 1959 that the prospects for South Africa's fulfilling this role were "dim," the theme was taken up by his successor, Dr. Hilgard Muller, when, for example in 1965, he argued that South Africans were "emi-

36. E. H. Louw, "The Union and the Emergent States of Africa," in SABRA, *South Africa in the African Continent,* p. 21. This speech is reproduced in RSA, Department of Information, *Fact Paper No. 70* (1959); the idea of South Africa as a bridge can be found in *Fact Paper No. 5,* February 1956, p. 12, and *Fact Paper No. 33,* April 1957, p. 9.

nently suited to serve as a bridge between Africa and the West, between the non-whites in Africa and the whites in the West."[37] Needless to say, nothing came of these overtures. Neither black African states nor the Western states needed an intermediary, least of all the RSA. Their links were continued as the transition from formal dependence to formal independence was made. Just why South African officials ever expected that they would ever be called upon to play this role is hard to determine. This theme died quietly as a more realistic "outward policy" was developed.

In many respects, South Africa's claimed magnanimity and concern for the well-being of independent black Africa grows out of a genuine, basically Afrikaner, distrust of Europe and European colonialism. The South Africans' cultural heritage has made them wary of the formal trappings of independence and the machinations of Britain. So they have repeatedly warned independent Africans of the dangers of "neo-colonialism" and "economic imperialism."[38] As the African states were about to become independent, Foreign Minister Louw warned African statesmen of the pitfalls in dealing with Europe. He spoke of "self-appointed advisers" from "outside" who sought only profit for themselves and those countries that sent them. Moreover, he mentioned "foreign financiers" who were seeking valuable concessions and guaranteed profits. Finally, he warned of foreign aid since "a political *quid pro quo* will be demanded (or at least be expected)."[39] This could easily have served as premature advice with regard to South Africa's outward-looking policy. Today's modifications of this message point to the dangers of communist expansion, particularly from China. However, Pretoria is not unaware of the opportunities that its own economic power afford it in black Africa.[40]

37. RSA, Assembly, *Hansard* (1965), cols. 456–57.
38. For example, Foreign Minister Muller's speeches, *The Republic of South Africa in a Changed World*, p. 5, and "South Africa's Africa Policy," *Africa Institute Bulletin*, VIII (1970), 256.
39. Louw's article in SABRA, *South Africa in the African Continent*, p. 12.
40. For an analysis of this thinking see Sparks, *New Perspectives in Africa*; also Marquard, *South Africa's Colonial Policy*.

In contradistinction, a case could also be made that the entire purpose (though by no means a public rationale) for the outward-looking policy in Africa is to sustain an outward policy toward the broadened European world. If this is the case, it might be argued that South Africa's Africa policy is designed to demonstrate to the West that South Africa wants to live in peace with and to help black Africans. Furthermore, South Africa's policies are sufficiently flexible to give the lie to those who maintain that the South African government is unable to adjust to the changing scene, and therefore that it ought to be abandoned and displaced. According to this reasoning, South Africa is chiefly interested in maintaining good relations with the West so that it can rely on Western political and economic cooperation and, if all goes well, protection also. Support for this sort of reasoning can be found in Dr. Muller's 1967 Potchefstroom speech, in which he said:

> To the extent to which the West is becoming aware of our fruitful cooperation with other countries in Africa, its attitude and disposition towards us are improving, and I believe that this will happen to an increasing degree. We must simply accept that our relations with the rest of the world are largely determined by our relations with the African states.[41]

In other words, South Africa's Africa policy is consciously designed to disarm advocates of strong opposition to apartheid in the more powerful states of Europe and North America, and if at all possible to enlist them in support of South Africa. In its most optimistic form this would involve the southern extension of NATO and the possible involvement of South Africa in that military alliance. For a relatively small investment, South Africa divides black Africa, causes a good deal of debate within key African and Western states, and even galvanizes support within South Africa from liberal whites and conservative blacks.

The Calvinist sense of mission is likewise embedded in South African thinking. Whether it is simply a blind conviction based on Biblical interpretation or communal identity or whether it is the more mundane but no less zealous sense of frustrated ideal-

41. Muller, *The Republic of South Africa in a Changed World,* p. 7.

ism makes little difference here. The first viewpoint might be illustrated by a former minister of Bantu administration and development when, in December 1959, he uttered these words:

> More than ever before I am convinced that we have been divinely chosen to reveal to Africa and the world the pattern in accordance with which racial and national groups may promote their material and spiritual progress on a peaceful and secure basis without the one becoming a danger or a threat to the other.[42]

Despite his missionary zeal, phrases like "the obvious market for our increasing industrial production" and our "natural sphere of influence" crept in.

An example of the other persuasion was given by Prime Minister Vorster, who appealed to South Africans to display a missionary spirit to propel the outward-looking policy. "We are of Africa," he said, "and our *destiny* lies in Africa. We do not want to escape our destiny. It is our challenge and we dare not fail in our *mission*. Africa has been good to us, and it is our *duty* to plough back part of what we have received."[43] Clergymen, businessmen, journalists, and politicians have taken up these themes, which contribute to both the motivation and the rationalization of the outward-looking policy. But in actual manifestation the best that has been achieved is a depressing paternalism. The worst is what has been called the "temptation of imperialism," for destiny and duty can justify a multitude of sins. Americans cognizant of what is referred to as the "winning of the West" ought to be aware of this.

Nevertheless, white South Africans are *in* Africa if not entirely *of* Africa, and they perceive their future as regional, if not continental in scope. With emphasis in the original, Mr. de Wet Nel stated, as would most South Africans, *"We are, always have*

42. Nel, "Our Task in Africa," *BaNtu,* February 1960, p. 78. See more recently the speech by Nationalist M.P. Dr. P. Bodenstein, in RSA, Assembly, *Hansard,* May 7, 1969, col. 5478.

43. Speech in November 1968, as quoted in Barratt, "The Outward Movement," *Newsletter* (SAIIA), no. 3, August 1969, pp. 17–18. Italics added. Barratt also mentions a lengthier treatment of this motif by the minister of information, Dr. Mulder, in a speech of June 24, 1969. An earlier expression of such a paternalistic viewpoint is Smuts, *The Basis of Trusteeship in African Native Policy,* pp. 11–12.

been and always will be [an] *indivisible part and parcel of Africa."*[44] Thus they seek to exercise their regional leadership in every conceivable field. Even so, the region, per se, has features in it that are regarded as possessing universal significance. First, it is felt that southern Africa is a key battleground for "white civilization" against the racial flood and the communist menace. Secondly, as Dr. Muller once contended, one reason why a relatively small country like South Africa should attract so much interest throughout the world is that South Africa is a microcosm of the whole world, with a white minority and a large nonwhite majority.[45] Whether or not these attitudes are in fact accurate perceptions of reality is unimportant. They prompt policy and enable the government and its followers to justify the outward-looking policy.

In reaching outward, regionally, South Africans maintain, indeed monotonously trumpet, their adherence to the principle of noninterference. South Africa is to be accepted as it is, a white-governed state, and what is more, it must be regarded as permanently so. In return for this recognition, South Africa promises not to interfere in the domestic affairs of other countries. In a moment of revealing candor, Prime Minister Vorster once stated: "South Africa has never interfered in the internal matters of other nations, *except when her interests have been directly touched.*" But he added: "I must keep in mind that South Africa's interests can be touched."[46] The point must be made, however, that South Africa is most sensitive about what constitutes its interests, particularly when matters of security are at stake. If its working definition of self-interest is as broad as are its working definitions of communism or sabotage, then we can expect to see South Africa conducting a most vigorous involvement in the domestic affairs of neighboring states. Figure 5 depicts Vorster as perceived by a cartoonist for the revolutionary ANC. To the ANC, South Africa's outward policy is a spider

44. Nel, "Our Task in Africa," *BaNtu,* February 1960, p. 76. Italics in original.

45. RSA, Information Service, *News from South Africa,* New York, no. 14, May 14, 1971, p. 1.

46. As quoted in the *Rand Daily Mail* and *The Star,* daily edition, October 14, 1967. Italics added.

Figure 5. African National Congress view of South Africa's African policy. Drawing by D. N. Osborn, on the cover of *Sechaba*, vol. V, no. 1 (January 1971). Reproduced with the permission of *Sechaba*, the official organ of the African National Congress, South Africa.

web of involvements that compromises and will ultimately destroy black leaders who become entangled in it. Nonetheless South Africa maintains a rigid adherence to legalisms in the question of involvement in the domestic affairs of other states—in bilateral and multilateral relations, in the United Nations and subsidiary organs, in the Commonwealth before its failure to reapply, and in official statement and overt behavior. In form, at least, South Africa adheres to its professed principles. But it must be remembered that one qualification, "when her interests have been directly touched," is central to South Africa's foreign policy behavior, as it is in the behavior of other states.

The rationalizations for the outward-looking policy have appeal among both Afrikaans- and English-speakers, among critics and advocates of apartheid, and among all economic segments of the white community. The rationalizations or their ideological antecedents have a long history in South African political rhetoric. Only a very few examples could be cited here. The appeal is, however, general rather than parochial, particularly among groups of increasing importance in the country: the young, the urban, the urbane, the affluent, and those conscious of (though not necessarily sensitive to) attitudes abroad and those interested in projecting an image of a progressive, dynamic, developing South Africa.

Emerging Contacts

In this section we shall review briefly the various forms which the outward-looking policy has taken in the years since 1965. Some have been described at length in earlier sections of this study. Other facets of the outward-looking policy have so far not been covered, and thus will be dealt with in some detail here. Those policy forms can be grouped into seven categories: (1) trade, (2) public relations, (3) further collaboration with regional white governments, (4) military preparedness and the offer to negotiate nonaggression pacts, (5) interference and involvement in the domestic affairs of neighboring states, (6) diplomatic exchanges and high-level visits, and (7) financial and technical assistance.

TRADE

Even before the contemporary outward-looking policy took shape, the dominant regional position of South Africa was evident. Things have not changed significantly since, except to reinforce already prevailing patterns. Even where the RSA has sought to protect itself and its African trading partners by refusing to publish country-by-country African trade data, the picture that emerges from the conscious obfuscation reveals a pattern of growing South African exports to the continent, and moreover an increasing number of black African trading partners (see table 13). Perhaps the most significant growth has oc-

TABLE 13
SOUTH AFRICAN EXPORTS TO AFRICA

Year	*To Africa (A)*	*Total exports (B)*	*Percent of A to B*
	In millions of rands		
1957	154	801	19
1963	107	916	12
1964	114	954	12
1965	147	1,061	14
1966	196	1,192	16.4
1967	226	1,356	16.8
1968	249	1,507	16.5
1969	255	1,532	16.6
1970	264	1,543	17.1
1971	293	1,555	18.8
1972	306	2,003	15.2

SOURCES: Figures for 1957–68 from *Africa Research Bulletin*, VII (no. 8), 1805C, September 30, 1970. Those for 1969 from *Standard Bank Review*, Johannesburg, no. 618, September 1970, p. 39, and for 1970, ibid., no. 627, June 1971, p. 28. Those for 1971 and 1972 supplied by the South African Embassy, Den Haag.

curred in exports to Malawi. In 1964 South Africa supplied but 6 percent of Malawi's imports. By 1969 the figure had risen to 15 percent.[47] The Rhodesian UDI served to extend Zambia's trade relations with South Africa despite ideological differences, and to expand immensely South Africa's exports to Rhodesia itself. Zambia will most likely reduce its imports from South Africa in the near future. It can be estimated that South Africa's share of the Rhodesian market has risen from 24 percent in 1964 to 54

47. Malawi, Department of Information, *Malawi 1969*, pp. 28–29. In 1970 Malawian imports from South Africa began to decline, representing only 12.6 percent. However, imports from Rhodesia showed a marked increase from 16.9 percent in 1969 to 21.7 percent in 1970. Malawi, *Malawi in Figures, 1971*.

percent in 1968 and perhaps as much as 80 percent in 1969. On the export side, Rhodesia in 1964 sent 7 percent of its exports to South Africa. In 1968 the figure was 29 percent. Even though the total effect of this growth on South African industry has been marginal, it does represent an important and successful manifestation of South Africa's Africa policy.

What should be stressed, however, is that the emphasis is on trade policies that enable the RSA to increase its exports of manufactured products to the rest of Africa, and that discourage the growth of indigenous industry in neighboring states. South African manufactured goods have not found and are not likely to find substantial markets in Europe, Asia, and America. Hence the RSA needs a protected market for them, and Africa seems to offer this at least as a possibility. The 1967 trade agreement with Malawi serves this need. So does the Customs Union agreement with the former HCT's. Rhodesia and, to some extent, the Portuguese territories are aware of this tendency and are attempting to shield their infant industries from South African competition. This is why they have, heretofore, resisted South Africa's appeals for increasing free trade arrangements on a regional basis. They are aware that they need, not inexpensive imports from South Africa, but protection from South African industry and access to the South African market. This is the awkward position in which they find themselves.

PUBLIC RELATIONS

The evidence seems to indicate that despite a more stringent application of various security regulations and a more conscious effort to separate races spatially as well as socioculturally, South Africa has managed to create in black Africa or among ruling elites in some black African states an improved image of itself. How this has been done is not entirely clear. But the idea that white South Africa can be dealt with openly, that South Africans are sufficiently open-minded or at least flexible to countenance and benefit from some contact with black Africans abroad, and the view that South Africa is legitimately a part of Africa, seem to have gained currency. The outward-looking policy seems to have won some converts in key positions in black

Africa. An optimistic South African characterization of the "success" of the outward policy can be seen in figure 6, in which Vorster is seen openly dealing with the black states to the north. Contributing to this has been efforts of various South African diplomats, particularly those in London, Washington, and New York. In some respects the alteration in attitude has come to black Africa not directly from South Africa, but by way of major Western countries who have to some extent persuaded and to some extent pressured black African states to reconsider their stand on southern Africa. Likewise, the changing situational component has prompted reconsideration of policies. Radio South Africa, the external service of the South African Broad-

'They've come to install the new hot line!'

Figure 6. Political cartoon from *The Argus*, Cape Town, March 31, 1971. Reproduced with the permission of *The Argus*.

casting Corporation, has been most active since 1966, transmitting to all regions of Africa and in English, French, Afrikaans, Portuguese, Chinyanja, Chichewa, and Swahili.[48] In general, the nadir of the RSA was the period from about 1960 to 1964. In the early 1960s South African propaganda, though extensive, was relatively unbending and heavy-handed. It improved immensely in quality and effect in the succeeding years, largely because of the expanded activities of the South Africa Foundation and Radio South Africa. The South African Foundation was founded in 1959, and is a well-financed non-governmental organization composed of businessmen who seek to promote South Africa abroad, largely through high-level contact with foreign governmental officials, businessmen, educators, and publicists.

COLLABORATION WITH RHODESIA AND PORTUGAL

The late 1960s saw the RSA throw in more completely with its regional white neighbors than in the 1950s or the early years of the decade of the sixties. Despite the geographical proximity of South Africa, Angola, Mozambique, and Rhodesia, intensive and extensive collaboration between their governments is relatively new. Contributing to the long-lasting lack of collaboration were a number of ethnic and ideological factors which are still highly pertinent. In the first place, South Africans committed to apartheid as a domestic "solution" to racial issues look at Rhodesia and the Portuguese territories with a measure of misgiving and distrust. Ideas of racial partnership and multiracialism, despite their practical effects, smack of halfway measures to the apartheid ideologues. Such policies represent a "weakness" that in their minds can lead to dangerous compromise and pressure. Insofar as apartheid is a product of a peculiar Afrikaner-Calvinist mentality, there has run throughout Afri-

48. On the effects of this extensive programing see Jaap Boekkooi, "South Africa's Subtle Soft-Sell Is Paying Off," *The Star*, May 15, 1971, p. 12. On South Africa's propaganda efforts see McKay, "The Propaganda Battle for Zambia," *Africa Today*, XVIII (April 1971), 18–26, and by the same author: "South Africa's Propaganda," *Africa Report*, XI (February 1966), 41–46, and "South African Propaganda on the International Court's Decision," *African Forum*, II (1966), 51–64.

kaner history a disdain for cultures less tempered by adversity. Thus, not only have Afrikaners looked down upon the Catholic and racially suspect Portuguese, but they have done battle over the years with the English. To reverse the coin, the dominant English element in Rhodesia has been unwilling, for ideological and nationalistic reasons, to be absorbed by the Afrikaners of South Africa. As of 1951 only 13.5 percent of the Europeans in Rhodesia were Afrikaners. This group has felt embattled. Ironically, when the English of Rhodesia sought to assert their national identity by their Unilateral Declaration of Independence in 1965, the price was a more intimate contact with the Republic of South Africa. Some would go so far as to say that Rhodesia has become a "satellite" of South Africa. Indeed, one of the rationalizations of Britain's Conservative government for its 1971 "settlement" proposals with the Smith government was that if no accommodation was reached, Rhodesia would have become virtually a province of South Africa.

In general, however, the various European groups in the region have a low opinion of each other's intellectual and political maturity. An Afrikaner leader in one breath called Rhodesia "a sort of extension of the White South African nation" and in the next referred to political life in Rhodesia as "a glorified divisional [county] council" manned by second-rate political hacks.[49] Another South African referred to the Smith government as a "cowboy" white regime.[50] The basic insecurity of the unsettled "Rhodesian question" has bedeviled many government officials who would prefer clarity and stability to the provocative and potentially dangerous Smith administration.

Thus the UDI created a delicate situation for South Africa, which apparently had advised the Rhodesians against such an act. South Africa would have preferred to stay out of the conflict, fearing a spillover from the international crisis that seemed imminent. Pretoria wanted to keep the UDI an issue strictly between Britain and the Smith government. It was made clear, however, that the RSA would not participate in boycotts or

49. Interview RSA–7, Cape Town, July 31, 1969.
50. Interview RSA–4, Cape Town, July 29, 1969.

sanctions. Both Prime Minister Verwoerd and his successor, Vorster, declared the issue to be outside the formal ambit of South Africa and urged Britain and Rhodesia to settle it honorably, "realistically," and amicably.

Nevertheless, the South African government, all things being equal, favored white rule in Rhodesia. The minister of transport declared that the government regarded Rhodesia as the "White frontier" on the Zambezi.[51] South African policy, despite an official policy of hands off and a formally "correct" legal stance on the Rhodesian issue, nevertheless, contributed immensely to the continuation of white rule in Rhodesia. Rhodesian pounds and later dollars were exchanged in South Africa at par. South Africa posted an "accredited diplomatic representative" to Salisbury and accepted Rhodesian reciprocation. South African private firms picked up the slack in Rhodesia's sanctioned trade. Private groups and individuals and public officials expedited contact with the outside world and enabled Rhodesia to withstand sanctions and external pressures. When Zimbabwe nationalists in concert with ANC of South Africa units made incursions into Rhodesian territory, South Africa requested the Smith government's permission to cooperate with the Rhodesian forces. To maintain the trappings of legality, Pretoria informed the British government of its action. In this way it recognized British sovereignty in Rhodesia while dealing openly with the de facto authority of the Smith government. The extent of this military collaboration is outlined in Chapter 6. Thus in small and not so small ways, South Africa managed to demonstrate its emotional, economic, and strategic interests in Rhodesian white rule. Portugal took much the same course. On the surface of it, the collaboration was successful. Smith is still in power, and external pressures have diminished. But all this time Rhodesia has been an irritant making the outward-looking policy more awkward and difficult. Pretoria was relieved when the 1971 "settlement" proposals with Britain were

51. *Sunday Times*, Johannesburg, November 14, 1965. These issues are discussed in Hill, "UDI and South African Foreign Policy," *Journal of Commonwealth Political Studies*, VII (1969), 96–103.

announced. The prime minister officially congratulated both governments.[52] However, not until some arrangements legitimize the Smith government and thereby normalize Rhodesia's international status can South Africa be satisfied that its own relatively calm existence will not be endangered by an international crisis set off by its northern neighbor.

Similarly, the RSA's growing interest in Portuguese-ruled Mozambique and Angola have found expression in military assistance, economic cooperation and investment, and technical association. To a large extent, these growing commitments have been developed in the past ten years.

MILITARY PREPAREDNESS

Throughout South Africa's "softening" of its policies toward independent black Africa, there has been a parallel expansion and improvement in its military and police establishments. Even before the Sharpeville lesson and its immediate aftermath, there was a determination to be prepared, militarily, for invasion or internal unrest. South Africa made important arms purchases just before the UN's arms embargo; sought to become self-sufficient in small weapons, ammunition, and military material production; sought to breathe activity into the Simonstown agreement and to engage Western forces in defense of the RSA; and even began testing and producing sophisticated equipment. The embargo, per se, did not deeply affect South Africa's military capabilities, and now that it has been effectively bridged, by France and Britain especially, its impact in practical terms is negligible.

At the same time that its guard was being raised, the RSA sought to neutralize the effects of the publicity accorded its military posture by offering to negotiate nonaggression pacts with African countries.[53] The prime minister followed his offer with a warning that South Africa would fight "terrorism" in any Af-

52. *The Star*, November 27, 1971, p. 2.

53. Ibid., September 19, 1970, p. 7; *News/Check*, IX, 7, September 18, 1970; and *ARB*, VII, 1862C–64A, October 15, 1970. Characteristic of this carrot-and-stick approach to foreign policy is the statement by Minister of Defense Botha in *The Star*, January 29, 1972, p. 15.

rican country that would allow it to do so. The immediate reaction in black Africa was outright rejection and denunciation or disinterested silence. The defense minister then stated that the republic was prepared to discuss with its friends and neighbors "contingency planning" arrangements aimed at resisting possible "terrorist" attacks and Russian military penetration.[54] In this statement the minister went further than any government spokesman in the past regarding South Africa's willingness to take part in multilateral or bilateral defense arrangements with either white or black states. The old communist bogey was raised and the promise of "stable" and "orderly" regional development was appealed to. Various ministers, including the prime minister, repeated these offers, urging a "common front" to resist communist "subversion and subjection."[55] The best response they could secure was a statement by President Houphouet-Boigny that subscribed to South African alarms about communist expansion. He intimated that he would like to see mutual defense pacts signed "eventually" between the RSA and the black African states.[56] Mentioning fear of the Chinese People's Republic's using Africa as a "dumping ground" for the "Asian multitudes" (a version of the "yellow peril" arguments heard decades earlier in the United States), he said he felt that South Africa's armed forces were Africa's strongest bulwark against Russian and Chinese communism. Prime Minister Vorster welcomed this expression. So far, however, no direct steps toward negotiations have taken place. South African regional policy has of late been a combination of carrot and stick, with the stick always in obvious readiness.

INTERFERENCE AND INVOLVEMENT IN DOMESTIC POLITICAL AFFAIRS

Many of the numerous relationships described in this and earlier chapters have the individual as well as the cumulative effect, either intended or fortuitous, of shaping domestic political configurations in neighboring states. Such causal linkages are virtually impossible to document. However, there are also certain measures taken by the South African government that

54. *The Star*, November 14, 1970, p. 4.
55. Ibid., May 15, 1971, p. 2.
56. Ibid., pp. 2, 3.

are specifically designed either to reinforce or strengthen elements sympathetic to the RSA or its policies in these states, or to weaken if not displace hostile forces. It has been reported that a fund of some R500,000 was established as early as 1965 (and renewed annually) to finance undercover political operations of this sort.[57] Naturally, the specific uses to which such funds have been put have never been disclosed.

Even more direct and overt interference can be seen in South Africa's role in the 1970 constitutional crisis in Lesotho. At that time Lesotho's chief justice, chief electoral officer, and principal legal adviser, among others, were white South Africans seconded from the Pretoria government. Available evidence seems to indicate that South African involvement took two forms. A few days after the January 27, 1970, election, as returns seemed to point to a narrow victory for the opposition Basutoland Congress Party headed by Ntsu Mokhehle, Chief Jonathan summoned his cabinet and several other senior officials to prepare to hand over power. Apparently several cabinet ministers, as well as some close South African legal advisers, objected to his stepping down. This position was also favored by the police. The prime minister consequently reversed his plans at this late stage and organized his continuance in office. Indications are that he was encouraged in this course by Pretoria and by his South African advisers. Vorster officially told the South African Parliament that his government's attitude toward Lesotho was exactly the same as its attitude toward Rhodesia: "We are continuing as if nothing happened"—since Chief Jonathan was in effective control. After all, he continued, Chief Jonathan's reasons were to combat communism, and it was an "undeniable fact" that the BCP leader was a "Peking Communist."[58] But the government, despite its repetitious professions of noninterference in the domestic affairs of Lesotho, recalled Lesotho's chief justice (a South African governmental official) on the day of the coup. This meant that Chief Jonathan's seizure of power could not be challenged in the court, nor could the plea of habeas corpus be litigated on behalf of the BCP detainees who had

57. Molteno, *Africa and South Africa*, p. 25.
58. *The Star*, February 7, 1970, p. 1. See esp. Khaketla, *Lesotho 1970*.

been arrested during the election campaign and shortly thereafter. Since there is no army in Lesotho, the government depends for its security on the white-officered paramilitary Police Mobile Unit, to which South Africa quickly extended financial aid.[59] Hence, what South Africa called its "noninterference" represented a crucial crutch for the Jonathan government. South Africa may have actually instigated Chief Jonathan's seizure of power rather than agree to a BCP government on its borders. Other less overt and less direct forms of interference, as well, add up to an active clandestine foreign policy of support for sympathizers and opposition to critics in black states in the region.

DIPLOMATIC EXCHANGES AND HIGH-LEVEL VISITS

Despite his reputation for lack of tact and sensitivity in dealing with black African states, Foreign Minister Louw at least had the courage and foresight to state as early as 1959: "Exchange of diplomatic representatives with Africa will come in due course, but it must not be hurried, and when the time arrives for such representation, it should be effected gradually."[60] His words reflect the cautious policy of the RSA on the issue of the exchange of representations with Black Africa. A good deal of publicity has attended its vigorous diplomatic activity since the exchange of diplomats with Malawi in 1967 and the visits of Chief Jonathan and others in 1966. Particularly with regard to high-level visits, the pace and tone of official contact has been impressive and is accelerating. One can surmise that the extent of unpublicized high-level contact would be surprising.[61] One

59. *Sunday Times*, Johannesburg, April 26, 1970; "Fred Roach—Lesotho's Para-Military Boss," *Sechaba*, IV (July 1970), 6–7. See also Frank, *The Basutoland National Party*, pp. 23–25, and Molteno, *Africa and South Africa*, pp. 23, 25.

60. Louw in SABRA, *South Africa in the African Continent*, p. 20. See also his 1958 statement in Union of South Africa, Assembly, *Hansard*, August 18, 1958, cols. 2373–74.

61. For example, in November 1970 Foreign Minister Muller told the Transvaal Nationalist Party congress that Secretary for Foreign Affairs Brand Fourie had held discussions during the preceding few weeks with heads of two neighboring states and that R. J. Montgomery, the head of the Africa Division, had visited "no fewer" than five

of the techniques of the government has been periodically to leak information about such contacts, presumably to impress critics and supporters with the government's circumspection and energy.

Highlighting this official policy were Prime Minister Vorster's state visit to Malawi and "informal" visit to Rhodesia in 1970.[62] The return visit of Dr. Banda to South Africa in 1971 further intimated the cordiality existing between the Malawian and South African governments. The Banda-Vorster visits were conducted with maximum fanfare, although, for security reasons, pre-visit preparations were couched in secrecy. Should the dialogue overtures and proposals gain support, contacts such as these should increase markedly. The simple fact is that so far, at least, domestic apartheid has not manifestly embarrassed visiting black dignitaries. They are carefully shepherded around the republic. However, there is evidence that the reality of apartheid has prompted some African states that might otherwise contemplate visits for their officials to be reticent for fear of incidents and of possible affront through diplomatic slight.

The fear of affront is especially pervasive. A number of African governments that have expressed a desire to exchange diplomats with the RSA have added the condition that they would expect black diplomats to be accorded the same treatment and freedom of movement as white diplomats in South Africa. It is practically impossible for South Africa to guarantee that a black foreign official stationed permanently in South Africa would not encounter racial incidents or insults. The embarrassing experiences of African diplomats in the United States in recent years may have given warning to both South Africa and its prospective diplomatic guests.

The problem would be compounded immensely when resident diplomats brought their families. The South African gov-

---

African countries during the preceding few months. *The Star*, November 7, 1970, p. 2. Had this announcement not been made, no public evidence on these contacts would have been available. See also Muller's disclosures reported in *The Star*, May 8, 1969, p. 7.

62. For details see Malawi, Department of Information, *Pioneers in Inter-African Relations*, and *The Star*, May 23, 1970, pp. 1, 10.

ernment is acutely aware of this delicate situation.[63] The expedient of high-level delegations on short and carefully ushered visits provides no long-range solution to the problem, either. Such visits are perplexing from two perspectives. First, how would they endanger otherwise cordial relations between South Africa and the sensitive state involved; second, what effects would smooth (as well as awkward) diplomatic relations have on partisan and domestic political affairs?

The government has sought to create diplomatic suburbs in Pretoria and Cape Town. Even so, there is little assurance that this form of ghettoization, even though it exists elsewhere in the world, would be acceptable to sensitive, new states anxious to demonstrate their sovereignty and newly found national dignity by open diplomatic interaction. When the exchange with Malawi was initiated in 1967, the ranking Malawi official was Chargé d'affaires Philip A. Richardson, who had been a British civil servant and was the former permanent secretary for external affairs in Malawi. He was also the last white career official left in the Malawi foreign service. The next in rank was First Secretary Joseph Kachingwe, who spent only the 1968 parliamentary session in Cape Town, where he was not especially happy. Thereafter he was posted to the UN and later was returned to Blantyre to become acting permanent secretary in the Foreign Ministry. He and his successor, Frank Ntoya, who arrived in September 1969, stayed in "white" hotels and lived in Rondebosch, a "white" suburb of Cape Town. In Pretoria, Ntoya became the first African to occupy the new "mixed" diplomatic enclave of Waterkloof Heights.[64] In July 1971, Malawi upgraded its mission and Kachingwe assumed the post of ambassador.

63. For an early discussion see Union of South Africa, Assembly, *Hansard*, June 10, 1957, cols. 7618, 7635. See Prime Minister Verwoerd's discussion in RSA, Assembly, *Hansard*, April 24, 1964, cols. 4900–4902. Note too the related incident in which the chief justice of Botswana was forced to spend a night in Jan Smuts Airport. *Sunday Times*, Johannesburg, February 6, 1972, p. 10.

64. *NYT*, November 16, 1969, p. 12; *The Star*, June 5, 1971, p. 6, and July 24 and 31, pp. 3, 4.

The South Africa government has moved quickly to expedite the transition. Even though it insists that "a diplomat is a diplomat," it has built a block of flats in Rondebosch to house junior-level African diplomats. It has also bought at least two houses in the same suburb for the use of their seniors.[65] But even careful preparation can go awry at the highest levels. A press row grew out of a statement attributed to the deputy minister of agriculture, Hendrick Schoeman, regarding a visit by two Lesotho delegates. "Do you think that I enjoyed dining with Blacks?" he told a Nationalist Party rally. "But I had to do it as it was beneficial to my country."[66] Thus, even the most conscientious efforts to avoid embarrassment have not been without incident. As the numbers increase the likelihood of major upsets increase. The South African government is well aware of this, despite the insensitivity of some of its members.

At least two additional and somewhat conflicting viewpoints must be accommodated by the Nationalist government. Both, in a sense, are saying the same thing, but for entirely opposite reasons. On the one hand, there is the right wing in the Nationalist Party and those parties and elements even farther to the right. For example, the Herstigte Nasionale Party (HNP), during its electoral challenge of the Nationalists in April 1970, expressed the fear that black diplomats, enjoying the ordinary immunities and privileges accorded visiting diplomatic personnel, were the thin edge of a wedge that would ultimately divide Afrikanerdom and render white civilization in Africa flaccid. According to one HNP leader, if the HNP should come to power its government would not exchange diplomats with black states, for the reason that diplomats would not be subject to South Africa's racial laws and "could go where they liked." Rather, the HNP would exchange consuls who, unlike diplomats, are subject to the laws of South Africa.[67]

65. *The Star,* February 6, 1971, p. 3. See the comments by the United Party foreign policy spokesman, J. D. du P. Basson, in RSA, Assembly, *Hansard,* May 6, 1969, cols. 5429–30.

66. *Sunday Express* and *Sunday Times,* Johannesburg, November 23, 1969.

67. Jaap Marais, HNP deputy leader, in *The Star,* January 24, 1970,

On the other hand, there are elements to the left of the present government who see, as does the HNP, the presence of black diplomats as committing South Africa to a policy that, for the sake of consistency, demands its logical extension to include officials from the Bantustans and also prominent Bantu leaders from outside the homelands. Even within the Nationalist Party, elements have called upon the government to receive African diplomats from the Transkei with the same courtesy and full diplomatic privileges accorded to African officials from states not encircled by South Africa.[68] Urban Africans in the RSA as well are aware of the differential treatment accorded foreign black visitors and that given their own leaders. They are asking why their leaders cannot be entertained in "white" hotels and cannot gain access to top government officials.[69] So are many whites. One of South Africa's top public relations firms has gone even farther and recommended that the government train nonwhite diplomats from the homelands to improve South Africa's popular image abroad.[70] The government is caught in the middle. To domestic whites it insists that the reception and residence of African diplomats will not jeopardize racial separation in the republic. In practice, its policy has been guarded. From 1967 to 1971, when Malawi appointed a black ambassador, there had been only one black diplomat resident in South Africa at any one time—the Malawi legation's first secretary. In the reception of visiting black dignitaries the government has been scrupulous in seeking to avoid incidents. Not always, however, has it been totally successful. The government certainly cannot be charged with plunging headlong into a policy whose ramifications it cannot foresee or control.

p. 6. See also HNP leader Dr. Albert Hertzog in the *Cape Times*, February 4, 1970.

68. Munger, *Bechuanaland*, pp. 82–83, mentions *Die Burger*, Cape Town, and *Dagbreek en Sondagnuus*, Johannesburg. The editor of the former, Piet Cillie, is an influential voice in Nationalist Party circles in the Cape Province. *Dagbreek en Sondagnuus* is a Sunday paper published by a company of which Dr. Verwoerd had been the chairman.

69. See the column by "Mhloli," in *The Star*, April 3, 1971, p. 10.

70. *The Star*, July 18, 1970, p. 12.

FINANCIAL AND TECHNICAL ASSISTANCE

The extent and meaning of South Africa's financial and technical assistance to neighboring black states has been reviewed in Chapter 2.

Domestic Reactions and Debate

All this activity has not gone without considerable discussion and debate among white South Africans. Under normal circumstances, a policy of establishing more cordial linkages with one's immediate neighbors would not precipitate major policy debates and widespread discussion. But South Africa is far from normal. Virtually all policy discussion involves consideration of racial issues and the long- and short-term consequences for white dominance. Hence foreign policy is not examined solely on its merits, in the sense of enabling a society to cope with (by altering or adapting to) its external environment.[71] In South Africa, foreign policy is viewed from the standpoint of the flexibility that is deemed necessary or possible in order to maintain the essential structures of society within acceptable limits. The profound cleavages that exist within the white population of South Africa are expressed openly in the difficult task of defining South Africa's essential societal structures, while among those who can reach some vague agreement on essential structures there still remains division on how to define acceptable limits.

Yet since the late 1960s that has been a striking range of agreement in white South Africa on the outward-looking policy. This agreement encompasses partisan conflict.[72] Even the Progressive Party endorses the government's Africa policy, though the party questions its motivations and impact, and demands its acceleration.[73] Agreement is even beginning to transcend eth-

71. See the theoretical discussion of foreign policy in Rosenau, *The Adaptation of National Societies.*
72. For example, the extended debate on the foreign affairs vote. RSA, Assembly, *Hansard,* May 6–7, 1969, cols. 5424–5503.
73. See the party's *Forging Links in Africa,* esp. p. 11, and my interview with Colin W. Eglin, national executive chairman of the party, RSA–8, Cape Town, July 31, 1969.

nic divisions within the white population. Afrikanerdom, within which one can find the chief sources of opposition to the outward-looking policy, has undergone several significant socioeconomic changes in the past several decades. Edwin Munger has characterized these changes as a movement from accepting the leadership and guidance of the *predikante* and the politician to accepting that of the politician and the Afrikaner businessman.[74] In Munger's view the *laager* (an Afrikaans word for the inward-looking character of the Afrikaner community) is being modernized and widened as the white oligarchy of South Africa grows more unified. Though this may be an exaggerated interpretation of South African social affairs, the trend is evident, and is most pronounced in the area of foreign policy. Many a South African liberal and government critic reluctantly admits that the only government policy with which he or she can agree is the outward-looking policy. Likewise, the English-language press and the business elite, long in opposition to domestic Nationalist policies, by and large enthusiastically endorse the outward-looking policy. To some extent their agreement is predicated on the feeling that they must agree with the government on some things in order to maintain their bona fides to oppose on affairs more controversial and closer to home. But, for the most part, the outward-looking policy has emerged as the epitome of the old American aphorism that partisan and divisive politics stops at the water's edge.

Opposition to the outward-looking policy, when it is expressed, develops from two polarized quarters. On the one hand, the most important and potentially dangerous challenge to the policy comes from the right—the verkramptes, who see the government's Africa policy as symptomatic of the malaise of Afrikaner culture. Although the importance of verkrampte pressures may be exaggerated in the political cartoon in figure 7, there is no question that Vorster has not had an easy time trying to balance off or outflank verligtes and verkramptes in his party. In rural areas, especially in the Transvaal and the Orange Free State, in the Dutch Reformed church, and among elderly

74. Munger, "New White Politics in South Africa," in Hance, ed., *Southern Africa and the United States*, pp. 33–84.

Figure 7. The Nationalist Party split between *verligte* and *verkrampte*. From the *Sunday Times*, Johannesburg, August 31, 1969, p. 17. Reproduced with the permission of the editor, the *Sunday Times*.

people can be found opponents of dealing cordially and intimately with black Africans. The fact that such dealings are on a diplomatic level and involve foreign Africans does not mean a great deal in the reasoning. God, history, the Bible, or destiny have willed absolute separation and white dominance. Any policy that smacks of compromise with these vague dictates can lead to the demise of the Afrikaner community and with it Calvinism and white civilization in Africa. Staunch anti-communists would go even further to contend that South Africa's white population is the linchpin of white civilization since, geopolitically, South Africa is ostensibly the key to the control of Africa, and Africa in turn is the target of communist "aggression" and hence the secret to world dominance. To some extent this viewpoint gained wide and ostensibly "legitimate" expression in the Africa Institute in Pretoria, particularly before Professor P. F. D. Weiss was dismissed as its director in November 1969, and in the South Africa Broadcasting Corporation under Dr. Piet Meyer.[75]

In partisan terms, the Herstigte Nasionale Party arose in

75. See *News/Check*, IX, 13, September 18, 1970.

1969-70 to articulate these views for the voters. It would be faulty to think that the HNP arose to oppose the outward-looking policy. The HNP's chief thrust centered on domestic racial issues and the matter of Afrikaner-English relations within the republic. But since, in verkrampte eyes, the outward policy would have profound and negative effects on South Africa's domestic structures, they opposed extended relations with neighboring black states. The HNP, its leader Dr. Albert Hertzog, its organ *Veg* (edited by Barry Botha), Dr. Ras Beyers, and the press on the right wing of the Nationalist Party led by Dr. Andries Treurnicht, an M.P. and former editor of *Hoofstad*, and S. E. D. Brown, of the *South African Observer*, have hammered away at the government, but have made little headway among the electorate.[76] Although the HNP stood 78 candidates in the April 1970 national parliamentary elections, none of its candidates were returned and all but three lost their deposits. Nationally they gained only 3.56 percent of the votes, almost all of them in the Transvaal.[77] In many respects, this is because of the nature of partisan competition in South Africa. The right still has an audience, particularly on domestic racial issues. The electoral challenge from the right, however, has been dissipated by the Nationalists, at least temporarily, particularly as it affects foreign policy, largely because the government has not been as flexible toward black Africa as it would like outsiders to believe.

The second source of opposition to the government's outward policy comes from what have been called the "super-verligtes." Some can be found within the Nationalist Party, but most of them would be members of the United Party (UP) or the Progressive Party. One consistent champion of greater and more correct interaction with black Africa has been Japie D. du Ples-

76. See Delius, "Internal Argument and External Policy," *African Affairs*, LXIX (1970), 371–74; Nolutshungu, "Issues of the Afrikaner 'Enlightenment,' " ibid., LXX (1971), 23–36. The tenor of this debate can be sensed in the following newspaper accounts: "It's Like a War between Moles," *Sunday Tribune*, Johannesburg, August 10, 1969, p. 16; "Verkramptes Rallying Forces," *Sunday Times*, Johannesburg, August 17, p. 2; J. H. P. Serfontein, "Full-Scale Verkrampte Press Attack on Vorster," ibid., August 3, p. 6; and articles by Serfontein and Stanley Uys, ibid., August 31, 1969, pp. 12, 7, and 2.
77. *The Star*, April 25, 1970, p. 2.

sis Basson, the UP spokesman on foreign affairs. As early as 1957 he was urging the government to establish friendly relations with emerging Africa.[78] Today his message is even stronger, demanding South African initiatives such as a round of invitations to hostile as well as friendly leaders in Africa, and the domestic rectification of what he labels "crude apartheid." In his estimation it is South Africa's racial policies, and particularly "crude [petty] apartheid," that create undue barriers to regional and wider cordiality. He feels that, given South Africa's domestic racial policies, it is remarkable that the republic has good relations with anybody.[79] Since Basson is a central figure in the UP and its shadow cabinet, and could be the successor to Sir de Villiers Graaf as opposition leader, his views deserve careful consideration.

Within the Nationalist Party, men such as Piet Cillie (editor of *Die Burger* and influential among Cape Nationalists), Schalk Pienaar (former editor of *Die Beeld*, Johannesburg), and Advocate R. F. "Pik" Botha (M.P. for the Pretoria constituency of Wonderboom and former officer in the Department of Foreign Affairs) are just a few of the influential members who are trying to stimulate governmental initiatives and activity in favor of the outward policy.[80] In party counsels and congresses the verkramptes continue to resist, but on the cautious outward-looking policy, at least, they have been eclipsed.

Thus, the pressures in support of an active Africa policy seem to be on the ascent in South Africa even if the reasons underlying these pressures are basically conservative. Anti-communism, strategic security, increased trade and economic dominance, missionary duty and destiny, and the preservation of the South African "way of life," with all this implies, provide

78. RSA, Assembly, *Hansard*, June 10, 1957, cols. 7660–63.
79. Interview with Basson, RSA–15, Johannesburg, August 5, 1969. See also *The Star*, May 8, 1971, p. 15, and "Can the UP Win with Japie Basson?" *News/Check*, IX, 9–11, November 13, 1970. See also Transvaal UP leader S. J. M. Steyn's speech in *The Star*, March 14, 1970, p. 4.
80. See *The Star*, November 7, 1970, p. 16; Hugh Murray, "Verligtes Start to Speak Out," *News/Check*, IX, 10, 13–14, September 4 and September 18, 1970; and interviews, RSA–7, Cape Town, July 31, 1969, and RSA–19, Pretoria, August 9, 1969.

the propulsions for reaching outward. There is a general tendency in the English-language South African press to exaggerate each division, each open criticism, each gesture of support and expression of change that occurs in white South Africa. Had one read all the copy generated by the verkramptes and verligtes and by the HNP electoral debate that ensued, one would have expected the HNP to garner more than 53,763 votes. A measure of caution is required to put change and dissent in perspective. For this reason, too much should not be read into reports of dissent in Afrikanerdom. To be sure, things are not the same as they were when the Nationalist Party came to power in 1948. But the outside observer must be wary of highly competitive press in search of salable copy, and the naïve hopes of editors and reporters wishfully thinking about and trying to encourage a progressive evolution of the white South African citizenry.

How Far Can the Outward-looking Policy Go?

To suggest answers—and only speculative answers, it might be added—to the question "How far can the outward-looking policy go?" we must re-pose the question from two differing viewpoints. We might ask "What are the domestic limitations and forces facing the outward policy?" We then could follow that up by a second question, "How far will the independent states of black Africa allow South Africa to become involved in their affairs?" The first question returns us to the vital issue of the perceived "essential structures" of South African society. To the preponderant white oligarchy, racial dominance is the sine qua non of any foreign policy. The moment it is perceived that interaction with black Africa jeopardizes continued white dominance and privilege, foreign policy will have failed the republic. By and large, it is not likely that interaction—at least on the level on which it now is conducted, or even on a foreseeably more intensive and extensive level—could affect the domestic racial structure. Most of the contact with black Africa has taken place outside South Africa, and contact in the republic is carefully controlled. It is the nature of diplomatic contact that the host country supervises contact on its own terms. This fact is known full well in Pretoria and is the subject of constant discussion there. Nevertheless there is an obvious commitment by the Vorster government to its outward policy, at least as the government understands it.[81]

The view that somehow or other contact with black Africa will convince white South Africans of the error and folly of their racist ways ignores the very purpose of the outward policy as seen by the South African government and its UP opposition. That purpose is to defend and sustain a sociopolitical structure that thrives on racial super- and subordination. If changes do occur in racial relations, they will most likely be superficial. It is unlikely that any government would consciously pursue a policy that, according to its own stated ends, would be counterproductive. We have seen above that political and social forces have unified a good portion of the white citizenry behind the outward policy, at least of those who are attentive to foreign policy matters. As they see it, even a stepped-up outward movement would not materially affect relations between Europeans and non-whites at home. Hence they support and encourage the government in its first halting steps toward black Africa.

A somewhat cynical but basically sound interpretation holds that the outward policy is designed to create sufficiently cordial relations with black Africa to buffer the republic in strategic terms and to enable its economic dominance to extend profitably northward. But insofar as the governments that deal with South Africa are unpopular and unstable, the outward policy may be self-defeating: in the long run, identification with South Africa may be the kiss of death to insecure black governments. In this context Anthony Delius has argued that the more South Africa involves itself in the affairs of black Africa, the more may its policies advance the opportunities for communist influence on the continent.[82] "South Africa might prove to be Peking's excuse for strengthening its influence." Until South Africa's racial policies are radically altered, he reasons, its efforts to fill

81. A major portion of Vorster's important speech at the republic's tenth anniversary festival was devoted to the government's commitment to its Africa policy. *The Star,* June 5, 1971, p. 8.

82. "China's Waiting Game in Africa," *Cape Times,* July 28, 1969, p. 8.

the vacuum created by British de-colonization will precipitate a symmetrical involvement by communist forces. He concludes that "In Africa, it is the race issue that prevents a greater drawing together of the potential resisters of communism in Africa." Thus, the outward-looking policy could set into motion the very counterforces it seeks to overcome.

Racial discrimination and exploitation is, ironically, both a raison d'être of the outward policy and the chief domestic obstacle to its fulfillment. Apartheid cannot be rendered neutral. It persistently intrudes itself into the outward policy because that policy is designed to defend and strengthen the system. Thus more than salesmanship and public relations will be needed to make the outward policy successful. There must be a product to sell, and domestic racial policies place inherent limitations on the market. Nevertheless, some African governments might become so desperate as to postpone or cancel their aspirations for majority rule on the continent. Those black states that take the pragmatic or "realistic" course—as they see it—and are dealing with South Africa do so because their choices are severely limited (or are perceived to be so), or because they see economic benefits in it. There are but a few states that "have to" deal with South Africa, and even fewer that could genuinely profit from the association. To be sure, there are individual politicians in black Africa who might gain by exploiting expanding relationships with the republic. It is not likely, however, that their constituents could, in more than a few cases, really gain economically. South Africa's resources are not unlimited, although in the regional setting they are relatively impressive. The American, British, and Russian experiences in Africa should have demonstrated that familiarity does not always breed cooperation and friendship, and that trade, capital, and technical aid will not in themselves yield economic growth and political stability. In many respects the apparent success of the outward-looking policy may represent its fullest possible extension. *The Star* expressed this viewpoint editorially when it argued: "The fact remains that our once promising outward policy seems to have ground to a halt on the frontiers of our immediate sphere of influence in Africa. . . . With foreign policy held firmly captive by policy at home, the prospect is one of just isolation and more isolation."[83] Any further or deeper penetration will be difficult, since Professor Kenneth Boulding's "loss of strength gradient" applies to southern African regional affairs.[84]

From the perspective of the newly independent states of Africa, further barriers face the outward-policy. First is the awkward situation created by Rhodesian independence. Even though South Africa would like to regard this as a dispute between Britain and Rhodesia, South Africa's reluctant support for the Smith government temporarily endangered the outward-looking policy in Black Africa. Uncertainty over the future nature of Rhodesia still obstructs the orderly development of the region and, hence, the flow of the outward movement. Until Rhodesia begins to establish working relationships with its black neighbors and other African states, South Africa's policies will be rendered generally suspect. South Africa has sought to facilitate the normalization of Rhodesia's relations with neighbor states, but without appreciable effect.

South Africa's relations with Zambia, although commercially fruitful, have been politically embittered and rendered stagnant by the Rhodesian situation. Zambia might possibly have gravitated southward toward a loose regional economic association. Though this was not likely, patterns at independence might have encouraged it. The UDI forced Zambia to look elsewhere, and events since then have furthered a northward orientation. President Kaunda's intense leadership of the anti-South African forces seems to mean that unless governments can be displaced by extra-legal means, future breakthroughs for South Africa in black Africa will come only among already conservative regimes closely identified with the West, especially with France.

There is not a black government in Africa that has openly voiced approval of South Africa's domestic racial policies. Thus an initial hurdle exists. To some extent the willingness to consider dialogue is a reaction to the failure of the advocates of guerrilla struggle or economic and diplomatic pressure. It would

83. *The Star*, May 6, 1972, p. 10.
84. Boulding, *Conflict and Defense*, pp. 227–48, 260–62, 268–69.

stand to reason that as dialogue and open diplomatic interaction likewise fail to yield changes in South Africa's racial patterns, they too may be abandoned as viable alternatives. Then only those who cannot possibly avoid open contact or who need South Africa's support to stay in power can be expected to deal with South Africa. It is to be expected that there will always be a handful of such governments in the region.

We can conclude that the outward policy is essentially an extension and reformulation of an old defensive line, prompted by an acute need for markets for industrial products and investment capital. It comes at a time when the RSA is better prepared (for domestic reasons) to extend its policies abroad, not in the sense that it wants to "export" apartheid, but in the sense that apartheid can be strengthened domestically by dealing with black-governed neighboring states. So, the coalescence of the white oligarchy, the economic growth and high-cost industrial expansion of South Africa, and the need to adjust foreign policy to the realities of African independence have stimulated the outward-looking policy. We cannot expect fundamental changes in the patterns of racial stratification within South Africa to occur because of the outward policy. If change should occur it would be a function of other massive domestic or external factors.

8

Conclusions: Hardened Positions and Pragmatic Responses

He who does not cultivate his field will die of hunger. —*Guinea*

The generalizations that follow will proceed on two levels: that of the regional sub-system and that of the foreign policies of individual nation-states. Obviously, there is an interaction between levels that makes any dichotomy artificial and misleading. Nevertheless, it is hoped that the conclusions drawn from the data presented above will indicate patterns of interaction and that the method chosen for presenting the findings will not unduly distort the information and its interpretation.

The Concept of "Border" in Southern Africa

Before moving directly into a discussion of the sub-system, we should devote some space to the widespread tendency to depict international relations in southern Africa as involving a clearly delineated and divisive "border," somewhat akin to the "iron" or "bamboo" curtains of the past three decades.[1] Journalists

1. In an earlier essay I have attempted to demonstrate the amorphous,

seem attached to neat, catchy concepts. Participants in regional politics, in particular, find such designations convenient, especially insofar as categorical postures may help enhance their domestic or international political stature. We may note that although, in Europe, the "iron curtain" was physically demarcated and the barriers were imposing, the division was not complete, especially after the passage of time.

The southern African "border," if there is such a phenomenon, is far less impressive, even though the criterion most commonly used to define it—racial dominance—is popularly thought to be physically demonstrable. The late Eduardo Mondlane wrote: "In Africa the dividing line between the white-dominated South and the independent states to the north is hardening."[2] ZAPU's *Zimbabwe Review,* in a curious and confusing interchange of defensive and aggressive metaphors, has referred to the "Zambezi Apartheid White Wall" and the "Zambezi Line of Aggression."[3] President Kaunda still speaks of a "holocaust" in which "the battlefront would be the Zambezi," President Nyerere has been quoted as saying that the whites seek to create a "political Maginot line along the Zambezi," and Swedish Prime Minister Olaf Palme has referred to that river as "the border of human decency."[4] One writer has asked whether the Zambezi or the Limpopo would constitute Africa's "Mason-Dixon Line."[5]

White southerners are no less taken by the concept of a frontier or battle line. In most cases they have spoken of their "defense line" or defensive perimeter. South Africa has variously located such a line at the "equator and beyond," thereby in-

---

permeable, and analytically elusive character of any such conception: "The 'Southern Border' of Africa," in Widstrand, ed., *African Boundary Problems,* pp. 119–60, 196–202.

2. *The Struggle for Mozambique,* p. 197.

3. *Zimbabwe Review,* Lusaka, I (December 1969), 7.

4. Kaunda quoted in *The Star,* March 20, 1971, p. 3; Nyerere in Hall, *The High Price,* p. 56; Palme in *The Times of Zambia,* November 26, 1971.

5. André Siegfried, *African Journey* (London, 1950), cited in Kirkwood, *Britain and Africa,* p. 111. Kirkwood himself, though rejecting Siegfried's emotional phrase, calls the Zambezi a "historical and policy frontier within British Africa."

cluding Kenya and Tanganyika, or at the Zambezi, but never back at the Limpopo.[6] The Rhodesians similarly have called the Zambezi a "Red Frontier," and, as do the Portuguese, see their territory serving as a dam against the flood of, variously (depending on the issue and the audience), black, red, and yellow hordes.

Although such designations often lack geographical precision, even when they possess identifiability, as in the case of a definable line such as the equator or the Zambezi or some other physical boundary, geographical precision does not necessarily provide us with analytical accuracy in political terms. The use of a border concept is a geopolitical device. But geopolitical concepts do not easily lend themselves to the definition of boundaries of sociopolitical systems or sub-systems. Indeed, in the case of the present study, the border approach would be positively perverse, presenting a deformed "map" of sociopolitical realities in the region. It becomes awkward to deal with, both in the historical sequence of events and in presenting the situation at any specific time.

Historically, the border has had a persistent habit of drifting, even when we lay down criteria for defining it. Let us, for the sake of a working definition, say that the "border" between the North and the South is the political division between states (or sub-divisions thereof) whose governments enjoy the support of the governments of South Africa and Portugal. There are tremendous difficulties in working with this definition, and indeed in the ostensibly simple task of defining a boundary in more than spatial terms. But such a challenge would only serve to reinforce the point I seek to make.

Before the demise of the British colonial empire in Africa, and after the rise to power of the Afrikaner Nationalist Party, the South African government had made its peace with Great Britain. Even though republican status and Commonwealth membership were controversial issues in South Africa, the Nationalist government found itself supporting continued British

6. See the several quotations in Vandenbosch, *South Africa and the World*, by Lord Selborne (p. 57), Cecil Rhodes (p. 58), Smuts (pp. 12, 33, 111), and Defense Minister Oswald Pirow (pp. 109, 155).

rule in East and Central Africa, though not necessarily in the High Commission Territories. South Africa had representatives in Salisbury and Nairobi, and did what it could, which was little, to retard the pace of African majority rule and independence. Likewise, it was represented in Leopoldville and Elisabethville, and it favored continued Belgian rule in the Congo. Thus one can say that, in a sense, for South Africa the "border" between southern Africa and the rest of the continent ran along the Congo River and included the line between Uganda and Kenya on one hand and the Sudan, Ethiopia, and Somalia on the other. Now this would, of course, be an absurdity. South Africa's economic influence was marginal north of Northern Rhodesia and Southern Rhodesia, and by and large, though she had contacts with colonial-ruled Africa, the relationships were exceedingly limited. In this regard, the border per se was fuzzy and basically indistinguishable. Once the prospect of independence became real, however, new patterns emerged.

When Congolese independence was impending in 1960, South Africa withdrew all seven diplomatic and consular officials from the territory, and the "border" moved southward to the boundary with Angola and Northern Rhodesia. The guerrilla war beginning in 1961 in Angola only pointed up more vividly the division between the independent Congo and Portuguese-ruled Angola. The secession of Katanga, which the South Africans supported, served to relocate the "border" northward again. The Tshombe government harassed Angolan nationalists, occasionally cooperated with Portuguese authorities, and enlisted European mercenaries, many of whom came from South Africa and Rhodesia. Recruiting offices were established in Johannesburg and Bulawayo.

Portugal, Rhodesia, and South Africa (among others) each sought to exert influence on Katanga's affairs and hence those of the Congo.[7] The Congo's independence had brought the "borders" of nationalist Africa to Angola and the Central African Federation. Black-ruled Africa now confronted white settler-ruled Africa. When war broke out in Angola, nationalists were

7. The extent of foreign involvement, especially regarding foreign mercenaries, is neatly outlined in Clarke, *The Congo Mercenary*.

based in the Congo. Portugal feared that it would be virtually impossible to close effectively Angola's long border with the Congo. Meanwhile, the Tshombe government sought allies. Portugal willingly collaborated. The Benguela railway became Katanga's lifeline for weapons and material. A marriage of convenience was struck up that was to outlast Tshombe's Katanga state.

The resident white leaders of the Federation of Rhodesia and Nyasaland were insecure, in that Britain maintained authority to deal with African nationalism, especially in Northern Rhodesia and Nyasaland. To Federal Prime Minister Sir Roy Welensky, the maintenance of Tshombe's government in Katanga was regarded as critical for the internal political system in Northern Rhodesia. Katanga became a buffer that Welensky encouraged, although, except for providing the security for Katanga's southern flank and acting as a bargaining lever for Katanga in Tshombe's meetings with UN and Belgian officials, the Federation government was not able to render direct or indispensable assistance. It supported the recruitment of mercenaries, obstructed UN activities against Tshombe, and sought to expedite shipments from the South.

An element in Salisbury even dreamed at one point of parlaying Nyasaland's drive to nationalist independence and Tshombe's malleability into an enriched and strengthened, white-dominated federation. It was felt that with Nyasaland out of the Federation, a closer control of nationalists in Northern Rhodesia might be maintained. It was conceded that this might necessitate establishing a security band (a new "border"?) across the 100-mile stretch between the Congo and Mozambique. Thus Nyasaland would be cut loose, the virtually unproductive Northern and Eastern provinces of Northern Rhodesia abandoned, perhaps to join with Tanganyika or Nyasaland, and the profitable sectors kept securely in white hands. It was even suggested that in this event Katanga and the Rhodesias might join, thereby creating an industrial heartland for Africa.[8] Tshombe's defeat by the UN forces in January 1963 put an end to such fatuity.

8. See Hall, *The High Price*, pp. 63–64.

South Africa saw Katanga's secession as an opportunity to protect the Federation and the Portuguese territories, which were regarded as its own buffers. By playing on Tshombe's professed anti-communism and open collaboration with southern white governments, Verwoerd was able to assist a "black" state. Katanga's foreign policies coincided with or furthered South Africa's and hence, from 1960 until January 1963, the "southern border" of Africa was temporarily shifted to the frontier between the central Congolese and Katangese forces.

From July 1964, when Tshombe became prime minister of the central Congolese government, until his removal in October 1965, the Katangese scenario was replayed on a grander scale. The Congo again came to be regarded as a battleground, or actually was included by some within the southern orbit. For example, the final communiqué released after the visit of Tanzania's President Nyerere to Mali in April 1965 said that the two countries wanted to alert the world to the fact that South Africa, Portugal, and Rhodesia had undertaken a war, in collusion with the government of the Congo, to exterminate the black man in Africa. The Congo, in their words, had fallen victim to "imperialist-inspired machinations."[9] After all, Tshombe relied heavily on mercenary units and former gendarmes, many of whom had been quartered in Angola by the Portuguese authorities from 1963 until 1964. The extent of the Tshombe-Portuguese collaboration was evident in the reduced effectiveness of the Angolan nationalists when the old Katangese fighting combination was reconstituted. Colonel Mike Hoare was recalled from South Africa and his agents began recruiting in Johannesburg and Salisbury. South African recruits were flown from Johannesburg to Kamina without any immigration formalities such as visas or the need for passports, an obvious demonstration of South African support.[10] The "medical" and "food" supplies sent to the Congo in August 1964 were more symbolically important than they were practical. There have

9. *East African Standard*, April 19, 1965, and *Daily Nation*, April 5, both of Nairobi.

10. Clarke, *The Congo Mercenary*, pp. 41–42; Hoare, *Congo Mercenary*, pp. 17–74.

been rumors that military material may have been included under these rubrics. At any rate, Moise Tshombe, not Dr. Banda, can be said to have been the first black African head of government to receive open assistance from the Republic of South Africa. In this regard, the outward policy received its first baptism of fire in the Congo in 1964. Secession and changing governments provided the impetus for the expansions and contractions of white southern Africa's sphere of influence.

The British-ruled territories of central Africa provide another example of the "rubber band" border between southern and central Africa. The Federation of Rhodesia and Nyasaland had been constituted in 1953 at the behest of white settlers and politicians in these territories, especially in Southern Rhodesia. Under the guise of "racial partnership" white dominance was maintained despite the continent-wide pattern of efflorescent African nationalism and more urgent demands for independence. With the breakup of the Federation in 1963 and the independence (under African rule) of Malawi and Zambia, it was felt that the Zambezi River was the logical dividing line. One British Conservative M.P. put it disparagingly: "Africa is divided by the Zambezi River. South of the Zambezi there is trade; north of it there is charity."[11] It was not long before this clear-cut division became more difficult to sustain. Malawi continued to look southward for support. The Rhodesian UDI seemed on the surface to harden the ideological positions of regional actors. Nevertheless, as Zambia attempted to offset its dependence upon Rhodesia, the new state found itself increasingly enmeshed by dependence upon Portuguese-controlled transport routes and upon imports from South Africa. Successive steps have been taken to lessen this pattern and it is likely that by 1975 the level of economic interaction between Zambia and white Africa will be considerably diminished.

To complicate the picture further, how should one deal with Botswana, Lesotho, and Swaziland? Geographically they

11. Walter Paget, *Parliamentary Debates,* Commons, *Hansard,* vol. 756, no. 34 (December 19, 1967), col. 1118. By way of contrast see Nyerere's speech on April 10, 1965 in his *Freedom and Unity,* p. 327, and the map in Nielsen, *African Battleline,* p. 1.

are part of the Southern orbit. Economically, as well, they fall within the Southern sub-system. But Botswana has undertaken policies (for instance, its determination to link up with Zambia, its diplomatic interaction with the Soviet Union, and its unwillingness to assent to South African overtures for assistance) which the Republic of South Africa and Rhodesia do not approve. In this context it may be inaccurate to regard Botswana as part of the Southern sub-system. These three black states may be anomalous in any geographical rendering of a "border."

It has been demonstrated elsewhere that, by and large, borders between black African states are historically and ethnically irrelevant, and that with a few exceptions they do not contain the seeds of major conflict.[12] Likewise, the boundaries chosen to represent any division between black and white Africa do not possess conflict potential per se. Rather it is the policies pursued by the governments on either side that lead to conflict. Thus the border is an uneasy one, not because of the nature of demarcation of the boundaries, but because there are far more serious issues at stake. The "southern border" is an unstable one because of disputes regarding the very legitimacy of neighboring governments. These governments are not struggling for a few hundred square miles of territory here or there, but for principles, and for whole states whose futures are bound up in those principles.

The picture has been one of a fluid "border" that tends to shift location with radical shifts of government—by and large (except for the case of Katanga) affecting whole states at a time. The "southern border" can only be regarded as a residual border reflecting the existence of two fluid sets of relationships dividing the continent. Should these groupings become crystallized, the "border" would assume a firm character of its own, tending to reinforce rather than reflect patterns of relationships. There are signs that this is increasingly the case. Yet it would be fundamentally inaccurate to stress such a characterization of international relations in southern Africa: there has been far

12. For instance, Kapil, "On the Conflict Potential of Inherited Boundaries in Africa," *World Politics*, XVIII (1966), 656–73, and Zartman, *International Relations in the New Africa*, pp. 105–19.

too much movement of the "border" with time, and there is still too much permeability in the "border" today.

If we could disregard changes over time, as well, the "border" concept would still leave a great deal to be desired. Even, given a fixed time, debate could occur as to where the "border" should be placed. The chief reason for this is that a delineation of the "border" depends upon the choice of criteria employed. So far, at least, it has been practically impossible to weigh criteria for all actors, and thus the amorphous nature of any such "border" must be admitted. Furthermore, boundaries are fine lines of division designed to demarcate sharp discontinuities. Given the extent of interaction among African territories, it becomes clear that boundaries cannot easily be fixed in zones of sociocultural transition. In the following sections, as we discuss the flexibility of "membership," and the multidimensionality of the sub-systems, the difficulties of creating discrete yet interlocking criteria will be evident, and thus the reason why the concept of "border" was not retained in this analysis will be demonstrated.

Flexible Non-Exclusive "Membership" in the Sub-System

At any given time, it could be said that there exist, superimposed upon one another, many regional sub-systems. Each one might be subsumed under a single criterion or under a combination of related criteria.[13] These sub-systems tend to overlap, but do not necessarily do so. In this section we shall discuss the concept of "membership" in the sub-system.

Membership in any sub-system is dependent upon two sets of variables: (1) the substantive criteria defining the sub-system, and (2) the varying degrees of commitment and identification with the sub-system so described. Let us take the second set first. The data presented in the preceding chapters indicate convincingly that there are degrees of involvement in sub-systemic af-

13. This general idea is also advanced in E. Raymond Platig, "International Relations as a Field of Inquiry," in Rosenau, ed., *International Politics and Foreign Policy*, pp. 17–18.

fairs and in commitment to the maintenance of the sub-system. The external behavior of Tanzania and Zambia further suggests that although they are deeply involved in sub-systemic affairs (the first in a political and strategic sense and the second according to several variables, especially the economic and strategic) they are also vigorous participants in another distinct yet related sub-system, that characterized by the OAU. The data on southern Africa does not appear to sustain the contention of Cantori and Spiegel that "every nation-state . . . is a member of only one subordinate system."[14] In the southern African context, it would be misleadingly simplistic to regard membership in one sub-system as exclusive.

Note should also be taken of the extent of commitment to the maintenance of the sub-system. Is an actor cooperative or supportive in its participation, or is it reluctant or, more extremely, disruptive within the sub-system? In many respects answers to these questions necessitate value judgments. We are also forced to make a decision as to whether we want to look at the intended or the fortuitous effects of a state's involvement. On the issue of commitment, if we regard the establishment of a southern African sub-system as a pattern of interaction that the Republic of South Africa seeks to extend, maintain, and institutionalize, we might ask an actor how far it would go toward greater regional integration—or, conversely, what risks would it assume to prevent the establishment or secure the destruction of such a sub-system?

The southern African regional sub-system bears some resemblance to the East European sub-system in one important respect. The pattern of interaction is a series of bilateral arrangements between the center on one hand and the other regional states on the other. South Africa can, like the Soviet Union, dominate the sub-system. In structural as well as political and economic terms South Africa has sub-systematic advantages. There are few important multilateral relationships. Thus, by serving as the institutional and communications hub of the region South Africa can maintain control of regional affairs and prevent or make difficult the collaboration of its neighbors against

14. Cantori and Spiegel, *The International Politics of Regions*, p. 5.

the republic. Regional relationships thereby take on the pattern of a wheel with little if any institutionalized contact between states on the extremities of the spokes. There have, however, been periodic expressions of support for schemes ranging from economic cooperation with weak or no central institutions to supranationality on certain narrow functional issues—for instance, water and soil resources, and the control of disease.

The terminology devised by Cantori and Spiegel might be usefully employed in analyzing our data. They identify three "sectors" of a regional sub-system: the core, the periphery, and the intrusive systems.[15]

1. "The core sector consists of a state or a group of states which form a central focus of the international politics within a given region." The existence of a core sector can be determined by its "level of cohesion." In other words, how much social, economic, and political similarity and complementarity exists among the particular states concerned? Has their cohesion been given organizational expression? The core is also identifiable by the nature of communications and the levels and distribution of power within the sub-system. Communications among core states and their residents would be more intense and core states would be obviously superior in various elements of state power.

2. "The peripheral sector includes all those states within a given subordinate system which are alienated from the core sector in some degree by social, political, economic, or organizational factors, but which nevertheless play a role in the politics of the subordinate system." The peripheral states do not always share all of the aspirations of the core actors. Nor do they interact with the core or with one another as extensively or intensively as do the core states among themselves. The peripheral sector may also be geographically removed from the core, and it is more than likely that other factors, such as the lower levels of cohesion, communication, and power on the periphery, will reinforce this isolation. Thus by choice and by policies imposed on them by more powerful states or by physical conditions beyond their control, they may be excluded from the core, though

15. Ibid., pp. 20–26.

patterned interactions are sufficiently evident to keep them within the sub-system.

3. "An intrusive system consists of the politically significant participation of external powers in the international relations of the subordinate system." It might be added that the intrusive sector is also involved in the internal affairs of the sub-system's member states. Naturally such involvement could be either significant or insignificant politically. Moreover, we could also speak of regionally adjacent intrusive states and of geographically distant intrusive states—those powers with deep interests in the regional sub-system or its component parts. If it is our intention to search for various degrees and kinds of involvement in the sub-system, the Cantori-Spiegel categorization seems to be suggestive of a fruitful line of analysis.

The Multidimensionality of the Sub-System

In this section we can summarize our data organized according to the various criteria employed to delimit the sub-system. The first criterion is the *geographic*.[16] If we use as our core those states under white governance we can designate (1) those states completely surrounded by white-ruled states or territories also as core members, (2) those black-governed states who share a small (less than 200 miles) common border with other black states as peripheral, (3) those states whose borders with black and white states are approximately equal as peripheral, and (4) those states that only share a small (less than 200 miles) common border with white Africa as outside the sub-system. The designation "intrusive" would not be included here since, by definition, intrusive actors are geographically distant from the region. Thus the core states by this map are: South Africa, Rhodesia, Mozambique, and Angola, plus Lesotho and Swaziland. Peripheral states, by degrees of propinquity, are Botswana, Malawi,

16. Brams has found that "geographical proximity" is the "most compelling force of attraction in the international system," but this does not get us far beyond the analytically obvious when answering questions about where regional sub-systems begin and end. "Transaction Flows in the International System," *American Political Science Review*, LX (1966), 880–98.

Zambia, the Congo, and Tanzania. The borders of the Congo could be both cooperative (Benguela railway) and disruptive (the movement of guerrillas, soldiers, and refugees); that of Tanzania with Mozambique is primarily disruptive of sub-systemic affairs. But the geographic map is essentially of little help in political terms, though it may be important in facilitating interpretation or in delimiting alternatives.

The *racial* picture is equally simplistic. Core states would be those governed by whites (South Africa, Rhodesia, Angola, and Mozambique) and peripheral states those with black governments but extensive white settler or expatriate participation at high (cabinet, or permanent secretary or advisory) levels, (Lesotho, Swaziland, Botswana, and Malawi).

A more complicated and more helpful picture is provided by various *economic* indices. Taking into consideration the various factors discussed in Chapter 2, external trade, economic aid and investment, labor supply and migration, transport routes, and formalized trade and customs agreements, a clear picture emerges. South Africa and Rhodesia are at the very core of the sub-system on each of these factors. As suppliers of labor, recipients of aid and investment, and being dependent on white-controlled transport routes, Lesotho, Swaziland, Botswana, and Mozambique would also be included, essentially as peripheral rather than core actors. Malawi, though less dependent, could be classified as a peripheral, supportive actor. Moving away from the center, Zambia is on the periphery in the areas of trade, investment, and transportation, being in these matters heavily dependent on the white South. Otherwise, Zambia has sought to divorce itself economically from the sub-system. Its government is more reluctant to continue such relationships as still exist and is taking positive measures to reduce its dependence. Yet Zambia is still in the sub-system, on the periphery, a disruptive force as much as a supportive one. The rest of the sub-system is comprised of Angola (transport, investments, and agreements), less so Madagascar (investments and agreements), and the Congo and Tanzania hardly at all.

It is important to note that racial distinctions do not appear to define or circumscribe economic patterns, except for Zambia's post-UDI polices. Four black-governed states outrank Angola in their degree of interaction with the core. Angola, in particular, seems to be outside the mainstream of white southern African economic affairs. Like Zambia, Bostwana has initiated steps to open transport contact with Zambia to extricate itself from the southern orbit. Both Zambia and Swaziland have sought association with the East African Community, thereby indicating that membership overlap in two or more sub-systems may be possible. If we look at trends in movement toward and away from the core, we can suggest that Mozambique, Angola, Rhodesia, and Malawi are increasing their involvement in the economic sub-system. The Congo, Zambia, Botswana, Madagascar, and Swaziland seem to be reducing theirs.

Moving into the even more treacherous realm of *political-diplomatic-strategic* indices a quite different picture of the sub-system emerges. In regard to voting at the UN, South Africa and Portugal have voted consistently against UN intervention in the region. Since Rhodesia is not a UN member, but is the subject of many resolutions, we can assume that its government would vote against such involvement. These states might be regarded as the core on this issue. Malawi, Lesotho, Swaziland, and Botswana, in that order, seem to constitute a periphery since they have abstained, absented themselves, or even voted with South Africa and Portugal on questions of UN involvement in regional affairs. Malawi, in particular, actively champions a position that is supportive of South Africa in committee sessions and at the General Assembly. Zambia and Tanzania, because of their concern about regional affairs and their active part in seeking to expand the UN's role in the region, might be categorized as disruptive peripheral actors.

On the basis of their behavior we might regard South Africa, Rhodesia, and Portugal, as non-members of the OAU, as the core. Malawi, Lesotho, Swaziland, and Botswana are members of the OAU. But in their opposition to the majority position on OAU resolutions on southern Africa and in their public refusal to cooperate with OAU directives and bodies on these matters they deserve to be viewed as supportive peripheral actors. Tanzania and Zambia, because of their openly attempting to use the OAU to assist those who seek to displace minority white governments, can be called disruptive peripheral actors.

The issue of the resumption of British arms sales to South Africa provided a further indicator. Only South Africa, Rhodesia, Portugal, and Malawi consistently supported the arms sales. Lesotho and Madagascar, by maintaining silence or an inconclusive stance, or by voicing what amounted to mild support for South Africa, were supportive of the core. All other regional states publicly opposed British arms sales.

The ideological core of the region would be those states that urge the maintenance and expansion of a stable regional subsystem that includes white-governed states. The white-governed states, plus Malawi and Lesotho, take this position. On the periphery are Swaziland, Madagascar, and Botswana—states that reluctantly yet positively collaborate in the maintenance of regional interaction patterns. Only three regional actors—Congo, Tanzania, and Zambia—openly seek and take positive steps to dismantle the regional patterns of white-dominated interaction.

The diplomatic pattern has already been discussed in some detail. Both Malawi and Swaziland send resident diplomatic representatives to or receive them from at least two of the white governments. Lesotho, Botswana, and Madagascar because of their quasi-diplomatic contact rest on the periphery.

On the controversial question of dialogue with white governments, Malawi and Lesotho have positively taken the lead in organizing and participating in dialogue. Madagascar, Botswana, and Swaziland have likewise publicly favored dialogue, though with some important reservations and not nearly so vocally or vigorously. Madagascar, since the military coup, and Botswana no longer can be regarded as proponents of dialogue. The Congo, Tanzania, and Zambia categorically oppose dialogue or even discussion of the dialogue question in intra-African councils. They seek to disrupt such talk until South Africa, Portugal, and Rhodesia conduct "dialogue" with their own African citizens regarding domestic political and race relations. In addition to this position the Congo, Tanzania, and Zambia also serve as host countries, conduits, and training grounds for nationalist parties pledged to unseat minority governments. Thus on the strategic dimension the core consists of those states that militarily resist revolutionary African nationalists: the white-ruled states plus Malawi and Lesotho. Swaziland and Botswana, by reluctantly cooperating with white governments in resisting or thwarting African nationalist movements against white rule, yet by providing haven for political fugitives from white states, can be considered on the periphery.

Taken as a whole, the political-diplomatic-strategic indices suggest that South Africa, Rhodesia, and Portugal are most committed to the sub-system. Malawi and Lesotho, and less so Swaziland and Botswana, and finally Madagascar also seem inclined to support the core of the sub-system. Tanzania, Zambia, and the Congo, in that order, are most intent on disrupting the present regional patterns.

What emerges is a political pattern considerably different from the economic "map" described above. Botswana and Zambia, for instance, rank far lower by political than economic criteria. In contrast, Angola and Malawi seem to be politically active and supportive in sub-systemic affairs, though by economic criteria they are on the periphery. It seems clear, then, that economic involvement (as in the case of Botswana or Zambia) need not dictate policy stances on vital regional questions.

Growing out of this summarization are two points that should be stressed: (1) a sub-system can be viewed in various ways, and (2) there is a great difficulty in generalizing without properly defining the indices to be employed. Components of the sub-system, particularly with regard to the nature and extent of their involvement, their commitment to or approval of the policies they and others pursue, and the changes in the patterns of interaction, present a fluid although identifiable and analyzable sub-system.

The Primary Factors in Regional Conflict and Tension

Two factors are chiefly responsible for tension and conflict in international politics in southern Africa. They are, first, racism and its expression in domestic and foreign policies as well as in inter-group and inter-personal relations, and, second, the economic imbalances that prevail, both in domestic and in inter-state aspects. In Chapter 1 we traced the evolution and hardening of racial relationships. Racism has become institutionalized, indeed even internalized in the thought patterns of peoples who see race as a convenient tool for maintaining sociopolitical and economic dominance. This fact has forced the majority population to be more race conscious, although reactive racism so far has not been nearly so pernicious or pervasive.

In this milieu, racist foreign policies thrive—policies that in an aggressive or defensive way seek to expand or prolong racial dominance and privilege. The outward-looking policy in many ways springs from the realization that to preserve the political order they have created, South Africa's whites must involve the African states of the region in a network of relationships that would constrain those states from cooperating with other states and groups anxious to erase minority racist governments from Africa. Before the independence of black Africa, settler and minority governments depended upon the European colonial order to buffer the "winds of change." But the windbreak has since been serially dismantled. Now minority white governments must probe for substitute arrangements to defend their privileged order. They seek to create a baffle of client states to check the thrust of revolutionary and anti-racist movements pressing them. Considering the social composition of the white states, this is no easy task. To construct these relationships with black states they must make certain concessions, concessions that, by and large, whites in southern Africa are not prepared to make ungrudgingly. In a sense they must be less racist in order to defend racism. This is one dilemma facing South African foreign policy today.

The dilemma poses problems as well as opportunities for the black governments. They are not without principles. Some sense that they are being used. But they rationalize that the contacts they develop with white governments will, in the long run, demonstrate to whites in Africa that racism is counterproductive, and that racial coexistence need not involve super- and subordination. Of course, the basic motivations are the hope for short-range economic rewards and the psychological buttressing they receive. For this they risk the hatred of their racial brothers to the north, and perhaps their own self-respect. No measure of economic gain or security can justify entirely the accusations of betrayal of one's own people.

The second reason for regional tension and conflict grows out of the gross economic imbalance among states. The white-ruled states enjoy tremendous advantages both in geography and productivity. Asymmetrical economic relationships lead to the temptation to assert unequal political relationships. Economically stronger states tend to seek to employ their economic superiority for political purposes, and in so doing cause tension and conflict. Even when they seem to withstand temptation, the weaker states quite naturally perceive that they are being exploited and thus they are often supersensitive to pressures. Neo-colonialism and the fear that economic penetration may overflow into political affairs are perceptual conditions. A state submits, adjusts, or resists on the basis of its perception of the threat. Different statesmen and different societies might react differently to the proximity of a stronger state. Nevertheless, it is clear that white southern Africa is inordinately more powerful, by a variety of economic indicators, then its black neighbors, and the resultant tensions, either real or imagined, precipitate and exacerbate many foreign policy issues.

Varieties of Foreign Policy in Southern Africa

One could construct a typology of foreign policy patterns in the southern African region. These might be labeled adaptation, symbiosis, isolation, penetration, and intervention. The first two strategies seem to be favored by the "bridge builders"; the latter three are identified with the policy pronouncements of the ideologically committed who seek either to upset or to maintain a racially dominant status quo in the region.

Under a policy of *adaptation* a state alters its external behavior and possibly its internal structure so that it can survive in a changed or hostile environment.[17] The officials of an adaptive state see few or no alternatives other than those emanating from the environment (usually a single, reputedly all-powerful neighbor). Likewise, they perceive that their state lacks the capacity to resist, alter, or deflect the demands of the environment. Rather than bargain they acquiesce. Such states have been called "client states," and "satellites," and in many areas of public endeavor they serve practically as an instrumental extension of the foreign policy machinery of the dominant state. So far, no regional black state can accurately be regarded as adaptive, except perhaps on only a few issue areas. Lesotho comes as close as any, but still maintains its autonomy in a number of critical issue areas.[18] This does not mean that South Africa does not support Chief Jonathan's government; it certainly does. Without that support his government probably would have collapsed. But the alternatives, as seen from Pretoria, are less desirable. Nevertheless, adaptation could be a future policy response given Lesotho's situation. Despite the immobilism of the UN and the OAU in taking strong and direct measures against racist and colonial governments in southern Africa, the international system maintains a protective umbrella, or at least the credibility of one, that lessens the danger of the destruction of Lesotho as a separate political entity. Moreover, South Africa would appear to prefer an "independent" Lesotho to the charge of expansionism and the international furor and perhaps action likely to develop from an open annexation. Thus Lesotho's leaders need not fully accept the demands of South Africa. Any direct intervention by Pretoria might trigger a regional or wider conflict that South Africa would wish to prevent. Despite Lesotho's precarious economic, geographical, and political existance, adaptation is not

17. The use of the term here is different from that of Rosenau, who provides a far more general definition in *The Adaptation of National Societies*, esp. pp. 2–3. My usage here would be closer to his "acquiescent adaptation" or Halpern's categories, "emanation" and "subjection"; see Halpern, *Applying a New Theory*, pp. 3–8.
18. For an explanation of the term "issue area" see Rosenau, "Foreign Policy as an Issue-Area," in Rosenau, ed., *Domestic Sources of Foreign Policy*, pp. 11–50.

perceived to be the only foreign policy alternative. This is, of course, an interpretive judgment since no state leader is going to admit that he is pursuing an adaptive foreign policy. Rather he would naturally claim to be securing something in return for his apparent acquiescence to strictures from a powerful neighbor. Hence he would insist that his policies were symbiotic.

By far the more common southern African response to environmental conditions has been *symbiosis*. Strictly speaking, a symbiotic relationship involves a mutually advantageous coexistence in which each partner sees its own future bound up with its opposite number. In international practice, however, one state usually perceives the possibilities and profitability of this sort of arrangement first, and then seeks to convince its potential partner of the efficacy of this policy while at the same time attempting to enmesh it in its sphere in influence. Later, however, the dominant partner comes to realize that its sphere of influence is not entirely subject to its own control, for it too has become dependent upon mutually beneficial ties with its partner. For black Africans, symbiosis has been asymmetrical; that is, the white-dominated states' economic and political strength usually results in unequal arrangements tending toward adaptation rather than symbiosis. However, this tendency has so far been resisted by the black governments largely because the total international environment has been passively protective—the regional environment has not been permitted to be solely determinative. White governments have been brought to realize that to hurt weaker black governments could well be to hurt themselves. But black governments cannot always depend upon the external environment and the white governments' perceptions of it. Black southern Africa must work to achieve conditions of symmetry and equality, if not between individuals across state lines, at least between states and groups. Some black governments now engaged in symbiotic policies with white-ruled states attempt to rationalize their policies to the rest of Africa by claiming that their policies are really designed to penetrate and thereby undermine racism in those states. In rebuttal, revolutionary black Africa brands relations with white southern Africa as adaptation. In other words, by dealing with the white states a black government is being penetrated and is adapting to white-dictated conditions. Symbiotic relationships and the conditions of interaction need not be static. On the contrary, if for black Africa they remain static, adaptation would probably eventually result.

A state may also seek to deal with regional conflict or tension by a policy of *isolation*.[19] Simply stated, isolation is a conscious effort to resolve a conflict situation by physically sealing off the actor regarded as the cause of the problem. This could be consummated in numerous ways, among them sanctions and boycotts in immigration, trade, communications, and diplomacy. This was the initial response of South Africa to impending black independence. In southern Africa, however, it is a policy virtually impossible for the black states to pursue, alone or in concert. They are, themselves, vulnerable, and too many links with the white-ruled states have been forged, before independence and since. Moreover, the target white governments are so manifestly objectionable to black Africans that turning one's back on the problem in question, racism, would not adequately resolve the matter at all. Rather, policies ostensibly designed to isolate or separate a state (for example, Rhodesia or South Africa) are basically penetrative or interventionist (see below). Their real purpose is not to isolate, but to induce a change in basic state policy (for example, racism) or to bring down the target government. Invariably such a policy is employed in concert with other strategies of foreign policy.

The fourth variety of foreign policy might be called *penetration*.[20] In this strategy, intentionally covert and nonviolent efforts are made to induce changes in particular policies on the part of another government without attempting to alter the government itself. While this has been a policy regularly employed by white governments, and it is often a common and acceptable form of foreign policy behavior, regional black states have been unable to secure the leverage necessary to employ

19. See Halpern's discussion of "isolation," "buffering," and "boundary-management" in *Applying a New Theory*, pp. 8–9.
20. Rosenau's concept of "penetration" is quite different. Cf. his "Pre-Theories and Theories of Foreign Policy," in Farrell, ed., *Approaches to Comparative and International Politics*, pp. 65–92.

penetration successfully. This has largely been due to disparities in the effective power of the participants. Nevertheless, one could hypothesize future efforts by various black states to undertake these policies toward one another (this indeed has probably occurred though documentary evidence is absent), and perhaps toward, the Bantustans—for instance, Lesotho toward the Transkei or Botswana toward Boputhatswana. The fact is, however, that they may possess far more leverage than they realize, given white Africa's efforts to legitimize its regimes and to break out of its isolated situation on the continent. Moreover, the potential for leverage also exists in black Africa's latent ability to communicate directly with the majority of South Africa's Bantu population. The establishment of Bantustans, the large numbers of alien African laborers in the South who have families in independent black states, and the ethnic, family, and linguistic linkages across state boundaries contain within them the capacity for penetration—in both directions, it should be added—not so much on a government-to-government basis but on a less formal but not necessarily less effective people-to-people or government-to-people basis.

Penetration could easily develop, if exposed or reacted to vigorously, into *intervention.* Intervention refers to "organized and systematic activities across recognized boundaries aimed at affecting the political authority structures of the target."[21] Such behavior may be either revolutionary, designed to replace existing structures, or conservative, to strengthen structures regarded as unstable. White governments in Africa have engaged in the latter sort of activity for some time, particularly toward Katanga, Portuguese Africa, and Rhodesia. But one suspects that they have also indulged surreptitiously in conservative intervention toward black governments as well. When, for example, a South African military attaché was appointed to the mission to Malawi in early 1969, it was widely suggested in

21. Young, "Intervention and International Systems," *Journal of International Affairs,* XXII (1968), 178. The term "intervention" has been widely employed in foreign policy analysis, but frequently usage is loose and general, sometimes as a synonym for influence: see, for example, Baldwin, "Foreign Aid, Intervention, and Influence," *World Politics,* XXI (1969), 425–47. I prefer a more narrow definition.

journalistic and diplomatic circles, that he was assigned the task not only of observing the liberation movements in nearby countries, but of exploring the possibilities for logistical assistance for the Banda government in case of external attack or internal uprising.

However, the black states boast another potential instrument for intervention. Revolutionary nationalists afford the host government a weapon for informal intervention against ideologically hostile neighbors without committing the host's own forces to battle outside its territory. Though it obviously poses knotty problems, the presence of refugees, exiles, and guerrillas provides the host governments a measure of access and choice otherwise lacking. Moreover, nationalists from neighboring territories become indebted to the host country and, in the long run, such obligations may be beneficial for the host. The coincidence of goals between nationalist forces and host governments enables the host to conduct a more active foreign policy toward the white-ruled states, a policy that otherwise would have been primarily limited and passive (statements, votes at the UN, sanctions, boycotts, resolutions, and other efforts to isolate the target governments). Only Zambia, the Congo, and Tanzania, of the regional states, have considered penetration and intervention as live options. The others have chosen, by and large, to coexist and deal peacefully with their white-ruled neighbors.

It should also be added that there are a number of hidden as well as obvious "costs" of penetration and intervention. First, the penetrator-intervener may find itself functioning in a foreign milieu it is incapable of adequately controlling—either directly or through a surrogate government. Second, chosen surrogates may not only be unable to control the situation, but may be unwilling to do precisely what they have been instructed to do. In this case, the penetrator-intervener may be faced with a difficult decision between trying to work within the constraints imposed by the "weaker" partner, assuming direct control, or reducing its involvement. It becomes chancy to allow others to make policy for you, especially others who, initially, were regarded as your agents. Third, the economic and social costs of maintaining penetration or intervention may become inflated. Conceivably, the military manpower demands on Portugal in Africa could do violence to its metropolitan social and political order. The same could happen to the South African economy and social fabric, both of which are patently delicate. Initial, perhaps limited, investments have a habit of escalating.[22] In the process, policy alternatives narrow as political and ideological stances are assumed. Ironically, a penetrator or intervener may arrive at a situation where it is doing the bidding of a government it does not entirely approve of and, indeed, may find embarrassing, uncontrollable, or dangerous. Finally, too direct and obvious involvement may lead to a situation that invites Great Power involvement designed to offset the influence of the original penetrator. It has been argued that in an extended conflict situation, contending forces tend to balance or neutralize each other at the same time that commitments are deepened and the stakes raised.[23] Applying this argument to southern Africa, white African involvement in black Africa could lead to the introduction or expansion of alien counter-elements, and thereby be counterproductive from the perspective of the white-ruled states.

The possibilities open to black Africa for the employment of these various strategies depend upon numerous variables, each deserving considerable discussion, and each dealt with throughout the text of this book. They include (1) the distribution of effective power in the region, (2) the extent to which extra-regional forces are willing and able to involve themselves in regional affairs, (3) the structure of the system itself and mechanisms that have been devised for intra-systemic exchange, (4) the internal viability of the individual actors in the system, and (5) the perceived level of interdependence among the actors.

The various types of policies outlined above are not clear-cut categories into which the foreign policy of a given government falls. On the contrary, they are suggested here as an analytical

22. See Yarmolinsky, "American Foreign Policy and the Decision to Intervene," *Journal of International Affairs*, XXII (1968) 231–35.

23. See the argument developed by Triska and Finley, "Soviet-American Relations," *Journal of Conflict Resolution*, IX (March 1965), 37–53.

tool to group the sorts of strategies either employed or considered possible. One state may pursue them all simultaneously although that would be not only unlikely but also dysfunctional. But it is evident that various combinations are regularly utilized, provided one views foreign policy as an aggregate of many policies concerned with a multiplicity of issue areas.

Pessimism and Optimism

The sub-systemic panorama described above is ever changing. In general it would appear that the situation, currently, is moving in a direction beneficial to the white-governments in southern Africa. Revolutionary black Africa has become defensive, diplomatically and economically and even militarily. A pessimism prevails, in marked contrast to conditions in the late 1950s and early 1960s. At that time African states were gaining independence and taking their places in various international bodies. They were starting to assert themselves in international councils and the Western European, American, and communist powers appeared to be listening. In the UN General Assembly Africa was becoming a force to be reckoned with. This spawned a widespread optimism in African capitals and a feeling that the corner had been turned, that racist and minority regimes would be displaced before long. After all, the world was thought to be mobilizable in the cause of racial justice. Before long it became evident that this was a naïve euphoria, that the forces of inertia and the status quo were far more deeply entrenched than had earlier been realized.

Event after event dampened the optimism of that post-independence era. The OAU and the UN had proved to be ineffectual in dealing with the southern African issues. The Congo syndrome of disorder, secession, military mutiny, white mercenaries, and general frustration sobered and soured many. The UDI in Rhodesia and the inability or unwillingness of the African and extra-African forces to end white rule there, vexing internal developmental and political problems, a series of military coups that replaced radical regimes with leaders less interested in stressing the southern African issues have led to a state of despair in Africa. To amplify these conditions, South Africa has launched an economic and diplomatic offensive in black Africa, the liberation movements have adopted longer-range time tables, the Western countries have apparently placed southern African racial justice lower on their priority scales—indeed, they have begun again to traffic in arms publicly, and some African states have openly brooked the ostensibly united front that existed in the early 1960s. By 1968 a reaction, an over-pessimism had set in. It may be that such a state of mind is as unwarranted as was the euphoria of the earlier era. There are, after all, real limits to South African, Rhodesian, and Portuguese policies. The white-ruled states are not rich by any but African standards. Their social structures are not monolithic or homogenous, and hence they are essentially unviable. Regional demographic trends are working against them. Their borders are not impregnable. It may be that they have nearly reached the peak of their influence in Africa. Unless their internal policies are radically changed, the debilitating realities of domestic racial exploitation and privilege will ultimately take their toll. Although black Africa should not fall victim to the naïve optimism of the past, the southern African sub-system seems to be, for many reasons, a fundamentally unstable one, despite its amazing staying power. In the long run, its core is predicated on what has historically proven to be an insecure as well as a morally objectionable foundation.

Appendix 1
Some Notes on the Analysis of Regional Sub-Systems

The reader may have perceived that the data, ideas, and analytical and organizational techniques employed in the foregoing study are rather eclectic and less than methodologically rigorous, at least in terms of modern political science. It is my opinion that the current state of political science and the unavailability of comparable over-time data renders such an eclectic approach imperative for the study of international relations in southern Africa. But to say this is not to solve important methodological problems. It might be helpful, by way of this afterthought, to reflect upon at least one of these methodological questions, even if the discussion departs somewhat from the approach of this study. We shall explore in this Appendix some issues relating to boundary definition, in the analytical sense, and the employment of the regional sub-system as a focus of analysis.[1]

The language of systems theory has become popular among political analysts; and understandably so. Whether they want

1. Two recent papers by Timothy M. Shaw that came to me after the completion of this study also deal with the methodological issues treated herein. They are chiefly concerned with fitting this problem into the scholarly literature of international relations and integration. They should be read in concert with this study. Moreover, they utilize some of the same techniques employed in this study, particularly the core-periphery classification and the idea of issue areas. See Shaw's "The Subordinate State System of Southern Africa" and "Linkage Politics and Subordinate State Systems" (listed in the Unpublished Papers section of the Bibliography).

to study functions, structures, processes, variables, or patterned relationships, scholars who wish to grasp the essentials of politics have found that quantities of important as well as extraneous information can be better sorted, organized, and analyzed by employing some type of systems approach. Although the concept of "system" is applicable to a wide variety of political phenomena, it must never be forgotten that "system" is but an analytical tool. It can be designed and accommodated to study political reality as the scholar desires, according to his choice of criteria. If this is born in mind, systems analysis can constitute a challenging and potentially fruitful avenue for research into regional international relations.

The choice of a loose regional systems perspective for this study grows out of a desire to survey the research problem broadly, with an eye to interactions rather than isolated incidents. The search for unique features of political entities, on whatever level, has led to some interesting but problematical and nongeneralizable findings. But we live in the era of comparison, the search for similarities and broader generalizations. Such an enterprise is not furthered by a case study or a country-by-country approach. Even so, my usage of the concepts of system and sub-system in this study has been much less stringent than would be expected in general systems theory. I have attempted throughout to make clear that the boundaries of the system depend on what data the student regards as important and how he organizes and manipulates that data. To conceptualize in systemic terms yet try to avoid the pitfalls of distortion is demanding. Of course, this danger cannot be entirely escaped. Any structural organization for such a study is to a large extent based on strategic research decisions made early in the undertaking. Otherwise, disorganization would prevail and accuracy, clarity, and interpretation would suffer.

It strikes me that international relations in southern Africa can be most fruitfully surveyed if we view the states involved collectively as a regional sub-system. The term regional sub-system is preferred here for several reasons. We are dealing with states that are geographically contiguous and that are, relatively speaking, removed from the general center of international political activity. Moreover, these states are racially heterogeneous and the bonds which link them in a sub-system are not so much cultural as they are geographical and regionally economic. To be sure, the element of race is the vital linkage for the governing bodies of the core states of the Republic of South Africa, Rhodesia, and the Portuguese-governed territories. But the other actors, only slightly less involved in patterned relationships of the sub-system, are not subject to this attraction. Their participation in the sub-system must be explained differently. Any regional sub-system then can be loosely defined as a group of states of which it can be said that (1) they occupy a geographically contiguous and identifiable territory, (2) they interact in regularized and patterned ways—so much so that decision makers in these states recognize that this sub-systemic interaction represents the most significant facet of the external relations of each participant, (3) among some actors regularized relationships have led or are leading to increased organizational expression of common and also conflicting interests, (4) events external to the sub-system affect relations within the sub-system more than relations within the sub-system can affect the larger system of which the sub-system is a part, and (5) the character of the relationships within the sub-system may be conflicting as well as cooperative, as long as they are sufficiently frequent, patterned, and intense.

It must be realized that by the choice of the state as the primary unit of analysis, arbitrary regional boundaries are imposed. To take one instance, economic regions do not always coincide with the imposition of state boundaries. The lower Katanga, for example, might sensibly be included in the southern African region even though the entire Congolese state is oriented, even economically, northward. But since it is the authority of the state that can ultimately impose its boundaries on other forms of relations, and since we are attempting to study international relations, it is tempting to adhere to this admittedly arbitrary division.[2] Geographical contiguity not only

2. See the monograph treating this: Kibulya and Langlands, *The*

facilitates more extensive and intensive interaction, but it also makes such relationships more necessary and withdrawal from them more difficult. Nevertheless, no one should ignore the fact that non-state actors participate in sub-systemic affairs. For example, guerrilla movements, international governmental and nongovernmental organizations, individuals, and ideologies have been considered. But the primary focus is usually on how these actors affect and are affected by inter-state behavior.

It is characteristic of actors in the sub-system to view intra-sub-systemic relations as more vital to their immediate interests than extra-sub-systemic affairs. Extra-sub-systemic relations are regarded as important chiefly insofar as they can enable an actor or actors to deal more effectively with sub-systemic issues and problems. Naturally, there are varying degrees of involvement in and commitment to the sub-systemic focus. It is for this reason that various categories of sub-systemic actors can be introduced. For those actors that are deeply committed to and substantively involved in the sub-system, called "core" actors, there is a perceived necessity to regularize and thereby strengthen, structurally and procedurally, the patterned relationships that are emerging. Other states, though enveloped in patterned sub-systemic relations, may regret their involvement and only continue the relationships because they fear possible repercussions of alternative arrangements. Still other actors, again enwrapped in sub-systemic affairs, may prefer to dismantle these attachments and assert an independence from the sub-system or to establish linkages with other sub-systems. This would probably occur in uneven fashion since a complete severance of deeply patterned relations is virtually impossible without strong and reliable support elsewhere. Ties can be continued in one issue area (for instance, economic) and yet be curtailed in other issue areas (military, diplomatic, cultural, and so on). Thus it is possible to talk of the multiple dimensionality of sub-systemic relations. Finally, conceivably some states that are geographically distant from the sub-system may regard themselves, and be

---

Political Geography of the Uganda-Congo Boundary, esp. the discussion of how economic and social patterns conformed to political boundaries, pp. 29–53.

so regarded by others, to be outside, indeed opposed to, the sub-system. Yet such states may be called "intrusive" members of the sub-system when their impact and their continuous and intensive association with sub-systemic actors (even if in a negative fashion) crucially affects sub-systemic affairs.

When relationships among a group of states reach a level of frequency and intensity that the states begin to routinize and to search out ways to give organizational expression to their patterned relationships, the germ of sub-systemic institutionalization has taken root. Within southern Africa we can see the routinization of military consultation and collaboration—both among the core states and among a counter-group of peripheral and intrusive actors. There is also a growing tendency towards the establishment of economic and functional organizations, and cultural-social collaboration at governmental as well as elite levels. One would expect that diplomatic-political coordination is not out of the question, although heretofore organizational expression has taken the form of wider than regional units (OAU, Commonwealth) or bilateral ties. At any rate, the regularization of existing and expanding patterned relations seems to be a rather natural development in the formation of a regional sub-system.

As a sub-system is part of a larger set of patterned relationships, it is to be expected that external forces can more deeply shape sub-systemic patterns than those patterns can affect external forces. This has led some scholars to refer to such sub-systems as "subordinate" state systems.[3] Although the terminology is not that essential, the word "subordinate" is somewhat objectionable on two counts. First, although the sub-systems in question are subordinate to the larger system in relative power terms, they are by no means always subordinate in the applica-

3. For example: Binder, "The Middle-East as a Subordinate International System," *World Politics*, X (1958), 408–29; Brecher, "International Relations and Asian Studies," ibid., XV (1963), 213–35; Zartman, "Africa as a Sub-State System," *International Organization*, XXI (1967), 545–64; Bowman, "The Sub-State System of Southern Africa," *International Studies Quarterly*, XII (1968), 231–61; Cantori and Spiegel, *The International Politics of Regions*, pp. 1–41; and the two papers by Shaw cited in note 1 above.

tion of the instruments of power. In other words, although the Great and Medium Powers may appear to be able to exercise predominant power when it is placed alongside the powers of the sub-systemic actors, there are numerous instances when global conditions do not permit the stronger states to dictate policies to and relations within the sub-system. This is particularly the case for southern Africa, where geographical isolation from the arenas of Great Power confrontation enable sub-systemic actors to pursue their policies without inordinate outside interference. Certainly there are situations in which external involvement is prompted and facilitated, but it is one of the vital preoccupations of sub-systemic actors to encourage or discourage certain types of external involvement, depending on their perceptions of their interests. Conversely, there are situations in which the larger global system or parts thereof are drawn into sub-systemic affairs and these situations can even lead to the eruption of a global crisis, or to a proto-war and possibly a general one.[4] To call a group of states that might detonate such an eventuality "subordinate" seems misleading. Second, the unfortunate political and ideological connotations for states either subject to or just emerging from colonial or neo-colonial status ought to be avoided at all costs. Since they are not subordinate in all circumstances, the term "regional sub-systems" may be preferred.

Heretofore much of the literature on systems, particularly as it applies to international relations, has been preoccupied with the Parsonian concern for a system's maintenance. Forces and factors that tended to weaken the system were regarded as extra-systemic. But, international relations refers to the sum total of the interactions between actors, however defined. Such interactions are not always cooperative and do not always work in the direction of system maintenance. Intensive antagonistic patterned relationships ought not be ignored or minimized. Conflict is as much a part of the international system as is cooperation. This is no less so regarding a regional sub-system. To ignore conflict in systemic affairs is to fall into the trap of

4. A more complete discussion of these conditions, regarding southern Africa, appears in Chapter 6 of my *Guerrilla Struggle in Africa*.

analyzing systems as static phenomena. This would be particularly deceptive in dealing with southern Africa. Something more than a static snapshot of the southern African sub-system is needed.

Analysts of international sub-systems, though taking pains to define what is meant by a sub-system and which states should be included in the sub-system, have approached membership in the sub-system somewhat simplistically. A state either is or is not a part of the sub-system. As long as the concentration is on actors committed to sub-systemic maintenance this predisposition does not pose insuperable problems of categorization or analysis. But insofar as this is a deformed image, it misrepresents the character of sub-systemic affairs. Such sub-systems truly would be "subordinate," for a good many more states and forces have a profound impact on the sub-system than are included as "members." The Cantori and Spiegel model deals with this issue by viewing a regional sub-system as being composed of three different types of actors, each with a different degree of involvement within the sub-system. One of the advantages of this more complex delimitation of membership is that it permits the existence of inclusive sub-systems that have overlapping memberships and that include, among their peripheral actors, states that are also members of other sub-systems.[5] The periphery can thereby be recognized as a fluid and active category with a few states moving from the periphery of one sub-system to that of another, and a few actually residing in more than one sub-system, depending on the boundary criteria employed for delimitation. Although forms of interaction tend to be reinforcing, making it less likely that a state belongs to more than one sub-system (in most cases), the possibility of dual membership must be admitted. The category of intrusive actors also serves to point up the fluidity of sub-system analysis and to make more manageable the actuality of linkage between sub-systems and the impact of external interactions with the sub-system. I

5. See also Zartman, op. cit. (in n. 3 above), p. 549. Exceptions to these generalizations include Shaw's papers (see n. 1 above), which utilize the concept of issue area to delineate the sub-system.

would agree with Inis L. Claude when he notes: "The world does not in fact break easily along neatly perforated lines."[6] To attempt to do so for analytical purposes may be necessary, but it must be realized that this may do violence to the realities of international relations.

A survey of the literature on southern Africa as a sub-system, region, or area quickly illustrates the challenges of delimitation. Russett, for example, did not even include Sub-Saharan Africa in his study of regions involving 54 variables and 82 countries. In his estimation "too few reliable data were present to make . . . inclusion worthwhile."[7] Such a judgment, though sobering, need not discourage further analysis. Table 14 illustrates the various constellations of "southern Africa" as expressed by recent scholars and publicists.

Although some of these configurations merely serve the convenience of editors of collections (Hance; Davis and Baker) and others emerge as residual or cursory groupings in treating a different aspect of the problems or issues (Nielsen; Cantori and Spiegel; Kuper), they nevertheless are based upon criteria, however implicit, and observations of the reality of southern Africa. The others are based on a more systemic study of the subject itself, especially the work of Bowman, Green and Fair, and Robson. The Robson article deals with economic integration, a far more exclusive and conscious effort at the creation of international groupings. With such a narrow focus, it is understandable that Robson includes only four states.

The Green and Fair study is more comprehensive and rigorous in its orientation and more akin to the sub-system analysis proposed herein. But the regional approach developed in that study concentrates solely on the issue of economic development and employs exclusively social and economic indices in the delimitation of what the authors call the "Southern African development region." It is a definitive study, though badly outdated in its data and outpaced by sociopolitical events. An unblush-

6. Claude, *Swords into Plowshares*, p. 113.

7. Russett, *International Regions*, p. 15. He was referring to the data presented in Russett et al., *World Handbook of Political and Social Indicators.*

TABLE 14
SOUTHERN AFRICA, VARIOUS GROUPINGS

Country, territory, or region	*A*	*B*	*C*	*D*	*E*	*F*	*G*	*H*	*I*
RSA	x	x	x	x	x	x	*C*	x	x
Rhodesia	x	–	x	x	x	x	*C*	x	x
Zambia	x	–	*F*	x	–	–	*P*	x	–
Malawi	x	–	*L*	x	–	x	*P*	x	–
Botswana	x	x	x	x	x	x	*P*	x	x
Swaziland	x	x	x	x	x	x	*P*	x	x
Lesotho	x	x	x	x	x	x	*P*	x	x
Mozambique	x	–	x	x	x	x	*C*	x	x
Angola	x	–	x	–	x	x	*C*	x	x
South West Africa	x	–	x	x	x	x	*C*	x	x
Malagasy Rep.	–	–	–	–	–	–	*P*	–	x
Mauritius	–	–	–	–	–	–	*P*	–	–
Congo	–	–	–	–	–	*P*	–	x	–
Tanzania	–	–	–	–	–	–	–	–	–

A. Hilda Kuper, "The Colonial Situation in Southern Africa," *Journal of Modern African Studies*, II (1964), 149–64. B. Peter Robson, "Economic Integration in Southern Africa," *Journal of Modern African Studies*, V (1967), 469–90. C. Eschel Rhoodie, *The Third Africa* (Cape Town, 1968), p. 8; *F* = future, *L* = likely (possible). D. L. P. Green and T. J. D. Fair, *Development in Africa*, (Johannesburg, 1962). E. William A. Hance, ed., *Southern Africa and the United States* (New York and London, 1968). F. Larry W. Bowman, "The Sub-State System of Southern Africa," *International Studies Quarterly*, XII (1968), 231–61; *P* = periphery. G. Louis J. Cantori and Steven L. Spiegel, *The International Politics of Regions*, (Englewood Cliffs, N.J., 1970); *C* = core, *P* = periphery. H. John A. Davis and James K. Baker, eds., *Southern Africa in Transition* (New York, 1966). I. Waldemar A. Nielsen, *African Battleline* (New York and Evanston, 1965), opp. p. 1.

ingly pro-South African government perspective is Eschel Rhoodie's *Third Africa*. Nevertheless, despite its journalistic and clearly biased orientation it is a fairly serious piece of data collection and analysis.

So far, the article by Bowman is the only published study of southern Africa as an international sub-system in political terms. He bases his study heavily on the six conditions developed by Brecher in his study of southern Asia.[8] Bowman seeks to demonstrate that the southern African "subordinate state system" is a separate, identifiable constellation of states that are deter-

8. Breecher, "International Relations and Asian Studies," *World Politics*, XV (1963), 220.

mined to coexist peacefully, build up relationships, and maintain their autonomy from the dominant international system.

In contrast to the Bowman findings, two studies have preferred to look at southern Africa as peripheral parts of larger, more inclusive sub-systems. Zartman argues that southern Africa (in this case the "white-ruled territories") might better be regarded as a "fringe area" of the larger African sub-system, not unlike Israel's role in the Middle East. Thus, he maintains, "The antagonistic relations between the system and the fringe area are one of the elements that help keep the system together."[9] Hence the geographical clarity of Africa and the racial composition of its inhabitants leads Zartman to see southern Africa as an unredeemed irredenta of the Africa sub-system, awaiting ultimate inclusion in the larger entity and yet all the while by its presence contributing to systemic unity elsewhere on the continent.

From a different perspective, George W. Shepherd, Jr., maintains that southern Africa (including the black-governed states) is a peripheral part of the "White Atlantic Sub-System."[10] Employing the Cantori and Spiegel categories, he includes most of the NATO states, Ireland, Spain, and Sweden in the core sector, and the Southern African periphery is linked with it, though not necessarily permanently. Although justice has not been done to the individual studies discussed above, they are mentioned to illustrate the great diversity of delimitations and approaches to southern Africa as an international region.

We now turn briefly to the question of the criteria to be employed in determining the components of an international sub-system. This can be discussed in conjunction with another central issue, that of the level and unit of analysis. In attempting to identify the southern African sub-system, then, we should be aware of at least these two dimensions of the problem. To some extent the level-of-analysis issue can be linked with the substantive criteria for inclusion to show the tremendous variety of "sub-systems" that could be isolated, analytically if not actual-

9. Zartman, op. cit. (in n. 3 above), p. 547.
10. Shepherd, "The White Atlantic Sub-System and Black Southern Africa" (see Bibliography, Unpublished Papers).

ly. The level-of-analysis problem, simply put, turns on the segment of the system that the observer brings into focus. This is a decision based upon the nature of the research problem and the most fruitful strategy open to the researcher. It should be a conscious rather than fortuitous decision. The "level" to be studied generally is expressed in spatial terms. The spatial or horizontal dimension, then, would include numerous levels: universal, continental, regional, inter-state, state, sub-state grouping, social class, and individual domestic interests. Theoretically one could also concentrate on the linkages between various levels—for instance, the relationships between sub-state groupings and the regional system or other regional systems (such as guerrilla movements and the OAU). It is distorting to say that the choice is simply between a micro- or a macro-level of analysis, between concentrating on the parts and concentrating on the whole.[11] We really are faced with two distinct but closely related matters—the issue of the unit of analysis and that of the level of analysis. Onc could, for example, decide that the unit of analysis will be the sub-state grouping and yet study such groupings as they interact in a far broader environment for instance, the continental sub-system.

When an additional dimension is introduced, that of substantive issue areas, the analytical challenge is compounded. Nevertheless, the total picture of the problem and the myriad combinations of analytical foci might be expressed in schematic form by a two-dimensional typology (see table 15).

To operationalize these categories is a problem in itself and one which further research can illuminate. These methodological notes are offered merely as a suggestive basis for further work on the analytical problems of research into regional international relations.

11. For example, Singer, "The Level-of-Analysis Problem in International Relations," in Knorr and Verba, eds., *The International System*, pp. 77–92. I would not for one moment minimize the importance of Singer's general work in this regard, for he was among the first to draw attention to this crucial issue in international relations. Rather, I simply want to point up the complexity of the issue in its operational context.

TABLE 15

A TWO-DIMENSIONAL MATRIX FOR THE STUDY OF INTERNATIONAL POLITICS

Substantive Dimension

Spatial Dimension	Chap. 2 Communication, Transportation, Economic	Chaps. 5, 6 Military	Chap. 3 Diplomatic, Organizational	Chaps. 3, 4 Political	Chaps. 1, 4, 5 Ideological	Chaps. 1, 7 Sociocultural
Transcontinental						
Continental						
Regional						
Inter-state						
States						
Communities and sub-state grouping						
Social classes						
Individuals						

Appendix 2

Fifth Summit Conference of East and Central African States Held in Lusaka, Zambia —April 14-16, 1969

Manifesto on Southern Africa

1. When the purpose and the basis of States' international policies are misunderstood, there is introduced into the world a new and unnecessary disharmony, disagreements, conflicts of interest, or different assessments of human priorities, which provoke an excess of tension in the world, and disastrously divide mankind—at a time when united action is necessary to control modern technology and put it to the service of man. It is for this reason that, discovering widespread misapprehension of our attitudes and purposes in relation to Southern Africa, we the leaders of East and Central African States meeting in Lusaka, 16th April, 1969, have agreed to issue this Manifesto.

2. By this Manifesto we wish to make clear, beyond all shadow of doubt, our acceptance of the belief that all men are equal, and have equal rights to human dignity and respect, regardless of colour, race, religion, or sex. We believe that all men have the right and the duty to participate, as equal members of the society, in their own government. We do not accept that any individual or group has any right to govern any group of sane adults, without their consent, and we affirm that only the people of a society, acting together as equals, can determine what is,

for them, a good society and a good social, economic, or political organisation.

3. On the basis of these beliefs we do not accept that any one group within a society has the right to rule any society without the continuing consent of all the citizens. We recognise that at any one time there will be, within every society, failures in the implementation of these ideals. We recognise that for the sake of order in human affairs, there may be transitional arrangements while a transformation from group inequalities to individual equality is being effected. But we affirm that without an acceptance of these ideals—without a commitment to these principles of human equality and self-determination—there can be no basis for peace and justice in the world.

4. None of us would claim that within our own States we have achieved that perfect social, economic, and political organisation which would ensure a reasonable standard of living for all our people and establish individual security against avoidable hardship or miscarriage of justice. On the contrary, we acknowledge that within our own States the struggle towards human brotherhood and unchallenged human dignity is only beginning. It is on the basis of our commitment to human equality and human dignity, not on the basis of achieved perfection, that we take our stand of hostility towards the colonialism and racial discrimination which is being practised in Southern Africa. It is on the basis of their commitment to these universal principles that we appeal to other members of the human race for support.

5. If the commitment to these principles existed among the States holding power in Southern Africa, any disagreements we might have about the rate of implementation, or about isolated acts of policy, would be matters affecting only our individual relationships with the States concerned. If these commitments existed, our States would not be justified in the expressed and active hostility towards the regimes of Southern Africa such as we have proclaimed and continue to propagate.

6. The truth is, however, that in Mozambique, Angola, Rhodesia, South-West Africa, and the Union of South Africa, there is an open and continued denial of the principles of human equality and national self-determination. This is not a matter

of failure in the implementation of accepted human principles. The effective Administration in all these territories are not struggling towards these difficult goals. They are fighting the principles; they are deliberately organising their societies so as to try to destroy the hold of these principles in the minds of men. It is for this reason that we believe the rest of the world must be interested. For the principle of human equality, and all that flows from it, is either universal or it does not exist. The dignity of all men is destroyed when the manhood of any human being is denied.

7. Our objectives in Southern Africa stem from our commitment to this principle of human equality. We are not hostile to the Administrations in these States because they are manned and controlled by white people. We are hostile to them because they are systems of minority control which exist as a result of, and in the pursuance of, doctrines of human inequality. What we are working for is the right of self-determination for the people of those territories. We are working for a rule in those countries which is based on the will of all the people, and an acceptance of the equality of every citizen.

8. Our stand towards Southern Africa thus involves a rejection of racialism, not a reversal of the existing racial domination. We believe that all the peoples who have made their homes in the countries of Southern Africa are Africans, regardless of colour of their skins; and we would oppose a racialist majority government which adopted a philosophy of deliberate and permanent discrimination between its citizens on grounds of racial origin. We are not talking racialism when we reject the colonialism and apartheid policies now operating in those areas; we are demanding an opportunity for all the people of these States, working together as equal individual citizens, to work out for themselves the institutions and the system of government under which they will, by general consent, live together and work together to build a harmonious society.

9. As an aftermath of the present policies it is likely that different groups within these societies will be self-conscious and fearful. The initial political and economic organisations may well take account of these fears, and this group self-

consciousness. But how this is to be done must be a matter exclusively for the peoples of the country concerned, working together. No other nation will have a right to interfere in such affairs. All that the rest of the world has a right to demand is just what we are now asserting—that the arrangements within any State which wishes to be accepted into the community of nations must be based on an acceptance of the principles of human dignity and equality.

10. To talk of the liberation of Africa is thus to say two things. First, that the peoples in the territories still under colonial rule shall be free to determine for themselves their own institutions of self-government. Secondly, that the individuals in Southern Africa shall be freed from an environment poisoned by the propaganda of racialism, and given an opportunity to be men—not white men, brown men, yellow men, or black men.

11. Thus the liberation of Africa for which we are struggling does not mean reverse racialism. Nor is it an aspect of African Imperialism. As far as we are concerned the present boundaries of the States of Southern Africa are the boundaries of what will be free and independent African States. There is no question of our seeking or accepting any alterations to our own boundaries at the expense of these future free African nations.

12. On the objective of liberation as thus defined, we can neither surrender nor compromise. We have always preferred, and we still prefer, to achieve it without physical violence. We would prefer to negotiate rather than destroy, to talk rather than kill. We do not advocate violence; we advocate an end to the violence against human dignity which is now being perpetrated by the oppressors of Africa. If peaceful progress to emancipation were possible, or if changed circumstances were to make it possible in the future, we would urge our brothers in the resistance movements to use peaceful methods of struggle even at the cost of some compromise on the timing of change. But while peaceful progress is blocked by actions of those at present in power in the States of Southern Africa, we have no choice but to give to the peoples of those territories all the support of which we are capable in their struggle against their oppressors. This is why the signatory states participate in the

movement for the liberation of Africa under the aegis of the Organisation of African Unity. However, the obstacle to change is not the same in all the countries of Southern Africa, and it follows therefore, that the possibility of continuing the struggle through peaceful means varies from one country to another.

13. In Mozambique and Angola, and in the so-called Portuguese Guinea, the basic problem is not racialism but a pretence that Portugal exists in Africa. Portugal is situated in Europe, the fact that it is a dictatorship is a matter for the Portuguese to settle. But no decree of the Portuguese dictator, nor legislation passed by any Parliament in Portugal, can make Africa part of Europe. The only thing which could convert a part of Africa into a constituent unit in a union which also includes a European State would be the freely expressed will of the people of that part of Africa. There is no such popular will in the Portuguese colonies. On the contrary, in the absence of any opportunity to negotiate a road to freedom, the peoples of all three territories have taken up arms against the colonial power. They have done this despite the heavy odds against them, and despite the great suffering they know to be involved.

14. Portugal, as a European State, has naturally its own allies in the context of the ideological conflict between West and East. However, in our context, the effect of this is that Portugal is enabled to use her resources to pursue the most heinous war and degradation of man in Africa. The present Manifesto must, therefore, lay bare the fact that the inhuman commitment of Portugal in Africa and her ruthless subjugation of the people of Mozambique, Angola, and the so-called Portuguese Guinea, is not only irrelevant to the ideological conflict of power-politics, but it is also diametrically opposed to the policies, the philosophies and the doctrines practised by her Allies in the conduct of their own affairs at home. The peoples of Mozambique, Angola and Portuguese Guinea are not interested in Communism or Capitalism; they are interested in their freedom. They are demanding an acceptance of the principles of independence on the basis of majority rule, and for many years they called for discussions on this issue. Only when their demand for talks was continually ignored did they begin to fight. Even now, if Portu-

gal should change her policy and accept the principle of self-determination, we would urge the Liberation Movements to desist from their armed struggle and to co-operate in the mechanics of a peaceful transfer of power from Portugal to the peoples of the African territories.

15. The fact that many Portuguese citizens have immigrated to these African countries does not affect this issue. Future immigration policy will be a matter for the independent Governments when these are established. In the meantime, we would urge the Liberation Movements to reiterate their statements that all those Portuguese people who have made their homes in Mozambique, Angola or Portuguese Guinea, and who are willing to give their future loyalty to those states, will be accepted as citizens. And an independent Mozambique, Angola, or Portuguese Guinea may choose to be as friendly with Portugal as Brazil is. That would be the free choice of a free people.

16. In Rhodesia the situation is different insofar as the metropolitan power has acknowledged the colonial status of the territory. Unfortunately, however, it has failed to take adequate measures to re-assert its authority against the minority which has seized power with the declared intention of maintaining white domination. The matter cannot rest there. Rhodesia, like the rest of Africa, must be free, and its independence must be on the basis of majority rule. If the colonial power is unwilling or unable to effect such a transfer of power to the people, then the people themselves will have no alternative but to capture it as and when they can. And Africa has no alternative but to support them. The question which remains in Rhodesia is therefore whether Britain will re-assert her authority in Rhodesia and then negotiate the peaceful progress to majority rule before independence. Insofar as Britain is willing to make this second commitment, Africa will co-operate in her attempts to re-assert her authority. This is the method of progress which we would prefer; it could involve less suffering for all the peoples of Rhodesia; both black and white. But until there is some firm evidence that Britain accepts the principles of independence on the basis of majority rule, and is prepared to take whatever steps are necessary to make it a reality, then Africa has no choice but

to support the struggle for the people's freedom by whatever means are open to her.

17. Just as a settlement of the Rhodesian problem with a minimum of violence is a British responsibility, so a settlement in South West Africa with a minimum of violence is a United Nations responsibility. By every canon of international law, and by every precedent, South West Africa should by now have been a sovereign, independent State with a Government based on majority rule. South West Africa was a German colony until 1919, just as Tanganyika, Rwanda and Burundi, Togoland, and Cameroon were German colonies. It was a matter of European politics that when the Mandatory System was established after Germany had been defeated, the administration of South West Africa was given to the white minority government of South Africa, while the other ex-German colonies in Africa were put into the hands of the British, Belgian, or French Governments. After the Second World War every mandated territory except South West Africa was converted into a Trusteeship Territory and has subsequently gained independence. South Africa, on the other hand has persistently refused to honour even the international obligation it accepted in 1919, and has increasingly applied to South West Africa the inhuman doctrines and organisation of apartheid.

18. The United Nations General Assembly has ruled against this action and in 1966 terminated the Mandate under which South Africa had a legal basis for its occupation and domination of South West Africa. The General Assembly declared that the territory is now the direct responsibility of the United Nations and set up an ad hoc Committee to recommend practical means by which South West Africa would be administered, and the people enabled to exercise self-determination and to achieve independence.

19. Nothing could be clearer than this decision—which no permanent member of the Security Council voted against. Yet, since that time no effective measures have been taken to enforce it. South West Africa remains in the clutches of the most ruthless minority Government in Africa. Its people continue to be oppressed and those who advocate even peaceful progress to

independence continue to be persecuted. The world has an obligation to use its strength to enforce the decision which all the countries co-operated in making. If they do this there is hope that the change can be effected without great violence. If they fail, then sooner or later the people of South West Africa will take the law into their own hands. The people have been patient beyond belief, but one day their patience will be exhausted. Africa, at least, will then be unable to deny their call for help.

20. The Union of South Africa is itself an independent sovereign State and a Member of the United Nations. It is more highly developed and richer than any other nation in Africa. On every legal basis its internal affairs are a matter exclusively for the people of South Africa. Yet the purpose of law is people and we assert that the actions of the South African Government are such that the rest of the world has a responsibility to take some action in defence of humanity.

21. There is one thing about South African oppression which distinguishes it from other oppressive regimes. The apartheid policy adopted by its Government, and supported to a greater or lesser extent by almost all its white citizens, is based on a rejection of man's humanity. A position of privilege or the experience of oppression in South African society depends on the one thing which it is beyond the power of man to change. It depends upon a man's colour, his parentage, and his ancestors. If you are black you cannot escape this categorisation; nor can you escape it if you are white. If you are a black millionaire and a brilliant political scientist, you are still subject to the pass laws and still excluded from political activity. If you are white, even protests against the system and an attempt to reject segregation will lead you only to the segregated and the comparative comfort of a white jail. Beliefs, abilities and behaviour are all irrelevant to a man's status; everything depends upon race. Manhood is irrelevant. The whole system of government and society in South Africa is based on the denial of human equality. And the system is maintained by a ruthless denial of the human rights of the majority of the population—and thus, inevitably of all.

22. These things are known and are regularly condemned in the Councils of the United Nations and elsewhere. But it appears that to many countries international law takes precedence over humanity; therefore no action follows the words. Yet even if international law is held to exclude active assistance to the South African opponents of apartheid, it does not demand that the comfort and support of human and commercial intercourse should be given to a government which rejects the manhood of most of humanity. South Africa should be excluded from the United Nations Agencies, and even from the United Nations itself. It should be ostracised by the world community until it accepts the implications of man's common humanity. It should be isolated from world trade patterns and left to be self-sufficient if it can. The South African Government cannot be allowed both to reject the very concept of mankind's unity, and to benefit by the strength given through friendly international relations. And certainly Africa cannot acquiesce in the maintenance of the present policies against people of African descent.

23. The signatories of this Manifesto assert that the validity of the principles of human equality and dignity extend to the Union of South Africa just as they extend to the colonial territories of Southern Africa. Before a basis for peaceful development can be established in this continent, these principles must be acknowledged by every nation, and in every State there must be a deliberate attempt to implement them.

24. We re-affirm our commitment to these principles of human equality and human dignity, and to the doctrines of self-determination and non-racialism. We shall work for their extension within our own nations and throughout the continent of Africa.

[Signatory states: Burundi, Central African Republic, Chad, Congo (Brazzaville), Congo (Kinshasa), Ethiopia, Kenya, Rwanda, Somalia, Sudan, Tanzania, Uganda, Zambia.]

Bibliography

Materials used in this study include public documents of governments and international organizations and institutions; official publications of non-governmental political organizations; newspapers, newsletters, journals, and other periodicals; books and monographs; various unpublished materials; and notes from personal interviews. The items are grouped accordingly. Thus an italic (book) title if not found in the books group will be found under public documents or official publications. Titles in quotation marks (articles) also appear under those headings and in the list of unpublished materials. A number of abbreviations are employed in the footnotes, as follows:

ARB Africa Research Bulletin. Citations are from the Political, Cultural and Social Series unless noted "(Econ)," in which case they are from the Economic, Financial and Technical Series.
ICJ International Court of Justice
JMAS Journal of Modern African Studies
NYT New York Times
RSA Republic of South Africa
SABRA South African Bureau of Racial Affairs
SAIIA South African Institute of International Affairs

With regard to the interviews, footnotes refer to my handwritten notes and, in order to preserve the anonymity of the interviewee, reference is made simply to the country in which the interview took place, the number of the interview according to my notes, the city, and the date. Researchers who may wish to follow up on my work should apply to me; in individual instances, some of the notes may be made available.

Government and United Nations Publications

Basutoland

See Lesotho.

Botswana

Central Statistical Office, Ministry of Development Planning. *Statistical Abstract: 1969*. Gaberone: Goverment Printer, August 1969.

Information Services. *Republic of Botswana–Fact Sheet*. Gaberone: Government Printer, 1968. Mimeographed.

Ghana

Ministry of Information. *Nkrumah's Subversion in Africa*. Accra-Tema: State Publishing Corp., 1966.

Great Britain

British Information Services. *Botswana*. London: HMSO, 1966.

———. *Swaziland*. London: HMSO, 1968.

Parliamentary Debates, Commons. *Hansard*, 1960–71.

International Court of Justice

International Status of South West Africa, Advisory Opinion. I. C. J. Reports 1950.

South West Africa Cases (Ethiopia v. South Africa, Liberia v. South Africa), Preliminary Objections, Judgment of December 21, 1962. I. C. J. Reports 1962.

South West Africa Cases, Second Phase, Judgment. I. C. J. Reports 1966.

Reports of Judgments, Advisory Opinions and Orders: Legal Consequences of the Continued Presence of South Africa in Namibia (South West Africa) Notwithstanding Security Council Resolution 276 (1970), Advisory Opinion of 21 June 1971. The Hague: International Court of Justice, [1971].

Lesotho

Basutoland Government. *Basutoland 1956 Population Census*. Maseru: Basutoland Government, 1958.

Bureau of Statistics. *1966 Population Census of Lesotho (14th–24th April, 1966), Interim Report: Release no. 1, 18th August, 1967*. Mimeographed.

Jonathan, Chief Leabua. *Address by the Honourable the Prime Minister at the First Anniversary Pitso of Lesotho's Independence, Held on the 4th October, 1967*. [Maseru?, 1967?]. Mimeographed.

Malawi

Banda, H. Kamuzu. *Agreements with South Africa and Portugal: Address to the Malawi Parliament by His Excellency the President, March 29, 1967*. [Blantyre?]: Department of Information, [1967?]

———. *The President, Ngwazi Dr. Kamuzu Banda Delivering His Opening Address to the Malawi Congress Party Convention at the Kwacha National Cultural Centre, Blantyre on Monday, September 1st, 1969*. Blantyre: Department of Information, [1969?]. Mimeographed.

———. *Press Conference Held at Chichiri House, Blantyre, on July 8th, 1969, Attended by His Excellency The President, Ngwazi Dr. H. Kamuzu Banda*. Blantyre: Department of Information, n.d. Mimeographed.

———. *Speech by His Excellency The President, Ngwazi Dr. Kamuzu Banda, at the Opening of Malawi Congress Party Annual Convention at Lilongwe, on September 16, 1968*. Blantyre: Department of Information, 1968. Mimeographed.

Department of Information. *Malawi 1969*. Blantyre: Blantyre Print, 1970.

———. *Pioneers in Inter-African Relations*. Blantyre: Department of Information, [1970?].

Ministry of Labour, Report 1963–1967. Zomba: Government Printer, 1969.

National Statistical Office. *Malawi in Figures, 1971*. Zomba: Government Printer, [1972?].

Parliament. *Debates. Hansard*, 1969–71.

Rhodesia

Economic Survey of Rhodesia for 1967. Salisbury: Government Printer, April 1968.

Economic Survey of Rhodesia, 1969. Salisbury: Government Printer, 1969.

Ministry of Finance. *Economic Survey of Rhodesia, 1970*. Salisbury: Government Printer, April 1970.

Ministry of Information, Immigration and Tourism. *Rhodesian Commentary*. Salisbury, 1967–71.

———. *Rhodesia in the Context of Africa*. Salisbury, 1966.

———. *Red for Danger*. Salisbury, November 1967.

———. *Zambezi—Red Frontier*. Salisbury, October 1968.

South Africa

Department of Customs and Excise. *Foreign Trade Statistics*. Vol. I.

Imports, Exports (South African Produce) and Imported Goods Re-Exported, Calendar Year, 1961. Pretoria: Government Printer, 1962. Also for subsequent years. In 1965 the subtitle was changed to *Imports and Exports, Calendar Year 1965.*

Department of External Affairs. *The Department of External Affairs List.* Pretoria: Government Printer, July 1948. Also subsequent lists dated July 1950, January 1952, July 1953, July 1954, January 1955, July 1955, January 1956, January 1957, July 1957, July 1958, and October 1959.

Department of Foreign Affairs. *The Department of Foreign Affairs List.* Pretoria: Government Printer, September 1961. Also subsequent lists dated February 1963, June 1964, and February 1966.

———. *South West Africa: South Africa's Reply to the Secretary-General of the United Nations (Security Council Resolution 269 of 1969).* Pretoria: Government Printer, September 1969.

Department of Information. *South African Digest,* Pretoria, 1961–71.

House of Assembly. *Debates. Hansard,* 1950–71.

Information Service. *News from South Africa.* New York, 1967–71.

———. *Progress through Separate Development.* New York, 1968.

Muller, Dr. H. *The Republic of South Africa in a Changed World: 31st August 1967.* Pretoria: Department of Information, 1968. *Fact Paper* series.

Tanzania

Ministry of Information and Broadcasting, Tanzania Information Services. *Why We Will Not Negotiate: A Statement by the Ministry of Foreign Affairs—February, 1971.* Dar es Salaam: Government Printer, 1971.

Nyerere, Julius K. *South Africa and the Commonwealth: Commonwealth Conference, Singapore, January 1971.* [Dar es Salaam?], January 1971.

———. *Tanzania Policy on Foreign Affairs: Address by The President, Mwalimu Julius K. Nyerere at the Tanganyika African National Union National Conference—16th October, 1967.* Dar es Salaam: Information Services Division, Ministry of Information and Tourism, n.d.

United Nations

General Assembly. *Official Records,* 21st–25th sessions, 1966–70.

———, High Commissioner for Refugees. *HCR Bulletin.* Geneva, 1968–71.

———, Executive Committee of the High Commissioner's Programme, 19th Session. *Report on UNHCR Operations in 1967* (A/AC.96/390), April 30, 1968.

Statistical Office, Department of Economic and Social Affairs. *Statistical Yearbook, 1970*. New York, 1971.

United States

Congress, House of Representatives, Committee on Foreign Affairs. *Report of Special Study Mission to Southern Africa*, 91st cong., 1st sess., October 10, 1969. Washington, D.C.: Government Printing Office, 1969.

Zambia

Zambian High Commission, London. *Details of Exchanges between President Kaunda of Zambia and Prime Minister Vorster of South Africa*. London: The Commission, April 29, 1971. Mimeographed.

Materials Issued by Political Parties, Movements, and Action-Oriented Research and Information Organizations

African National Congress. *Sechaba*. London, 1968–71.

African National Congress. *Spotlight on South Africa*. London, 1969–71.

Ainslie, Rosalynde. *The Unholy Alliance*. London: Anti-Apartheid Movement, 1963.

Liberation Support Movement. *Daniel Chipenda [MPLA], Interview*. Seattle: Liberation Support Movement, [1969?].

Minty, Abdul S. *South Africa's Defense Strategy*. London: Anti-Apartheid Movement, October 1969.

Mozambique/Angola Soldiers' Comforts Fund. *What This War Means to South Africa*. Cape Town and Durban, n.d., 4 pp.

Pan-African Freedom Movement for East, Central and Southern Africa, Addis Ababa Conference, February 2–10, 1962. Addis Ababa: African Department of the Foreign Office, 1962.

Progressive Party. *Forging Links in Africa: Speeches Made by Mr. Colin Eglin, of the Progressive Party of South Africa, and by Mr. B. C. Thema, of the Botswana Government, at Gaberones on 26th March, 1967*. Cape Town, n.d.

South West Africa Peoples' Organization. *Namibia News*. London, 1968–71.

Toivo, Toivo Herman Ja. *Statement by Toivo Herman Ja Toivo*. New York: SWAPO Office, April 1968.

Zimbabwe African National Union. *Zimbabwe News.* Lusaka, 1969–71.

Zimbabwe African Peoples Union. *Zimbabwe Review.* Lusaka, 1969–70.

Materials Issued by Politically Committed Research and Information Organizations

Africa Bureau

X-Ray. London, 1970–72.

Molteno, Robert. *Africa and South Africa: The Implications of South Africa's "Outward-Looking" Policy*. London: Africa Bureau, February 1971.

Africa Institute

Africa Institute Bulletin. Pretoria, 1967–72.

Breytenbach, W. J. *Vreemde Bantoewerkers in Suid-Afrika en Rhodesie.* Pretoria: Afrika Institut, 1971. Communications Series, no. 17.

Leistner, G. M. E. *South Africa's Development Aid to African States.* Pretoria: Africa Institute, 1970.

Muller, Hilgard. "South Africa's Africa Policy," *Africa Institute Bulletin,* VIII (1970), 256.

Smit, P. "Botswana Railway Line," *Africa Institute Bulletin,* VII (1970), 272–80.

Angola Committee or Comité.

Facts and Reports. Amsterdam, 1971.

Bosgra, Dr. S. J., and Van Krimpen, Chr. *Portugal and NATO.* Amsterdam: Angola Comité, October 1969.

South African Bureau of Racial Affairs

South Africa in the African Continent: Papers Read at the Tenth Annual Conference, 1959. Stellenbosch: SABRA, 1959.

South African Institute of Race Relations

Brett, E. A. *African Attitudes: A study of the Social, Racial and Political Attitudes of Some Middle Class Africans.* Johannesburg: South African Institute of Race Relations, 1963. Fact Paper, no. 14.

Friedman, Dr. Bernard, Sutherland, John, and Ballinger, R. B. *Looking Outwards: Three South African Viewpoints.* Johannesburg: South African Institute of Race Relations, 1961.

Horrell, Muriel. *South-West Africa.* Johannesburg: South African Institute of Race Relations, 1967.

Marquard, Leo. *Our Foreign Policy: The 1969 Presidential Address.* Johannesburg: South African Institute of Race Relations, 1969.

Marquard, Leo. *South Africa's Colonial Policy: Presidential Address, 1957.* Johannesburg: South African Institute of Race Relations, 1957.

Smuts, J. C. *The Basis of Trusteeship in African Native Policy.* Cape Town: South African Institute of Race Relations, 1942. New Africa pamphlet, no. 2.

Sparks, Allister. *New Perspectives in Africa.* Johannesburg: South African Institute of Race Relations, 1967. Topical Talks, no. 5.

World Council of Churches.

Programme to Combat Racism. *Cabora Bassa and the Struggle for Southern Africa.* London: The Council, 1971.

———. *Cunene Dam Scheme and the Struggle for the Liberation of Southern Africa.* N.p.: The Council, December 1971.

Books and Monographs

Abshire, David M., and Samuels, Michael A., eds. *Portuguese Africa: A Handbook.* New York: Praeger, 1969.

Adam, Heribert. *Modernizing Racial Domination: South Africa's Political Dynamics.* Berkeley: University of California Press, 1971.

Booth, Richard. *The Armed Forces of African States, 1970.* London: Institute for Strategic Studies, May 1970. Adelphi Papers, no. 67.

Boulding, Kenneth E. *Conflict and Defense: A General Theory.* New York: Harper, 1960.

Bwanausi, A. W. et al. *Dr. Banda's Malawi: A Neo-Colonialist Puppet.* [Cairo? 1965?]

Cantori, Louis J., and Spiegel, Steven L. *The International Politics of Regions: A Comparative Approach.* Englewood Cliffs, N.J.: Prentice-Hall, 1970.

Carter, Gwendolen. *The Politics of Inequality: South Africa Since 1948.* 2d ed., rev. London: Thames and Hudson, 1959.

Carter, Gwendolen M., Karis, Thomas, and Stultz, N. J. *South Africa's Transkei: The Politics of Domestic Colonialism.* Evanston, Ill.: Northwestern University Press, 1967.

Chapman, David. *The Infiltrators.* Johannesburg: Macmillan, 1968. A novel.

Clarke, S. J. G. *The Congo Mercenary: A History and Analysis.* Johannesburg: South African Institute of International Affairs, 1968.

Claude, Inis L. *Swords into Plowshares.* New York: Random House, 1959.

Cox, Richard. *Pan-Africanism in Practice: PAFMECSA, 1958–1964.* London: Oxford University Press, 1964.

Dale, Richard. *The Racial Component of Botswana's Foreign Policy.* Denver: Center on International Race Relations, 1971. Race and Nations Monograph Series, II, no. 4 (1970–71).

———, and Potholm, Christian P., eds. *Southern Africa in Perspective: Essays in Regional Politics.* New York: Free Press, forthcoming.

Davidson, Basil. *In the Eye of the Storm: Angola's People.* London: Longman, 1972.

Davis, John A., and Baker, James K., eds. *Southern Africa in Transition.* New York: Praeger, 1966.

Day, John. *International Nationalism: The Extra-Territorial Relations of Southern Rhodesian African Nationalists.* London: Routledge, 1967.

Falk, Richard A. *The Status of Law in International Society.* Princeton, N.J.: Princeton University Press, 1970.

Feit, Edward. *African Opposition in South Africa.* Stanford, Calif.: Hoover Institution, 1967.

———. *South Africa: The Dynamics of the African National Congress.* London: Oxford University Press, 1962.

———. *Urban Revolt in South Africa, 1960–1964: A Case Study.* Evanston, Ill.: Northwestern University Press, 1971.

Frank, Lawrence. *The Basutoland National Party: Traditional Authority and Neo-Colonialism in Lesotho.* Denver: Center on International Race Relations, 1970. Studies in Race and Nations, II, no. 3 (1970–71).

Glass, Harold M. *South African Policy towards Basutoland.* Johannesburg: South African Institute of International Affairs, 1966.

Green, L. P., and Fair, T. J. D. *Development in Africa: A Study in Regional Analysis with Special Reference to Southern Africa.* Johannesburg: Witwatersrand University Press, 1962.

Gruhn, Isebill V. *British Arms Sales to South Africa: The Limits of African Diplomacy.* Denver: Center on International Race Relations, 1972. Race and Nations Monograph Series, III, no. 3, 1971–72.

Grundy, Kenneth W. *Conflicting Images of the Military in Africa.* Nairobi: East African Publishing House, 1968.

———. *Guerrilla Struggle in Africa: An Analysis and Preview.* New York: Grossman, 1971.

Haefele, Edwin R., and Steinberg, Eleanor B. *Government Controls on Transport: An African Case.* Washington: Brookings Institution, 1965.

Hailey, Lord. *The Republic of South Africa and the High Commission Territories.* London: Oxford University Press, 1963.

Hall, Richard. *The High Price of Principles: Kaunda and the White South.* London: Hodder and Stoughton, 1969.

Halpern, Jack. *South Africa's Hostages: Basutoland, Bechuanaland and Swaziland.* Baltimore: Penguin, 1965.

Halpern, Manfred. *Applying a New Theory of Human Relations to the Comparative Study of Racism.* Denver: Center on International Race Relations, 1969. Race and Nations Monograph Series, I, no. 1 (1969–70).

Hamrell, Sven, ed. *Refugee Problems in Africa.* Uppsala: Scandinavian Institute of African Studies, 1967.

Hance, William A. *Population, Migration, and Urbanization in Africa.* New York and London: Columbia University Press, 1970.

———, ed. *Southern Africa and the United States.* New York and London: Columbia University Press, 1968.

Harrigan, Anthony. *Defence against Total Attack.* Cape Town: Nasionale Boekhandel, 1965.

Herrick, Allison Butler, et al. *Area Handbook for Angola.* Washington, D. C.: Government Printing Office, August 1967.

———, et al. *Area Handbook for Mozambique.* Washington, D. C.: Government Printing Office, 1969.

Hoare, Mike. *Congo Mercenary.* London: Robert Hale, 1967.

Hovet, Thomas, Jr. *Africa in the United Nations.* Evanston, Ill.: Northwestern University Press, 1963.

Institute for Strategic Studies. *The Military Balance, 1970–71.* London: Institute for Strategic Studies, 1970.

———. *The Military Balance, 1971–72.* London: Institute for Strategic Studies, 1971.

Kaplan, Irving, et al. *Area Handbook for Zambia.* Washington, D. C.: Government Printing Office, 1969.

Kaunda, Kenneth D. *A Humanist in Africa: Letters to Colin D. Morris.* London: Longmans, 1966.

———. *Zambia Shall Be Free: An Autobiography.* London: Heinemann, 1962.

Kibulya, H. M., and Langlands, B. W. *The Political Geography of the Uganda-Congo Boundary.* Kampala: Department of Geography, Makerere University College, 1967. Occasional Paper, no. 6.

Kirkwood, Kenneth. *Britain and Africa.* Baltimore: Johns Hopkins Press, 1965.

Khaketla, Bennett Makalo. *Lesotho 1970—An African Coup under the Microscope*. London: C. Hurst, 1972.

Kuper, Leo. *An African Bourgeosie: Race, Class, and Politics in South Africa*. New Haven and London: Yale University Press, 1965.

———. *Passive Resistance in South Africa*. New Haven: Yale University Press, 1957.

Legum, Colin. *Pan-Africanism: A Short Political Guide*. New York: Praeger, 1962.

———, and Drysdale, John, eds. *Africa Contemporary Record—1968–1969*. Exeter: Africa Research Ltd., 1969.

———, ———, eds. *Africa Contemporary Record—1969–1970*. Exeter: Africa Research Ltd., 1970.

———, and Legum, Margaret. *South Africa: Crisis for the West*. London: Pall Mall, 1964.

Leiss, Amelia C., ed. *Apartheid and the United Nations Collective Measures: An Analysis*. New York: Carnegie Endowment for International Peace, 1965.

Lombard, J. A., et al. *The Concept of Economic Co-operation in Southern Africa*. Pretoria: Econburo (Pty.) Ltd., 1969.

MacCrone, I. D. *Race Attitudes in South Africa: Historical, Experimental and Psychological Studies*. London: Oxford University Press, 1937.

Marcum, John. *The Angolan Revolution*, vol. I: *The Anatomy of an Explosion (1950–1962)*. Cambridge, Mass., and London: M. I. T. Press, 1969.

Marquard, Leo. *A Federation of Southern Africa*. New York and London: Oxford University Press, 1971.

Mazrui, Ali A. *The Anglo-African Commonwealth: Political Friction and Cultural Fusion*. London: Pergamon Press, 1967.

———. *Towards a Pax Africana: A Study of Ideology and Ambition*. London: Weidenfeld and Nicolson, 1967.

———. *Violence and Thought: Essays on Social Tensions in Africa*. New York: Humanities Press, 1969.

Mbeki, Govan. *South Africa: The Peasants' Revolt*. Baltimore: Penguin, 1964.

Mboya, Tom. *Freedom and After*. London: Deutsch, 1963.

Mlambo, Eshmael. *Rhodesia: The Struggle for a Birthright*. London: C. Hurst, 1972.

Mondlane, Eduardo. *The Struggle for Mozambique*. Harmondsworth: Penguin, 1969.

Morris, Michael. *Terrorism: The First Full Account in Detail of Ter-*

rorism and Insurgency in Southern Africa. Cape Town: Howard Timmons, 1971.

Munger, Edwin S. *Bechuanaland: Pan-African Outpost or Bantu Homeland?* London: Oxford University Press, 1965.

———. *Notes on the Formation of South African Foreign Policy*. Pasadena, Calif.: Grant Dahlstrom/The Castle Press, 1965.

Nielsen, Waldemar A. *African Battleline: American Policy Choices in Southern Africa*. New York and Evanston: Harper and Row, 1965.

Nkrumah, Kwame. *Neo-Colonialism: The Last Stage of Imperialism*. New York: International Publishers, 1965.

Nyerere, Julius K. *Freedom and Socialism—Uhuru Na Ujamaa: A Selection from Writings and Speeches, 1965–1967*. Dar es Salaam: Oxford University Press, 1968.

———. *Freedom and Unity: Uhuru Na Umoja*. Dar es Salaam: Oxford University Press, 1966.

Orpen, Neil. *Total Defence: The Role of the Commandoes in the Armed Forces of South Africa*. Cape Town: Nasionale Boekhandel, 1967.

Rhoodie, Eschel. *The Third Africa*. Cape Town: Nasionale Boekhandel, 1968.

Rhoodie, N. J., and Venter, J. J. *Apartheid: A Socio-Historical Exposition of the Origin and Development of the Apartheid Idea*. Cape Town: National Commercial Printers, 1961.

Rose, Peter I. *They and We: Racial and Ethnic Relations in the United States*. New York: Random House, 1964.

Rosenau, James N. *The Adaptation of National Societies—A Theory of Political System Behavior and Transformation*. New York: McCaleb-Seiler, 1970.

———, ed. *Domestic Sources of Foreign Policy*. New York: Free Press, 1967.

———, ed. *International Politics and Foreign Policy: A Reader in Research and Theory*. Rev. ed. New York: Free Press, 1969.

Royal United Service Institution. *The Cape Route: Report of a Seminar, 25 February 1970*. London: The Institution, 1970.

Royal United Services Institute for Defence Studies. *The Security of the Southern Oceans—Southern Africa the Key: Report of a Seminar, 16 February 1972*. London: The Institute, 1972.

Russett, Bruce M. *International Regions and the International System: A Study on Political Ecology*. Chicago: Rand McNally, 1967.

———, et al. *World Handbook of Political and Social Indicators.* New Haven: Yale University Press, 1964.

Segal, Ronald, ed. *Sanctions against South Africa.* Baltimore: Penguin, 1964.

Shepherd, George W., Jr. *Nonaligned Black Africa: An International Subsystem.* Lexington, Mass.: Heath Lexington Books, 1970.

Smuts, J. C. *Africa and Some World Problems.* Oxford: Clarendon Press, 1930.

Spence, J. E. *Lesotho: The Politics of Dependence.* London: Oxford University Press, 1968.

———. *Republic under Pressure: A Study of South African Foreign Policy.* London: Oxford University Press, 1965.

———, and Thomas, Elizabeth. *South Africa's Defense: The Problem of Internal Control.* Los Angeles: University of California at Los Angeles, 1966. Security Studies Paper, no. 8.

Standard Bank Group. *Annual Economic Review: Botswana, Lesotho, Swaziland.* London, October 1970.

Teixeira, Bernardo. *The Fabric of Terror: Three Days in Angola.* Cape Town: Human and Rousseau, 1965.

Thompson, W. Scott. *Ghana's Foreign Policy, 1957–1966: Diplomacy, Ideology and the New State.* Princeton, N. J.: Princeton University Press, 1969.

Vandenbosch, Amry. *South Africa and the World: The Foreign Policy of Apartheid.* Lexington, Ky.: The University Press of Kentucky, 1970.

Vatcher, William Henry, Jr. *White Laager: The Rise of Afrikaner Nationalism.* New York: Praeger, 1965.

Venter, Al J. *The Terror Fighters: A Profile of Guerrilla Warfare in Southern Africa.* Cape Town: Purnell, 1969.

Walker, Eric A. *A History of South Africa.* 2d ed. London: Longmans, 1940.

Wallerstein, Immanuel. *Africa—The Politics of Unity: An Analysis of a Contemporary Social Movement.* New York: Random House, 1967.

Weisfelder, Richard F. *Defining National Purpose in Lesotho.* Athens, Ohio: Ohio University Center for International Studies, 1969. Papers in International Studies, Africa Series, no. 3.

Wood, David. *The Armed Forces of African States.* London: Institute of Strategic Studies, April 1966. Adelphi Papers, no. 27.

Wright, Quincy. *A Study of War.* Chicago: University of Chicago Press, 1942.

Zartman, I. William. *International Relations in the New Africa.* Englewood Cliffs, N. J.: Prentice-Hall, 1966.

Articles and Chapters

Alger, Chadwick F., and Brams, Steven J., "Patterns of Representation in National Capitals and Inter-Governmental Organizations," *World Politics,* XIX (1967), 646–63.

AlRoy, Gil Carl. "Insurgency in the Countryside of Underdeveloped Societies," *Antioch Review,* XXVI (1966), 149–57.

Anglin, Douglas G. "Confrontation in Southern Africa: Zambia and Portugal," *International Journal,* XXV (1970), 497–517.

———. "The International Arms Traffic in Sub-Saharan Africa." In *Working Papers: Conference on Arms Trade and International Politics,* pp. 7–37. Ottawa: School of International Affairs, Carleton University, May 1971. Occasional Papers, no. 12.

Baldwin, David A. "Foreign Aid, Intervention, and Influence," *World Politics,* XXI (1969), 425–47.

Barnekov, Christopher C., Jr. "Sanctions and the Rhodesian Economy," *Rhodesian Journal of Economics,* III, no. 1 (March 1969), 44–75.

Bender, Gerald L. "The Limits of Counterinsurgency: An African Case," *Comparative Politics,* IV (1972), 331–60.

Binder, Leonard. "The Middle-East as a Subordinate International System," *World Politics,* X (1958), 408–29.

Bowman, Larry W. "The Sub-State System of Southern Africa," *International Studies Quarterly,* XII (1968), 231–98.

Brams, Steven J. "Transaction Flows in the International System," *American Political Science Review,* LX (1966), 880–98.

Brecher, Michael. "International Relations and Asian Studies: The Sub-State System of Southern Asia," *World Politics,* XV (1963), 213–35.

Caplan, Gerald L. "Zambia, Barotseland, and the Liberation of Southern Africa," *Africa Today,* XV, no. 4 (1969), 13–17.

Cefkin, J. Leo. "The Rhodesian Question at the United Nations," *International Organization,* XXII (1968), 649–69.

Chipembere, Henry B. Masauko. "Malawi's Growing Links with South Africa—A Necessity or a Virtue?" *Africa Today,* XVIII, no. 2 (1971), 27–47.

Craig, James. "Zambia-Botswana Road Link: Some Border Problems." In *Zambia and the World: Essays on Problems Relating to Zambia's*

Foreign Policy—Articles Collected for the Occasion of the Non-Aligned Summit Conference Held in Lusaka, September 1970, pp. 25–32. Lusaka: University of Zambia, School of Humanities and Social Sciences, 1970.

Dale, Richard. "Ovamboland: 'Bantustan Without Tears?'" *Africa Report*, XIV, no. 2 (1969), 16–23.

Davidson, Basil. "Angola in the Tenth Year: A Report and an Analysis, May–July 1970," *African Affairs*, LXX (1971), 37–49.

———. "Arms and the Portuguese," *Africa Report*, XV, no. 5 (1970), 10–11.

Delius, Anthony. "Internal Argument and External Policy in South Africa," *African Affairs*, LXIX (1970), 371–74.

Deutsch, Karl W. "External Influences on the Internal Behavior of States." In R. Barry Farrell, ed., *Approaches to Comparative and International Politics*, pp. 5–26. Evanston, Ill.: Northwestern University Press, 1966.

———. "External Involvement in Internal War." In Harry Eckstein, ed., *Internal War*, pp. 100–110. Glencoe, Ill.: Free Press, 1964.

Diamond, Robert A., and Fouquet, David. "Portugal and the United States," *Africa Report*, XV, no. 5 (1970), 15–17.

Doxey, Margaret. "International Sanctions: A Framework for Analysis with Special Reference to the UN and Southern Africa," *International Organization*, XXVI (1972), 527–50.

Feit, Edward. "Urban Revolt in South Africa: A Case Study," *Journal of Modern African Studies*, VIII (1970), 55–72.

Galtung, Johan. "On the Effects of International Economic Sanctions: With Examples from the Case of Rhodesia," *World Politics*, XIX (1967), 378–416.

Glickman, Harvey. "Where Exiles Plan—and Wait," *Africa Report*, VIII, no. 7 (1963), 3–6.

Gruhn, Isebill V. "The Commission for Technical Co-operation in Africa, 1950–65," *Journal of Modern African Studies*, IX (1971), 459–69.

Grundy, Kenneth W. "The 'Southern Border' of Africa." In Carl Gösta Widstrand, ed., *African Boundary Problems*, pp. 119–60, 196–202. Uppsala: Scandinavian Institute of African Studies, 1969.

Hill, Christopher. "UDI and South African Foreign Policy," *Journal of Commonwealth Political Studies*, VII (July 1969), 96–103.

Hovet, Thomas, Jr. "African Politics in the United Nations." In Herbert J. Spiro, ed., *Africa: The Primacy of Politics*, pp. 116–49. New York: Random House, 1966.

Jeeves, Alan H. "The Problem of South Africa," *International Journal,* XXVI (1971), 418–32.

Kapil, Ravi L. "On the Conflict Potential of Inherited Boundaries in Africa," *World Politics,* XVIII (1966), 656–73.

Khama, Sir Seretse. "A Policy of Prudence," *Africa Report,* XI, no. 7 (1968), 19–20.

Kitchen, Helen. "Conversation with Eduardo Mondlane," *Africa Report,* XII, no. 8 (1967), 31–32, 49–51.

Kotsokoane, J. R. L. "Lesotho and Her Neighbours," *International Affairs* (London), LXVIII, no. 271 (1969), 135–38.

Kuper, Hilda. "The Colonial Situation in Southern Africa," *Journal of Modern African Studies,* II (1964), 149–64.

Lawrie, G. G. "South Africa's World Position," *Journal of Modern African Studies,* II (1964), 41–54.

Legum, Colin. "Guerrilla Warfare and African Liberation Movements," *Africa Today,* XIV, no. 4 (1967), 5–10.

McKay, Vernon. "The Propaganda Battle for Zambia," *Africa Today,* XVIII, no. 2 (1971), 18–26.

———. "South Africa's Propaganda: Methods and Media," *Africa Report,* XI, no. 2 (1966), 41–46.

———. "South African Propaganda on the International Court's Decision," *African Forum,* II, no. 2 (1966), 51–64.

McKinnell, Robert. "Sanctions and the Rhodesian Economy," *Journal of Modern African Studies,* VII, no. 4 (1969), pp. 559–81.

Marcum, John. "The Exile Condition and Revolutionary Effectiveness: Southern African Liberation Movements." In Dale, Richard, and Potholm, Christian P., eds., *Southern Africa in Perspective,* forthcoming.

Marcum, John. "Three Revolutions," *Africa Report,* XII, no. 8 (1967), 9–22.

Matthews, Robert O. "Refugees and Stability in Africa," *International Organization,* XXVI, no. 1 (1972), 62–83.

Mazrui, Ali A. "The United Nations and Some African Political Attitudes," *International Organization,* XVIII, no. 3 (1964), 499–520.

Miller, J. D. B. "South Africa's Departure," *Journal of Commonwealth Political Studies,* I, no. 1 (1961), 56–74.

Modelski, George. "The International Relations of Internal Wars." In Rosenau, James N., ed., *International Aspects of Civil Strife,* pp. 14–44. Princeton, N. J.: Princeton University Press, 1964.

Mondlane, Eduardo. "Our Chances: An Interview," *The New African,* IV (1965), 104–5.

———. "Violence: Not Whether, but How Much." In Vickers, George, ed., *Dialogue on Violence*, pp. 34–38. Indianapolis: Bobbs-Merrill, 1968.

Morgenthau, Hans J. "A Political Theory of Foreign Aid," *American Political Science Review*, LVI (1962), pp. 301–9.

Mudge, George Alfred. "Domestic Policies and UN Activities: The Cases of Rhodesia and the Republic of South Africa," *International Organization*, XXI (1967), 55–78.

Nel, M. D. C. de Wet. "Our Task in Africa," *BaNtu*, February 1960, pp. 69–78.

Niblock, Timothy C. "Tanzanian Foreign Policy: An Analysis," *African Review*, I, no. 2 (1971), 91–101.

Nkoana, Matthew. "The Struggle for the Liberation of Southern Africa, Part II," *Africa and the World*, IV, no. 39 (1968) , 14–17.

Nolutshungu, Sam C. "Issues of the Afrikaner 'Enlightenment,' " *African Affairs*, LXX, no. 278 (1971), 23–36.

Ostrander, F. Taylor. "Zambia and the Aftermath of Rhodesian UDI," *African Forum*, II, no. 3 (1967), 50–65.

Potholm, Christian P. "Transaction Flows and Policy Formation: The Limits of Choice for Swaziland in the Southern African Complex." In Dale, Richard, and Potholm, Christian P., eds., *Southern Africa in Perspective*, forthcoming.

Pratt, R. C. "African Reactions to the Rhodesian Crisis," *International Journal*, XXI (1966), 186–98.

Rake, Alan. "Black Guerrillas in Rhodesia," *Africa Report*, XIII, no. 9 (1968), 23–25.

Rhoodie, E. M. "Luke-Warm Liberation," *To the Point*, I, no. 3 (February 12, 1972), 51–52.

Robson, Peter. "Economic Integration in Southern Africa," *Journal of Modern African Studies*, V (1967), 469–90.

Rosenau, James N. "Intervention as a Scientific Concept," *Journal of Conflict Resolution*, XIII (1969), 149–71.

———. "Pre-Theories and Theories of Foreign Policy." In Farrell, R. Barry, ed., *Approaches to Comparative and International Politics*, pp. 27–92. Evanston, Ill.: Northwestern University Press, 1966.

St. Jorre, John de. "Zambia's Economy: Progress and Perils," *Africa Report*, XII, no. 9 (1967), 36–39.

Scott, Andrew M. "Internal Violence as an Instrument of Cold Warfare." In Rosenau, James N., ed., *International Aspects of Civil Strife*, pp. 154–69. Princeton, N. J.: Princeton University Press, 1964.

Shamuyarira, N. M. "The Lusaka Manifesto on Southern Africa," *African Review,* I, no. 1 (March 1971), 66–78.

Singer, J. David. "Inter-Nation Influence: A Formal Model," *American Political Science Review,* LVII (1963), 420–30.

———. "The Level-of-Analysis Problem in International Relations." In Knorr, Klaus, and Verba, Sidney, eds., *The International System,* pp. 77–92. Princeton: Princeton University Press, 1961.

"The Skirmishes Aren't the Real War," *The Economist,* January 25, 1969, pp. 37–38.

Spence, J. E. "The Implications of the Rhodesia Issue for the Former High Commission Territories," *Journal of Commonwealth Political Studies,* VII, no. 2 (July 1969), 104–111.

Sprout, Harold, and Sprout, Margaret. "Environmental Factors in the Study of International Politics," *Journal of Conflict Resolution,* I, (1957), 309–28.

Stevens, Richard P. "The History of the Anglo-South African Conflict Over the Proposed Incorporation of the High Commission Territories." In Dale, Richard, and Potholm, Christian P., eds., *Southern Africa in Perspective,* forthcoming.

Sutcliffe, R. B. "Zambia and the Strains of UDI," *The World Today,* XXIII (1967), 506–11.

Tandon, Yash, and Shaw, Tim. "Contrasting Attitudes and Behaviour towards Southern Africa: Tanzania and Malawi," In *Proceedings, University of East Africa, Social Science Council Conference (1968–1969),* III, pt. 5, 306–23. Kampala: Makerere Institute of Social Research, 1969.

Tandon, Yashpal. "The Organization of African Unity as an Instrument and Forum of Protest." In Rotberg, Robert I., and Mazrui, Ali A., eds., *Protest and Power in Black Africa,* pp. 1153–83. New York: Oxford University Press, 1970.

Triska, Jan F., and Finley, David D. "Soviet-American Relations: A Multiple Symmetry Model," *Journal of Conflict Resolution,* IX (1965), 37–53.

Turner, Biff. "A Fresh Start for the Southern African Customs Union," *African Affairs,* LXX, no. 280 (1971), 269–76.

Wallensteen, Peter. "Dealing with the Devil: Five African States and South Africa," *Instant Research on Peace and Violence* (Tampere, Finland), no. 3, 1971, pp. 85–99.

Ward, Michael. "Economic Independence for Lesotho?" *Journal of Modern African Studies,* V (1967), 355–68.

Watson, Graham. "The Process of Passing for White in South Africa: A Study in Cumulative Ad Hoc-ery," *Canadian Review of Sociology and Anthropology*, IV (1967), pp. 141–47.

Wheeler, Douglas L. "The Portugese Army in Angola," *Journal of Modern African Studies*, VII (1969), 425–39.

Yarmolinsky, Adam. "American Foreign Policy and the Decision to Intervene," *Journal of International Affairs*, XXII (1968), 231–35.

Young, Oran R. "Intervention and International Systems," *Journal of International Affairs*, XXII (1968), 177–87.

Zartman, I. William. "Africa as a Sub-State System in International Relations," *International Organization*, XXI (1967), 545–64.

Newspapers and Periodicals

Africa Diary, New Delhi, 1961–68

Africa Confidential, London, 1967–72

Africa Digest, London, 1963–72

Africa Report, Washington and New York, 1960–72

Africa Research Bulletin, Exeter, 1964–72 (Political, Cultural and Social Series; Economic, Financial and Technical Series)

Die Burger, Cape Town, January 28, 1964

Cape Times, Cape Town, 1966–71

Daily Nation, Nairobi, 1965–68

East African Standard, Nairobi, 1965–72

Financial Mail, Johannesburg, 1967–71

Malawi News, Blantyre, 1968–71

Manchester Guardian Weekly, 1969

Le Monde, Paris, November 6, 1970

The Nationalist, Dar es Salaam, 1965–71

New York Times, 1960–72

News/Check, Johannesburg, 1965–70

The Observer, London, 1961–71

Rand Daily Mail, Johannesburg, 1960–72

Rhodesia Herald, Salisbury, 1965–71

South African Financial Gazette, Johannesburg, April 28, 1967

Standard Bank Review, Johannesburg, 1967–72

The Star, Johannesburg, 1962–72 (daily editions; weekly air edition)

Sunday Express, Johannesburg, 1967–69

Sunday Times, Johannesburg, 1967–72

Sunday Tribune, Johannesburg, August 10, 1969

Tanganyika Standard, Dar es Salaam, December 22 and 31, 1964

The Times, Blantyre, 1969–71

The Times, London, 1960–71
Times of Zambia, Ndola, 1971
West Africa, London, 1960–71
Zambia Mail, Lusaka, 1971

Unpublished Papers and Materials

Barratt, John. "Dialogue in Africa." Private paper, mimeographed. Johannesburg: South African Institute of International Affairs, June 1971.

Barratt, John. "The Outward Movement in South Africa's Foreign Relations," *Newsletter* (South African Institute of International Affairs), no. 3, August 1969, pp. 13–34.

Barratt, John. "South Africa and the United Nations," *Newsletter* (South African Institute of International Affairs), no. 1, February 1969, pp. 22–39.

Chilcote, Ronald H. "Conflicting Nationalist Ideologies in Portuguese Africa: The Emergence of Political and Social Movements, 1945–1965." Paper prepared for the meeting of the African Studies Association, Montreal, October 15–18, 1969. Mimeographed.

Corsi, Thomas. "The Tan-Zam Rail Project." B.A. honors paper, Department of Political Science, Case Western Reserve University, Cleveland, Ohio, May 13, 1971. Typescript.

Curran, James C. "Communist China in Black Africa: The Tan-Zam Railway, 1965–1970." Research paper, U. S. Army War College, Carlisle Barracks, Pa., April 26, 1971.

Dale, Richard. "Botswana's Post-Independence Relations with South Africa: The Limits of Statecraft." Paper prepared for the Faculty Seminar of the African Language and Area Center, Ohio University, Athens, Ohio, February 15, 1969. Mimeographed.

———. "South African Counterinsurgency Operations in South West Africa." Paper presented at the meeting of the African Studies Association, Los Angeles, October 16–19, 1968. Mimeographed.

"Economic Costs of Zambia's Alternative Rail Routes." Mimeographed. [Lusaka? 1969?]

Egeland, Leif. "South Africa's Role in Africa: Address, 6th November, 1967." Mimeographed. Johannesburg: South African Institute of International Affairs.

"Impact of the Nacala Link upon the Economy of Malawi." Mimeographed. [Blantyre? 1969?]

Legassick, Martin. "The Consequences of African Guerrilla Activity for South Africa's Relations with Her Neighbors." Paper presented to the meeting of the African Studies Association, New York, November 3, 1967. Dittoed.

Marcum, John. "The United States and Portuguese Africa: A Perspective on American Foreign Policy." Paper presented at the meeting of the African Studies Association, Denver, November 3–6, 1971. Mimeographed.

Shaw, Timothy M. "Linkage Politics and Subordinate State Systems: The Case of Southern Africa." Paper presented at the meeting of the Canadian Political Science Association, Montreal, June, 1972. Mimeographed.

———. "The Subordinate State System of Southern Africa: Prospects for Regional Order." Halifax, Nova Scotia: African Studies Seminar, Dalhousie University, January 1971.

Shepherd, George W., Jr. "The White Atlantic Sub-System and Black Southern Africa." Paper presented to the Colloquium on International Law and Development in Southern Africa, African Studies Center, University of California, Los Angeles, April 8, 1970. Mimeographed.

Utete, Charles Munhamu Botsio. "South Africa and Independent Africa: Continued Confrontation or Peaceful Coexistence?" Ph.D. dissertation, Department of Political Science, Carleton University, Ottawa, Canada, 1971.

Whitaker, Paul M. "The Liberation of Portuguese-Held Africa: Assistance to the Nationalists from Africa and Abroad." Paper prepared for the meeting of the African Studies Association, Montreal, October 15–18, 1969. Typescript.

Index

Abe Bailey Institute for Inter-Racial Studies: study of white South African elite attitudes, 3n
Accra Conference on Positive Action and Security (1960), 22
Adaptation: as form of foreign policy, 293–95
Adjei, Ako, 234
Adoula, Cyrille, 171
Africa Institute, 268
African Liberation Committee, 109–11, 112, 194–97; finances, 112, 195; Angola war, 175–76; and FRELIMO, 180; and Namibia, 186; recognition by, 194–95, 196–97; aid to guerrillas, 195, 196, 224; seeks unity among movements, 219, 220
African National Congress (South Africa) (ANC), 188–90, 194; at PAFMECSA meeting, 22–23; ideology of, 24, 158n, 161, 166n; and USSR, 166n; alliance with ZAPU, 166n, 181, 219, 221, 257; image of Vorster and "outward policy," 249–50
African Nationalist Council (ANC-Zimbabwe), 180
Afrikaners: early dealings with African nations, 230; expansionism, 231–32; criticism of Smuts, 232; distrust of Europe, 246; dislike of Portuguese, 255–56; in Rhodesia, 256; and "outward policy," 267–71
Afro-Malagasy and Mauritius Joint Organization, 141, 144–45
Algeria, 26, 173, 183, 186, 197; and violence, 21–22; impact on guerrilla thought, 163, 164; guerrilla training, 199
All-African Peoples' Conference (Accra, 1958), 21–22
Anglo-American Corporation, 41, 94
Angola, xiv, 13, 14, 17, 21, 26, 77, 119, 182, 187, 192, 196, 206, 218, 222, 224, 255, 287, 288, 289, 291; agriculture, 31; trade, 34; and Kunene project, 46; and Namibia, 46, 184, 185, 240; economic relations with RSA, 48–49, 79; transport routes, 50–51, 210–11; guerrilla movements, 157–58, 159, 171–73; war in, 163–64, 168, 170–76, 210–11, 279–80; refugees from, 200, 203; Corpo Voluntário Angolano de Assistência dos Refugiados, 203; Serviço de Assistência dos Refugiados de Angola, 203; and Katangese mercenaries, 281
Apartheid, 241, 255–56, 275; philosophy of, 20; and importation of foreign laborers, 68–69; Ivory Coast view of, 142–43; and RSA foreign policy, 147, 268, 270, 273; African criticism of within RSA, 189; and black visitors and diplomats, 262–65
Apollus, Emile, 167
Armaments Development and Production Corporation of South Africa (ARMSCOR), 217
Assegai, 167
Assimilation, racial, 18–21
Azores: US military base, 214

Bakongo, 157, 171, 200, 207
Banda, Dr. H. Kamuzu: on white settlers, 6–7; and "bridge building," 13–14, 15–18, 122–23; on racism, 14, 15–18; on Rhodesia, 16–

17; on war with white South, 16–17, 226, 227n; status in black Africa, 17, 126–31; on Southern African Customs Union, 39; and FRELIMO, 57–58; and OAU, 109–12; visit to Lisbon, 125; criticisms of Nyerere, 126, 127–28; visit to RSA (1971), 126, 262; personal relations with Kaunda, 128–29; intermediary in Zambia-Portugal dispute, 131; image in RSA, 132; political style, 138; mentioned, 133, 140, 178, 282

Bantustan leaders: in regional relations, 141; as "Black Dubčeks," 238, 240; prefer dialogue, 239; diplomatic status for, 265

Bantustans: in regional affairs, 141, 297; and RSA foreign policy, 235–41

Basotho National Party, 136

Basson, Japie D. du Plessis, 269–70

Basutoland Congress Party, 134, 260–61

Beaupré, Maurichot, 143

Bechuanaland. *See* Botswana

Beira, port of, 50, 53

Belgium: and Katanga, 280

Benguela Railway, 50–51, 53, 55, 56–57, 288; and Angola war, 175; services disrupted, 210–11; and Katanga secession, 280

Beyers, Dr. Ras, 269

Border, as analytical concept, 276–84

Botha, Barry, 269

Botha, P. W.: on preemptive strikes, 169, 208

Botha, R. F. "Pik," 270

Botswana: export of labor, 31, 62, 63, 67; and Southern African Customs Union, 34, 36–38; RSA investment in, 48, 49; transport routes, 50, 51, 55, 58–59, 124; "Government Representative" in RSA, 67, 89–90; economic assistance from UK, 69–70; economic assistance from USA, 71, 137; and infrastructural imbalances, 78; and RSA's "co-prosperity sphere," 78; formal diplomatic relations, 84, 85; relations with RSA, 87–88, 136–38, 210, 238–41, 283; relations with black states, 88; Malawi "Government Office" in, 89; visit from Kaunda, 95; votes at UN, 102–4; and OAU, 111–12; regulates liberation movements, 112, 220; geographical factors in foreign policy, 120, 123–24; border with Zambia, 123, 137; RSA offers of aid, 136–37; as "bridge builder," 136–38, 146; diplomatic relations with Czechoslovakia and USSR, 137, 283; position on RSA arms sales, 138; Ramotse case, 210; and Namibia, 240; and "border" concept, 283; and Rhodesia, 283; relations with Zambia, 283; and Bantustans, 297; mentioned, xiv, 111n, 119, 131, 170n, 181, 183, 236, 287, 288, 289, 290, 291. *See also* High Commission Territories

Boulding, Kenneth, 274

Bowman, Larry W., 310, 311–12

Brecher, Michael, 311

"Bridge building," 10–11, 13–21, 93, 118–51; defined, 118–19; economic inducements, 120–21; South Africa as link between black Africa and Europe, 245–46

British Aircraft Corporation: missiles, 209

Broederbond, 4

Brown, S. E. D., 269

"Buffer" states: for RSA, 243–44

Burger, A. B. F., 143

Burundi, 116

Busia, Dr. Kofi: 14n, on the Commonwealth, 107–8; and dialogue, 145

Buthelezi, Chief Gatsha, 239

Cabinda, 174, 175, 176

Cabora Bassa project, 41–44; and Conferences of Heads of State and Government of East and Central Africa, 116; in Mozambique war, 177, 180; mentioned, 46, 78, 180

Calvinism: 247–48; and Portuguese-RSA collaboration, 255–56

Canada: and RSA arms embargo, 212

Cantori, Louis J. and Spiegel, Steven L.: concept of subordinate system, 285–87; types of sub-systemic membership, 309, 312; mentioned, 310

Capital City Development Corporation, 76

Central African Railways, 92
Central African Republic, 116–17
Central American Common Market, 39
China, People's Republic of: and Tan-Zam Railway, 53, 54, 56; relations with Zambia, 71; ideological impact on liberation movements, 161–62, 163, 166; and Angola war, 176; guerrilla training, 178, 197, 198; and Namibia, 183, 186, 240; aid to revolutionary movements, 192–94, 195, 197; missiles in Tanzania, 209; encourages "Congo Alliance," 221; RSA fear of, 244, 246; Ivory Coast fear of, 259; RSA paves way for CPR's increased influence, 272–73; mentioned, 141
Chipembere, Henry B. Masauko, 127
Chirwa, Dr. Orton, 127
Chisiza, Yatuta, 127, 128n
Chona, Mainza: negotiates in Lisbon, 93
Chou En-lai, 54
Christianity: "defended" by RSA, 166–67
Cillie, Piet, 270
Claude, Inis L.: quoted, 310
Clausewitz, Carl von, 25
Coloureds: assimilation of, 19
Comité Revolucionário de Moçambique, 93, 177, 179, 192, 219–20
Committee for Technical Cooperation in Africa, 47
"Common Market": proposed for southern Africa, 38–40
Commonwealth: 105–8; composition, 105–6; South African membership, 106–7, 250, 278; Rhodesian independence, 107; British arms sales to RSA, 107–8; and South Africa's early relations with Africa, 231; Nkrumah-Louw agreement, 234; mentioned, 47, 83, 307
Communism: in RSA foreign policy rhetoric, 249, 259; as bogey in Lesotho crisis (1970), 260
Conference of Independent African States (Accra): and South Africa, 234
Conferences of Heads of State and Government of East and Central Africa, 43, 83, 113–17. *See also* Lusaka Manifesto
Conferência das Organizações Nacionalistas dos Colónias Portuguesas (CONCP), 116n, 220–21
Congo (Brazzaville), 116; and Angola war, 176; training guerrillas, 198, 199
Congo (Zaïre): trade, 34; "Route Nationale," 53, 56, 59; and infrastructural imbalances, 78; formal diplomatic relations, 84, 85; relations with Portugal, 84, 170–76, 209; issue at the UN, 98; participation in Conferences of Heads of State and Government of East and Central Africa, 113–14; and Angola war, 157–58, 170–75; as "host" to refugees and guerrillas, 170–73, 200, 203, 206; member of ALC, 197; guerrilla training, 199; insurgents, 206; territory violated, 209; economic pressures on, 210–11; encourages "Congo Alliance," 221; relations with RSA, 235, 279; Nyerere criticism of, 281; Tshombe government supported by RSA, Portugal, and Rhodesia, 281; intervention and penetration, 298; mentioned, xiv, 29, 31, 111n, 142, 182, 280, 288, 289, 290, 291, 300, 305
"Congo Alliance," 220–21
Copper: transport routes, 50, 51, 53–57, 59, 93; shipments and Angola war, 210–11
"Co-prosperity sphere," southern African, 38, 39–40
COREMO (Comité Revolucionário de Moçambique): 177, 179, 192; kidnaps Portuguese technicians, 93; cooperation with PAC, 219–220
Core sector of sub-system: defined, 286; delimited, 287–91; commitment to system maintenance, 306
Cuba: and Angola war, 176; guerrilla training, 197–98
Customs Union, Southern African, 34, 36–38, 77–78, 253; as diplomatic medium, 87–88
Czechoslovakia, 137

Dahomey, 111n, 143
Dar es Salaam: transport terminus, 50, 53; port inadequacies, 55
Davis, John A. and Baker, James K., 310

Debray, Régis, 161–62, 183
De Gaulle, Charles, 140, 143
Delius, Anthony, 238, 272
Deutsch, Karl W.: and linkage groups, 203–4
De Villiers Graaf, Sir, 270
Dhlamini, Prince Makhosini: 40; on violence and "bridge building," 138–39
"Dialogue" with white southern Africa, 119, 141–51, 274–75; Conference of Heads of State and Government of East and Central Africa (1970), 116; and Lesotho, 133; and Swaziland, 139; and Malagasy, 140–41; and Houphouet-Boigny, 141–46; preferred by Bantustan leaders, 239; and regional actors, 290
Diplomacy, secret, 92–97, 125
Diplomatic relations: formal representation, 83–87; quasi-diplomatic links, 87–88; sub-diplomatic representation, 88–90; official and state visits, 90–92; irregular contacts, 92–96; use of private "'unofficial" persons, 93–96
"Domestic colonialism," 238
"Domino theory," 167
Dutch East India Company, 230

East African Community, 289; and Zambia, 40; and Swaziland, 40, 139
East and Central Africa, Conferences of the Heads of State and Government of, 83, 113–17; and Cabora Bassa, 43. *See also* Lusaka Manifesto
Economic Commission for Africa (UN), 47
Economics: assistance, 69–77; and politics, 78–82; as factor in regional conflict, 292, 293
ESCOM (Electricity Supply Commission of South Africa), 41–42
Ethiopia, 88, 197, 279; and Namibian cases, 100; insurgency in, 206
European Economic Community, 39; British entry, 108
European Free Trade Area, 39

Fanon, Frantz, 21
Field, Winston, 125
Foccart, Jacques, 143
Food and Agriculture Organization, 47, 99, 200
Foreign policy: and external environment, xi–xiii; purposes, xii; domestic instability, xvii; "operational environment," 82; "psychological environment," 82, 120; geographical determinents of, 119–20, 123–25; varieties of, 293–300
Fourie, Brand, 261n
France: relations with Malagasy, xv, 140, 141; and Cabora Bassa, 42; and Tan-Zam Railway, 54; votes at UN, 102; condemned by OAU, 111; and dialogue, 145; weapons sales to RSA, 213, 258; military supplies for Portugal, 214; mentioned, 22, 31, 143, 164, 274
FRELIMO (Frente Libertação de Moçambique), 176–80, 194; Cabora Bassa and Tete offensive, 42, 127; and rail routes, 57–58; and Makonde, 157–58; on political education, 161, 163; on duration of liberation struggle, 164; leadership struggle and ethnic divisions, 176, 179–80; training, 178, 192n, 198; financial aid, 192–94; and liberated territory, 192n; in Tanzania, 206
Frente de Luta pela Independência Nacional da Guiné (FLING), 197
Front for the Liberation of Zimbabwe (FROLIZI), 180
Functional cooperation, 40–48

Gabon: relations with RSA, 75n, 145; votes at UN, 104; as "bridge builder," 146; mentioned, 111n, 142, 143, 146
Gandhi, Mohandas K., 21–22, 23, 24
Gardiner, Robert, 234
Gerdener, T. J. A., 221n
Germany, Federal Republic of: and Cabora Bassa, 42, 43; condemned by OAU, 111; and RSA arms embargo, 213; military supplies for Portugal, 214; mentioned, 85
Ghana: on dealing with white Africa, 14n; and Commonwealth, 105–6, 107–8; relations with Malawi, 130; training guerrillas, 198; early relations with South Africa, 234–35; mentioned, 135, 142, 143, 183

Governo Revoluciónario de Angola no Exílo (GRAE), 173–76; and Bakongo, 157–58; assistance to, 192; and refugees, 203; competition with MPLA, 220
Great Britain: and Southern African Customs Union, 36; and Kariba Dam, 44, 45–46; and Tan-Zam Railway, 54; economic assistance, 69–71, 72; competition with RSA in Malawi, 75; relations with Portugal, 90; passports used by South Africans, 94; and Commonwealth, 105–8; arms sales to RSA, 107–8, 213, 250, 290; and Rhodesia, 107, 180–81; condemned by OAU, 111; Swaziland's position on G. B.'s arms sales to RSA, 139; effect of "bridge building" policies on, 149; arms sales to Zambia, 209; naval retrenchment, 214–15; treaties with African chiefs, 230; early relations with South Africa, 231–32, 278–79; High Commission Territories and RSA, 236; Afrikaner distrust of, 246; Rhodesian settlement proposals (1971), 256, 257–58; and RSA military assistance to Rhodesia, 257; mentioned, 4, 31, 273
Great North Road, 53, 59
Green, L. P. and Fair, T. J. D., 310
Guerrilla warfare, 152–227; Banda opposes, 16–17; Botswana's alternatives, 124; in Lesotho, 135; and Swaziland, 138–39; theory of, 153–70; and ethnic heterogeneity, 159; Marxist-Leninist theory of, 160–61; patterns of political-military interaction, 160–63; movements and "liberated areas," 162–63; and protracted war, 163–65; counter-guerrilla thinking, 165–70; in Angola, 170–76; in Mozambique, 176–80; in Zimbabwe, 181–83; in Namibia, 183–86; in RSA, 187–90; sources of assistance for movements, 192–99; training for fighters, 197–99; fighters sell weapons, 205–6; in Congo, 206; in Sudan, 206; mentioned, 1
Guevara, Ernesto "Che," 161, 166
Guinea, 197
Gulf Oil Company (Mozambique), 58
Hance, William A., 310
Heath, Edward, 149
Herero, 186
Herstigte Nasionale Party, 264–65, 268–69, 271; on Banda, 17
Hertzog, Dr. Albert, 269
High Commission Territories: and Southern African Customs Union, 34, 36–38; RSA forces in, 221; and incorporation into South Africa, 231, 235–36; Malan's reaction to possible independence, 233; mentioned, xvi, 279. *See also* Botswana; Lesotho; Swaziland
Hoare, Mike, 281
"Host" governments, 199–212; relations with ALC, 196; aid to guerrillas, 224–25
Houphouet-Boigny, Félix: on dealing with white Africa, 14n, 141–46; on violence, 142; on RSA defenses against communism, 259
Hydroelectric projects, 40–48

Ideology, 28; elite and popular attitudes, 1; polarization of, 2, 3. *See also* Racism; Violence
India, 105
Industrial Development Corporation (SA), 48, 49, 75–76; and Cabora Bassa, 43; and Kunene project, 46; loan for Malawi railway construction, 57
International Civil Aviation Organization, 47
International Court of Justice (ICJ): Namibia cases, 8–9, 100–1, 185
International governmental organizations, 96–117
International Labor Organization (ILO), 47, 99, 200
International Telecommunications Union, 47
Intervention, 211; defined, 211n; as form of foreign policy, 296, 297–99
Intrusive actors, 309–10; defined and delimited, 287; and regional subsystem, 287, 306–7
Investments, private, 48–49
Ireland, 312
Isolation: as form of foreign policy, 296
Israel: preemptive military strikes, 14n, 169, 208; doctrine of "antici-

patory counter-attack," 208; as example for RSA, 208; Vorster's opinion of, 244; mentioned, 312
Italy: and Cabora Bassa, 43; financed pipeline, 53; relations with Zambia, 71, 72
Ivory Coast: RSA aid to, 75n; votes at UN, 104; policy on RSA, 141, 142–46; fear of communism, 259; mentioned, 111n. *See also* Houphouet-Boigny, Félix

Japan: and Tan-Zam Railway, 54–55; aid to Congo, 56n; mentioned, 19
Jonathan, Chief Leabua: on Southern African Customs Union, 39; criticizes OAU, 112; on "bridge building," 122, 133–34, 135–36; visits Malagasy, 135–36; political style, 138; on war with RSA, 226, 226n–227n; in constitutional crisis (1970), 260–61; visits RSA, 261; mentioned, 18
Jordan, 205

Kachingwe, Joseph, 263
Kafue hydroelectric project, 44, 45
Kankonbe, Samuel, 179
Kapwepwe, Simon, 54
Kariba Dam, 44–46, 78
Katanga, 56–57, 305; transport routes, 50; and Angola war, 173, 174, 175; Portuguese cooperation with, 209, 279–80; relations with RSA, 223, 235, 279, 281; military cooperation with white South, 223, 279; in orbit of white South, 279–81; and Federation of Rhodesia and Nyasaland, 280; and border concept, 283; and conservative intervention, 297–98
Kaunda, Kenneth D.: anti-racism, 5–6; and non-violence, 21, 22–24; and Cabora Bassa, 42–43; and Tan-Zam Railway, 53–57; and Harold Wilson, 70–71; and diplomatic exchange with RSA, 86, 235; exchanges with Vorster, 94–95; visit to Botswana, 95; personal relations with Banda, 128–29; criticized by Malagasy, 140; on guerrilla training, 198; accuses RSA of border violations, 223n; as leader of anti-RSA bloc, 274; on Zambezi "border," 277; mentioned, 93, 94n, 182
Kavandame, Chief Lazaro, 179
Kenya: policy toward RSA, 99; and Conferences of Heads of State and Government of East and Central Africa, 116, 117; relations with Malawi, 133; insurgency in, 206; in South African defense perimeter, 243; Vorster opinion of, 244; mentioned, 26, 88, 117, 142, 278, 279
Kenyatta, Jomo, 132
Khama, Sir Seretse: on "prudence," 119; diplomatic skills, 136, 138; on dialogue, 146
Khartoum Alliance, 220–21
Kitenge, Gabriel: visits South Africa, 235n
Kitwe, Jean: visits South Africa, 235n
Kommando, 167
Korea, Democratic People's Republic of (North): guerrilla training, 183, 197
Krause, Otto: and origins of "outward policy," 229–30
Kunene project, 46, 78
Kuper, Hilda, 310

Labor: supply and migration, 59–69
League of Nations: mandate system, 97, 102
Lebanon, 205
Lenin, V. I.: theory of imperialism, 77
Lesotho: constitutional crisis (1970), xvi, 134–35, 260–61; and "bridge building," 13, 133–36, 146; export of labor, 31, 59–62; and Southern African Customs Union, 34, 36–38; Oxbow scheme, 46–47; transport routes, 50, 51; representation in RSA, 67, 89–90; U.S. economic assistance to, 71; relations with RSA, 75, 87–88, 133–35, 136, 238–41, 264, 297; and infrastructural imbalances, 78; formal diplomatic relations, 84, 85; regular contact with RSA, 87–88; relations with black states, 88, 135–36; votes at UN, 102–4; and Commonwealth, 108; and OAU, 111–12; survival

of, 119; systemic determinants of policy, 120, 134; economic determinants of policy, 134; relations with Malagasy, 135–36; claims "conquered" territory in Orange Free State, 136; opposes guerrillas using its territory, 220; Police Mobile Unit, 261; visitors to RSA, 264; and border concept, 283; and adaptation, 294–95; and Bantustans, 297; mentioned, xiv, 48, 111n, 122, 123, 131, 138, 143, 226, 236, 287, 288, 289, 290, 291. *See also* High Commission Territories

Level of analysis problem, 312–13

Liberation movements: reject racism, 6; Chief Jonathan on, 133–34, 135. *See also entries under specific parties and movements*

Liberia: and Namibia cases, 100

Lobito, 51

Lourenço Marques, 50, 64–65

Louw, Eric: and Ghana, 234; on South Africa's role in Africa, 245; warns about European neo-colonialism, 246; on diplomatic exchanges with black Africa, 261

Lusaka Manifesto, 113–17, 315–23; rejects racism, 6, 113, 115; and RSA UN membership, 99; South African reactions to, 115n, 117; and dialogue with RSA, 133, 146

Lutheran World Federation, 200

Luyt, Sir Richard, 94n

Machel, Samora, 179–80

MacKinder, Sir Halford, 167

Madagascar. *See* Malagasy, Republic of

Makonde, 157, 177, 179, 200

Malagasy, Republic of: foreign policy, xv; relations with France, xv, 140, 141; and "bridge building," 13, 15, 140–41; Narinda port project, 58, 72; relations with Portugal, 58, 85; economic relations with RSA, 75, 76, 96, 96n; visit by Chief Jonathan, 135–36; military coup, 140; relations with RSA, 140–41; as economic broker for RSA, 145; mentioned, xiv, 111n, 135, 143, 144, 288, 289, 290, 291

Malan, Dr. Daniel F., 232, 233

Malawi: and "bridge building," 13–18, 93, 125–33, 146; state visit of Tsiranana, 15; official and state visits, 15, 90–92; agriculture, 31; bilateral trade agreements, 38, 40; and Cabora Bassa, 43, 58; hosts regional tourism conference (1970), 47–48; RSA investment in, 48, 49; transport routes, 50, 51–53, 57–58; and Rhodesian Railways, 52–53; RSA aid to, 58, 75, 76; relations with Portugal, 58, 84, 93, 178, 209; labor agreement with RSA, 63; labor migration, 63–64, 65, 66, 67; Mozambique migrants in, 64; labor offices in RSA, 67; economic assistance from UK, 69, 70; economic assistance from U.S.A., 71; Department of Information, 76; RSA personnel employed by, 76; formal diplomatic relations, 84–85, 90, 122–23, 125–26, 132, 141; relations with black states, 88; sub-diplomatic representation, 89; relations with RSA, 89, 130–32; relations with Zambia, 90, 122–23, 126, 128–30, 131, 132; as intermediary between Portugal and Zambia, 93; votes at UN, 102–4; and Commonwealth, 108; in OAU, 109–13; participation in Conferences of Heads of State and Government of East and Central Africa, 113–17; determinants of policy, 120; diplomatic exchange with RSA, 125–26, 141, 261, 263, 265; relations with white South, 125–27; relations with Tanzania, 126, 127–28, 129–30; military relations with RSA, 126–27, 178, 297–98; boundary dispute with Tanzania, 128; claims Zambia territory, 129; and Rhodesian sanctions, 129, 252n; relations with Ghana, 130; relations with United Arab Republic, 130; and Mozambique war, 177, 178, 179; regulates liberation movements, 220; RSA view of, 244; trade with RSA, 252, 252n; trade with Rhodesia, 252n; Vorster visit to, 262; diplomats in RSA, 263, 265; independence, 280, 282; mentioned, xiv, 6, 16, 18, 48, 50, 79, 81, 92, 135, 138, 143, 145, 281, 288, 289, 290, 291. *See also*

Rhodesia and Nyasaland, Federation of
Malawi Broadcasting Company, 76
Malawi Congress Party (MCP), 127, 129
Malawi Development Corporation, 76
Mali, 281
Malvern, Godfrey Martin Huggins, Lord, 44
Mandela, Nelson: on violence and revolution, 22–23, 24, 26, 188
Mangope, Chief Lucas, 239
Mao Tse-tung: military doctrines, 161–62; read in white Africa, 166
Marcum, John, 163–64, 199
Marquard, Leo, 238
Massamba-Débat, Alphonse: visits South Africa, 235n
Matanzima, Chief Kaiser, 239
Mauritius, 48, 135
Mazrui, Ali A.: on Commonwealth, 105–6
Mboya, Tom, 25–26
Meyer, Dr. Piet J., 4, 268
Middle East, 138; OAU resolutions on, 111
Migration. *See* Labor; Refugees
Military: force levels, 215–19; "alliances" among black nationalists, 219–21; "alliances" among white minority governments, 221–24
Mogadishu Declaration, 116–17
Mokhehle, Ntsu, 260
Molotsi, Peter, 22n
Mondlane, Dr. Eduardo: 176, 178–79; on assimilation, 19; on violence, 153; emphasized political education, 161, 163; on duration of liberation struggle, 164, 165; on race and geography, 277
Monroe Doctrine: applied to Africa, 244
Montgomery, R. J., 261n–262n
Movimento Popular de Libertação de Angola. *See* MPLA
Mozambique: agriculture, 31; RSA investment in, 48–49; transport routes and facilities, 50–51, 58, 92–93; pipeline to RSA, 58; rail link with Swaziland, 58; labor migration, 64–65; labor office in RSA, 67; war in, 153, 176–80; guerrilla movements, 157–58, 159; refugees from, 200, 202; mentioned, xiv, 13, 14, 15, 17, 58, 97, 119, 168, 181, 187, 192, 196, 206, 210, 218, 224, 255, 280, 287, 288, 289. *See also* Cabora Bassa
Mozambique/Angola Soldiers' Comforts Fund, 221n
MPLA: 174–76, 194; cooperation with SWAPO, 186, 219–20; guerrilla training, 198; and refugees, 203; competition with GRAE, 220
Muller, Dr. Hilgard: on RSA's position in UN, 104n; on RSA as a bridge, 245–46; on "outward policy" as foundation for RSA foreign policy, 247; on RSA's importance, 249; discloses RSA contacts in Africa, 261n–262n
Multidimensionality. *See* Regional sub-systems
Mulungushi reforms, 55
Munger, Edwin S., 267

Nacala: rail link, 55n, 57–58
Namibia: relationship to South Africa, xiv, 231; issue at UN, 7–8, 97, 101–4; International Court of Justice, 8–9, 100–1; mining, 31; and Kunene project, 46; UN Council for, 167; explosions in Caprivi strip, 182; guerrila war, 183–86; labor strike, 184–86; revolutionary parties, 192; South African forces in South West Africa, 221; and Bantustans, 239–40; RSA's relations with UN about, 239–40; mentioned, xiv, 13, 124, 187, 196
Narinda, port of, 58, 72
Nationalist Party (South Africa), 4, 14n, 94, 268–71; and "outward policy," 229, 230; debate over black diplomats, 265; and Great Britain, 278–79
National People's Union (Rhodesia): and Banda, 16–17
NATO. *See* North Atlantic Treaty Organization
Ndola, 50
Nel, M. D. C. de Wet, 248–49
"Neo-colonialism": RSA warns black states about, 246
Neto, Dr. Agostinho, 174
News/Check: and origins of "outward policy," 229–30
Ngwane National Liberatory Congress, 139

Nielsen, Waldemar A., 310
Niger, 111n, 143
Nigeria, 105, 135, 197
Nixon, Richard M., 149
Nkama, Moto, 116
Nkrumah, Dr. Kwame: and non-violence, 22; "positive action," 24; on military cooperation, 219; relations with South Africa, 234
Nogueira, Alberto Franco, 178, 207
Nonaggression pacts: RSA offer of, 258–59
Noninterference: as principle of RSA foreign policy, 121–22, 134–35, 143, 245, 249–51
Non-violence, 21–23, 24, 25. *See also* Violence
North Atlantic Treaty Organization: and Portugal, 213–15; relations with RSA, 214–15, 215n, 247; in southern hemisphere, 214–15, 224; mentioned, 312
Northern Rhodesia. *See* Zambia
Norway, 214
Ntoya, Frank, 263
Nujoma, Sam, 164, 183
Nyanja, 179
Nyerere, Julius K.: anti-racism, 5–6; and non-violence, 21, 23, 25; and Tan-Zam Railway, 54; and Commonwealth, 106–7; disagreements with Malawi, 110, 127–28; and FRELIMO, 180; on Zambezi "border," 277; and Congo, 281

OAU. *See* Organization of African Unity
OCAMM: and dialogue with RSA, 141, 144–45
Odendaal Commission, 46, 185
Okavango: and Botswana, 240
Oppenheimer, Harry, 94
Organization of African Unity, 108–13; resolutions, 10; and violence, 23; and Cabora Bassa, 43; caucus at UN, 102; Council of Ministers, 107; "dual strategy," 109; Summit Conferences, 109–10, 111, 112, 194n; unity on Southern African questions, 109–13; on arms sales to RSA, 111; reservations on resolutions, 111–12; Lesotho policy at, 133–34, 135; and dialogue, 144–45; recognizes GRAE, 173; supports FRELIMO, 176, 180; establishes African Liberation Committee, 194; investigates ALC, 195–96; on military cooperation, 219; aid to guerrillas, 224; as a sub-system, 285; and southern African members and non-members, 289–90; mentioned, 83, 88, 123, 294, 300, 307
—African Liberation Committee. *See* African Liberation Committee
Orpen, Commandant Neil: and white guerrillas, 226
Ovambo, 183–86, 198, 240
Ovamboland People's Organization, 183
Oxbow scheme, 46–47, 78
Oxford Famine Relief Committee, 200

Pakistan, 105
Palme, Olaf: on Zambezi "border," 277
Pan-African Freedom Movement of East and Central Africa (PAFMECA): and non violence, 22–23; aid to revolutionary movements, 194n
Pan-African Freedom Movement of East, Central and Southern Africa (PAFMECSA), 127; and violence, 22–23; aid to revolutionary movements, 194n
Pan-Africanist Congress (South Africa): ideology, 5, 24; at PAFMECSA meeting, 22n–23n; opposes Malawi, 111n; link with Poqo, 188; revolutionary effectiveness, 189; in Tanzania, 206n; cooperation with COREMO, 219–20; mentioned, 192
Parsons, Talcott, 308
"Peaceful coexistence": as theme in regional relations, 119, 245
Pearce Commission, 180–81
Peasantry: as theme in guerrilla thought, 156–60
Penetration: as form of foreign policy, 296–97, 298–99
Peripheral sector of sub-system: defined, 286–87; delimited, 287–91, 309
Pienaar, Schalk, 270
Pirow, Oswald, 222
Pompidou, Georges, 143
Pondoland: violence in, 188–89

Poqo, 188

Portugal: and Cabora Bassa, 41–42, 43–44; excluded from international functional organizations, 47; permits foreign investments in African territories, 48–49; relations with Malawi, 58, 72, 84; and Malagasy, 58, 85; relations with RSA, 75–76, 255–56; formal diplomatic relations, 84–85; relations with Swaziland, Lesotho, and Botswana, 84–85, 138; relations with Congo, 84, 170–76, 281; relations with Zambia, 86, 92–93, 131, 174–75, 208–11; relations with UK, 90; relations with Rhodesia, 90, 222–24, 257; and UN, 97, 102–4; counterinsurgency training and thought, 167–68, 226; relations with Tanzania, 176–78; espionage and unconventional warfare, 178–79; doctrine of "legitimate retaliation," 178, 207; and Namibia war, 184; leafletting refugees in Tanzania, 202n; violates territory and airspace, 208–9; weapons procurement, 212, 213–14; in NATO, 213–15; military expenditures, 218; military cooperation with RSA and Rhodesia, 222–24, 244; assistance to Katanga, 223, 279–80; and intervention, 299; mentioned, 48, 289, 290, 291, 301

Portuguese Africa: UN, 7–8; assimilation in, 19–20; OAU policy on, 109–10; transport advantages, 282; and conservative intervention, 297–98; mentioned, 2, 16, 80, 159. *See also* Angola; Mozambique

Preemptive military strikes: against Zambia and Tanzania, 14n; RSA threats, 168n, 168–70, 207–8; Rhodesian threats, 169n

Preemptive violence against domestic revolutionaries, 26–27

Progressive Party (RSA): and "outward policy," 266, 269

Protracted war, 163–65

Racism: 1–21; defined, 2–3; and foreign policy, 2, 4, 291–93, 301, 305; institutionalized, 2–11; opposition to, 2–11; Lusaka Manifesto on, 113, 115; Malagasy statements on, 140, 141; impact of "bridge building" on, 146–49; and RSA's "outward policy," 255–56, 262–65, 271–75; and black diplomats in RSA, 262–65

Radio South Africa, 254–55

Ramotse, Benjamin: arrested in Botswana, 210

"Rand diplomacy," 147

Red Cross Societies, League of, 200

Refugees, 59; from Angola, 171, 200, 203; from Mozambique, 177, 178, 200, 202; from Namibia, 184; and "host" countries, 199, 200–5; from RSA, 202; as linkage groups, 203–5

Regional sub-systems: defined, xiii–xiv, 304–5; delimitation of boundaries, xiv, 309–13; levels and units of analysis, xv–xvi; multidimensionality, xv–xvi, 287–91, 306, 313; and global system, xv, xvii; "membership" issue, 284–87, 306–7, 309–13; delimited according to geographic criteria, 287–88; delimited according to racial criteria, 288; delimited according to economic criteria, 288–89; delimited according to diplomatic-political-strategic criteria, 289–91; divided on arms sales to RSA, 290; divided on dialogue issue, 290; divided ideologically, 290; strategic dimension, 290–91; factors in conflict and tension, 291–93; typology of foreign policies, 293–300; methodological problems, 303–314; preference for term, 304–5, 307–8; and systems maintenance, 307, 308–9; substantive issue areas, 313

Rhodes, Cecil J.: on South Africa's place in Africa, 121, 230–31, 232, 232n

Rhodesia: UN sanctions, 7, 8, 97; economy, 31; trade, 32, 33, 34, 35, 252–53, 252n; and Cabora Bassa, 43; Kariba Dam, 44–46; RSA investment in, 48, 49; and Rhodesia Railways, 52–53; rail links with RSA, 58–59, 124; as importer of foreign labor, 63–64, 65–66, 68–69; alleged aid to "neighboring government," 72; RSA aid to, 76; relations with RSA, 76, 90, 255, 256–58, 262; formal diplomatic relations, 84, 85; Malawi "Government Representative" in, 89; diplomatic relations with Portugal, 90; currency restrictions on, 93; OAU policy on, 109; relations with Botswana, 136, 283; urban opposition, 158; guerrilla movements and ethnic unity, 159; "domino theory," 167; threatens Zambia, 169n; and Mozambique war, 177; espionage, 181; violates territory and airspace, 208–9; weapons procurement, 212; RSA forces in, 219, 221–22, 223–24, 244; military cooperation with RSA and Portugal, 222–24; counterinsurgency training, 226; Vorster visit to, 262; on Zambezi "border," 278; early South African economic influence, 279; mercenaries to Katanga and Congo, 279–281; assists Tshombe's Congo, 281; and isolation, 296; and conservative intervention, 297–98; mentioned, xiv, xv, 2, 8, 13, 14, 15, 16, 17, 130, 134, 170n, 187, 190, 206, 210, 287, 288, 289, 290, 291, 301. *See also* Rhodesia and Nyasaland, Federation of

Rhodesia and Nyasaland, Federation of: dissolution of, xvi, 50, 52–53; Kariba Dam, 44; effect of dissolution on transport patterns, 50, 52–53; and military cooperation with Portugal and RSA, 222, 223; and Congo independence, 279–80; and shifting "border," 282; mentioned, 128

Rhodesian African Labour Supply Commission, 63

Rhodesia Railways, 50, 52–53, 124

Rhodesian Unilateral Declaration of Independence: and RSA, 4, 256, 274; effects on transport patterns, 50; effect on regional affairs, 182–83, 282; mentioned, 24, 70, 86, 90, 92, 107, 256, 300

Rhoodie, Eschel, 311

Richardson, Philip A., 263

Roberto, Holden, 170, 174

Robson, Peter, 310

Ronga, 179

Rupert, Anton, 73

Rwanda, 111n, 173

Salazar, Antonio de Oliveira, 125

Santos, Marcelino dos, 179–80

Savimbi, Jonas, 210–11, 211n

Schoeman, Hendrick, 264

Schramm, Colonel Jean, 173

Scientific Council for Africa, 47

Senegal, 197

"Separate development." *See* Apartheid

Shanga, 179

Sharpeville shootings, 187, 229, 242, 258

Shepherd, George W., Jr., 312

Sierre Leone, 143

Simango, Uria: on guerrilla warfare, 161, 179

Simonstown agreement, 258

Singer, J. David: quoted, 81

Smith, Ian: on white rule, 3–4; global perspectives, 166–67

Smuts, Jan Christian: on South African expansion, 231–32, 231n–232n, on defense of South Africa, 243

Societa Anonima Eletrificazione (SAE), 43

Somalia, 197, 206, 279

South Africa, Republic of: mentioned, xi, xiv, xvii, 2, 5, 13, 14, 15, 17, 50, 92, 117, 287, 288, 289, 290, 291. *See also* Dialogue

—economic affairs and infrastructure, 86; economic hegemony, 29–32, 32–40 *passim*, 77–82 *passim*; industry, 31; trade, 32–40, 145, 251–53; and Southern African Customs Union, 34, 36–38, 38–40; and Cabora Bassa, 41–42, 43–44; and Kunene project, 46; Oxbow scheme, 47; private investments in region, 48, 49, 279; pipeline from Mozambique, 58; and Narinda project, 58; rail link with Swaziland, 58; railway expansion, 58–59, 124; economic assistance to black Africa, 58, 72–77; as importer of foreign labor, 59–69; rail link with Rhodesia, 124

—foreign affairs: relations with Rhodesia, 4, 90, 181–82, 219, 252–53, 255, 256–58; in "white world," 4, 312; UN, 7–10, 97, 98–100, 102–5; and racial assimilation, 20; relations with Malawi, 38, 58, 63, 89, 125–27, 130–32, 252, 262, 297–98; excluded from international functional organizations, 47; and principle of "noninterference," 74,

249–51, 299; competition with UK in Malawi, 75; formal diplomatic relations, 84, 85, 279; relations with Zambia, 86, 94–95, 223n, 235, 252, 274; relations with Lesotho, 87–88, 89, 133, 134–35, 136, 220, 238–41, 260–61, 294–95; relations with Botswana, 87–88, 89, 136–38, 210, 238–41, 283; relations with Swaziland, 87–88, 90, 138–39, 238–41; Department of Foreign Affairs, 87–88, 132; official and state visits, 90–92; use of "private" diplomats, 93–96; relations with Malagasy, 96, 96n, 140–41; Namibia cases, 100–1; Terrorism Act of 1967, 103; and Commonwealth, 106–7, 232–33; OAU policy on, 109–13; opposition to Botswana-Zambia border claims, 123; transit permission, 131–32; extradition treaty with Swaziland, 139; vulnerability to oil embargo, 213; relations with Portugal, 222, 255–56; relations with Katanga, 223, 235, 279, 281; incorporation of South West Africa, 231; early relations with Great Britain, 231–32, 279; expansionism, 231–33, 243–44; incorporation of High Commission Territories, 231, 235–36; post-1948 relations with Great Britain, 232–33; and independence for black African states, 233–34; early relations with Ghana, 234–35; relations with and assistance to Congo, 235, 279, 281–82; "domestic colonialism," 237–38; a status quo power, 241–42; isolation of, 242–43, 296; anti-communism, 244; as link between black Africa and Europe, 245–46; Calvinism, 247–48; frustrated idealism, 247–48; as part of Africa, 248–49; propaganda, 254–55; offers nonaggression pacts, 258–59; proposed employment of black diplomats, 265; and commitment to sub-system, 285–86; and intervention, 299

—military affairs and revolution: threats of preemptive military strikes, 14n, 168n, 168–70, 207–8; British arms sales to RSA, 107–8, 138, 290; military relations with Malawi, 126–27, 297–98; urban violence, 157, 158; duration of liberation struggle, 164; counterinsurgency training, 166, 226; espionage and unconventional warfare, 168–69, 181, 244, 260; fears of black uprising, 168–70; regional military perspective, 168–70, 221; cooperation with Rhodesia and Portugal, 181, 182, 219, 222–24; military casualties, 187; African nationalist movements, 187–90, 192; violates territory and airspace, 208–10, 223n; weapons procurement and defense expenditures, 212–13, 215, 217; air defenses, 213; strategic importance to NATO, 214–15, 215n; force levels, 216, 217; self-sufficiency in armaments, 217–18, 218n; Defense Act of 1913, 221; views of wars in Angola and Mozambique, 221; defensive perimeter, 243, 277–78

—"outward policy," 228–75, 301; black responses, 13, 15–16; and economic relations, 32, 49, 77–78, 79–82, 251–53; praised by *The Star*, 37; background, 228–41; Verwoerd defines basis of, 237; official rationale, 241–51; and "buffer" states, 243–44; as mission, duty, destiny, 247–48; domestic reactions and debate, 251, 266–71; public relations, 253–55; and collaboration with Rhodesia and Portugal, 255–58; and military preparedness, 258–59; interference in domestic politics of other states, 259–61; diplomatic exchanges and high level visits, 261–66; limitations upon, 271–75; supports Congo, 282; and racism, 292

South Africa Foundation, 255

South African Broadcasting Corporation, 4, 254–55, 268

South African Chamber of Mines. *See* Witwatersrand Native Labour Association

South African Institute of Race Relations: and "outward policy," 229; RSA's "domestic colonialism," 238

South Africa-Rhodesia Association, 167n

Southern Africa: geographical de-

limitation, xiv; relative isolation, xvii; as delimited by scholars, 310–12
Southern African Customs Union: 34, 36–38, 77–78, 253; as diplomatic medium, 87–88
"Southern African development region," 310
Southern African Regional Committee for the Conservation and Utilization of Soil (SARCCUS), 40
South West Africa. *See* Namibia
South West Africa National Union (SWANU), 186, 192
South West African National Liberation Front (SWANLIF), 186
South West Africa People's Organization. *See* SWAPO
Spain, 84, 175, 312
Stamp, Sir Maxwell and Associates, 54
State: as unit of analysis, xv
Strijdom, J. G., 3, 233, 234
"Subordinate" state systems: criticism of term, 307–8, 311
Sudan, 206, 279
SWANU, 186, 192
SWAPO: 153, 164, 183–86, 194; guerrilla training, 198; cooperation with MPLA, 219–220; and Khartoum Alliance, 221; and Namibian unity, 240
Swaziland: and "bridge building," 13, 138–39; agriculture, 31; and Southern African Customs Union, 34, 36–38; bilateral trade agreements, 40; and East African Community, 40, 139; electricity link with South Africa, 48; transport routes, 50, 51; rail link with Mozambique, 58; rail link with RSA, 58; labor migration, 62–63; economic assistance from UK, 70; economic assistance from USA, 71; relations with RSA, 75, 87–88, 90, 138–39, 238–41; and infrastructural imbalances, 78; relations with Portugal, 84, 138; relations with black states, 88; votes at UN, 104; and OAU, 111–12; systemic determinants of policy, 120, 138–39; on guerrilla warfare, 138–39; on arms sales to RSA, 139; position on dialogue, 139; extradition treaty with RSA, 139; on Rhodesian issue, 139; relations with Zambia, 139; regulates liberation movements, 220; and border concept, 283; mentioned, xiv, 123, 131, 135, 236, 287, 288, 289, 290, 291. *See also* High Commission Territories
Sweden, 42, 116, 312
"Swiss device," 93
Switzerland: and RSA arms embargo, 213
Symbiosis: as form of foreign policy, 295–96
Systems analysis, xiii, 303–4; and linkage groups, 203–5. *See also* Regional sub-systems

Tanganyika. *See* Tanzania
Tanganyika Concessions Limited: Benguela Railway, 210
Tan-Zam Railway, 50, 53–56, 78, 124
Tanzania: preemptive military strikes, 14n; agriculture, 31; and infrastructural imbalances, 78; formal diplomatic relations, 84, 85; positions at UN, 103; and Commonwealth, 106, 107; in OAU, 110; participation in Conferences of Heads of State and Government of East and Central Africa, 113–14, 116; relations with Malawi, 126, 127–28, 129–30; opposition to dialogue, 145n; and war in Mozambique, 157–58, 177; relations with Portugal, 176–78, 207, 208–9; as refugee "host," 177, 200, 202; and Zimbabwe war, 182; in Namibia struggle, 183; and RSA revolutionary movements, 189, 197; and ALC, 195; guerrilla training, 198, 199, 206; hosts FRELIMO, 206; threatened by Portugal, 207; territory violated, 208–9; air defenses, 209; in South African defense perimeter, 243; RSA view of, 244; and Northern Rhodesian "partition," 280; as member of two sub-systems, 285; intervention and penetration, 298; mentioned, xiv, 29, 142, 278, 288, 289, 290, 291
Technical assistance. *See* Economic assistance
Toivo, Toivo Herman Ja: on violence, 153–54

Tokenism, international: policy and philosophy, 11–21
Trade patterns, regional, 32–40, 79, 251–53
Transportation routes, 49–59, 78, 92, 93, 124, 175, 210–11, 280, 288
Treurnicht, Dr. Andries, 269
Tshombe, Moise, 279, 280–81; and Angola war, 173, 174; military cooperation with white South, 223; relations with RSA, 235, 282
Tsiranana, Philibert: and "bridge building," 15; on racism, 15; visits Malawi, 132–33; mentioned, 136, 140
Tunisia, 111n, 171
Turkana: border raiders, 206

Uganda, 195, 197, 279
Ullmann, Pierre-Jerome, 96n
Umkonto we Sizwe, 188
UNESCO, 47
"Unholy alliance," 222–24
União das Populações de Angola. *See* UPA
União para la Independência Total de Angola, 175, 192, 198, 210–11
Union of Soviet Socialist Republics (USSR): and Botswana, 137, 283; in Indian Ocean, 141, 214–15; influence on liberation movements, 166n; and Namibia, 183, 186, 240; aid to revolutionary movements, 192–94, 195, 197; guerrilla training, 197, 198; missiles in Tanzania, 209; Union Republics and Bantustans, 237; RSA warnings on, 244, 259; and East Europe, 285; mentioned, 5, 273
UNITA, 175, 192; guerrilla training, 198; disrupts Benguela Railway, 210–11
United Arab Republic (UAR), 183, 186, 197; relations with Malawi, 130
United National Independence Party (UNIP), 23, 86
United Nations (UN), 83, 97–105, 123, 208, 210, 234, 237, 294, 300; resolutions, 7–8, 10; and Kunene project, 46; African member states, 97–99; and Namibia, 100–5, 167, 183, 240; Lesotho policy, 133–34, 135; and Katanga, 173, 280; and Angola war, 175; and RSA, 212–13, 250, 258; Banda on ineffectualness of, 227n; voting patterns, 289
—Council for Namibia, 167
—Development Program: Oxbow scheme, 47
—High Commission for Refugees, 200
United Party (RSA), 269–70, 272
United States of America (USA), 34, 259, 273, 300; racial problems, xii, 11–13, 20; finances Great North Road, 53; and Tan-Zam Railway, 54–55; Peace Corps, 71; Public Law 480, 71; Agency for International Development, 71–72; aid to Botswana, 137; effect of "bridge building" policies on, 149; Central Intelligence Agency, 211n; and RSA arms embargo, 212; Azores base, 214; military supplies for Portugal, 214; black diplomats in, 262
Unit of analysis, 305, 312–13
Universal Postal Union, Congress of the, 47
UPA, 170–71, 176; and refugees, 203; and Katanga, 223

Van der Merwe, Dr. P., 14n
Van Eck, Dr. H. J., 43, 46
Verkramptes: opposition to "outward policy," 230, 267–69
Verligtes: and foreign policy, 31–32, 230
Verwoerd, Dr. Hendrik W.: on white supremacy, 3; on Rhodesian UDI, 4, 257; on regional economic cooperation, 38–39; as intermediary between Zambia and Rhodesia, 93n; and Commonwealth, 106–7; and High Commission Territories, 236; and "outward policy," 237; and Katanga, 281
Vietnam, 138
Violence, 1, 13, 14–15; in South Africa, xi, 187–90; ideologies of, 21, 27; and economic development, 73; OAU policy, 109; Rhodesian issue, 109; Lusaka Manifesto on, 115; Mogadishu Declaration on, 116; Khama on, 137–38; Prince

Dhlamini on, 138–39; Houphouet-Boigny on, 142; Mondlane on, 153; utility of, 153–54

Vorster, J. B., 254, 259, 272; exchanges with Kaunda, 94–95; visit to Malawi and Rhodesia, 126, 262; on relations with Lesotho, 134–35, 260; on dialogue and "outward movement," 147, 230; on preemptive strikes, 169; threatens Zambia, 207–8; announces incursions into Zambia, 209–10; on military coordination, 222; on military aid to Rhodesia, 223, 224; on Zambezi as RSA defense perimeter, 243; and anti-communism, 244; on RSA "destiny," 248; ANC view of, 249; on noninterference, 249; and Rhodesian UDI, 257; and division in Nationalist Party, 267–69

Waldheim, Kurt: visit to RSA and Namibia, 102

Weiss, P. F. D., 268

Welensky, Sir Roy, 125, 280

Western civilization: as "defended" by RSA, 166–67, 215, 249

"White Atlantic Sub-System," 312

Wilson, Harold: and Kaunda, 70–71

Witwatersrand Native Labour Association, 66–67; in Lesotho, 59–62; in Malawi, 63–64; in Mozambique, 64–65; in Namibia, 185

World Bank, 45–46, 47, 53

World Council of Churches, 200

World Food Program, 200

"Yellow peril," 244, 259

Yugoslavia: finances Kafue project, 45

Zaïre. *See* Congo

Zambezi River: as RSA defense perimeter, 243, 257; as border between white and black Africa, 277–78, 282

Zambia: relations with Rhodesia, xv; military threats by RSA and Rhodesia, 14n, 169, 169n, 207–8; mining, 31; trade, 40, 252; and East African Community, 40; and Cabora Bassa, 42–43; and Kariba Dam, 44–46; South African private investment in, 48, 49, 279; transport patterns, 50, 51, 52–56, 57, 59, 92–93; petroleum, 50, 53; and Rhodesia Railways, 52–53; domestic politics, 55–56, 211; relations with Malawi, 57, 90, 122–23, 126, 128–30, 131, 132, 133; Malawi laborers in, 63; labor migration, 64, 65, 66; relations with UK, 70–71, 209; relations with CPR, 71; relations with USA, 71–72; relations with Italy, 71, 72; and RSA's "co-prosperity sphere," 78; economic pressures on, 78, 210–11, 282; relations with Portugal, 86, 92–93, 174–75, 208–11; formal diplomatic relations, 84, 85; relations with RSA, 86, 94–95, 235, 274; official and state visits, 90–92, 95; territory violated, 92–93, 131, 208–11, 223n; Portuguese border incursions, 92–93, 131; and Anglo-American Corporation, 94; use of non-black "unofficial" diplomats, 94–95; relations with Botswana, 95, 123, 137, 283; at UN, 103; in OAU, 110; participation in Conferences of Heads of State and Government of East and Central Africa, 113–14, 116; relations with Swaziland, 139; and Angola war, 174–76; as refugee host, 177, 200, 202, 203; and Zimbabwe struggle, 181–82, 183; and Namibia, 184, 186, 240; and RSA revolutionary movements, 189; and ALC, 195, 197; Refugee (Control) Bill, 202; as host to revolutionary movements, 206; air defenses, 209; RSA violates territory, 223n; RSA view of, 244; possible partition of, 280; independence, 282; as member of two sub-systems, 285; intervention and penetration, 298; mentioned, 29, 124, 135, 142, 170n, 288, 289, 290, 291. *See also* Rhodesia and Nyasaland, Federation of

ZAMCO (Consórcio Hidroelétrico do Zambeze), 41, 42–43, 44

ZANU, 180, 181, 182, 192; on racism, 6; criticism of Malawi, 126; competition with ZAPU over refugees, 203

ZAPU, 180, 181, 182, 194, 223; alliance with ANC (South Africa),

166n, 181, 189–90, 219, 221; competition with ZANU over refugees, 203; on Zambezi "border," 277

Zartman, I. William, 312

Zimbabwe: revolutionary parties and activities, 164, 180–83, 192, 196. *See also* FROLIZI; Rhodesia; ZANU; ZAPU

Zimbabwe African National Union. *See* ZANU

Zimbabwe African People's Union. *See* ZAPU

Zwane, Dr. Ambrose, 139